24⁹⁹

Cities in the Telecommunications Age

T

Cities in the Telecommunications Age

THE FRACTURING OF GEOGRAPHIES

James O. Wheeler, Yuko Aoyama,
and Barney Warf, Editors

ROUTLEDGE
New York and London

Published in 2000
by
Routledge
29 West 35th Street
New York, NY 10001

Published in Great Britain by
Routledge
11 New Fetter Lane
London EC4P 4EE

Printed in the United States of America on acid-free paper.
Design: Jack Donner

Library of Congress Cataloging-in-Publication Data

Cities in the telecommunications age : the fracturing of geographies /
James O. Wheeler, Yuko Aoyama, and Barney Warf, editors
p.   cm.
Includes bibliographical references and index.
ISBN 0–415–92441–3 (hb.). — ISBN 0–415–92442–1 (pb.)
1. Cities and towns—Effect of technological innovations on—United States.
2. Telecommunications—Social aspects—United States.
I. Wheeler, James O. II. Aoyama, Yuko. III. Warf, Barney, 1956– .
HT167.C483 2000
384'.0973—dc21   99–35013
CIP

To: Alan, Dian, Elise, and Walter

To: Noriko and Gozo Aoyama

To: Derek

CONTENTS

ACKNOWLEDGMENTS

We wish to acknowledge funding from Dr. Wyatt Anderson, Dean of the Franklin College of Arts and Sciences at the University of Georgia, in support of the "Telecommunications and the City" conference held in Athens, Georgia, in March 1998, in which these book chapters were first presented in oral form. Thanks especially to Dr. George A. Brook, who served as Head of the Department of Geography at the University of Georgia during the period of this conference and who provided additional departmental financial support for the conference, leadership in initiating an ongoing series of state-of-the-art conferences in various topics in human geography, and dedicated personal support for our efforts. Thanks also to Ms. Audrey Hawkins, Department of Geography at the University of Georgia, who helped prepare material for the conference and who contributed invaluably to coordinating the conference and, in particular, in assisting in the preparation of the book manuscript chapters. We also gratefully acknowledge the assistance of Ms. Jodie Guy, Assistant Editor of *Urban Geography* at the University of Georgia; Ms. Loretta Scott, Ms. Kim Smith, and Ms. Emily Duggar, members of the office staff in the Department of Geography at the University of Georgia; and several graduate students (Mr. Christopher Bertaut, Mr. Jonathan Smith, and Ms. Selima Sultana). Thanks also go profoundly to each of the chapter authors for adhering to our deadlines for initial manuscript submissions and subsequent revisions. Our book enterprise has been possible only through the considerable support and aid of a committed group of professionals. We would also like to thank Emily E. Wheeler for her assistance during the conference.

PART I.

Introduction

1

INTRODUCTION

CITY SPACE, INDUSTRIAL SPACE, AND CYBERSPACE

James O. Wheeler, Yuko Aoyama,
and Barney Warf

Cities in the Telecommunications Age: The Fracturing of Geographies grew out
of a conference on "Telecommunications and the City" sponsored by the
Department of Geography at the University of Georgia and held in Athens,
Georgia, in March 1998. These chapters were drawn from more than forty-five
papers presented at the conference, and were extensively revised for publication in this volume. The conference brought together many of the world's leading scholars conducting research on the telecommunications revolution.

The word *telecommunications* has a new meaning today. My 1978 *Web-
ster's Dictionary* defines telecommunications as "communication by radio, telephone, telegraph, television," where the Greek stem word *"tele"* means "over
a distance." "Telecommunications" is today used almost exclusively to refer to
electronic transmission of information via computer networks. The Internet, a
complex of networks linking computers worldwide, became accessible to people only very recently. The way to access documents over the Internet, stored
in many different computers, was conceived only in 1989 by researchers in
Geneva, Switzerland, and the halting use of what became known as the World
Wide Web (WWW) did not begin until 1993, when a number of academics
and online enthusiasts began traversing the Web (Shipley and Fish, 1996). In
1996, fewer than 40 million people were connected to the Internet; by 1997,
the figure had risen to more than 100 million. In 1998, the volume of traffic
on the Internet doubled every three months (Segaller, 1998).

It is within this exploding telecommunications revolution that this collection of chapters is set. A surprisingly large background of scholarly work has
been accomplished in the area of telecommunications in the past few years,
especially given the recency of developments. Castells's *The Informational City*
(1989) set a broad view of how "information" was restructuring capitalism,
capital-labor relationships, new industrial space, and the "space of flows."
Hepworth's *Geography of the Information Economy* (1990) was among the first
books to comprehend the role of computer networks on multilocational firms,

flexible production, and "wired cities." The Brunn and Leinbach collection of essays (1991) revealed the complexity and potential of the geographical consequences of communications and information. Kellerman (1993) focused on how telecommunications were impacting the global system of cities and the spatial arrangements of activities within cities. In a comprehensive survey of the literature, Graham and Marvin (1996) examined the extant research on telecommunications and the city, and provided a solid foundation for understanding the rapidly changing impacts of information technologies. It is Castells's trilogy (1996, 1997, 1998) that best places the context for *Cities in the Telecommunications Age: The Fracturing of Geographies*. Castells's thoughtful tour de force will long be read and valued as the most encompassing rendering and understanding of society and the economy in this early stage of the telecommunications age.

TELECOMMUNICATIONS AND URBAN SPACE

For nearly the first two hundred years of urban settlement history in North America, cities that prospered economically by creating employment opportunities and hence population growth were cities located strategically with respect to transportation routes. Large cities of the early to middle 1800s were positioned in coastal areas and had port functions that were almost exclusively tied to Europe. These important port cities included Boston, New York, Philadelphia, and Baltimore on the East Coast, and the lesser ports of Charleston, Savannah, and New Orleans in the South. Thereafter river cities (St. Louis, Cincinnati, Louisville, Pittsburgh) and later cities on the Great Lakes (Chicago, Buffalo, Cleveland, Toronto, Milwaukee, and Detroit) came into prominence. All of the early port, river, and Great Lakes cities got a head start on urban growth and continue to be large centers today. The West Coast cities of San Francisco, Los Angeles, San Diego, Seattle, and Portland emerged later as principal centers.

The railroad superimposed advantages on many of the port, river, and lake cities and led to the widespread diffusion of the population in the U.S. and Canada, opening up "gateway" cities such as Kansas City, Omaha, and Fort Worth to westward settlement. Air and highway transportation completed the urbanization process by allowing inland cities such as Indianapolis, Atlanta, Denver, and Dallas to grow to considerable size. And all through these technologically evolving transport eras, manufacturing was the engine of urban growth. A strategic location on the extant water and rail transportation networks meant advantages in moving materials to the manufacturing centers and shipping commodities to market.

All of this has suddenly changed. Manufacturing, after nearly two hundred years of ascendancy as a city-builder, has suffered massive relative and absolute declines in North America, with the centers that specialized predominately in manufacturing undergoing the greatest declines. Almost all new jobs being created today are in some area of services, and the high-paying jobs are in the producer or advanced services, such as marketing, advertising, finance, legal services, accounting, and other business services associated with large corporations. The point is that all of this advanced service employment has been increasingly dependent upon new communications technology.

We tend to forget today that the initial impact of telephone technology brought about tremendous changes in the way business enterprises conducted their operations and how the social structures of individuals' lives were altered. But the changes engendered by the telephone were insubstantial in comparison with other changes in communications, and especially modern telecommunications. Although facsimile technology existed in the 1930s, it was not commonly used until the late 1980s. FedEx overnight delivery of letters, packages, and boxes began in 1974 but did not come into extensive use until the early 1980s and did not intensify until the mid-1990s. Most major corporations and institutions make daily, routine use of fax machines and overnight delivery.

It is the Internet that has had the greatest, most far-reaching, and most permanent impact on the world economy and the transformations of society, especially in today's advanced world economies of North America, Western Europe, Japan, and Australia. It is a brand-new technological development. The Internet is a whole series of interconnected computer networks, a network of telecommunications connections, sometimes described as a network of networks (Shipley and Fish, 1996). It was only in 1993, when the National Center for Superconducting Applications released the Mosaic Web browser (developed at the University of Illinois at Urbana-Champaign), that academic researchers realized the possibilities available by using the Web. Since then, there has followed the most explosive growth in communications in all of human history. As Castells (this volume) reminds us, "Our historic time is defined by the transformation of our geographic space."

With the transformation from a manufacturing-based to a service-based economy within one generation, and with the telecommunications age superimposed on this new service economy, cities have undergone colossal and permanent change. A few large urban centers have emerged throughout the advanced economies of North America, Europe, and Japan that rightly deserve the standing of "global cities." These are not necessarily the largest urban centers in the world, as Mexico City, São Paulo, Shanghai, Seoul, Calcutta, and Bombay—among the world's ten largest cities—are not deemed global cities. Global cities, instead, include New York, Tokyo, and London at the top of the hierarchy. At a slightly lower level are the global cities of Hong Kong, Singapore, Paris, and Osaka. These large urban centers, as well as others, achieve the designation because of their intense utilization of global interdependent telecommunications, not merely because of their considerable population size. The reason these global cities are set apart is due to the nature of the capitalist activities housed within them, especially major transnational and multilocational corporations, as well as the concentrations of governmental, institutional, and education establishments.

Despite the worldwide possibilities of instantaneous telecommunications via fiber-optic cables and satellites, only a few cities have yet achieved global

JAMES O. WHEELER, YUKO AOYAMA, AND BARNEY WARF

status in this early period of the telecommunications age. These are the cities whose economic dominance necessitates a central position on the worldwide Internet. These are the centers that are most intently wired with other global cities. In spite of the geographically emancipating possibilities of electronic telecommunications, only a few places on the earth have in fact developed the communications infrastructure and have the pent-up requirements for widespread information exchange. Rather than creating a system of information flow that is independent of distance, the telecommunications age has instead caused the concentration in only a limited number of places of the sources of information genesis, particularly high-order information and knowledge. These places are the global cities within the capitalist world.

The recent and rapid spread of fiber-optic cables within and among urban areas in the United States and Canada and, more particularly, the explosion in the placement of transoceanic cable lines have significantly increased the speed and efficiency of telecommunications around the globe. Prior to 1993, the number of voice paths across the Atlantic Ocean was greater via satellites than cables. Since then, however, fiber-optic cables with improved light pulse technology in digital computer code have easily eclipsed satellite communications, whose advantage is largely to serve inland and remote locations not yet reached by fiber-optic cable. (Satellites still handle most of the broadcast video.) Most global Internet and telephone messages now flow through hair-thin threads of glass propelled by laser light pulses.

It was not until 1988 that glass fiber started to replace copper telephone signals. The fiber-optic system proved to be overwhelmingly advantageous. In the year 2000, more than 400,000 miles of fiber-optic cable will lie on the ocean floors, enough to circle the earth sixteen times. By the year 2003, more than 600,000 miles of cable will connect some 175 countries and virtually all the major cities of the world. Using lasers that split light into colors, the newest cable crossing the Atlantic ocean can transmit 2.4 million voice conversations simultaneously, and the recently completed cable link with China will handle 4 million at one time. Developing technologies promise even more messages per hairlike fiber, with each cable housing multiple glass fibers.

The current reality and these future developments are astounding in the consequences for telecommunications among global cities and emerging world cities. Whereas inexpensive and instantaneous transmission of routine messages and data can take place worldwide, the limited number of global cities will continue to function as select gathering places — centers of people concentrations — for the necessary face-to-face human interactions required for high-level decision making. Despite the tons of data that can be sent via the Internet, that amount pales in comparison to the volume of information humans provide one another simply by being in one another's presence — with body language, voice, eye contact, handshake, small talk, and so much more. In spite of the worldwide extension of human telecommunications from one's own home or office, human beings have been conditioned to communicate face to face since human speech first developed. Agglomerations of humans will be intensified by telecommunications.

CYBERSPACE AND THE CITY

A significant part of the world's expanding telecommunications matrix, particularly within the economically developed world, is "cyberspace," a term popularized by Gibson's notoriously influential novel, *Neuromancer* (1984). Born out of the microelectronics revolution and the digitization of information, cyberspace loosely encompasses the realm of the Internet and related technologies, a domain in which telecommunications merged with computers to form integrated networks. However, the term is often used casually in other ways and has suffered from its popularity. It is important to note that while cyberspace is large and growing, it certainly does not encompass the broad entirety of telecommunications. Indeed, the most common form of telecommunications, the telephone, frequently utilizes analog technology and often involves communication entirely outside the domain of cyberspace.

Nonetheless, the Internet is incontestably the largest electronic network on the planet, connecting an estimated 100 million people in more than one hundred countries (Warf, 1995), but still less than 2 percent of the world's population. Even more important is the stupendous rate of growth: spurred by declining prices of services and equipment and enormous media hype, the number of users worldwide has doubled roughly every year. From its military origins in the United States in the 1960s, the Internet emerged on a global scale through the integration of existing telephone, fiber optic, and satellite systems, which was made possible by the technological innovation of packet switching and Integrated Services Digital Network (ISDN), in which individual messages may be decomposed, the constituent parts transmitted by various channels, and then reassembled, virtually instantaneously, at the destination. Popular access systems in the United States such as CompuServe, Prodigy, and America Online, allow any individual with a microcomputer and modem to "plug in" to cyberspace. The widespread use of such systems and others forms a fundamental part of what Castells (1996) calls the "space of flows" in which virtually all localities are embedded today.

Considerable confusion about the real and potential impacts of telecommunications on cities in part reflects the exaggerated claims made by "postindustrial" theorists (for instance, Toffler, 1980), which often hinge upon a simplistic, utopian, technological determinism that ignores the complex, often contradictory, relations between telecommunications and urban form. For example, repeated proclamations that telecommunications would allow everyone to work at home via telecommuting, dispersing all functions and spelling the obsolescence of cities, have fallen flat in the face of the persistence of growth in dense, urbanized places. In fact, telecommunications are generally a poor substitute for face-to-face meetings, the medium through which most sensitive corporate interactions occur, particularly when the information involved is irregular, proprietary, and unstandardized in nature. Most managers spend the bulk of their working time engaged in face-to-face contact, and no electronic technology can allow for the subtlety and nuances critical to such encounters. For this reason, a century of telecommunications, from the telephone to fiber optics, has left most high-wage, white-collar, administrative command and control functions clustered in downtown areas (despite their high rents). In contrast, telecommunications are ideally suited for the transmission of routinized, standardized forms of data, facilitating the dispersal of functions involved with their processing (that is, back offices) to low-wage regions. By allowing multinational firms to stay in contact with their operations around the world, telecommunications have contributed to the centralization of key activities in global cities such as New York, London, and Tokyo, which rely upon their extensive connections to the global telecommunications infrastructure to serve as the nerve centers of the world economy. In short, there is no *a priori* reason to believe that telecommunications inevitably lead to the dispersal or deconcentration of functions; by allowing the decentralization of routinized ones, information technology may enhance the comparative advantage of inner cities (albeit with jobs generally filled by suburban commuters). Telecommunications thus facilitate the simultaneous concentration and deconcentration of economic activities (Moss and Carey, 1995).

Within cities, cyberspace has contributed to a substantial reconstruction of urban space (Graham, 1992ab; Graham and Marvin, 1996), creating a social environment in which "being digital" is increasingly critical to knowledge, wealth, status, and power (Negroponte, 1995). As Graham and Aurigi (1997, p. 26) note, "Large cities, based, in the past, largely on face-to-face exchange in public spaces, are dissolving and fragmenting into webs of indirect, specialized relationships." Information systems such as the Internet may reinforce existing disparities in wealth, connecting elites in different nations who may be increasingly disconnected from the local environments of their own cities and countries. Indeed, in a sociopsychological sense, cyberspace may allow for the reconstruction of "communities without propinquity," groups of users who share common interests but not physical proximity (Anderson and Melchior, 1995). In the age of the "City of Bits" (Mitchell, 1995), in which social life is increasingly mediated through computer networks, the reconstruction of interpersonal relations around the digitized spaces of cyberspace is of the utmost significance.

One increasingly important effect of cyberspace is "telework" or "telecommuting," in which workers substitute some or all of their working day at a remote location (almost always home) for time usually spent at the office (Grantham and Nichols, 1994–95; Office of Technology Assessment, 1995). The self-employed do not count as teleworkers because they do not substitute teleworking for commuting. Telework is most appropriate for jobs involving mobile activities or routine information handling such as data entry or directory assistance (Moss and Carey, 1995). Proponents of telework claim that it enhances productivity and morale, reduces employee turnover and office space, and leads to reductions in traffic congestion (especially at peak hour), air pollution, energy use, and accidents (Handy and Mokhtarian, 1995; Van Sell and Jacobs, 1994). The U.S. Department of Transportation (1993) estimated that 2 million people (1.6 percent of the national labor force) telecommuted one to two days per week in 1992, while the Department of Energy estimated in

1994 that 4.2 million (3.3 percent) did so, a volume expected to rise to 7.5 to 15.0 million (5 to 10 percent) of the labor force by 2002. If this phenomenon grows as expected, it will lead to further decentralization of economic activity in suburban areas.

However, as Graham and Marvin (1996) point out, there are countervailing reasons why telecommunications may *increase* the demand for transportation rather than decrease it. First, while telecommuters spend fewer days at their workplace, it is not at all clear that they have shorter *weekly* commutes overall; indeed, by allowing them to live farther from their workplace, the total distances traveled may actually rise. Second, time freed from commuting may be spent traveling for other purposes, such as shopping or recreation. Telecommuting may alter the reasons for travel, but not necessarily the frequency or volume. Third, by reducing congestion, telecommuting may lead to significant induced effects whereby others formerly inhibited from driving may be induced to do so. In short, the substitutability, rather than complementarity, of telecommunications for commuting is far from clear.

Differentials in access to the skills, equipment, and software necessary to gain entrée to the electronic highway threaten to create a large (predominantly minority) underclass deprived of the benefits of cyberspace (Wresch, 1996). This phenomenon must be viewed in light of the growing inequalities throughout industrialized nations generated by labor market polarization (that is, deindustrialization and growth of low income, contingent service jobs). Modern economies are increasingly divided between those who are comfortable and proficient with digital technology and those who neither understand nor trust it. This development disenfranchises the latter group, denying them the possibility of citizenship in cyberspace. Indeed, those who may need access to such information the most—the poor and relatively powerless—may have least ability to purchase or use it. Despite the falling prices for hardware and software, basic entry-level machines for Internet access cost less than roughly $1,000, an exorbitant sum for low-income households. For employees in poorly paying jobs that do not offer access to the Internet at work, the obstacles to access are formidable, including cost and lack of familiarity with computer systems. Even within the most digitized of cities there remain large pockets of "off-line" poverty (Thrift, 1995; Resnick and Rusk, 1996; Sawicki and Craig, 1996; National Telecommunications and Information Administration, 1995).

Like other telecommunications systems such as the telephone or Geographic Information Systems (Pickles, 1995), the Internet is a social product, interwoven with relations of class, race, and gender and the formation and transformation of communities, and inevitably subject to the uses and misuses of power (Jones, 1995; Shields, 1996). A growing body of critical literature has detailed how electronic systems are used to monitor everyday life, including credit cards, visas and passports, tax records, medical data, police reports, telephone calls, utility records, automobile registration, crime statistics, and sales receipts (Lyon, 1994). In this light, the Internet is more akin to Foucault's famous panopticon that surveys and controls all it sees than to some mythical unfettered frontier region. The unfortunate tendency in the popular media to engage in technocratic utopianism has largely obscured these power relations. *Contra* the postindustrial utopian perspective popular with the mass media, social categories of wealth and power are inevitably reinscribed in cyberspace.

TELECOMMUNICATIONS AND INDUSTRIAL SPACE

While the role of technologies in urban space has generally led to the refortification of the existing urban hierarchy, their impacts on industrial space are far less clear. Traditionally, the role of technologies in industrial space was examined by focusing on the behavior and locational dynamics of high-tech manufacturing industries (Markusen, Hall, and Glasmeier, 1986). The picture is far more complicated today, as telecommunications serve as a basic infrastructure for every industry with various technological components. The spatial dynamics have become particularly complex when industrial networks cross international borders and when extensive use of telecommunications infrastructure is required for frequent coordination between parts suppliers or client firms.

Amid the possibilities offered by back offices, electronic cottages, and telecommuting, the past few decades have seen further concentration of advanced producer services in global cities, suburbanization of mass production assembly plants, globalization of various sectors from footware to semiconductors, and formation of highly specialized industrial districts of networked variety. Thus, on the one hand, telecommunications technologies have offered an enormous opportunity for decentralization of industrial activities at regional, national, and international levels; on the other hand, we continue to observe the emergence of specialized agglomerations, and particularly in such functions as corporate headquarters and research and development (R&D), high-tech manufacturing, and advanced producer service functions.

In most instances, the widely advocated "death of distance" did not result in dismantling of specialized industrial districts and manufacturing agglomerations. In fact, agglomeration has become a new focus of research, not simply as a pervasive phenomenon, but also as an important source of competitive advantage. By minimizing high transaction costs for innovation, firms can compete more effectively through forming agglomerations. Alternatively, firms can induce innovation more effectively through agglomerating.

In analyzing competitiveness of industries, economists have placed increasing attention to geographical perspectives. The rebirth of interests was most recently induced by Paul Krugman (1992), whose contribution includes an effort to integrate geographical perspectives into economic paradigms. However, there are numerous critical spatial issues that the economists either neglect or fail to acknowledge as influential factors in production functions. The issue of agglomeration and its relationship to innovation is one of these issues. Some contend that innovative activities are promoted by knowledge spillovers, which are typically contained and occur within a selected region. Only a limited set of regions is able to form an "innovative milieu" (Castells, 1985) or "territorial innovation complex" (Stohr, 1985). These millieux emerge based on a particular mix of government policy, industrial organization, and technical skills. More recently, attention has been placed on the social and regional cultures on which industries are founded, emphasizing territorially embedded relationships between innovation and entrepreneurship (Saxenian, 1994). Others emphasize firms' locational decisions that are increasingly based on climate and cultural amenity for employees. Despite differences, they all agree that innovative activities are not readily transferred across space: in the United States and elsewhere, it is clearly evident that high-level manufacturing and R&D functions are still located in or near high-order metropolitan areas, and evidence shows no trend toward massive decentralization. The unequal distribution of innovative activities highlights the spatial disparity of high-technology industries, and serves as a key indicator for regional growth.

Similar to innovations being restricted within certain geographical space, new industries continue to concentrate in large metropolitan areas. New industries of the 1990s, such as information services, are seen agglomerating at the core of the metropolitan economy. However, they are also rapidly growing in rural areas. As Beyers shows (Chapter 11), information-related industries are growing faster in rural America than in cities. Although face-to-face contacts continue to play an important role in business transactions, the use of telecommunications technologies has broadened their export base. These information merchants have largely managed to acquire and maintain clients at distant locations, in part because of the specialized nature of their product and service delivery. Thus the emerging spatial patterns of new industries are fundamentally different from the classic notion of time-space convergence, partly because the current patterns of expanded markets for many industries are based on heightened levels of specialization both for supply and demand. The market demand has become increasingly segmented, and the suppliers have correspondingly become specialized and niche-market-oriented. These supply-and-demand conditions can take place at far greater distances through telecommunications infrastructure.

These new trends bring us to a new hypothesis on the relationship between firms and space. Rather than economic efficiency, corporate strategies, and innovation-driven locational decisions of firms, is location increasingly a factor that drives economic efficiency, corporate strategies, and innovation? The importance of spatial dynamics in today's economy involves far-reaching effects both at the regional and international levels. No doubt telecommunications technologies have expanded options for locational choices for industries. They have also expanded the potential market size for companies, from local to international. The success of the Internet bookstore, Amazon.com, is a prime example of technologies expanding the market size. Yet the most sought-after locations remain industry-specific, and firms are faced with increasing competition from out-of-state and out-of-the-country competitors.

The specialization of activities and resulting reconfiguration of industrial space pose a serious challenge to regional policy makers. Not only are regions faced with a continuous updating of physical and technological infrastructure, they are also faced with direct global competition and the need to identify their locational niches, which are no longer solely based on wage and skill levels of workers. For policymakers, making a local industrial base to develop competitive and specialized products and services — combined with technological capability in reaching out to clients and suppliers at short and long distances — remains a major challenge.

CHAPTER COVERAGE

The recent surge of interest in telecommunications has resulted from the combined effects of regulation (for example, the Telecom Act of 1996), mergers, technological change, and globalization. This edited volume focuses on the role of contemporary telecommunications in creating new geographies of space and in redefining our traditional concepts of urban places and spaces. Unlike distance- and cost-based transport, telecommunications at once both unlocks space constraints and concentrates high-order functions. This volume offers insight into urban cyberspace and the considerable challenges and implications for urban planning in the age of telecommunications, analyzes the impacts of how changes and innovations in the economic system are being fueled by developments of networks of telecommunications, and provides case studies of how communications technologies bring about the restructuring of cities.

In addition to Part I, consisting of this introductory chapter and Manuel Castells's most recent statement on the space of flows, the book is organized into four parts: "Cyberspace," "Telecommunications Infrastructure and Urban Planning," "Impacts of Telecommunications," and "Case Studies of the Effect of Communications Technology on Urban Space." Part I introduces the reader to the major issues of how telecommunications is affecting activities within and among cities and sets the foundations for understanding how our historic time is defined fundamentally by the transformations of geographic space. Part II, on cyberspace, explores the configuration of nodes and linkages among them, different in concept and kind from traditional place-bound locations. Part III elaborates how telecommunications infrastructure is related to urban and regional planning and to public policy and governance issues. Part IV examines impacts of telecommunications on how humans carry out their social and economic functions. Part V offers insightful case studies demonstrating urban restructuring and telecommunications impact and change in Atlanta, Phoenix, and Sunderland, England.

Specifically, Part II includes three chapters treating the salient features of cyberspace, the use of electronic computers to interact via complex networks of networks over geographic space, or computer network space substituted for physical space. Moss and Townsend argue and provide evidence that the new telecommunications technology is altering all the key features of urban society: "the home, the office, the automobile, and even the hotel room and public parks and streets." This transformation of urban life by the diffusion of intelligence and awareness is changing our cities and city relationships in ways even more profound than the changes brought about by factory-based mass production or the interstate highway system.

The chapter by Martin Dodge and Narushige Shiode is the first attempt to create a map of cyberspace. The invisible communications system known as the Internet does have a geography, and the authors have mapped it for the United Kingdom, revealing London in particular and other sizable cities (for instance, Birmingham, Manchester, Liverpool) as well as smaller cities that are major Internet uses such as Cambridge (University of Cambridge), and Oxford (Oxford University). Their map of IP (Internet Protocol) addresses for Britain includes nearly 44 million data points.

Barney Warf reminds us that the human body has recently emerged as an important topic of social analysis. Although they appear "natural," bodies are social constructions, playing a crucial role in the construction of identity. A key function of telecommunications has been to "disembody" information, allowing the social and physical aspects of individuals to be separated. Cyberspace is commonly represented as the immaterial antithesis of the body, but in fact the location and nature of bodies deeply condition the ways in which telecommunications are deployed. To some extent, conversely, digital spaces also condition the body. Warf draws from telemedicine, electronic security systems, cyberpornography, and virtual reality. He concludes that the Cartesian distinction that views the body and cyberspace as physical and mental opposites must be jettisoned in favor of an approach that firmly integrates these dimensions.

Part III, focusing on telecommunications infrastructure and urban planning, includes five chapters. Extending their ideas from their seminal *Telecommunications and the City* (1996), Stephen Graham and Simon Marvin examine how planning strategies can creatively address the complex linkages between telecommunications, urban form, and transportation. They explore the broad relations between new information technologies, the changing form and development of cities, and systems of physical mobility and location; they review planning and policy initiatives that try to shape the articulation between urban built forms and electronic interactions; and they assess the significance of these policies by suggesting innovative ways to integrate telecommunications into urban policy and planning strategies. Within the context of national, state, and local government's policies affecting telecommunications, Grant and Berquist explore the potential impacts of the next generation of networks on urban infrastructure, the role of telecommunications in economic development, and the role of networks on the quality of urban life.

Stephen McDowell analyzes the passage and implementation of the Telecommuncations Act of 1996, focusing on zoning authority over the siting of communication towers to provide wireless services, state and municipal taxation of communication services, the provision of telecommunications infrastructure and services by city governments, and the role of local institutions (libraries, schools, and hospitals). He situates his discussion within the context of shifts in telecommunications governance, the introduction of new technologies, and the geographic reorganization of production and consumption on a local and global basis.

Stanley Brunn and Thomas Leinbach examine the Finnish company, Nokia, a global leader in the production of cellular telephones. Using Porter's (1990) model of international competitiveness, they conclude that Nokia's success represents a convincing example of the Porter model, showing how this firm achieved national and international leadership in cellular telephone production.

Bishwapriya Sanyal relates information technology and urban poverty. He finds sharp contrasts in the attitudes of low-income communities toward the benefits of technology, as perceptions have shifted from skepticism and distrust in the 1960s to widespread interest in communications technology today. Sanyal concludes that the loss of "real communities" in low-income areas due to various social and economic problems has created the need for "virtual communities." He also argues that local, state, and federal governments should see that all schools are connected to the Internet in order that all communities are fully integrated into the national and international economy.

Part IV treats the various impacts of telecommunications. William B. Beyers concludes, based on hundreds of interviews with urban and rural businesses nationally, that face-to-face interaction remains as important as ever to businesses in the producer services, though it is being increasing supplemented—not supplanted—by other modes of communications. Beyers foresees greater locational freedom for business firms in which most enterprises will have an urban location at the same time that more businesses will select exurban locations.

David Audretsch and Maryann Feldman argue that the two fundamental characteristics of new knowledge as input to economic activity are (1) the high level of uncertainty, and (2) the high cost of transmission across geographic space. The first characteristic leads to the result that the mobility of agents, especially in terms of their ability to start new firms, increases the degree to which new knowledge is produced and commercialized. The latter leads to knowledge-based activity being localized at the source of that knowledge. They find that a paradox of the telecommunications revolution is that in the high-cost locations of North America and Europe, local proximity has grown in importance in generating economic activity that is competitive in globally linked markets. Similarly, but at the intrametropolitan level, Darrene Hackler examines the issue of decentralization of firms from central cities to the suburbs, relating the shift to information technology. She finds that traditional manufacturing centers and older cities should pursue policies to recreate cities, as high information technology-intensive manufacturing tends to be footloose in distribution.

14

Robert Mugerauer reports on a pilot study based on forty-two open-ended interviews with CEOs and professional employees in high-technology industries about how and where they decided to locate their companies. The analysis reveals four factors that combined to form milieu preferences and location-site decisions: natural setting, and utilitarian, social, and amenity features.

Andrew Gillespie and Ronald Richardson explore several myths associated with electronic communications and cyberspace, including "the disappearing city," "the disappearing workplace," and "the disappearing need to travel." After debunking the assumptions on which these myths are based, the chapter presents empirically informed discussion of the implications of "teleworking" for the spatial form of the future city. They conclude that, far from reducing travel, "new communications technology seem, conversely, to be associated with mobility-intensive and spatially dispersed activity patterns."

Part V provides four case studies of the role of telecommunications within metropolitan areas. Alan Southern uses Sunderland in the northeast of England to examine how communications technologies are involved in the restructuring of cities. Elizabeth Burns describes a large commuting survey in Phoenix and finds that flexible work scheduling is more common than telecommuting. She concludes: "Telecommuting, at this time, is an option currently limited to a small percentage of commuters in selected economic sectors and at limited work sites." Christopher Bertaut focuses on Gwinnett County, an Atlanta suburban area, to examine the density and spatial configuration of cellular towers to provide insight into the dispersal of knowledge-based workers (roaming users). He finds that roadway traffic volume largely determines the areal extent and spatial patterning of cellular telephone base-station facilities. Finally, Nancey Green Leigh explores the influence of new flexibility and technology requirements in the delivery of advanced services to central city offices, using case studies in Chicago and Atlanta. She finds that, especially in Atlanta, the edge city office sector is not back-office development but, rather, a recreation of the central business district (CBD) in the metropolitan suburbs.

Because of the burgeoning interest in the topics covered in this book, a diverse group of scholars will be interested in the book. It is expected that this book will be used by practicing urban and regional planners, academic geographers, and social scientists such as political scientists and sociologists, as well as those in public administration and urban governance. Because of the interdisciplinary group of authors, the book should appeal to a range of social scientists.

REFERENCES

Anderson, T. and A. Melchior. (1995). "Assessing Telecommunications as a Tool for Urban Community Building." *Journal of Urban Technology* 3:29–44.

Brunn, Stanley D. and Thomas Leinbach, eds. (1991). *Collapsing Space and Time: Geographic Aspects of Communications and Information*. London: Harper.

Castells, Manuel, ed. (1985). *High Technology, Space, and Society*. Beverly Hills, CA: Sage.

———. (1989). *The Informational City*. Cambridge, MA: Blackwell.

———. (1996). *The Rise of the Network Society*. Oxford: Blackwell.

———. (1997). *Power and Identity*. Malden, MA: Blackwell.

———. (1998). *End of Millennium*. Malden, MA: Blackwell.

Gibbs, D. (1993). "Telematics and Urban Development Policies." *Telecommunications Policy* (May/June): 250–256.

Gibbs, D. and K. Tanner. (1997). "Information and Communication Technologies and Local Economic Development Policies: The British Case." *Regional Studies* 31:768–774.

Gibson, W. (1984). *Neuromancer.* London: Harper Collins.

Graham, S. (1992a). "Electronic Infrastructures and the City: Some Emerging Municipal Policy Roles in the U.K." *Urban Studies* 29:755–781.

———. (1992b). "The Role of Cities in Telecommunications Development." *Telecommunications Policy* (April): 187–193.

Graham, S. and A. Aurigi. (1997). "Virtual Cities, Social Polarization, and the Crisis in Urban Public Space." *Journal of Urban Technology* 4:19–52.

Graham, Stephen and Simon Marvin. (1996). *Telecommunications and the City: Electronic Spaces, Urban Places.* London: Routledge.

Grantham, C. and L. Nichols. (1994–95). "Distributed Work: Learning To Manage at a Distance." *The Public Manager* (Winter): 31–34.

Handy, S. and Mokhtarian, P. (1995). "Planning for Telecommuting—Measurement and Policy Issues." *Journal of the American Planning Association* 61: 99–111.

Hepworth, Mark. (1990). *Geography of the Information Economy.* New York: Gilford Press.

Howland, M. (1993). "Technological Change and the Spatial Restructuring of Data Entry and Processing Services." *Technological Forecasting and Social Change* 43:185–196.

Jones, S., ed. (1995). *CyberSociety: Computer-Mediated Communication and Community.* Beverly Hills, CA: Sage.

Kellerman, Aharon. (1993). *Telecommunications and Geography.* New York: Belhaven Press.

Krugman, Paul. (1992). *Geography and Trade.* Leuven, Belgium: Leuven University Press.

Lyon, D. (1994). *The Electronic Eye: The Rise of Surveillance Society.* Minneapolis: University of Minnesota Press.

Markusen, Ann, Peter G. Hall, and Amy Glasmeier. (1986). *High Tech America: The What, How Where and Why of the Sunrise Industries.* Boston: Allen & Unwin.

Mitchell, W. (1995). *City of Bits: Space, Place, and the Infobahn.* Cambridge, MA: MIT Press.

Moss, M. and J. Carey. (1995). "Information Technologies, Telecommuting, and Cities." In J. Brotchie, M. Batty, E. Blakely, P. Hall, and P. Newton, eds. *Cities in Competition: Productive and Sustainable Cities for the 21st Century.* Sydney, Australia: Longman.

Moss, M. and A. Dunau. (1986). "Offices, Information Technology, and Locational Trends." In J. Black, K. Roark, and L. Schwartz, eds. *The Changing Office Workplace.* Washington, DC: Urban Land Institute; 171–182.

National Telecommunications and Information Administration, U.S. Department of Commerce. (1995). *Falling through the Net: A Survey of the Have Nots in Rural and Urban America.* Washington, DC: U.S. Government Printing Office.

Negroponte, N. (1995). *Being Digital.* New York: Knopf.

Office of Technology Assessment. (1995). *The Technological Reshaping of Metropolitan America.* Washington, DC: U.S. Government Printing Office.

Pickles, J., ed. (1995). *Ground Truths: The Social Implications of Geographic Information Systems.* New York: Guilford.

Porter, Michael E. (1990). *The Comparative Advantage of Nations.* New York: Macmillan.

Resnick, M. and N. Rusk. (1996). "Access is Not Enough: Computer Clubhouses in the Inner City." *The American Prospect* (July-August): 60–68.

Sawicki, D. and W. Craig. (1996). "The Democratization of Data: Bridging the Gap for Community Groups." *Journal of the American Planning Association* 68:219–231.

Saxenian, AnnaLee. (1994). *Regional Advantage: Culture and Competition in Silicon Valley and Route 128.* Cambridge, MA: Harvard University Press.

Segaller, Stephen. (1998). *Nerds: A Brief History of the Internet.* New York: TV Books.

Shields, R., ed. (1996). *Cultures of Internet: Virtual Spaces, Real Histories, Living Bodies.* London: Sage.

Shipley, Chris and Matthew Fish. (1996). *How the World Wide Web Works.* Emeryville, CA: Ziff-Davis Press.

Stohr, Walter B. (1985). "Territorial Innovation Complex." *Papers of the Regional Science Association* 95: 29–44.

Thrift, N. (1995). "A Hyperactive World." In R. Johnston, P. Taylor, and M. Watts, eds. *Geographies of Global Change.* Oxford: Blackwell.

Toffler, A. (1980). *The Third Wave.* New York: William Morrow.

U.S. Department of Energy. (1994). *Energy, Emissions and the Social Consequences of Telecommuting: Energy Efficiency in the U.S. Economy.* Technical Report One, Doe/Po-0026: Washington: U.S. Government Printing Office.

U.S. Department of Transportation. (1993). *Transportation Implications of Telecommuting.* Washington, DC: U.S. Department of Transportation.

Van Sell, M. and S. Jacobs. (1994). "Telecommuting and Quality of Life: A Review of the Literature and a Model for Research." *Telematics and Informatics* 11; 2: 81–93.

Warf, B. (1995). "Telecommunications and the Changing Geographies of Knowledge Transmission in the Late 20th Century." *Urban Studies* 32: 361–378.

Wresch, W. (1996). *Disconnected: Haves and Have-Nots in the Information Age.* New Brunswick, NJ: Rutgers University Press.

GRASSROOTING THE SPACE OF FLOWS

Manuel Castells

INTRODUCTION

Our historic time is defined fundamentally by the transformation of our geographic space. This is a key dimension of the multilayered social and technological transformation that ushers in the so-called Information Age. To understand such a spatial transformation, I proposed ten years ago the concept of space of flows. The aim at that point was to acknowledge the reality and the significance of the transformation without yielding to the simplistic notions of futurologists announcing the death of distance and the end of cities.

Empirical evidence showed—and shows—that new information and communication technologies fit into the pattern of flexible production and network organization, permitting the simultaneous centralization and decentralization of activities and population settlements, because different locations can be reunited in their functioning and in their interaction by the new technological system made out of telecommunications, computers, and fast reliable transportation systems, as well as dispatching centers, nodes, and hubs. So new communication technologies allow for the centralization of corporate activities in a given space precisely because they can reach the whole world from the City of London and from Manhattan without losing the dense network of localized, ancillary firms as well as the opportunities of face-to-face interaction created by territorial agglomeration.

At the same time, back offices can decentralize into the suburbs, newly developed metropolitan areas, or in some other country and be part of the same system. New business centers can be created around the country and around the world, always following the logic of clustering and decentralizing at the same time, of concentrating and networking, so creating a selective worldwide web of business services. As well, the new industrial space is characterized by its similar pattern of the spatial dispersion of activities and concentration of innovation and strategic decision-making—around what Peter Hall and I propose to label as "milieux of innovation," following the evidence gathered by a series of studies undertaken in the 1980s at Berkeley by the Institute of Urban and Regional Development. The new media have also become built around the double process of globalization of capital and customization/networking of information and images that respond to the localization of markets and segmentation of audiences. In territorial terms, in fact, the age of information is not just the age of spatial dispersal, it is the age of generalized urbanization. In the next decade it is likely that most people of the world will be, for the first time, living in the cities. Yet cities are, and will be, of very different kinds, depending on cultures, institutions, histories, and economies, but they share, and they will share in the forseeable future, a spatial logic that is specific to the Information Age. This logic is characterized by the combination of territorial sprawl and locational concentration. Thus intrametropolitan, interregional, and international networks connect with global networks in a structure of variable geometry that is enacted and modified by flows of information and electronic circuits and fast, information-based, transportation systems. In the last decade, studies by Peter Hall, Peter Daniels, AnnaLee Saxenian, Michael Batty, Jim Wheeler, Barry Wellman, Jeff Henderson, Roberto Camagni, Stephen Graham, Simon Marvin, Amy Glasmeier, and so many other scholars have substantiated, empirically, the emergence of a new spatial structure. This structure is defined by articulated territorial concentration and decentralization in which the unit is the network. This particular model of spatial organization, which seems to be characteristic of the Information Age, is the model that I tried to conceptualize, ten years ago, as the space of flows.

THE SPACE OF FLOWS

By space of flows, I understood, and I understand, the material arrangements that allow for simultaneity of social practices without territorial contiguity. It is not a purely electronic space. It is not what Batty has called a cyberspace, although cyberspace is a component of the space of flows. It is made up first of all of a technological infrastructure of information systems, telecommunications, and transportation lines. The capacity and characteristics of this infrastructure and the location of its elements determine the functions of the space of flows and its relationship to other spatial forms and processes.

The space of flows is also made of networks of interaction, and the goals and task of each network configurate a different space of flows. Thus financial markets, high-technology manufacturing, business services, entertainment, media news, drug traffic, science and technology, fashion design, art, sports, or religion constitute a specific network with a specific technological system and various territorial profiles. So they all operate on the logic of the space of flows but they specify this logic.

Second, the space of flows is made up of nodes and hubs. These nodes and hubs structure the connections and the key activities in a given locale or locales. For instance, Wall Street or Ginza are such nodes, as well as Cali and Tijuana in their specific trade, or Berkeley, Stanford, and MIT in computer sciences. Hubs are communication sites, airports, harbors, train, or bus stations that organize exchanges of all kinds, as they are increasingly interconnected and spatially related. However, what characterizes the new role of these hubs and nodes is that they are dependent on the network, that their logic depends on their place in the network, and that they are sites to process signals that do not originate from any specific place but from endless recurrent interactions in the network.

Third, the space of flows is also made of habitats for the social actors who operate the networks, be it residential spaces adjacent to the nodes, spaces of consumption, protected and secluded, or global corridors of social segregation separating these corridors from the surrounding places around the globe (VIP lounges, the virtual office, computing on the run, standardized international hotels).

Fourth, the space of flows comprises electronic spaces such as Web sites, spaces of interaction, as well as spaces of one-directional communication, be it interactive or not, such as information systems. A growing proportion of activity is from the Web, and the visual design of Web sites, as well as the structure of an operation of their content, is becoming a fundamental frame for decision-making, information making, and communication.

SPACE OF PLACES

I have sketched out the new spatial structure of the Information Age, the space of flows. But we really need to know that not all space is organized around the space of flows. As has been the case throughout the whole history of humankind, most people live, work, and construct their meaning around places. I defined, and I define, a place, as the locale whose form, function, and meaning are self-contained within the boundaries of territorial contiguity. People tend to construct their life in reference to places, be they their homes, their neighborhoods, their cities, their regions, their countries. Now this is not to say that the local community is thriving. In fact, research shows that all over the world, there has been a process of individualization and atomization of place-based relationships. The loss of community is, in fact, the founding theme of urban sociology, since the Chicago School. Yet you may have no community and still refer to your place as your main source of experience. Social organization and political representation are also predominately place-based. And cultural identity is often built on the basis of sharing historical experience in a given territory.

So, when analyzing spatial transformation in the Information Age and showing the emergence of a new spatial form, the space of flows, I also emphasized the persistence of the space of places as the most usual form of spatial existence for humankind. And I observed that while most dominant activities were constructed around the space of flows, most experience and social interaction was and still is organized around places. For dominant activities, I refer to financial flows and to the management of major corporations in services and manufacturing, as well as to their ancillary networks of firms, to media, entertainment, professional sports, science and technology, institutionalized religion, military power, the global criminal economy. Thus I added that, in fact, the constitution of the space of flows was in itself a form of domination, since the space of flows, even in its diversity, is interrelated and can escape the control of any locale, while the space of places is fragmented, localized, and thus increasingly powerless vis-à-vis the versatility of the space of flows, with the only chance of resistance for localities being to refuse landing rights for overwhelming flows—only to see that they land in the locale nearby, inducing therefore the bypassing and marginalization of rebellious communities.

This was my analysis some time ago, presented in various publications during the last decade. I still sustain most of this analysis, and I think it can be backed up empirically. However, what was an analysis of transformation of the space in a given historical moment—that is, the moment of the dawn of the Information Age—should not be cast in stone as an iron rule of spatial development. Yes, there are two different forms of space: flows and places. Yes, the space of flows is historically new in its overwhelming prevalence because it can deploy its logic through a new technological medium. Yes, dominant activities in our society are organized around the logic of the space of flows, while most forms of autonomous construction of meaning and social and political resistance to the powers that be are being constructed, for the time being, around places. But two major qualifications may be introduced:

First, the space of flows includes some places. Indeed, the space of flows is not simply an electronic space. Electronic spaces—such as the Internet or global communication media—are but one dimension, however important, of the space of flows.

Second, both electronic spaces and the space of flows at large are not exclusively organized around and by social/economic/cultural domination. Societies are not closed systems, they are always open processes, characterized by conflict. History, in fact, is a very tiresome experience. It never ends, against the claims of the neoliberal illusion. Wherever there is domination, there is resistance to domination. Wherever there is imposition of meaning, there are projects of construction of alternative meaning. And the realms of this resistance and this autonomous meaning are ubiquitous—which means, concretely, that while the space of flows has been produced by and around dominant activities and social groups, it can be penetrated by resistance and can be diversified in its meaning. The grass roots of societies do not cease to exist in the Information Age. And after an initial moment of exclusion and confusion, people and values of all kinds are now penetrating and using the space of flows, Internet and beyond, in the same way as the Parisian Champs-Élysées dreamed by Hausman to escape the populace of the *rive gauche*, have become, in the 1990s, the hangout place for the festive and multiethnic young people of the Paris *banlieues* (suburbs). While the space of flows remains the space in which dominant activities are spatially operated, it is experiencing at the same time the growing influence and pressure of the grass roots and the insertion of personal meaning by social actors, in a process that may alter the cultural and political dynamics of our societies and ultimately may alter the space of flows itself. So let me review the main dimensions of this grassrooting of the space of flows.

First, I will refer to a series of dimensions of autonomous expression of social meaning in the space of flows, with emphasis on electronic spaces but in interaction with the space of places. First is personal interaction—people using the Net for themselves and electronic mail as recuperating letter writing as a form of communication. And people are finding ways to be together with much more diversity and importance than has been the experience before in history: chat groups, multidimensional communication, cultural expressions of all kinds, people building their Web sites. People build their fantasies, but they also experience their needs and exchange their information. They are inhabiting the space of flows and thus transforming it. Am I talking maybe about a small global elite? Well not so small, and not so elite.

A second dimension for autonomous expression is represented by purposive, horizontal communication, not just personal feelings of casual communication. Horizontal communication occurs among people and across countries, and establishes information systems that are alternative to the media. And they are in fact doubling the media. There is, indeed, much gossip and irresponsible information. As you know, the news that triggered one of the latest scandals relating to President Clinton was first sent from the Internet through a news bulletin that is a one-man operation out of his home office in Los Angeles, while *Newsweek* was considering publication of the story. There are people and institutions very concerned about the lack of control of information on the Net. Many governments are terrified of losing control of information, a fundamental source of power throughout history. They usually argue in terms of controlling child pornography. I think child pornography is terrible. But what happens in countries like France or Spain, for instance, is that it is perfectly legal to sell child pornography—it is not legal to produce the images, and it is not legal to hire or kidnap the children to do it, but selling it is not a problem. But you cannot do it on the Internet. Why? Because the Internet is a mass medium, or so the statist argument goes. The fact is that horizontal communication on the Internet, by bypassing both media and government controls, is becoming a most fundamental political issue which, ultimately, reflects who we are collectively, as a society. And if some of us are enjoying child pornography, if we are this kind of monsters, this appears reflected on the Internet. The Internet brings us face to face with the mirror of who we actually are. So I would rather work on ourselves than close down the Net. The fight is against the self, not against the Net.

Third, there is a fast growth of networks of solidarity and cooperation on the Internet, with people bringing together their resources to live and to survive. To give an example, Senior Net in the United States not only brings information (for instance, to counter the monopoly of medical information by doctors) and resources together: it also develops solidarity ties between senior people, thus reinforcing the group to which all of us belong—or will belong if we are lucky. Thus, at the time the welfare state, at least as constructed in the last half-century, is being challenged economically and politically, people are reconstructing networks of solidarity and reflecting and debating about them at the same time.

The fourth dimension is social movements. The Net is increasingly used by social movements of all kinds as their organizing ground and as their privileged means to break their isolation. The greatest example here, and one that has become a classic, is the Zapatistas in Chiapas, Mexico. Without fully presenting the case, on which I have written in my latest book, let me remind you of some interesting facts about this social movement. The Zapatistas organized solidarity groups around the world on the Internet. And they used the Internet very effectively to diffuse their information and to obtain interactive communication between their different solidarity groups. They have also used the Internet as a protective way to fight repression when, in February 1995, there was a major military offensive that forced them to escape to the forest. They sent a message over the Internet asking everybody to flood the White House with messages, because at that point the White House had put money into the Mexican bailout. A major crisis in Mexico would jeopardize the entire stability of the region, ultimately wasting U.S. taxpayers' money. So in one day more than 30,000 messages came to the White House. That does not mean that street demonstrations in front of the White House are not important; they continue to be important, but you cannot organize them in twenty-four hours, and in this particular case it was a matter of life and death in these twenty-four hours. This ability of the Zapatistas to work on the Net does not come from Subcommandante Marcos, as people say, whether he was a communications professor or from the Indian communities. It came from women's groups in Mexico. In 1993, women's groups organized an Internet network in Mexico to support women's solidarity funded by the Catholic Church and organized instrumentally by the Institute of Global Communication in San Francisco, a group of progressive, computer people in Silicon Valley. The institute and the women's groups sent several people to Chiapas, and they organized an extension of the women's network that was called La Neta. La Neta is an interesting expression because on the one hand it is the Spanish feminine term for the Net, but in Mexican slang it also means the truth. So this La Neta network organized by women's groups branched out and trained a number of people in Chiapas who, through human rights groups, were the ones who were able to link up with the Zapatistas and provide both the technological and the knowledge support for their Internet operations.

However, not only progressive movements are on the Internet. Everybody is on the Internet, and our societies are on the Internet. The Internet has played a major role in the development of American militia groups. The Internet is as real as life itself. Increasingly, global movements of solidarity, environmentalists, and human rights and women's groups are organized on the Internet, again on the basis of local/global connection. One of the greatest and latest examples in the United States was the fall 1997 One Million Women March organized by two black women in Philadelphia. There was practically no organization, no sponsorship, and yet a small group of women in Philadelphia went on the Net and called a demonstration, obtaining an extraordinary level of support and mobilization. But going to a place, I think is the most interesting thing. The space of flows is not just being on the Net, it is organizing on the Net to be in Philadelphia on a given day; that is, using the Net to control space.

Fifth, linkages are a development to which we have to pay close attention, increasing linkages between people and institutions in an interactive process. The creation of what some people call virtual cities is renewing local governments and citizen democracy. May I say that we have some relatively old experiments, such as in 1986, when Santa Monica's PEN program allowed public debate between citizens, including debates on major issues such as homelessness in Santa Monica, with the homeless themselves being able to get into the debate. European cities are organizing participation in information systems. Graham and Aurigi have studied these experiments and they say that they are usually one-directional information systems. So it is still not a full-fledged participatory democracy; it is more information than participation and democracy, but still evolving and changing.

And there is a potential for much more. I am personally struck by the experience of Amsterdam's Digital City, an autonomous group originally supported by the municipality of Amsterdam. It is a private foundation that has organized a system of citizen participation and citizen interaction. You have to register to take part—anyone can visit the site, but to really participate to go to the homes, you have to be registered. By 1998, they had 80,000 fully registered participating "residents." They have activities organized around different squares: bigger squares and then micro squares. Each square relates to different activities, cultural politics, sports, business, then homes. People have built their homes, they also sometimes have marriages between the families that live in these homes; they do recall elections, they certainly do debates, and from time to time they link this to real life in a very close interaction. So the Digital City experience has shown the possibility of mobilizing the population at dramatically different levels, from the most political activist level to chat groups. What strikes me too is how much the group is connected to the local, political, and spatial experience in Amsterdam. On the one hand, this is a movement that grew out of the squatters movement in Amsterdam. Caroline Nevejan and Marlene Strikker, the two women who lead the movement and who lead this program, were members of this squatters movement and, in their own view, they have not changed their values much. They have continued their ability to mobilize people and change society through the new medium without abandoning the idea of the city as a place. Even symbolically, the city has ceded to them as their headquarters one of the most historic buildings in Amsterdam, the Waag, the building that in the sixteenth century used to close the canals for trade when the ships were coming to Amsterdam. This building also housed the School of Medicine where autopsies were performed that were illegal because of the church's repression. In that building, there is a room where Rembrandt painted his famous "Anatomy Lesson." In this very room is located the Digital City server. I think this kind of historical continuity, this linkage between history and information flows, place and electronic networks, is representative of something new happening in the space of flows.

Another example of this linkage between institutions, civil society, and grass roots groups, something that is less known because it is only in the project stage, is the Barcelona Internet Citizen Project. This project is being sponsored by the city of Barcelona and is linked to a megaproject they called Forum 2004. It is in fact a good example of connecting the global to the local, Internet to grass roots. Remember that the 1992 Olympic games created a great transformation in Barcelona. Among other things, Barcelona opened up to the sea by building a whole new neighborhood connecting to the harbor, seaside promenade, and beaches. Now a group of local leaders, with the support of the municipality, have conceived a new project, an Olympics of sort: the Forum 2004, with the sponsorship of UNESCO and the Pope. Over the course of the next six months, the project will make plans to bring in half a million young people from all over the world into Barcelona in 2004 to discuss what to do with the world in the twenty-first century. And of course they need to build a city to organize this project—therefore another 20 kilometers of seaside development.

Furthermore, the project includes the idea of linking up the world to these thousands of youth and sharing the debate on the Net. To ensure Barcelona citizens are up to the task, there is a project to set up an Internet citizen center to train and diffuse the uses of the Internet to people at large. Most people in Barcelona are unaware of the potential uses of the Internet, so a literacy campaign directly linked to an event and with the purpose of participating in a global debate could be key in bringing Barcelona as a whole into the Information Age.

As you can see, there is a gradual opening up of the Information of Age to different avenues. So through a blossoming of initiatives, people are taking on the Net without uprooting themselves from their places. And through this practice they transform both forms of the space. However, are we talking about only a small elite? Are people not in fact being massively excluded from the Net? Well, first of all, the recent data show there is a large elite—about 128 million users in 1998. Yes, data are shaky, but the same shaky data were indicating about 30 million users in 1995/1996. What seems to be a little bit more solid is the rate of diffusion among users, which seems to be nearly doubling every year. By the end of 2000, we should be approaching 500 million Internet users. Serious experts in the communication business predict about 1 billion users by the middle of the first decade of the twenty-first century, considering a slowdown in the rate of diffusion when less-advanced countries and less-educated and less-affluent groups become the new frontier of expansion. Computer capacity and telecommunications capacity are already there; the issue is how to bring people onto the Net. And for what?

Yet there is certainly a social bias in terms of who uses the Internet. There is a gender bias, with the proportion of men to women being 3 to 1. There is also an ethnic bias, with ethnic minorities having much lower rates of Internet use, although in the case of Hispanics in the United States, the rates of incorporation are extremely high. There is a country bias too. In fact, Scandinavia is advancing over everybody else. Finland has decided to become the first information society in the world. In 1998 there was one Web site for every ten people in Finland, and projections are that by 2000 there will be more Web sites in Finland than Finnish people. Still, in absolute terms, there is a dominance of the Internet by American users.

However, more importantly, the bias is not only in terms of use, but use for what purpose, that is the level of education required to look for and retrieve information. I have proposed a notion that we are living in a world that is made up of the interactive and the interacted. We interact, but many people are just interacted. For many people the Net may become an extension of a multimedia-based, one-directional system, so that they may receive some basic information to which they just have to react, as in some marketing device. However, if we look historically into the diffusion of information, and the diffusion of technology, and the ability to upgrade the level of consciousness and the level of information, there has always been a connection between open-minded, educated social groups and the uneducated masses who, through this connection, become educated. In the historic example of the development of the labor movement, printing workers were critical in that they knew how to read, whereas most workers did not know how to read nor want to read. Printing workers were the ones who, in many countries, created the basis for self-training, self-development, and self organization of these uneducated masses. And this is happening now in many countries. Low income communities are being brought onto the Internet in different ways by local community groups.

I also personally know of some important experiences that are highly developed, such as in the working class periphery of Barcelona, an area called the Lower Llobregat, in which the unions and the municipalities decided that they have to move into the Information Age and develop social struggles and social consciousness. They have created a cultural organization and a network of Internet-based, publicized activities around a journal titled *La Factoria* that you can access on the Net. Thus they have started a process of mass education and social debate, mixing print, the Net, the city, and the factory, and ultimately grass-rooting the Net.

Finally, even if there is still a minority of users (but a minority that is going to be numbered in the hundreds of millions), their eruption on the Net, with the creative cacophony of their social diversity and the plurality of their values and interests expressed on the Net, and the linkage between places and information flows transform the logic of the space of flows and make it a contested space—a plural and diversified space.

26 CONCLUSION

Whither the theory of the space of flows? Not necessarily. This is because it was always based on the linkage between electronic space and places through networks of flows—and this is becoming increasingly the space in which most important activities operate in our societies. There is interaction; there is connection. Moreover, it remains true, I think, and can be empirically sustained that strategically dominant activities are operated essentially through the space of flows, and that global elites ensure their domination in this process, bypass-ing segmented, isolated localities. And trenches of resistance to the domina-tion of flows of capital and information are being built primarily around places.

However, a new dynamics is operating, a dynamics of interpenetration of uniformity and autonomy, of domination and resistance, of instrumentality and experience, within the space of flows. So, historically produced forms of space, even as complex and new as the space of flows, by their very existence are trans-formed through the process of their enactment. They become contested spaces as well, freedom is carved in their hallways, and cultural identity is built and affirmed on the Net. So the geography of the new history will not be made, after all, of the separation between places and flows, but out of the interface between places and flows and between cultures and social interests, both in the space of flows and in the space of places. The attempt by capital, media, and power to escape into the abstraction of the space of flows, bypassing democ-racy and experience by confining them in the space of places, is being chal-lenged from many sources by the grassrooting of the space of flows.

PART II.

Cyberspace

3

HOW TELECOMMUNICATIONS SYSTEMS ARE TRANSFORMING URBAN SPACES

Mitchell L. Moss and Anthony M. Townsend

INTRODUCTION

All too often, telecommunications systems are treated as an alternative to transportation systems, as a substitute for the physical movement of people and services. The growing use of telecommunications systems is doing far more than influence where people work and live, but is actually changing the character of activities that occur in the home, workplace, and automobile. This chapter examines the way in which information and telecommunications are transforming everyday urban life; making the home into an extension of the office, shopping mall, and classroom; allowing the automobile and airplane to become workplaces; and converting the office building into a hub for social interaction and interpersonal contact. The diffusion of information technologies drastically increases the complexity of cities by increasing the number and type of interactions among individuals, firms, technical systems, and the external environment. Information systems are permitting new combinations of people, equipment, and places; as a result, there is a dramatic change in the spatial organization of activities within cities and large metropolitan regions.

Telecommunications has made the fundamental elements of urban life — housing, transportation, work, and leisure — far more complex logistically, spatially, and temporally. Despite the rapid integration of information and telecommunications into everyday life, our theories and policies rarely consider the role of information technology in urban growth and development. In this chapter, we explore the way in which new information and telecommunications systems are altering the structure of urban development in the United States.

For the past century, cities have sought to control land use and guide economic development by designating areas for distinctly different types of activities. The zoning regulations that govern most cities and suburbs reflect the industrial-era value placed on the separation of activities into distinct zones for residential, commercial, and industrial uses. The dirt, dust, and fumes from factories led to a concern for public health that imposed restrictions on where manufacturing activities could occur. With the advent of the electric streetcar, commuter railroad, and the automobile, it became possible to develop residential communities far from the industrial portions of cities.

As we enter the twenty-first century, telecommunications technologies are transforming the mix of activities within the home, office, and automobile in ways that are only beginning to be recognized and understood. We have invested far more resources to study the influence of transportation systems on urban development than to understand the relationship of telecommunications technologies to urban and regional growth. The popular and academic literature on new information technologies reflects a long-standing belief that electronic communications will lead to the economic decline of cities as they make it possible to replace the face-to-face activities that occur in central locations. More than a quarter century ago, Ronald Abler (1970), a pioneer in the study of communications and urban space suggested that:

> [A]dvances in information transmission may soon permit us to disperse information-gathering and decision-making activities away from metropolitan centers, and electronic communications media will make all kinds of information equally abundant everywhere in the nation, if not everywhere in the world.

George Gilder (1995) extended this argument when he wrote that: "we are headed for the death of cities" due to the continued growth of personal computing and distributed organizations advances. Gilder further claimed that: "cities are leftover baggage from the industrial era." By this reasoning, cities are no longer needed to access a wide range of cultural activities and information sources, because telecommunications can bring the library, concert hall, or business meeting into any home or office.

Peter Gordon and Harry W. Richardson (1997), of the University of Southern California, have argued that communications technologies are reinforcing the movement out of cities that the automobile had initiated: "Rapid advances in telecommunications are now accelerating the decentralization trends set in motion by the advent of the automobile." They contend that: "Proximity is becoming redundant.... Entertainment already is, and instruction is more likely to be, transmitted over broad-band radio frequencies rather than seen in traditional theaters or lecture halls. Today's cities continue to become less compact; the city of the future will be anything but compact."

Most observers believe that technology will eliminate the need for cities as centers of interaction. The leading media guru, Nicholas Negroponte (1995), has stated that "[T]he post-information age will remove the limitations of geography. Digital living will include less and less dependence upon being in a specific place at a specific time, and the transmission of place itself will start to become possible." Even the concept of the "edge city," a label that Joel Garreau (1991) applied to clusters of suburban office parks linked by freeways, is a reflection of how both transportation and communication technologies are treated as forces that have fostered the outmigration of work and housing from the central city.

Admittedly, geographers such as John Goddard, Jean Gottman, Allen Scott, and James Wheeler have carefully analyzed the way in which telecommunications can both centralize and decentralize activities, reflecting geography's concern for understanding communications technology and the location of human activities. Gottmann (1983) proposed that communications technologies work in two directions by making it possible both to concentrate and to disperse economic activities, and had a "dual impact" on office location: "First, it has freed the office from the previous necessity of locating next to the operations it directed; second, it has helped to gather offices in large concentrations in special areas." The authors of this paper have also succumbed to this spatial imperative and emphasized the role of technology in reinforcing the position of major cities in the United States. (Moss and Townsend, 1996, 1997, 1998)

Nigel Thrift (1996) provided a new rationale for face-to-face contact in an era of high-speed communications by claiming that telecommunications networks were generating a demand for instant information in the financial services sector that was best done in a face-to-face context. Thrift argued that the principal function of major financial centers is interpreting in real time the massive amounts of information that are generated each day: "Since the international financial system generates such a massive load of information, power goes to those who are able to offer the most convincing interpretations of the moment." Interpreting information depends as much on face-to-face interaction as on advanced technologies, an activity that is necessarily and increasingly centralized in the leading world financial centers.

A NEW APPROACH TO TELECOMMUNICATIONS RESEARCH

While telecommunications technologies are certainly a space-adjusting phenomena, the emergence of the Internet, the growth of mobile telephony, and the diffusion of new information technologies are doing far more than merely rearrange the spatial pattern of activities in cities and metropolitan regions. New telecommunications systems are redefining the fundamental elements of modern urban society—the office, the automobile, the home, and the street—and generating a need for a new conceptual framework to understand the way in which telecommunications systems are influencing the character of activities in cities and metropolitan regions.

Simply put, telecommunications systems have progressed faster and deeper into our society than the theories we use to guide research on such technologies. Michael Batty (1997) states: "the city itself is turning into a constellation of computers." Batty highlights the way in which new information systems are "generating new opportunities for understanding and planning cities," and makes a powerful case for a new approach to the study of cities that builds upon the "synthesis of computers and telecommunications." As he states:

[C]omputers which were once thought of as solely being instruments for a better understanding, for science, are rapidly becoming part of that infrastructure, and thus affecting space and location. In one view, the line between computers being used to aid our understanding of cities and their being used to operate and control cities has not only become blurred but has virtually dissolved. In another sense, computers are becoming increasingly important everywhere and the asymmetry posed by their exclusive use for analysis and design in the past and their all pervasive influence in the city is now disappearing. In both cases, the implication is that computers will have to be used to understand cities which are built of computers.

In recent years, new theoretical and empirical studies have offered insights into the way in which information systems are influencing urban activity patterns. Jed Kolko has suggested that telecommunications has led to the "death of distance" but not the "death of cities." He also found that "city size is positively related to domain density, and significantly so" (Kolko, 1998). Daniel Sui has proposed the need for new urban models that reflect an "organic view of cities based upon analogies in biology" and that emphasize that "cities are formed more from local actions without centralized planning or macro control " (Sui, 1998). The growth of electronic communications is also forcing changes in how we think about regions, according to Harvey and Macnab. They assert that "the fundamental geographical notion of the region" is in need of a temporal overhaul and ask "to what degree will traditional east-west channels . . . give way to north-south alignments more win keeping with the time of day?" (Harvey and Macnab, 1998).

This chapter makes a simple argument: the deployment of new telecommunications systems is altering the activities that occur in the key elements of urban society—the home, the office, the automobile, and even the hotel room and public parks and streets. Telecommunications systems are blurring the separation between the home and the workplace, radically changing office design and function, transforming the automobile into an extension of the workplace, and moving street crime into the shadows of cyberspace.

TELECOMMUNICATIONS AND THE WORKPLACE

The modern office building is the single greatest human artifact explicitly designed to generate, process, and manage information. The merger of computers and telecommunications systems has profoundly altered the physical design of office buildings and the type of activities that occur within them. At the macroscopic level, new office buildings increasingly feature advanced telecommunications infrastructure built into their walls and floors to accommodate the growing use of data and video transmission equipment. For large financial institutions, the floorplate of a building has become the critical factor, as large floor areas are required for modern trading rooms where hundreds of traders are situated in close proximity to each other. In cities such as New York and London, many older office buildings are unable to meet today's technological requirements, generating a demand for new buildings that can meet today's spatial and technological requirements. As a result, Canary Wharf in the London Docklands and the World Financial Center in New York City's Battery Park City have attracted leading financial institutions to areas that are not contiguous to the city's traditional financial district.

At the same time, there is also a new emphasis on interior office design that eliminates the physical boundaries within offices in order to promote human interaction. Francis Duffy (1969), was among the first to observe that modern office buildings are increasingly designed to accommodate the face-to-face exchange of information through meetings, conferences, and informal conversations at the watercooler. As Duffy states, "Office work is generally becoming more mobile, more complex, and more plural. And yet there is often the need for some concentrated, individual work in the same place. This has led to one of the eternal conflicts in office design: the need to accommodate communication and interaction as well as individual work" (Duffy, 1998). Firms such as IBM (Young, 1992) have reduced the size of individual offices and rely on flexible office assignments such as "hot-desking," but there is simultaneously a greater emphasis on the use of conference rooms and centers for mobilizing workers, encouraging interaction, and bringing experts together to work in team efforts.

Telecommunications technologies have also influenced the scale and mix of activities that occur within office buildings. The modern office building has remained the epicenter of electronic and face-to-face communication by adapting to new technological requirements and organizational priorities only through investments in new equipment, which have dramatically expanded the buildings' information-processing capabilities. An example of such modernization is the New York Information Technology Center, a 400,000-square-foot building in Manhattan's Financial District that was previously the headquarters of an investment bank. Although the building stood empty for years, in 1995 it was totally renovated with new telecommunications systems and has become a center for New York's multimedia industry (Conway, 1997).

While technological innovation has strengthened the role of the office building in certain areas of the financial sector, it has also led to the dispersion of routine and retail financial services. Nowhere is this more apparent than in the consolidation of local banks into interstate banking companies and the replacement of the local branch offices with automated teller machines (ATMs). Retail banks, once built to resemble elaborate temples in order to reassure depositors that their savings were safe and secure, are no longer defined by real estate but by electronic networks. This has led many communities to protest the loss of the locally owned and managed bank, while also hastening the spread of 24-hour banking into local communities through the supermarket, drugstore, and gas station.

Of even more significance, banks now operate solely in electronic space rather than physical space. Three Internet banks, Security First Network Bank and Atlanta Internet Bank offer 24-hour service at their Websites, and a third, CompuBank opened in mid-1998. These banks may be the harbinger of banking in the future; an activity once confined to a distinct physical building in the geographic center of a community that can now be conducted from a terminal anywhere in the world. However, these new ways of banking presuppose access to and literacy in information technology and telecommunications, which are lacking in many poor inner-city and rural communities.

Another place-based activity, the auction market—whether in rare art, commodities, or financial instruments—has traditionally relied on face-to-face contact that took place in specific cities and at specific times. Telecommunications has totally disrupted the traditional physical marketplace in which goods are bought and sold. For example, the auction of tea leaves, an activity based in London for more than three hundred years, can now be conducted wherever tea is grown—in Sri Lanka, India, China, and Africa—as a result of advanced telecommunications systems. Electronic trading in futures and options is being done through a global network that links the Chicago Mercantile Exchange, the Paris Bourse, and the Singapore International Monetary Exchange and will eventually replace the traditional "open outcry" system, in which buyers and sellers shout out bids on the crowded floor of an exchange.

Even the secretive world of buying and selling art has adapted to telecommunications. More than seven hundred art dealers are linked to ArtNet, an online service that allows potential buyers to see collections online and to compare prices, a previously impossible task. Jacob Weisberg notes that "the Web will expand the art market not only by spreading information but also by making art into a more liquid asset" (Weisberg, 1999). The potential growth of the art market through electronic auctions does not mean that cities will decline as centers for culture, but that the world of art, like the world of finance, will soon be driven by information, and that those people and places with the skill and capacity to participate in the electronic flow of art will benefit greatly. If history is any guide, explaining, interpreting, and conveying information about the art market will soon be as valued as the production of art itself.

THE HOME ENVIRONMENT

Just as the office environment has been influenced by telecommunications technology, the home is undergoing a fundamental change in its function and design as a result of new telecommunications technologies. Information has traditionally been delivered to the home through a single telephone line, broadcast radio and television, and by hand (whether delivered by mail carriers or newspaper delivery personnel, or carried in by the residents). For much of the last one hundred years, the home has functioned primarily as a site for social-emotional functions of the family, explicitly designed as a refuge from the workplace. A relic of Victorian-era philosophers, this separation of home and work appears to be disappearing as new information technologies are becoming widely available.

Information brought into the home through satellite dishes, coaxial cable, and high-speed phone lines dramatically expands the number and type of activities that can occur within the confines of a residence. According to a recent study by the US Department of Labor (1998), more than 21 million Americans did some part of their primary job at home in 1997, and more than half of those used a computer for their home-based work. For many small businesses and self-employed individuals, personal computers equipped with modems, reliable overnight delivery services, sophisticated voice mail systems, and the proliferation of neighborhood office centers such as Kinko's have allowed the home to become the firm's headquarters, workplace, and distribution center. In Manhattan, San Francisco, Chicago, and Boston, underutilized industrial structures have been converted into combined "work-and-live space" with advanced telecommunications systems to serve home-based workers.

The capacity to extend the workplace into the home has generated new demands for high-speed telephone lines in the home. Home contractors now treat telecommunications infrastructure as the equivalent of "electronic plumbing," and new homes are being equipped with high capacity phone conduits to accommodate information services. Electrolux has even developed an Internet-connected refrigerator with an LCD touch screen and bar-code scanner that could be used to order groceries over the Web. New housing developments across the United States are being marketed to sophisticated buyers, based on the speed of their Internet access and services available through their own intranet. A developer of townhouse and single-family housing in the Washington, D.C., metropolitan area offers Local Area Network (LAN) wiring as an option in all new homes it constructs, at a price of $1,500 to $2,000 (Tueting, 1997).

The diffusion of new information-based services in the home—for security, climate control, and entertainment—has led a consortium of semiconductor, computer, and telecommunications companies to develop a "Shared Wireless Access Protocol" that would interconnect electronic devices within the home using the same technology employed by cordless telephones. Even low-income communities are participating in the information explosion in the house. In Oakland, California, the Acord complex, a 206-unit housing project, is equipped with fiber-optic cables, computers in each home, and a learning center for job training.

Public services, once provided solely within designated public buildings such as schools, libraries, or prisons are now also being provided in the home, albeit for different reasons. For example, the growth of "home-schooling" has been facilitated by the Internet; an estimated 1.2 million children now learn at home, and in California there is a California Homeschool Network that links home-schooling parents. Amazon.com even has a link for home-schoolers on its Web site. At the same time, many government agencies have adopted advanced technologies remotely to monitor parolees as a way to control costs. The home has evolved into a site for the incarceration for nonviolent offenders. Electronic bracelets simply activate a modem to contact corrections officers when a convict attempts to leave his or her home.

In the twenty-first century, a home's attractiveness will be judged by the speed of its dial-up connections and extent of its intelligent infrastructure, rather than conventional measures such as the number of bedrooms or bathrooms.

John Chambers, President of Cisco Systems, believes that "everything" in the home will be connected to the Internet—not just electronic devices, but the piano, the fireplace, the window blinds (Beiser, 1999). According to some experts, it will even be possible to create "rooms or environments where humans can interact with otherwise inanimate objects and machines; . . . consumers will be able to turn their homes into full-fledged intelligent environments" (Patch and Smalley, 1998). Clearly, the movement of information into the home will expand its role in the economy, allowing all members of a household to participate in a wide array of different economic and social functions and making the home far more than a site for housing family members.

TELECOMMUNICATIONS AND TRAVEL

Wireless telephony has transformed transportation and travel across the world, converting the automobile, the hotel room, and even the airport into an information-intensive infrastructure. It is conceivable that telecommunications will eventually make the automobile commute into a productive part of the workday, once it is possible to send and receive e-mails, faxes, and telephone calls from any street or highway. "Hands-free" voice recognition technology should overcome many of the safety concerns about mobile phones. Traffic jams and congestion may even be tolerated as a chance to catch up with telephone messages and e-mail. Traffic congestion may even intensify in cities and suburbs, as the automobile evolves into a communications as well as transportation device.

There are a variety of new technological innovations that have been designed to take advantage of the automobile's new role. Traffic information, once delivered by radio stations, is now a commercially available service provided by mobile phone in many metropolitan areas. Subscribers can even purchase customized traffic reports on their routes in Southern California. And in the State of Washington, a demonstration project is testing a voice-activated computer, the AutoPC, that provides instant traffic information to cars equipped with this technology (A. Reid, 1998 and Whitely, 1999).

However, information technology is also being deployed to assist motorists eager to make face-to-face contact with drivers they identify on the freeway. Traffic Gems, a company in Long Island, New York, provides subscribers with a bumper sticker that contains an e-mail alias so that motorists who want to meet a fellow driver can visit the Traffic Gems Web site, find out more about other subscribers, and e-mail a message (Slayton, 1998). When the automobile was first invented, it was commonly called a "horseless carriage," but with information technology, it has become possible to do far more in a car than one could do in a horse-drawn carriage.

PUBLIC LIFE, PUBLIC SPACES, AND TELECOMMUNICATIONS

Cities have often been defined by their great public spaces, where people meet and share common experiences, whether in a stadium, a cathedral, or even a music club. Telecommunications systems are gradually affecting even the activities and events that occur in those distinctly urban settings. For example, the capacity to download music from Internet sites may soon diminish the recorded music industry but could invigorate nightclubs and concert halls where live music is produced. Telecommunications technology makes it possible for every club and concert hall to be a site for transmitting music over the Internet to audiences around the world.

Airports and hotels are also being transformed into centers for information-based activities so that travelers can conduct business while waiting for flights or during layovers. A company called Laptop Lane rents offices, phone lines, and equipment to air travelers in several major airports across the United States. Similarly, hotels now recognize the need to provide their guests with access to sophisticated information infrastructure. At the Ritz-Carlton Hotel in Kuala Lumpur, there is an on-call "technology butler" to provide high-tech support to business travelers. Hotel chains are increasingly providing a variety of telecommunications services, ranging from "virtual offices" in each hotel room to computing kiosks in public areas. The hotel room, once a place to rest, has also become a place to do business.

The character of urban street life is also changing due to the deployment of communications technologies by law enforcement agencies and criminal organizations. Telecommunications has always been an important tool in law enforcement, but a broad array of new technologies is increasing the effectiveness of crime prevention and prosecution. New geographic information systems being used to map and identify crime-prone locations, and remote surveillance cameras being deployed to monitor drug dealing in many cities are widely used in many urban precincts. In Redwood City, California, the police are able precisely to identify the location of gunshots with a new system of directional microphones connected by phone lines to a central computer. In St. Louis, police cars are equipped with laptop computers so that police can rapidly obtain information about suspects and perform live scanning of fingerprints without using a radio dispatcher as intermediary.

Perhaps the most innovative use of new telecommunications has been by drug dealers and prostitutes who increasingly use beepers, Web sites, and mobile phones to conduct their business transactions. In big cities, drug dealers rely on beepers to receive requests from purchasers and can avoid selling drugs in public places by using mobile phones to arrange deliveries.

Telecommunications is also converting the "streetwalker," the oldest urban profession into an online industry. Web sites such as www.redlightnet.com allow prostitutes to advertise their services and to reach customers without leaving their home. While the actual service may entail interpersonal contact, the negotiation over price and schedule can be done electronically, off the streets. In New York City, street level prostitution is reserved for the low-cost provider and customer. Surely, prostitutes will never be eliminated from city streets, but the emergence of erotic Web sites and online sex is diverting some of the traffic that might once have frequented adult entertainment districts in large cities. While this may be an improvement in the "quality of life," it is not clear how tourists will respond to such changes in urban street activity.

CONCLUSION

This chapter has sought to provide an alternative perspective on how scholars can study the effects of telecommunications in cities and metropolitan regions. The information-based city is increasingly differentiated from previous urban forms by its extensive and interconnected networks for moving information. Unlike previous upheavals that followed the advent of large-scale technological innovations such as factory-based mass production or the interstate highway system, the transformation of the metropolis is being driven by the diffusion of intelligence and awareness (via technology) across many components of urban life. Telecommunications technologies are changing the character of activities in the office, home, automobile, and even the street. This essay has identified—at a very preliminary level—the need to expand our research on telecommunication so that we can understand how commuting, the home, work, and even public spaces are being affected by new telecommunications systems.

REFERENCES

Abler, Ronald. (1970). "What Makes Cities Important." *Bell Telephone Magazine.*

Asimove, Nanette. (1999). "Teaching the Kids at Home: Internet Swamped with Home-school Resources." *San Francisco Chronicle* January 29.

Batty, Michael. (1997). "The Computable City." *Online Planning* 2. (http://www.casa.ucl.ac.uk/planning/articles2/city.htm)

Beiser, Vince. (1999). "Networking Everything." *Wired News* January 8. (http://www. wired.com/news/news/culture/story/17237)

Conway, Andrew. (1997). "55 Broad Street: The Digitization of Physical Space." Institute for Technology and Enterprise, Polytechnic University, Brooklyn, New York. April 1. (http://www.poly.edu/ite/55broad/begin.htm)

Duffy, Francis Cuthbert. (1998). "The New Office." *Facilities Design and Management* October 12. (http://www.fdm.com/db_area/archives/1998/9808/newoffice.htm)
———. (1969). "Organization, Behavior, and Office Buildings: Some Proposals for Analysis and Design." Thesis (Master of Architecture), University of California, Berkeley. September.

Garreau, Joel. (1991). *Edge City: Life on the New Frontier.* New York: Doubleday.

Gilder, George. (1995). *Forbes ASAP* February 27: 56.

Gordon, Peter and Richardson, Harry W. (1997). "Are Compact Cities a Desirable Planning Goal?" *Journal of the American Planning Association* (Winter) Vol. 63, No.1.

Gottman, Jean. (1983). "Urban Settlements and Telecommunications." *Ekistics.*

Harvey, Andrew S. and Paul A. Macnab. (1998). "Who's Up? Global Interpersonal Temporal Access." Paper presented at the NCGIA Specialist Meeting: Measuring and Representing Accessibility in the Information Age, November 19–22, Monterey, California. Time Use Research Program, Department of Economics, Department of Geography, Saint Mary's University, Halifax, Nova Scotia, Canada.

Kahney, Leander. (1999). "The Coolest Internet Appliace." *Wired News* February 12. (http://www.wired.com/news/news/email/explode-infobeat/technology/story/17894.html)

Kelley, Tina. (1998). "Places to Do Business on the Fly." *The New York Times*, November 5. (http://www.nytimes.com/library/tech/98/11/circutis/articles/05airp.html)

MITCHELL L. MOSS AND ANTHONY M. TOWNSEND

Kolko, Jed. (1998). "The Death of Cities? The Death of Distance? Evidence from the Geography of Commercial Internet Usage." Unpublished manuscript, Harvard University, October. Contact Mr. Kolko at kolko@nber.nber.org.

Moss, Mitchell L. and Townsend, Anthony M. (1996). "Leaders and Losers on the Internet," Taub Urban Research Center, New York University, September. (http://urban.nyu.edu/research/l-and-l/report.html)

———. (1997). "Tracking the 'Net: Using Domain Names to Measure the Growth of the Internet in U.S. Cities." *Journal of Urban Technology* Vol. 4, No. 3. December.

———. (1998). "Spatial Analysis of the Internet in U.S. Cities and States." Paper presented at "Urban Futures—Technological Futures" conference in Durham, England, April 23–25. (http://urban.nyu.edu/research/newcastle/newcastle.html)

Negroponte, Nicholas. (1995). *Being Digital*. New York: Knopf.

Patch, Kimberly and Eric Smalley. (1998). "The Walls Have Eyes—and Ears and . . ." *Boston Globe* July 20. (http://www.ai.mit.edu/people/mhcoen/Globe/Globe.html)

Reid, Alice. (1998). "High-Tech Traffic Help Is En Route." *Washington Post* August 10. (http://www.washingtonpost.com/wp-srv/frompost/aug98/traffic10.htm)

Reid, T. R. (1998). "Traders Lament End of London Auction?" *Washington Post* June 29. (http://www.washingtonpost.com/wp-srv/frompost/june98/london20.htm)

Silberman, Steve. (1999). "Minding Bits at the Ritz." *Wired News* January 5. (http://www.wired.com/news/news/culture/story/17095 .html)

Slayton, Joyce. (1998). "Driving on the Freeway of Love." *Wired News*, December 21. (http://www.wired.com/news/print_version/culture/story/16956.html?wnpg=all)

Sui, Daniel Z. (1998). "Geography of the E-merging Information Society: Accesibility of Adatability?" Paper delivered at NCGIA Project Varenius Specialist Meeting. Asilomar, California, November. (ftp://www.artsci.washington.edu/nsfpapers/dsui.doc)

Thrift, Nigel. (1996). "New Urban Eras and Old Technological Fears: Reconfiguring the Goodwill of Electronic Things." *Urban Studies* Vol. 33, No. 8.

Tueting, S. M. (1997). "Hard-Wired to the Future; Differentiation: A Virginia Homebuilder Offers Advanced Computer, Phone, Video, and Audio Wiring." *Baltimore Sun*, October 19.

United States Department of Labor, Bureau of Labor Statistics. (1998). "Work at Home in 1997." March 11. (http://stats.bls.gov/news.release/homey.toc.htm)

Wesiberg, Jacob. (1997). "Picasso.com: the Internet Breaks Open the Art Market." *Slate* February 5.

Whitely, Peyton. (1999). "With New PC, Your Car Can Talk Back." *Seattle Times* February 12. (http://www.seattletimes.com/news/local/html98/auto_021299.html)

Young, H. (1992). "Workplace Solutions." Paper presented to the Beacon Group Teleworking 92 Conference, September 15, Brighton, England. Cited in Gillespie, Andrew, and Richardson, Ranald. "Tele-Activities and the City: Emerging Technologies, emerging Mythologies". Paper presented at the "Telecommunications and the City" Conference, Athens, Georgia, March 23, 1998.

WHERE ON EARTH IS THE INTERNET?

AN EMPIRICAL INVESTIGATION OF THE GEOGRAPHY OF INTERNET REAL ESTATE

Martin Dodge and Narushige Shiode

INTRODUCTION

The Internet is largely an invisible communications phenomenon. It is used by millions of people every day, yet there is little physical evidence of its existence (Batty, 1990, 1993). For many people the Internet is a "place" that lies somewhere beyond their computer screens in a new domain popularly known as cyberspace. However, the invisible territories of the Internet do have a geography and, in an attempt to reveal its topography, we are analyzing the spatial patterns of the *ownership* of Internet space. In this chapter we draw an analogy between the space of the Internet and physical space of the real world; we refer to the virtual space of the Internet as "*Internet real estate.*"

To aid our understanding of the spatial patterns of Internet real estate, we are mapping it onto real geographical space — geospace — to provide a familiar grid. It is also hoped that mapping the ownership of Internet real estate onto geospace will provide useful insights into where the Internet and the emerging digital economy (Kelly, 1997; Commerce, 1998; Davis and Meyer, 1998) are focused in the real world and what the impacts may be on the cities. The impact of cyberspatial technologies on location, distance, and geography in the real world is the subject of recent academic debate (Couclelis, 1994, 1996, 1998; Graham and Marvin, 1996; NCGIA, 1996), as well as the focus for more populist economic commentators looking at "weightless worlds," "friction-free economies," and the "death of distance" (Coyle, 1997; Cairncross, 1997; Lewis, 1998).

STATEMENT OF PURPOSE

We begin by defining what we mean by Internet real estate and how space and location are created within the Internet. Next we describe the source of our empirical data on the United Kingdom's Internet real estate and how it was mapped onto geospace. We then present the preliminary results of our analysis mapping Internet real estate in the United Kingdom using density surfaces.

OTHER RELEVANT RESEARCH

There has been little academic empirical research examining the geography of Internet infrastructure and usage at a detailed geographic scale. In addition, there has been no one looking at IP address space from a geographical perspective that we are aware of. The majority of the studies have examined the geography of the Internet at the global scale working with data that is readily available at the national scale (Batty and Barr, 1994; ITU, 1997; Press, 1997). In this work there is a reliance on descriptive measures, such as Internet linked computers per capita. The paper by Larry Press provides a good overview of these types of statistical sources (Press, 1997). In terms of traffic flows, TeleGeography Inc., a research consultancy, provides one of the best sources of data and analysis from a geographical perspective (Staple, 1997). There are also a seemingly endless number of demographic and marketing surveys of Internet usage, perhaps the best is the GVUWWW User Survey series (GVU, 1998). However, many are of dubious quality and few have any geographical discrimination.

There is even less empirical work looking at the geography of the Internet at the subnational level of regions and cities. This is due in large part to the dearth of comprehensive and reliable data on the Internet's users and infrastructure at this local scale. There are two notable exceptions; first, a study by Greenstein on the geography of the commercial Internet service provider (ISP) industry in the United States (Greenstein, 1998). His study examined potential access to the Internet at the county level using the availability of dial-up ISPs in local call areas as an empirical measure, the context for the research being the changing notion of universal service as the Internet increases in significance, particularly in relation to differential access between rural and urban populations. From a geographical perspective, he concluded that approximately 15 percent of the U.S. population has only costly access to the Internet.

The other exception worthy of note is the research by Moss and Townsend looking at the geography of ownership of Internet domain names in the United States (Moss and Townsend, 1996, 1997, 1998). From their research on the density and growth of domains in major cities, they conclude that major "information-based" urban centers have been in the vanguard of Internet development; in particular; ". . . New York City has the largest Internet presence of any city in the United States, and in all likelihood, the entire world" (Moss and Townsend, 1997, page 52). In their most recent work they have also examined the capacity of Internet network links between U.S. metropolitan areas. Townsend also contributed significantly to a recent nonacademic study of "America's 100 Most Wired Cities & Towns" in a popular Internet magazine (Greenman, 1998). An index of "most wired" cities was constructed for the article using various measures, such as the density of Web sites, Internet hosts, users, and bandwidth. Perhaps unsurprisingly, the winner was San Francisco, "the undisputed west coast leader in software, hardware, geeks per capita, and more—S.F. is plugged in" (Greenman, 1998). There is also notable work by Matthew A. Zook (1998), Department of City and Regional Planning at University of California, Berkeley. Zook made a detailed analysis of the geography of domain name ownership in the United States, including mapping down to street level.

Finally, an honorable mention should go to John S. Quarterman and his Matrix Information and Directory Services (MIDS) research consultancy. Quarterman is a real Internet veteran having been involved in networking for many years. He published one of the first books on the Internet and other computer networks, entitled *The Matrix* (Quarterman, 1990). His MIDS consultancy is one of leading companies collating and mapping the geography of Internet hardware and users for many countries around the world. However, the results, such as those published in the *Matrix Maps Quarterly* magazine, are available only at commercial consultancy prices. In addition, little analysis of the results beyond simple descriptive mapping is attempted.

WHAT IS INTERNET REAL ESTATE?

Space on the Internet is not an infinite and unbound electronic domain, as often presented in populist "cyber" writings. Fundamentally, Internet space is defined and in a sense created by the addressing standard used to identify and locate computers on the network. This is a globally unique numeric code called an *IP address* (short for Internet Protocol address). An IP address looks something like 128.40.59.170, consisting of four numbers ranging from 0 to 255, separated by dots.

The IP address defines a massive spatial array, containing more than four billion unique locations (4,294,967,296 to be precise). However, in practice the actual usable Internet address space is smaller than this because of how it has been partitioned and allocated (Huston, 1994; Semeria, 1997). IP addresses are fine for computers to use but are not easily remembered by people. Hence the invention of the domain name system, which matches more memorable names (such as *www.ucl.ac.uk*) to the numeric IP addresses.

The IP address can be compared, in principle, to postcodes (zip codes) used by postal services to identify real world locations (mailboxes) for the delivery of letters and parcels. Postcodes define a distinct and widely used form of spatial referencing (Raper, Rhind, and Shepherd, 1992), and the IP address is the Internet equivalent, allowing parcels of data to be delivered to the correct computer "mailbox." IP addresses are usually allocated in large blocks. Taking our postcode analogy further, blocks of IP addresses can be thought of as forming chunks of valuable "real estate" on the Internet onto which computers can be "built."

So who actually owns this Internet real estate? This is somewhat of a moot question at present. It can be argued that no one really owns the space of the Internet because it is a public good belonging to the whole Internet community. The ownership and management of key Internet standards and protocols, such as IP address space and domain names, have been a source of considerable debate in recent years (Conrad, 1996; Foster, Rutkowski, and Goodman, 1997; Kahin and Keller, 1997). The Internet is in a period of rapid commercialization and globalization, undergoing a somewhat difficult transition from a network effectively run by the U.S. government and academia to a global communications medium and commercial entity. The control of domain names, in particular the much sought after global *.com* ones, has been particularly contentious (Shaw, 1997; Diamond, 1998).

In practical terms, the management of the global IP address space is handled by the Internet Assigned Number Authority (IANA), which, in turn, delegates large blocks of addresses to regional Internet registries (RIRs) to administer (Foster, Rutkowski, and Goodman, 1997). There are three such registries responsible for different geographical areas. They are :

ARIN (American Registry for Internet Numbers), covering North and South America, the Caribbean and sub-Saharan Africa

RIPE (Réseaux IP Européens), covering Europe and surrounding countries

APNIC (Asia—Pacific Network Information Center), covering Asia and the Pacific

In some cases the regional registries further delegate management responsibility to local Internet registries (LIRs) at the national level. For example, APNIC delegates responsibility down to JPNIC (Japan Network Information Center), which then manages IP address space in Japan. Individual organizations and companies that need Internet addresses then make requests to the appropriate regional or local registries for the required size range of IP address space. This IP space is allocated free (excluding a small registration fee) to the organization for its exclusive use as it sees fit. Allocation is on a first-come, first-served basis (Hubbard, et al., 1996). Due to the extremely rapid growth of the Internet in the recent years, concerns were raised that available IP address space could quickly become exhausted; in effect the Internet would run out of "vacant land" for new development (Huston, 1994). In response, various technical and management solutions have been implemented by the Internet community to mitigate the dangers of "overdevelopment" of Internet space (Halabi, 1997; Semeria, 1997).

Once an organization has been allocated a block of IP address space, it is free to "build" whatever it wants on its plot of Internet real estate, with no planning constraints. However, organizations do have to prove a genuine need for the Internet real estate in the first place, as space has become a scarce resource. Using our real-estate analogy again, the management of IP address can be conceptualized along the lines of the planning process in the real world, as shown in Figure 4.1. At the top of the process we have central government (IANA in the case of the Internet), which sets the strategic planning framework, with the

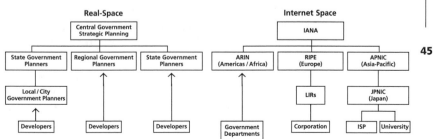

Figure 4.1 Planning Real and Internet Space

actual planning being done at the level of regional and local government (the RIRs and LIRs), which does the detailed land-use zoning and handles the requests from the developers (organizations and companies, particularly ISPs, that want to be on the Internet) to build.

DATA SOURCES AND LIMITATIONS

Réseaux IP Européens (RIPE) is responsible for the management and allocation of IP address space in Europe and surrounding countries. It allocates blocks of IP numbers from a large pool of available numbers that have been delegated by IANA for use in Europe. The RIPE network coordination center (NCC), based in Amsterdam, maintains a large database of operational Internet information known as the "RIPE Network Management Database" (Magee, 1997). One component of this database is the "IP address space allocation and assignment registry." We obtained a copy of this from the RIPE NCC FTP site, dated March 21, 1997. We proceeded to analyze this registry to determine the geography of ownership of Internet real estate in the United Kingdom.

The registry of IP address space lists all the companies and organizations to which allocations have been made, along with details of two designated contact people in the organization concerned. A complete mailing address is given for these contact people, and we used these mailing addresses to locate geographically the IP space allocations. Continuing with our real-estate analogy, we view these designated people as the *de facto* landowners of that block of IP address space, and their mailing addresses are taken to be the point in geospace where the IP addresses are located.

We felt it was important to protect privacy of the individuals and organizations listed in the IP address registry, as their information was provided expressly for the purposes of the operational management of the Internet. Consequently, once the designated person's mailing address had been used to give each IP allocation record a geographic coordinate, all personal information was removed and formed no further part in our analysis. Details on the organizations were used to classify them into three categories—commercial, government, and academic/nonprofit. Once they had been categorized, all details on the organizations were also removed.

The IP address space registry contained 10,660 records of allocations of blocks of IP space to organizations and companies for use in the United Kingdom. This yielded a total number of unique IP addresses allocated to the United Kingdom, in March 1997, of just under 44.7 million. This represents slightly more than 1 percent of the total global IP address space. We then pinpointed a geographical location for the ownership of these 44.7 million IP addresses. This was done using the mailing address details. We were able to match 99.6 percent of the U.K.'s IP address space to a geographical location. Interestingly, just under 1 percent of this address space was actually registered to owners located outside the United Kingdom, in some twenty-five different countries. The breakdown of IP address space by type of organization is shown in Figure 4.2. More than 75 percent of the space is owned by commercial organizations.

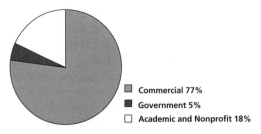

Commercial 77%
Government 5%
Academic and Nonprofit 18%

Figure 4.2 U.K. Address Space by Type of Organization

There are several limitations with the IP address data available for our analysis that require discussion. The source of the data may not be wholly accurate or suitable for the purposes of geographical analysis, as the RIPE database is maintained for the purposes of operational management of the Internet in Europe. One must be aware of the dangers of taking data collected and maintained for one purpose and then using it for another, possibly unforeseen and unrelated, application such as ours. However, the RIPE database is the only readily available source of information on the ownership and distribution of IP address space for the United Kingdom. From our hands-on knowledge of data gained through processing it, we are quite satisfied with the general accuracy of it, including the mailing address information that we used to pinpoint geographically the location of blocks of IP addresses.

It must be stressed we are analyzing the spatial distribution of the *ownership* of blocks of Internet real estate. The geographical location at which the IP address space is owned may not necessarily be the same as where the space is actually used, that is, where the Internet-linked computers are located. Returning to our real-estate analogy, we know where the landowner lives, but this may or may not be on a particular plot of his or her land. Also, Internet landowners may own lots of different plots of land in different places. In addition, we are unable to determine how much "construction" the landowner has done on the land. So we do not know, from our current data, how much of the allocated IP address space is actually being used. Even if the real estate is being developed, we cannot tell whether it is being used by "detached homes" (PCs), a "supermarket" (a big file server) or a huge "tower block" (a corporate mainframe).

The analysis presented here examines the geographical distribution of IP address space ownership at a single point in time—March 1997. Clearly the situation is likely to change due to the rapid growth of the Internet. The spatial patterns evident at the beginning of 1997 should not be assumed to be representative of later points in time. To overcome this limitation we are going to try and track the geographical growth in the ownership of IP address space over time.

EMPIRICAL FINDINGS ON THE IP ADDRESS DENSITY IN THE UNITED KINGDOM

We present results of our preliminary analysis of spatial patterns of Internet real estate in the United Kingdom on a geospace framework using continuous density maps. For the convenience of this element of our analysis, we used a subset of the U.K. data covering just Britain, so data for Northern Ireland, the Channel Islands, the Isle of Man and non-U.K. registered IP address allocations were excluded. A total of 10,183 allocation records, representing some 43.85 million IP addresses, were used to create density surface maps for Britain. The location of the 10,183 allocation records are mapped in Figure 4.3, with each dot representing one record. There is a wide spatial distribution of dots, covering all parts of Britain from Penzance in Cornwall up to the Shetland Islands. The majority of the allocation records are located in the major cities. Central London clearly stands out with a very dense cluster of data points, along with the towns in London's hinterland to the west and north. Other notable concentrations include Birmingham, Manchester, and Newcastle.

In Figure 4.3, each data point represents widely varying numbers of IP addresses. To take account of this variation, we created continuous density surfaces as an effective means of visualizing the data. The number of IP addresses at each point was used as the data value in the creation of the density surfaces. Figure 4.4 shows the IP address density surface for the whole of

[Total No. Data Points = 10,183]

Figure 4.3 Location of IP Address Allocations

Britain based on 43.85 million addresses. The surface is "spotty" in appearance, with much of the country effectively flat apart from a relatively few spikes of high IP address density. The highest densities (represented by solid black in Figure 4.4) are in the range of 9090 to 639,422 IP addresses per square kilometer. There is a concentration of high-density IP space spikes evident within and around London. Additional spikes are found in Nottingham, Birmingham, and Cambridge, with IP address densities of 639,000, 18,500, and 82,000 per square kilometer respectively. From Figure 4.4 we conclude that the majority of IP space is owned by organizations and companies located in southern Britain and particularly in London and its hinterland towns.

Figure 4.5 shows the density surface for the midlands and southern England. To help give the map context, county boundaries and motorways are also shown. The "spotty" density surface is evident, with major peaks of high densities outside the London region, in Cambridge, Birmingham, and Oxford. Perhaps weaker-than-expected densities are exhibited by Bristol and Portsmouth. Figure 4.6 provides a close-up view of Greater London and its hinterland, revealing the complexity of IP address density patterns in this region. A particular trend apparent in this map is the much higher densities of IP addresses

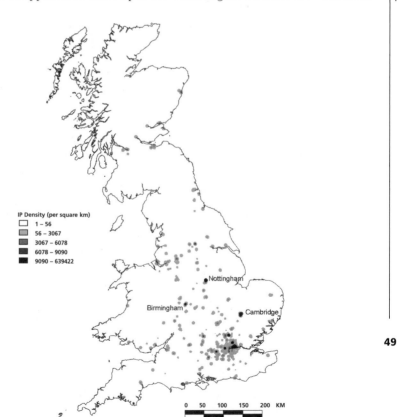

IP Density (per square km)
- 1 – 56
- 56 – 3067
- 3067 – 6078
- 6078 – 9090
- 9090 – 639422

Nottingham

Birmingham   Cambridge

0   50   100   150   200 KM

[Total No. IP Addresses = 43.85 Million]

Figure 4.4 IP Address Density Surface

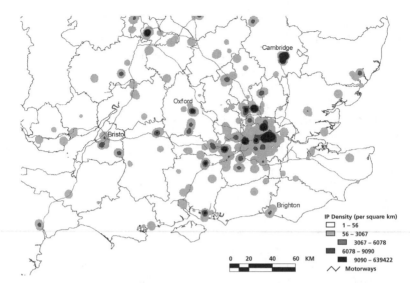

Figure 4.5 IP Address Density Surface for the London Area

found on the western side of London compared to the east. Central London clearly stands out, with a large oblong-shaped zone of very high Internet address density, peaking at 154,500 per square kilometer. This zone covers the area from the City across to the West End. There are two other notable high-density areas inside the boundaries of Greater London. The one to the west of Central London is the area around Heathrow Airport, with an IP address density of 18,600 per square kilometer. The other dense batch in North London, with a peak density of 22,900, is due in part to the headquarters of a major ISP.

Looking at the immediate hinterland surrounding London itself, many of its smaller satellite towns have high IP address densities. These satellite towns have experienced considerable growth in high-technology, computer-related industries in the last ten to fifteen years. Heading north out of London, along the M1 motorway (one of England's key transportation corridors), high densities are apparent in Watford, Hemel Hempstead, and particularly St. Albans, with 33,800 IP addresses per square kilometer. (St. Albans's particularly high IP address densities are largely caused by the headquarters of the Internet operations for a major telecommunications company). Following the M4 motorway west out of London, several other "hot spots" can be observed; these are the towns of Slough, Reading, and particularly Bracknell with 11,900 IP address per square kilometer.

50

CONCLUSION

We have presented some of the first results from our exploratory analysis of the geography of the real estate of Internet space in the United Kingdom, using the density of IP addresses at a detailed spatial scale. The majority of the U.K.'s Internet space is owned by commercial organizations concentrated in a few urban centers; these are Central London and its surrounding satellite towns, along with Nottingham, Cambridge, and Birmingham. Nottingham's high IP density is caused by one very large block of address space allocated to an ISP. Cambridge is noted in the United Kingdom as "Silicon Fen," with a high concentration of computing and research-oriented companies, plus its world-renowned university. The dominance of Central London in the ownership and control of Internet space is as one would expect, as it is the capital city and enjoys the position as the preeminent center for corporate and government headquarter functions in the United Kingdom. The current analysis revealed interesting spatial patterns of high IP address density in London and its hinterland towns of Bracknell and St. Albans.

As we mentioned above, we are also interested in performing time-series analysis on the growth in ownership of Internet address space in the United Kingdom and how the geographical patterns may be shifting. To begin we captured another "snapshot" of IP address space from the RIPE database in March 1998, exactly a year since the last data was captured, and we are looking at the growth over this period. We are also keen to undertake a comparative study of Internet real estate, examining the spatial patterns in the United Kingdom against other countries, particularly Japan. We are also developing a more explanatory model of the relationship between the existing economic geography of Britain and the spatial patterns exhibited by the ownership of Internet real estate.

We hope that our work mapping Internet address space will contribute to a better understanding of the geography of the Internet by making it visible and amenable to spatial analysis. We propose that Internet address space, when related to real-world geospace, could provide a potentially useful surrogate measure of the location of the centers of production in the emerging cyberspace economy.

ACKNOWLEDGMENTS

The authors gratefully acknowledge the RIPE Network Coordination Centre for their permission to use the RIPE database that made this research possible. In particular, we would like to thank John LeRoy Cain at the RIPE NCC for his assistance. Please note the views expressed in this chapter are solely those of the authors and in no way reflect those of RIPE or RIPE NCC. Thanks are also due to Sarah Sheppard and Simon Doyle for their help in processing and analyzing the data. The digital base-map data used in the research was made available by the ESRC and the Midas and U.K. Borders data services.

REFERENCES

APNIC. Asia-Pacific Network Information Center. (http://www.apnic.net/)

ARIN. American Registry for Internet Numbers. (http://www.arin.net/)

Batty, M. (1990). "Invisible Cities," *Environment and Planning B: Planning and Design* Vol. 17: 127–130.

———. (1993). "The Geography of Cyberspace," *Environment and Planning B: Planning and Design* Vol. 20: 615–16.

Batty, M. and B. Barr. (1994). "The Electronic Frontier: Exploring and Mapping Cyberspace," *Futures* Vol. 26, No. 7: 699–712.

Cairncross, F. (1997). *The Death of Distance: How the Communications Revolution Will Change Our Lives*. Boston: Harvard Business School Press.

Conrad, D. R. (1996). "Administrative Infrastructure for IP Address Allocation," paper at the *CIX/ISOC Internet Infrastructure Workshop*, February 2. (Available online at http://www.aldea.com/cix/randy.html)

Couclelis, H. (1994). "Spatial Technologies," *Environment and Planning B: Planning and Design* Vol. 231: 142–143.

———. (1996). "The Death of Distance," *Environment and Planning B: Planning and Design* Vol. 23: 387–389.

———. (1998). "The New Field Workers," *Environment and Planning B: Planning and Design* Vol. 25: 321–323.

Coyle, D. (1997). *Weightless World: Thriving in the Age of Insecurity*. Oxford: Capstone Publishing.

Davis, S. M. and C. Meyer. (1998). *BLUR: The Speed of Change in the Connected Economy*. Reading, MA: Addison-Wesley.

Diamond, D. (1998). "Whose Internet Is It, Anyway?" *Wired* April; Vol. 6.04: 172ff.

Foster, W. A., A. M. Rutkowski, and S. E. Goodman. (1997). "Who Governs the Internet?" *Communications of the ACM* August; Vol. 40, No. 8: 15–20.

Graham, S. and S. Marvin. (1996). *Telecommunications and the City: Electronic Spaces, Urban Places*. London: Routledge.

Greenman, B. (1998). "America's 100 Most Wired Cities & Towns" *Yahoo! Internet Life* March Vol. 4, No. 3: 74ff.

Greenstein, S. (1998). "Universal Service in the Digital Age: The Commercialization and Geography of US Internet Access," report by Kellogg Graduate School of Management, Northwestern University, U.S. January 21.

GVU. (1998). *GVU's WWW User Surveys*. Georgia Tech, Graphics, Visualizations, and Usability Center. (http://www.cc.gatech.edu/gvu/user_surveys/)

Halabi, B. (1997). *Internet Routing Architectures*. Indianapolis: New Riders Publishing.

Hubbard, K., et al. (1996). "Request for Comments (RFC) 2050: Internet Registry IP Allocation Guidelines" (Available online at: ftp://ftp.ripe.net/rfc/rfc2050.txt)

Huston, G. (1994). "Request for Comments (RFC) 1744: Observations on the Management of the Internet Address Space" (Available online at ftp://ftp.ripe.net/rfc/rfc1744.txt)

IANA. Internet Assigned Numbers Authority. (http://www.iana.org/)

ITU. (1997). "Challenges to the Network: Telecommunications and the Internet," report by the International Telecommunication Union (ITU), September.

JPNIC. Japan Network Information Center. (http://www.nic.ad.jp/)

Kahin B. and J. Keller, eds. (1997). *Coordinating the Internet*. Cambridge, MA: MIT Press.

Kelly, K. (1997). "New Rules for the New Economy," *Wired* September; Vol. 5.09: 140ff.

Lewis, T. G. (1998). *Friction-Free Economy: Strategies for Success in a Wired World*. New York: HarperBusiness, USA.

Magee, A. M. R. (1997). "RIPE NCC Database Documentation," RIPE Network Coordination Centre. Document reference: ripe-157, May. (Available online at: http://www.ripe.net/docs/ripe-157.html).

MIDS. Matrix Information and Directory Services. (http://www.mids.org/)

MIDS. (1997). "The Internet by U.S. County," *Matrix Maps Quarterly (MMQ)* No. 402, January.

Moss, M. L. and A. Townsend. (1996). "Leaders and Losers on the Internet," report from the Taub Urban Research Center, New York University.

———. (1997). "Tracking the Net: Using Domain Names to Measure the Growth of the Internet in U.S. Cities," *Journal of Urban Technology* Vol. 4, No. 3, December: 47–59.

———. (1998). Spatial Analysis of the Internet in U.S. Cities and States, paper presented at Technological Futures—Urban Futures Conference at Durham, England, April 23–25.

NCGIA. (1996). *Spatial Technologies, Geographic Information, and the City*, September 9–11, Baltimore: National Center for Geographic Information and Analysis, Technical Report 96–10.

Press, L. (1997). "Tracking the Global Diffusion of the Internet," *Communications of the ACM* Vol. 40, No. 11, November: 11–17.

Quarterman, J. S. (1990). *The Matrix: Computer Networks and Conferencing System Worldwide*. Burlington, MA: Digital Press.

RIPE. Réseaux IP Européens Network Coordination Centre. (http://www.ripe.net/)

Raper, J., D. Rhind, and J. Shepherd. (1992). *Postcodes: The New Geography*. Harlow, England: Longman Scientific and Technical.

Semeria, C. (1997). *Understanding IP Addressing: Everything You Ever Wanted to Know*. (Available online at http://www.3com.com/nsc/501302.html)

Shaw, R. (1997). "Internet Domain Names: Whose Domain Is This?" In B. Kahin and J. Keller, eds., *Coordinating the Internet*. Cambridge, MA: MIT Press.

Staple, G. C. (1997). *TeleGeography 199/98: Global Telecommunications Traffic Statistics and Commentary*, TeleGeography, Inc., October.

U.S. Department of Commerce. (1998). *The Emerging Digital Economy*, U.S. Department of Commerce report, May.

Zook, M. A. (1998). "The Web of Consumption: The Spatial Organization of the Internet Industry in the United States," paper at the Association of Collegiate Schools of Planning 1998 Conference, Pasadena, Calif., November 5–8.

COMPROMISING POSITIONS

THE BODY IN CYBERSPACE

Barney Warf

The body has recently emerged as an important topic of social analysis. Although they appear "natural," bodies are social constructions, playing a crucial role in the construction of identity. A key function of telecommunications has been to "disembody" information, allowing the social and physical aspects of individuals to be separated. Cyberspace is commonly represented as the immaterial antithesis of the body, but in fact the location and nature of bodies deeply condition the ways in which telecommunications are deployed. To some extent, conversely, digital spaces also condition the body. Examples are drawn from telemedicine, electronic security systems, cyberpornography, and virtual reality. Throughout, this chapter argues that the Cartesian distinction that views the body and cyberspace as physical and mental opposites must be jettisoned in favor of an approach that firmly integrates these dimensions.

The interface between body and mind is an ancient topic of philosophical consideration; the fact that we both *have* bodies and that we *are* bodies presents an endless list of fascinating questions about the intersections of mind and matter. The body is where the mind resides, tangible and corporeal evidence of its existence, giving existential and phenomenological depth to lived experience. We cannot escape our bodies anywhere, including cyberspace. Merleau-Ponty wrote "The body is the vehicle of being in the world. To have a body is, for a living being, to join itself to a certain environment, to involve itself with certain projects and therein to engage itself continuously" (quoted in Nguyen and Alexander, 1996, page 117). The body is thus fundamental to understanding our engagement with the world. The body is also the locus of self-consciousness; as Campbell (1994, page 7) puts it, "The unique closeness of the individual's body to himself as a perceiver results because his body is the only perceptual field which he simultaneously perceives and is also a part of himself." Our flesh is simultaneously "it" and "I."

Epistemological treatments of the body have fluctuated greatly over time. As Synnott (1993) argues, the body is an ever-changing matrix of attributes and functions that is redefined with each passing age. Classical Greek philosophy held that as mind and body are inseparable, both should be cultivated with ardor. Later interpretations came to reject this view, privileging the mind over body. Lefebvre (1991, page 407) argues that "Western philosophy has *betrayed* the body; it has actively participated in the great process of metaphorization that has *abandoned* the body; and it has *denied* the body. The living body, being at once 'subject' and 'object,' cannot tolerate such conceptual division, and consequently philosophical concepts fall into the category of the 'signs of the non-body'" (italics in original). The Enlightenment witnessed a renewed obsession with the body, with physicality and spectacle, which resonated widely throughout the historic emergence of modernism, including the exultation of war, blood sport, high adventure, the revival of the Olympics, and the racist cult of the body in Nazi Germany (Segel, 1998). Today, we live in a culture that worships the body, including bodybuilding, obsessive self-monitoring of calories and fat (for example, anorexia) and drug use, the cult of personal hygiene and beauty (for example, cosmetic surgery), and excessive fears of contamination (for example, from HIV). Because academics and intellectuals are typically more concerned with the cerebral than the physical, we tend to forget how important bodies are to most people.

In contemporary poststructural social theory, the human body has become an inspirational topic of academic analysis (Synnott, 1993). While bodies appear as "natural" in their form, they are in fact social constructions deeply inscribed with multiple, contingent meanings, "embodiments" of class, gender, ethnic, and other relations, staged performances of personal identity. The body is the vehicle through which prevailing economic and political institutions affect our selves and how we experience the world, a bundle of signs that encodes, reproduces, and contests prevailing notions of identity, order and discipline, morality and ethics, sensuality and sexuality (Schatzki and Natter, 1997). In *The Production of Space*, Lefebvre (1991) goes so far as to argue (page 405) that "the whole of (social) space proceeds from the body . . . the passive body (the senses) and the active body (labour) converge in space." Similarly, Foucault (1979) dwells at length on what he calls "biopower" and the "micropolitics of desire," the specific forms of power/knowledge in societies that produces healthy, secure, and productive individuals. In this light, the body is the most personalized type of politics; all power is, ultimately, power over the body, as the debates over abortion and incarceration amply illustrate. Recent feminist perspectives on the body have highlighted the importance of gender, sexuality, and the legal regulation of bodies, which are vehicles for the construction, expression, and enforcement of social codes stratified by sex (Sawicki, 1991; Butler, 1993; Davis, 1997; Hyde, 1997). A growing literature has examined cyberspace and the body (Featherstone and Burrows, 1995; Shields, 1996). In geography, interest in this topic has been dominated by the postmodern focus upon the complex, multiple ways in which identity, subjectivity, the body, and place are sutured together (Keith and Pile, 1993; Duncan, 1996; Kirby, 1996; Pile and Thrift, 1995).

Following two centuries of industrialization, any contemporary theory of the body must include its relations to machines. The field of cybernetics, originating with Weiner (1948), offered a novel means to represent the body; as Tomas (1995, page 31) notes, "New terms of reference such as feedback, message and noise functioned to reduce heterogeneous fields such as telephone engineering and the body's nervous system, the analogue computer and the human brain to a common viewpoint originating in control and communications theory and their engineering practices." Computer technology allowed for a far-reaching rescripting of the "natural" body. Haraway (1991) persuasively argued that in the current age the boundaries between bodies and machines, the natural and the artificial, have become progressively blurrier, a notion manifested in her famous use (but not invention) of the term "cyborgs" (cybernetic organisms), complex articulations of tissue and technologies rather than simple binary oppositions. Transcending gender or ethnicity, Haraway's cyborgs became a dominant metaphor for the critical politics (particularly feminism) of technology. Similarly, Graham and Marvin (1996, page 107) note that "Humans and machines (have) become fused in ways that make the old separations between technology and society, the real and the simulated, meaningless." Such a trope problematizes dominant conceptions of "nature" as nonmechanical when almost all of our bodies rely heavily, and even incorporate as prosthetics, machines in many forms (Luke, 1997). Thus, the human/machine threshold has shifted over time, and never more so than in the aftermath of the microelectronics revolution of the late twentieth century.

Today, "being digital" is increasingly critical to knowledge, wealth, status, and power (Negroponte, 1995) as well as identity (Turkle, 1997). Current forms of commodity production, typified by hypermobile capital, confront us with disorienting notions of time and space that can change at the speed of light (Thrift, 1996). Leslie and Butz (1998) note how cybernetic systems are used to code the body in post-Fordist capitalism. The current social construction of the body is thus part of the contemporary wave of time-space compression, or "distanciation," to use Giddens's (1984) term for how societies are stretched over time and space. Given the widespread use of electronic communications, interpersonal relations are increasingly, but never completely, freed from face-to-face contact (Warf, 1994). In the same vein, Jameson (1984, page 83) notes that postmodern hyperspace "has finally succeeded in transcending the capacities of the individual human body to locate itself, to organize its immediate surrounding perceptually, and cognitively to map its position in a mappable external world." A key task in this regard is to extend understandings of the body to include some of the most important contemporary technologies: telecommunications and cyberspace.

TELECOMMUNICATIONS AND THE BODY

Telecommunications have had a long history of reshaping the relations among bodies. Since the inception of the telegraph in 1844, telecommunications have allowed information to become "disembodied," separating communications and transportation through the first "out of body" experiences. From the telephone to the Internet, telecommunications enable the social and physical dimensions of human life to be disentangled, allowing individuals to form "communities without propinquity," spaces of shared interest without physical proximity, so that even television viewing can be seen as comprising a community of disparate individuals linked by a common intersection with the screen (Adams, 1992). Despite the air of anonymity that telecommunications impart to interpersonal communication, bodies form an important part of how individuals interact with one another electronically, ranging from how we appropriate information through our senses (computer screens, and so forth) to the speed with which we type (in chat groups, for example) to metaphors such as "surfing" the Internet's "backbones" to the emoticons (for example, :)) that convey facial expressions, emotions, and other paralinguistic cues. Conversely, but to a lesser extent, telecommunications often help to shape bodies, including the effects of television on obesity, the relations between video games and eye-hand coordination, and the various ways in which electronic systems substitute for travel (for example, telecommuting, teleshopping), altering the biorhythms of everyday life.

One of the most telling examples of how important the body is to social relations is the highly imperfect substitution of telecommunications for face-to-face interaction. The exaggerated claims of early postindustrial theorists that telecommuting would render face-to-face interaction obsolete (and geography unimportant) were simply untrue; at best, information systems facilitate the transmission of standardized forms of data associated with low value-added jobs such as back offices, not the highly irregular forms of contact that necessitate in-person communication. Occupations that command high salaries and generate high degrees of value-added, in contrast, are invariably those that involve in-person meetings, in which multiple and irregular sources of information are collected and shared, usually in large cities (Warf, 1995). Telecommunications simply cannot perform this function adequately. Thus, despite decades of declines in the price of videoconferencing, corporations pay enormous sums to set up offices in expensive downtown areas and to fly executives thousands of miles, all because of the need to communicate face to face (Kutay, 1986). Apparently, face-to-face contact allows more "bits" of information to be communicated per unit of time, including the critical dimension of body language and nonverbal cues, than any other medium, which is why meetings occupy so much work time for many professionals.

Geographers have occasionally analyzed bodies in space in intriguing ways. Hagerstrand's (1970) seminal paper launching time-geography, for example, focused upon the daily routines of individuals as their bodies moved through time and space subject to capacity, authority, and coupling constraints, forming a "weaving dance" that reproduces social relations (Giddens, 1984). Janelle's (1969) and Harvey's (1989, 1990) notion of time-space compression brought bodies firmly into the realm of relative space. More recently, Adams (1995) has extended time-geographic models to include telecommunications, which transform the body into an electronic "amoeba," allowing an extensibility in which individuals can occupy more than one space at one time (Figure 5.1). He argues (page 275) that telecommunications facilitate a distinction between the person and the body: "the body is self-contained and spatial and temporally finite, while the person is other-contained and spatial and temporally unbounded." By conferring a certain degree of anonymity (the opposite of the advantages of face-to-face communication), telecommunications allow us to escape the parts of our identities associated with our bodies. In cyberspace, people become more than their bodies, for electronic extensibility allows them to "live in the minds of others" at great distances from their physical selves.

CYBERSPACE AND THE BODY

At first glance, cyberspace would appear to be the antithesis of the body. The former is by definition intangible, inorganic, and infinitely flexible; the latter is the most tangible representation of human existence possible. Cyberspace is where our minds can go but our bodies cannot; we exchange thoughts through e-mail, but not our physical selves. Electronic interactions thus acquire an aura of sanitary detachment from the messy, organic world of the body. Indeed, many cybergeeks have an open contempt for the flesh even as they

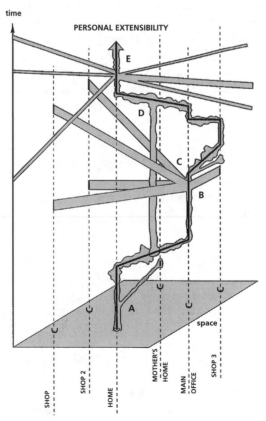

Figure 5.1 Time-Geography Diagram Modified to Include Telecommunications
Source: Adams, 1995.

spend ever greater portions of their lives sitting in chairs, staring at screens, disdaining bodies as "meat" that is obsolete as soon as consciousness is uploaded into the network (Stone, 1992; Dery, 1997), a view greatly distant from the classic Greek ideal. Nguyen and Alexander (1996, page 116) argue "As cyberspace erases the boundaries of time and space, it also erases the materiality of our bodily boundaries. Online, we seem to break free from the limitations of bodily existence." This argument rests upon the long-standing and pervasive Cartesian distinction between mind and body, which portrays them as discrete categories. Further, it presumes that space has become unimportant, that cyberspace has conquered geography, that e-mail or videoconferencing perfectly substitute for face-to-face communication, a widespread utopian fantasy bequeathed by classic postindustrial theory and contemporary observations infatuated with the space-conquering potential of telecommunications (for example, Cairncross, 1997).

But are the body and cyberspace as separate as they first appear? Might there not be a subtle unity, or at least interconnection, lurking beneath the Cartesian schism? A growing, feisty literature on the culture of cyberspace frequently employs body-related metaphors, likening the Internet to an extension of our nervous system (Stone, 1991; Jones, 1995, 1997; Negroponte, 1995; Shields, 1996). Similarly, in popular films such as *Tron* or *The Lawnmower Man*, bodies are shown being incorporated into cyberspace. Dery (1996) offers a comprehensive catalogue of cyberspace intersections with the body, including digital music, body art, and "robocopulation."

Yet bodies are important to cyberspace in other, more immediate ways as well. One approach to demonstrate this interconnection is to consider the physical distribution of bodies relative to the Internet. Profound spatial inequalities exist in access to cyberspace across the globe; indeed, given the overwhelming U.S. and European dominance, the "World Wide Web" hardly lives up to its name. These inequalities reflect the long-standing bifurcation between the First and Third Worlds. In terms of Internet hosts per 100,000 individuals —perhaps the best index of accessibility—the leading nations are located in Scandinavia, Canada, and Australia; the United States, surprisingly, is relatively low in this regard, a reflection of its vast population of poorly served people, primarily low-income minorities (Figure 5.2). Access to the Internet thus reflects where people's bodies are located (which itself is highly political), for bodies are the hinge between physical space and cyberspace.

To illustrate the ways in which bodies and cyberspace are shot through with each other, four examples are offered from widely varying spheres of social life: telemedicine, electronic security systems, cyberpornography, and virtual reality.

The Digital Medical Body

Along with finance and other industries, telecommunications has revolutionized the theory and practice of medical care. The microelectronics revolution allowed for a host of new technologies to explore the body in unprecedented

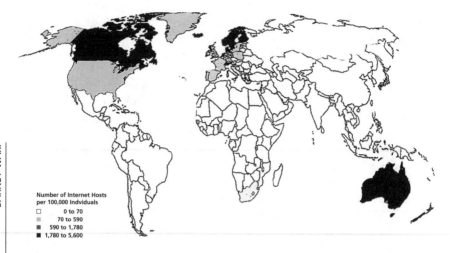

Number of Internet Hosts
per 100,000 Individuals
☐ 0 to 70
▨ 70 to 590
▨ 590 to 1,780
■ 1,780 to 5,600

Figure 5.2 Global Distribution of Internet Hosts Per 100,000 Person, January 1997
Source: Compiled by author from data at
http://www.nw.com/zone/WWW/dist-byname.html.

ways, digitizing human anatomy and allowing the resultant data to be analyzed and transported instantaneously over great distances. Thus telemedicine, in which physicians at one location use remote viewing techniques to diagnose and provide advice to patients located somewhere else, has grown in popularity, particularly in rural areas with inadequate access to health care. In some cases, such technologies facilitate the training of physicians engaged in virtual surgeries (Merril, 1993; Satava, 1994). The Internet has also become an important source of medical information, dramatically changing the traditional doctor-patient relationship: two thirds of everyone online have searched for health-related information there, although much of it is inaccurate or misleading (Hafner, 1998). The centralization of sensitive medical information in centralized databases also raises concern for the protection of individuals' privacy.

One dramatic instance in which the medical body and cyberspace converge is the Body Voyage Project sponsored by the National Library of Medicine's Visible Human Project, in which the cadaver of a convict executed in Texas in 1995 was sliced into 1,878 pieces at one-millimeter intervals and photographed using Computerized Axial Tomography (CAT) scans. The resulting 45 gigabytes of data were then loaded into the Internet to produce a visually stunning fly-through in which the viewer can peel away skin and muscle layers (*http://www.nlm.nih.gov/research/visible/visible_human.html*). This individual became the first person to be "immortalized" in cyberspace, uploading not just his mind but his body into the Internet.

Future advances in computing and health care may extend the medical applications of cyberspace in unexpected ways. Digital prosthetics, already found in pacemakers, hearing aids, and personal digital assistants, may include snap-in organs connected by electronic nerves. Mitchell (1996, page 31) offers intriguing speculation about this possibility:

Think of yourself on some evening in the not-so-distant future, when wearable, fitted, and implanted electronic organs connected by bodynets are as commonplace as cotton; your intimate infrastructure connects you seamlessly to a planetful of bits, and you have software in your underwear. It's eleven o'clock, Smarty Pants; do you know where your network extensions are tonight?

In this context, the boundary between interiority and exteriority has become fuzzy to the point of meaninglessness.

The Body as Password

Recently the proliferation of a host of new biometric identification technologies has made the body an important part of security systems that employ cyberspace (Davis, 1997; Hansell, 1997). Employers, retail trade merchants, and governments are increasingly developing the capacities to read and store the unique biological characteristics of individuals electronically, using scanners that map retinal patterns, fingerprints, knuckle creases, and acoustic head resonances. More than 10,000 establishments in the United States, from bank vaults to blood banks, require presentation of a body part to access secure locations. Davis (1997, page 134) gives several examples:

> Inmates must submit to retinal scanning in Cook County, Illinois, coming and going from jail to court appearances. Connecticut and Pennsylvania are two of several states that now use digitized finger imaging to match welfare records with recipients. Frequent travelers crossing into Canada from Montana can zip through an automated voice-verification system run by the U.S. Immigration and Naturalization Service. In the private sector, Lotus employees pass through a hand-geometry scanner to pick up their children from in-house day care. Coca-Cola is using hand geometry at the time clock to prevent workers from "buddy punching" a late colleague's time card.

One particularly popular biometric technology is the retinal scan, in which users place their eyes a few inches from an incandescent light beam that maps the vein patterns of the eyeball's innermost layer. Firms such as IriScan, in Mount Laurel, NJ, argue that the iris is the most unique feature of the human body. Producers of automated teller machines are increasingly turning to this technology. The corporation Identification Technologies goes even further, using digital maps of the face and the slogan "Your Face Is Your PIN," an option currently being explored by Mastercard. Finger scanners, which map fingers and the tops and sides of the hand with a video camera, are used at immigration checkpoints at the San Francisco airport and to verify the identity of donors at sperm banks. IBM is developing travelers' credit cards that rely on handprints (Hansell, 1997). Even body odors (from the hand) can be digitized using a new device called Scentinel, currently being tested by the Saudi National Guard and private Indian and Japanese security companies. Exploratory technologies include wrist-vein recognition and signature verification, although such systems tend to be expensive and can be fooled, intentionally or inadvertently, by scarring, beards, weight gain or loss, and other bodily changes.

While such systems can be used to guarantee privacy and security of access, and given the slippage around previously secure numbers such as Social Security, there is little to guarantee that cyberspace may be used inappropriately or unethically. For example, retinal scans used to prove that an individual is a legal immigrant might also be used to catch suspected drug users. Cyberspace is already used for surveillance and incarceration: already, more than four million Americans are under "correctional supervision" at home, monitored by electronic anklet transponders linked to police computers via telephone modems (Gowdy, 1994), constituting a panopticon of the sort envisioned by Bentham and Foucault. In more benign terms, marketers who purchase credit card, banking, and consumption data play significant roles in monitoring—and shaping—the time-space prisms of daily life. The fact that such data are commodified and traded raises severe doubts about the sanctity of the digital individual (Curry, 1997), a phenomenon similar to the marketing of consumer profiles through geodemographic systems (Goss, 1995), and recalls Habermas's (1987) warning about the colonization of lifeworlds, the penetration of commodity relations into ever deeper realms of thought and behavior.

Cyberpornography

One of the most hotly debated dimensions of cyberspace concerns the widespread prevalence of pornography (Wallace and Mangan, 1996). It is images of bodies that arouse the most controversy, even passion, about cyberspace, a subject that has otherwise elicited relatively little political debate. Pornography in cyberspace is an extension (and for some, a sad substitute for) the physical sexuality of the body, revealing that the mind is the most erotic organ of all. Computer pornography combines aspects of the public and private spheres: in the privacy of the home, consumers can participate in Usenet discussion groups, WWW sites, private chat rooms, and bulletin-board services (BBS). Given that the vast majority (roughly 80 percent) of Internet users are male, many of them young (Doctor, 1994; Doheny-Farina, 1996; Miller, 1996), the content of the Internet may well reflect the testosterone levels of its users.

No aspect of cyberspace has generated as much political friction as cybersex, particularly the ease with which children may have access to explicit pictures and stories about sexual acts. In 1996, the U.S. Congress passed the Communications Decency Act (CDA), an attempt to limit children's access to pornography (however loosely defined) on the Internet by facilitating government censorship, essentially catering to the political agenda of the Christian Right. The Supreme Court, however, overturned the CDA, granting the Internet the same First Amendment protection as print, not the lower standard applied to broadcasting, on the grounds that cyberspace is not as "invasive" as radio or television.

One of the most famous legal cases involving cyberspace revolved around the body in two ways, including pornography and the physical location of its consumer. In, 1991, the Thomases established a computer bulletin board system run from their home in Milpitas, California, which gave subscribers the opportunity to download sexually explicit images (Wallace and Mangan, 1996). The site was billed as "the nastiest place on the planet." In 1993, a Memphis, Tennessee postal inspector downloaded a series of such images and proceeded to charge the Thomases with interstate trafficking in pornography on the grounds of violating the "community standards" of Tennessee. As the lawsuit proceeded, the case increasingly hinged upon the question: Exactly where is one when one is in cyberspace? What community's standards were being violated by the Milpitas bulletin-board system? The U.S. Supreme Court ruled (*United States* v. *Robert Alan Thomas*) that although "community" (as in "community standards") included cyberspace, when logged in, legally one is located in the place of his/her body, and found the Thomases innocent.

Virtual Bodies

A version of cyberspace that has captured the public imagination is virtual reality (VR), an apparent oxymoron. Although the term has been overused and abused, true VR departs from traditional film and computer screen technologies by *surrounding* the individual with a fully interactive interface, allowing users to immerse themselves in, see, and touch a completely digital world, providing instantaneous feedback between mind, body, and computer, utterly collapsing the distance between spectator and the digital environment and decoupling the phenomenal world from the realm of representations (Clark, 1995). Users, often separated by vast physical distances, can "inhabit" the same virtual world at the same time, along with virtual characters that exist nowhere outside of cyberspace. VR worlds display varying degrees of realism; some simply resemble animated films, while others are difficult to distinguish from the real nondigital world. In every case, however, it marks a marked departure from the passive, mimetic orientation of photography to one in which the viewer/user plays an active role.

VR technology can be traced back to World War II flight training and simulation programs (Hillis, 1996). Advances in medical and molecular modeling, architectural walk-throughs, and computer-aided design (CAD) technology, particularly at MIT's Servomechanism Lab and at NASA (Woolley, 1994), made VR environments increasingly realistic and user-friendly. A key step was the development of computers in the, 1980s "capable of juggling the vast ocean of data bits required to synthesize eye-hand real-time coordination in cyberspace at sufficient speeds to overcome the disorienting and reflexivity-inducing perception of time lag" (Hillis, 1996, page 85). This innovation allowed for a complete mapping of the virtual world onto human perceptions, fusing the senses digitally in a universe neither actual nor imaginary, but virtual. The most sophisticated VR technologies (in universities rather than commercial contexts) allow disembodied cybernauts to be suspended in computer space in a state akin to other altered states of consciousness such as dreams, hallucinations, drug use, and religious visions. VR hence should not be construed in opposition to "real" reality, but rather as an extension of it.

VR is just beginning to percolate into the everyday world. Most VR applications are in entertainment, where private firms have created a variety of video games and CD-ROM fantasies, both realistic and fantastic, involving one or more real or computer-generated players (Schroeder, 1996). MUDs, or Multi-User Domains, already have a devoted following. Other applications include flight training for pilots and astronauts, military battlefield simulations, architecture, education, and medicine. All of these uses are designed for an overwhelmingly male clientele. Future developments hold wild possibilities; Dery (1996, page 213) notes, for example, that "Cybersex will grow exponentially stranger as virtual reality technology develops."

The body forms a key dimension in the development and utility of VR. Indeed, "whether the body should be represented at all, and if so, in what form, is still an open question among researchers and developers of VR systems" (Schroeder, 1996, page 58). This issue is of some significance given that the design of VR interfaces is heavily affected by their relations to the body and how it is represented in cyberspace. In the 1980s, VR technology relied upon "data gloves" and bodysuits, although these proved to be too cumbersome for most users; today, the vast majority of commercial VR systems employ handheld 3-D mice in conjunction with head-mounted displays, VR's most distinctive feature (Figures 5.3 and 5.4). Research on such environments finds that having a virtual body typically greatly enhances users' sense of presence and ability to move within cyberspace. The success of VR thus depends upon its ability to simulate the body, to trick the senses into believing the virtual world is "real," much like Baudrillard's (1993) notion of the simulacra, where the simulation becomes more real than reality itself.

Virtual bodies may presage a digital evolution of the cybernetic body that has several stages. Clark (1995, page 115–16) argues that this process reflects the progress of computer technology itself, from alphanumeric to visual media,

Figures 5.3 and 5. 4 Examples of User of Virtual Reality
Source: Schroeder, 1996.

then to artificial intelligence: "The first generation of cyberbodies belongs to the previsual era of computational practices; the second to the phase in which cybernetic spaces take on a visual dimension, so that interacting subjects require some form of body descriptor. In the third phase, entities 'evolve' their own structure and appearance." The latter is reminiscent of computer-generated avatars in cyberpunk novels such as Gibson's famously influential *Neuromancer* (1984) or Stephenson's *Snow Crash* (1992). In this reading, cyberspace does not simply extend or enhance the body, it displaces it altogether. Thus the potential for cyberbodies ranges from "pure" human beings to fully simulated disembodied creatures that can exist only in cyberspace.

CONCLUDING THOUGHTS

Although bodies as concrete flesh, the *terra firma* of human existence, and cyberspace as intangible, ethereal webs of digital information are commonly conceived as polar opposites, they in fact deeply shape one another. Our bodies inescapably condition how we enter cyberspace, who enters, where, and for what purposes. Contemporary telecommunications, in turn, increasingly play a central role in how we view, construct, and display our bodies. The negation of the body has proven difficult, if not impossible. As Nguyen and Alexander (1996, page 121) argue, "Bodies can no longer serve as the last outpost of a vanishing world of finite spacetime and bounded order."

Computer-mediated interaction has become highly significant in the everyday lives of millions, if not billions, of people, changing not simply what we know, but how we know it (Barrett, 1986; Poster, 1990). For those who drift in and out of digital realities, cyberspace becomes an extension of the body as well as the mind, a prosthetic comparable to artificial limbs, pacemakers, wheelchairs, eyeglasses, and other devices that make the body thoroughly denaturalized (Brahm and Driscoll, 1995). Broadly speaking, everyone who uses the Internet becomes a cyborg, to reiterate Haraway's (1991) famous conception, a fusion of person and machine, rendering the old duality largely meaningless. Similarly, Thrift (1996) argues: "there is a very high degree of interactivity between machines and humans, and even in which, in certain cases, machines become parts of the human subject's body." Thus, the physical body and the circulating pixels of cyberspace exist in constant interplay, a state of creative tension in which each transforms the other. The long standing Cartesian distinction between mind and body, mental and material, therefore, must be regarded with increasing skepticism, if not jettisoned altogether. As Argyle and Shields argue in an essay appropriately titled "Is There a Body in the Net?" (1996, page 58), "The simple dichotomies of on-line versus off-line, of the virtual and the real have been the fodder of both the ecstatic boosters of computer-mediated communications and the dour critics of the time 'lost' to virtual simulations of neighbourhoods and to online interaction."

Acknowledging that the body shapes cyberspace, and vice versa—to the point where we must consider them increasingly to be simultaneously determinant—has important implications for our conceptions of the Internet. The digital world, like our bodies, is not simply some free floating set of concepts in a state of suspended animation above time and space, but an organic, concrete entity rooted in the politics and spaces of everyday life. Viewed in this way, questions of access, identity, and use of the Internet rise to the foreground, whereas such issues have been marginalized by prevailing hype that celebrates cyberspace as an unfettered frontier of rugged individualism, that is, in asocial, purely technological terms. The intersections between the body and cyberspace, therefore, serve as a necessary reminder that telecommunications systems are inescapably political and geographical in origin, nature, and consequence.

REFERENCES

Adams, P. (1992). "Television as Gathering Place." *Annals of the Association of American Geographers* 82: 117–135.

———. (1995). "A Reconsideration of Personal Boundaries in Space-Time." *Annals of the Association of American Geographers* 85: 267–285.

Argyle, K. and R. Shields. (1996). "Is There a Body in the Net?" In R. Shields, ed. *Cultures of Internet: Virtual Spaces, Real Histories, Living Bodies*. London: Sage.

Barrett, W. (1986). *Death of the Soul: From Decartes to the Computer*. Garden City, NY: Anchor Press.

Baudrillard, J. (1993). "Hyperreal America." *Economy and Society* 22: 243–252.

Brahm, G. and M. Driscoll, eds. (1995). *Prosthetic Territories: Politics and Hypertechnologies*. Boulder, CO: Westview Press.

Butler, J. (1993). *Bodies That Matter*. New York: Routledge.

Cairncross, F. (1997). *The Death of Distance: How the Communications Revolution Will Change Our Lives*. Boston: Harvard University Business School Press.

Campbell, J. (1994). *Past, Space and Self*. Cambridge, MA: MIT Press.

Clark, N. (1995). "Rear-View Mirrorshades: The Recursive Generation of the Cyberbody." In M. Featherstone and R. Burrows, eds. *Cyberspace, Cyberbodies, Cyberpunk: Cultures of Technological Embodiment*. London and Thousand Oaks, CA: Sage.

Curry, M. (1997). "The Digital Individual and the Private Realm." *Annals of the Association of American Geographers* 87: 681–699.

Davis, A. (1997). "Body as Password." *Wired* July: 133–176.

Davis, K., ed. (1997). *Embodied Practices: Feminist Perspectives on the Body*. Beverly Hills: Sage.

Dery, M. (1996). *Escape Velocity: Cyberculture at the End of the Century*. New York: Grove Press.

———. (1997). "The Cult of the Mind." *New York Times Magazine* Sept. 28: 96–97.

Doctor, R. (1994). "Seeking Equity in the National Information Infrastructure." *Internet Research* 4: 9–22.

Doheny-Farina, S. (1996). *The Wired Neighborhood*. New Haven: Yale University Press.

Duncan, N., ed. (1996). *BodySpace*. London: Routledge.

Featherstone, M. and R. Burrows, eds. (1995). *Cyberspace, Cyberbodies, Cyberpunk: Cultures of Technological Embodiment*. London and Thousand Oaks, CA: Sage.

Foucault, M. (1979). *Discipline and Punish*. New York: Vintage.

Gibson, W. (1984). *Neuromancer*. London: HarperCollins.

Giddens, A. (1984). *The Constitution of Society: Outline of the Theory of Structuration.* Berkeley: University of California Press.

Goss, J. (1995). "'We Know Who You Are and We Know Where You Live': The Instrumental Rationality of Geodemographic Systems." *Economic Geography* 71: 171–198.

Gowdy, V. (1994). "Alternatives to Prison." *The Futurist* Jan.–Feb.: 53.

Habermas, J. (1987). *The Theory of Communication Action* Vol. 2. Boston: Beacon.

Graham, S. and S. Marvin. (1996). *Telecommunications and the City: Electric Spaces, Urban Places.* London: Routledge.

Hafner, K. (1998). "Can the Internet Cure the Common Cold?" *New York Times* July 9: D1.

Hagerstrand, T. (1970). "What about People in Regional Science?" *Papers of the Regional Science Association* 24: 7–21.

Hansell, S. (1997). "Is This an Honest Face? Use of Recognition Technology Grows in Everyday Transactions." *New York Times,* August 20: C1, 3.

Haraway, D. (1991). *Simians, Cyborgs and Women: The Reinvention of Nature.* New York: Routledge.

Harvey, D. (1989). *The Condition of Postmodernity.* Oxford: Basil Blackwell.

———. (1990). "Between Space and Time: Reflections on the Geographical Imagination." *Annals of the Association of American Geographers* 80: 418–434.

Heim, M. (1991). "The Erotic Ontology of Cyberspace." In M. Benedikt, ed. *Cyberspace: First Steps.* Cambridge, MA: MIT Press.

Hillis, K. (1996). "A Geography of the Eye: The Technologies of Virtual Reality." In R. Shields, ed. *Cultures of Internet: Virtual Spaces, Real Histories, Living Bodies.* London: Sage.

Hyde, A. (1997). *Bodies of Law.* Princeton, NJ: Princeton University Press.

Jameson, F. (1984). "Postmodernism, or The Cultural Logic of Late Capitalism." *New Left Review* 146: 53–92.

Janelle, D. (1969). "Spatial Reorganization: A Model and Concept." *Annals of the Association of American Geographers* 59: 348–365.

Jones, S., ed. (1995). *CyberSociety: Computer-Mediated Communication and Community.* Beverly Hills, CA: Sage.

———, ed. (1997). *Virtual Culture: Identity and Communication in Cybersociety.* London: Sage.

Keith, M. and S. Pile, eds. (1993). *Place and the Politics of Identity.* London: Routledge.

Kirby, K. (1996). *Indifferent Boundaries: Spatial Concepts of Human Subjectivity.* New York: Guilford.

Kutay, A. (1986). "Effects of Telecommunications Technology on Office Locations." *Urban Geography* 7: 243–257.

Lefebvre, H. (1974/1991). *The Production of Space.* Oxford: Blackwell.

Leslie, D. and D. Butz. (1998). "GM Suicide: Flexibility, Space, and the Injured Body." *Economic Geography* 74: 360–378.

Luke, T. (1997). "At the End of Nature: Cyborgs, 'Humachines,' and Environments in Postmodernity." *Environment and Planning* A 29: 1367–1380.

Lyon, D. (1994). *The Electronic Eye: The Rise of Surveillance Society.* Minneapolis: University of Minnesota Press.

Merril, J. (1993). "Surgery on the Cutting Edge: Virtual Reality Applications in Medical Education." *Virtual Reality World* Nov.–Dec.: 17–21.

Miller, S. (1996). *Civilizing Cyberspace: Policy, Power and the Information Superhighway.* New York: ACM Press.

Mitchell, W. (1996). *City of Bits: Space, Place, and the Infobahn*. Cambridge, MA: MIT Press.

Negroponte, N. (1995). *Being Digital*. New York: Knopf.

Nguyen, D. and J. Alexander. (1996). "The Coming of Cyberspacetime and the End of the Polity." In Shields, R., ed. *Cultures of Internet: Virtual Spaces, Real Histories, Living Bodies*. London: Sage.

Pile, S. and N. Thrift. (1995). *Mapping the Subject: Geographies of Cultural Transformation*. London: Routledge.

Poster, M. (1990). *The Mode of Information*. Chicago: University of Chicago Press.

Satava, R. (1994). "Update on Virtual Reality in Health Care: The New Future for Medicine and Surgery." In S. Helsel, ed. *Proceedings of the Fourth Annual Conference on Virtual Reality*. London: Meckler.

Sawicki, J. (1991). *Disciplining Foucault: Feminism, Power, and the Body*. New York: Routledge.

Schatzki, T. and W. Natter, eds. (1997). *The Social and Political Body*. New York: Guilford.

Schroeder, R. (1996). *Possible Worlds: The Social Dynamic of Virtual Reality Technology*. Boulder, CO: Westview.

Segel, H. (1998). *Body Ascendant: Modernism and the Physical Imperative*. Baltimore: Johns Hopkins University Press.

Shields, R., ed. (1996). *Cultures of Internet: Virtual Spaces, Real Histories, Living Bodies*. London: Sage.

Stephenson, N. (1992). *Snow Crash*. New York: Bantam Books.

Stone, A. (1991). "Will the Real Body Please Stand Up? Boundary Stories about Virtual Cultures." In M. Benedikt, ed. *Cyberspace: First Steps*. Cambridge, MA: MIT Press.

Synnott, A. (1993). *The Body Social: Symbolism, Self and Society*. New York: Routledge.

Thrift, N. (1996). "Inhuman Geographies: Landscapes of Speed, Light and Power." In P. Cloke, M. Doel, D. Matless, M. Phillips, and N. Thrift, eds. *Writing the Rural: Five Cultural Geographies*. London: Paul Chapman.

Tomas, D. (1995). "Feedback and Cybernetics: Reimaging the Body in the Age of Cybernetics." In M. Featherstone and R. Burrows, eds. *Cyberspace, Cyberbodies, Cyberpunk: Cultures of Technological Embodiment*. London and Thousand Oaks, CA: Sage.

Turkle, S. (1997). *Life on the Screen: Identity in the Age of the Internet*. New York: Touchstone.

Wallace, J. and M. Mangan. (1996). *Sex, Laws, and Cyberspace*. New York: Henry Holt.

Warf, B. (1994). "Structuration Theory and Electronic Communications." in D. Wilson and J. Huff, eds. *Marginalized Places and Populations: A Structurationist Agenda*. Westport, CT: Greenwood.

———. (1995). "Telecommunications and the Changing Geographies of Knowledge Transmission in the Late 20th Century." *Urban Studies* 32: 361–378.

Wiener, N. (1948). *Cybernetics: or Control and Communication in the Animal and the Machine*. New York: Wiley.

Woolley, B. (1994). *Virtual Worlds: A Journey in Hype and Hyperreality*. Oxford: Blackwell.

PART III.
Telecommunications Infrastructure and Urban Planning

6

URBAN PLANNING AND THE TECHNOLOGICAL FUTURE OF CITIES

Stephen Graham and Simon Marvin

INTRODUCTION

It is now widely argued that the increasingly pervasive applications of linked computer, media, and telecommunications technologies constitute nothing less than a wholesale shift of our economy, society, and culture. Social scientists regularly now talk of a new, emerging "digital age," an "information society," or a "network society" (see Gosling, 1997; Castells, 1996). Such a transition is widely believed to be a new industrial revolution, a societal, technological, and economic shift across capitalist civilization of similar magnitude to the industrial revolution through which every aspect of society is transformed (Graham and Marvin, 1996).

As part of this shift, cities, and the corridors between them, are being permeated with widening arrays of telecommunications grids—conventional phone networks, wireless and radio systems, cable networks, satellite systems, and Internet, data, and video networks. These silently and (usually) invisibly underpin booming flows of voice, data, video, and images across all walks of city life and development. Indeed, every aspect of the life of advanced industrial cities is now crosscut with all manner of computerized and "tele-mediated" communications exchanges, and transactions, most of which are now based on digital principles (meaning that they are based on the streams of zeros and ones used in computers). As Geoff Mulgan (1991) once put it, "the re-definition of the city as a system for producing and switching information is highly visible."

IT and telecommunications networks are thus becoming, in a very real sense, the very sinews of our society. For our profoundly urban societies, and for the whole gamut of actors, agencies, policy-makers, organizations, and individuals who currently depend on cities in various ways, the relationship between new media and telecommunications technologies and the future of our cities is clearly of critical importance. But what does this so-called "digital age" really mean for our cities? What future is there for our urban areas, as more and more of the traditional roles and functions that first generated the need for urban concentration seem likely to be possible across distance via advanced telecommunications links? Will our cities face some electronic requiem, some nightmarish *Blade-Runner*-style future of decay and polarization? Or can they be powerhouses of economic, social, and cultural innovation in the new electronic media? And, perhaps most important from the perspective of urban planning, what roles are there for urban policies, plans, and strategies, and for urban design, community development, and transport policies, within the shift to a so-called "tele-mediated" urban life, based more and more on all types of online interactions?

The coevolution of cities and electronic interactions is increasingly emphasized in technological debates within academia. Debates about cyberspace, telecommunications, and the future of cities are currently proliferating within disciplines as diverse as architecture, cultural studies, communications studies, science and technology studies, and urban sociology and geography (see, for example, Mitchell, 1995; OTA, 1995; Graham and Marvin, 1996; Castells, 1996). Attention is increasingly being directed to exploring how the economic, social, and cultural aspects of cities interact with the proliferation of advanced computer-based telecommunications networks in all walks of urban life (Graham, 1998). Here, the common, 1980s assumption that the new communicational capabilities of new media technologies will somehow "dissolve" the city has waned. Rather, it is now clear that most IT applications are largely metropolitan phenomena. They are developing out of the older urban regions and are associated with new degrees of complexity within cities and urban systems, as urban areas across the world become relationally combined into a globally interconnected, planetary metropolitan systems (Graham and Marvin, 1996). Research here now centers on the degree to which city economies can be maintained in a world of online electronic flows; the ways in which place-based and "virtual communities" interact; and the related interactions between urban cultures rooted in traditional public spaces, and "cybercultures" operating within the virtual spaces accessed from computers (see Mitchell, 1995, and Graham and Marvin, 1996, for reviews).

Despite the central importance of the "urban" in cyberspace debates, however, issues of urban policy and planning have been virtually absent within both the popular and academic sides of the discussions. New information and communications technologies are usually seen to be some disembodied, external "wave" of change. Their urban "impacts" are usually seen to follow inevitably from their effective "collapse of distance" as a constraint on human life (*The Economist*, 1995). Such scenarios also usually imply that all cities (say, for Europe, London, Leeds, Charleroi, and Athens) will somehow all be "impacted" in the same ways. Such so-called "technological determinism" is attractive because it creates powerful scenarios and clear stories, and because it accords with the dominant experience in the West, where, as Stephen Hill (1988) puts it, the pervasive experience of "technology is one of apparent inevitability."

Questions of agency and local policy and planning therefore tend to be ignored in the simple recourse to either generalized, future-oriented debates, or to macrolevel, binary models of societal transformation. In these, new technologies are seen to be somehow autonomously transforming society *en masse* into some new "information age," "information society," or "cyberculture." As the American geographer Robert Warren (1989, page 344) argues, "benign projections [about telecommunications and the future of cities] give little indication that there are significant policy issues which should be on the public agenda." In the emphasis on private entrepreneurship and the transcendence of place, the discourses of the "information society" thus tend to imply that local municipalities, policy agencies, and planners might even be little more than irrelevant distractions in this exciting and epoch-making transformation driven by private media, communications, and property interests. Consequently, little thought is being put toward how urban policies, plans, and strategies can *engage with* new technologies as policy agents to try to help shape *desired* urban futures in a purposive manner.

With utopianism and crude technological determinism often dominating popular and, in many cases, academic debates, it is not surprising that the potential roles of urban policy-makers and planners in "socially shaping" new technologies in cities at the local level are usually overlooked (see, for example, Negroponte, 1995; Martin, 1995). This neglect, however, is problematic. It means that a fast-growing wave of urban experimentation with telecommunications, which is currently emerging across advanced industrial cities, is largely ignored within urban planning and policy debates. This is a problem because such innovation promises to have major practical and theoretical implications for how we might consider the future of cities, urban policy, and planning. It may also offer lessons on the broader question of how we might best understand the relations between cities and new communications technologies, and how we might address the crucial question of thinking about the "local" and the "urban," in an increasingly tele-mediated and globalized era.

This chapter attempts to address this problem by inserting urban planning into debates about new technologies and the future of cities. It has three parts. In the first, we set the context for local, planned intervention on IT and telecommunications by reviewing the evidence on the complex interdependence between cities, transportation, and face-to-face interactions and electronically mediated interactions. We do this by looking in turn at transport-telecommunications relations, the broad links between urban economies and the so-called "information economy," the relations between urban and so-called "cybercultures" based on IT systems, and, finally, the ways in which urban communities and "virtual," IT-based communities are interdependently linked. In the second part of the chapter we go on to review a broad, international range of emerging policy initiatives that aim to help shape the articulation between the built form and socioeconomic development of cities, and the electronic interactions within such cities and between them and the "outside" world. Finally, in the third section, we assess the significance of these policies and suggest ways for creatively integrating telecommunications into urban policy and planning practices and strategies.

THE METROPOLITAN DOMINANCE OF THE DIGITAL AGE

To understand why cities will be central to the "digital age," we need to explore the *complex interrelationships* between electronic and urban interactions in the economy, culture, and society. We need, in short, to understand how our urban life stands in a state of subtle, two-way, *articulation* with electronic interactions (see Robins, 1995). We also need to understand why the level of the city and urban region might be a crucial one for exploring new policy innovations that make the most of the potential of new technologies in a way that has meaning in relating to the urban worlds in which the vast majority of us live, work, and act out our lives. To further explore the coevolution of cities and telecommunications, which is essential as a basis for successful urban policy and planning innovation in these areas, we need to look in more detail at its four key aspects: transport-telecommunications interactions; the links between urban economies and the "information economy"; interactions between urban cultures and cybercultures; and the subtle interactions between place-based and "virtual" communities in cities.

Transport-Telecommunications

Conventional approaches to transport-telecommunications relations stress the environmentally beneficial role of telecommunications technology. It is often assumed that telecommunications can unproblematically substitute for physical transport flows and movement, reducing the need for travel and so lowering levels of pollution and urban congestion. For example, British Telecom's (BT) Environmental Manager argues that: "telecommunications technology is likely to play an increasingly important role in offering a more environmentally sound alternative to travel. . . . Apart from a saving in energy, the switch to telecommunication services would have other environmental benefits such as reduced noise levels, fewer new roads and lower levels of urban pollution" (Tuppen, 1992, page 81). Jonathon Porrit, one of the United Kingdom's leading environmentalists, "hails this fusion of communications and computing technologies as one of the 'tools for sustainability.'"

Early research on the potential for trade-offs between telecommunications and transportation networks was commissioned by the U.S. government in the mid-1970s in response to the energy crisis. This work simply compared the energy costs associated with communications through the telephone, and physical forms of communication such as personal travel by car, train, and aeroplane (Nilles, et al., 1976). The energy savings associated with communications by telecommunications created much excitement about the potential for trade-offs between telecommunications and transportation.

Initial interest in the role of telecom–transport trade-offs focused on the potential for the displacement of work-related commutes. In the mid-1970s, Jack Nilles invented the term "telecommuting" to describe home or neighborhood-based working using computers and telecommunications technology (see Nilles, et al., 1976). Tele-based communication was seen as a solution to the problem of congested urban environments and long commutes to centralized offices. It was assumed that telecommunications would simply substitute electronic flows for the transportation of people and freight along more polluting road, rail, and air networks. There were a number of attempts to demonstrate the potential substitution effects of teleworking on travel patterns and to estimate energy savings. In the U.S. context, these demonstrate that telecommuting has the potential to save between 1 percent and 3 percent of national energy consumption, figures that were not as great as the early proponents of teleworking might have expected (Nilles, 1988). These reports also have highlighted some of the "rebound" implications of teleworking, including extra energy consumed in the home, movement out to higher-amenity areas, increasing total commute distances, and the rapid filling of road space through high latent demand. (see Marvin, 1997).

The U.K. Department of Environment, Transport and the Regions' traffic projections show how demands for mobility and movement, both within and between cities, are unlikely to reduce, even whilst telecommunications use continues to burgeon. Overall, transport and telecommunications *actually feed off and fuel, more than simply substitute for, each other.* While telecoms undoubtedly have some potential to substitute for journeys and more routine interactions, there is considerable evidence that the relationship between transport and telecoms is more complex (Graham and Marvin, 1996). Rather than simply substituting, telecoms have highly *complementary* relationships with physical travel. This, we would argue, can actually result in three forms of traffic *growth*.

First, telecommunications play a central role in *improving the efficiency and effectiveness of transport networks,* so reducing the cost of travel. Complex computer ticketing, transaction systems, and air-traffic control systems help reduce the costs of air travel, making it more attractive as our perceptual understanding of the world increases. Electronic information exchange also plays a major role in the organization and management of transport networks. Such innovations help to extend the reach, reliability, and usefulness of transport flows through air travel, auto-route guidance, fax, mobiles, e-mail, real-time information, and electronic data interchange-based "just-in-time" logistics systems. A single flight of a 747, for example, has been estimated to generate 50,000 electronic exchanges in booking, maintenance, refueling, airport management, and so on.

Second, access to cheaper telecommunications increases an individual's or organization's "perceptual space," creating more opportunities for physical travel. The more we get to know about the world, whether from a leisure, recreation, or business opportunities point of view, the more we demand new forms of physical travel to support flows of goods or directly to experience the quality of interaction that can only be achieved through physical contact—usually in cities. The people with the greatest demands to use phones and mobile computers are business travelers. People who telework and move far from cities may actually travel farther overall because they travel farther for other trips like shopping or because their fewer commutes are over longer distances.

Finally, congested roads create new demands for telecommunications. Mobile phones may actually help to sustain larger traffic jams because they allow "dead" time to be converted to "live" working time. It is no accident that some car manufactures now sell cars with car phones, faxes, or mobile computers—the ideal way of staying in touch with work and home once a driver is stuck in a gridlock or slow-moving traffic. In this way telecommunications helps overcome our resistance to traveling by cars on congested roads, as real-time information overcomes many of the uncertainties and difficulties of travel. In short, what appears to be happening is a major expansion in all forms of communications. Although some substitution may undoubtedly be taking place, overall growth of electronic and physical mobility simply overwhelms the contribution of substitution.

Urban Economies/Information Economy

Current advances in telecommunications are a phenomenon which is overwhelmingly driven by the economic dynamism of cities, particularly larger, internationally oriented, metropolitan regions. City-regions have important assets in an internationalizing economy, based more and more on flows of information, services, and "symbolic" products such as media, advertising, cultural services, and electronic entertainment (as well as movement of people, goods, and commodities). They support face-to-face interactions, especially for higher-level decision-making functions, in a world of fast flows and great volatility. We should not forget the sheer infrastructural advantages of cities. Cities also have the high-quality physical, service, and telecommunications infrastructures to extend access efficiently to distant places and markets. Whilst remote, rural areas might still have the old-fashioned and poor quality analog telecom infrastructure of the old monopoly (BT), our main city centers now have three or more separate, high-capacity, digital systems competing in price and quality (with many others selling specialized services). London's City and West End districts have at least four superimposed fiber-optic grids (those of BT, Cable and Wireless, MFS, and COLT) and countless other service providers who deliver over these networks. Eighty percent of investment in telecoms in France goes to the Paris city-region.

But cities still offer unrivaled place-based, as well as electronic, contact potential. Today's uncertain and globalizing economies make trust, constant innovation, and reciprocity more and more important, which can only be fully forged through ongoing face-to-face contact. Stressing "the extraordinarily social nature of modern economies," the geographers Nigel Thrift and Kris Olds (1996, page 316) write that: "it is clear that face-to-face interaction has not died out. Indeed, in some sense it has become more important as reflexivity (including and enhanced ability to see oneself as others see us) has become built into economic conduct." Tony Fitzpatrick (1997, page 9) the Director of Ove Arup, argues that: "cities reflect the economic realities of the 21st century. Remote working from self-sufficient farm steads via the Internet cannot replace the powerhouses of personal interaction which drives teamwork and creativity. These are the cornerstones of how professional people add value to their work. Besides, you cannot look into someone's eyes and see that they are trustworthy over the Internet." On the consumption side, too, the whole range of consumer services, now so important in urban economies—tourism, shopping, visiting museums and leisure attractions, eating and drinking, sport, theatre, cinema, and so on— are all growing and seem likely to resist any simple, substantial substitution by online equivalents.

Major urban places support dense webs of face-to-face links, transactional opportunities, agglomeration economies, access to wide pools of specialized labor, services, property and infrastructure, and "soft" cultural and social advantages. Here the emphasis is increasingly on the *qualitative* aspects of urban economies and urban places, and the increasing dominance of urban economies by symbolic and representational flows and outputs, which may or may not be linked closely to commodity flows and outputs—what Lash and Urry (1994) term "economies of signs and space." Thus, in today's urban economies, the spiraling use of telecommunications becomes combined with the spiraling use of transport and a continuing, perhaps even growing, reliance on face-to-face contacts and meetings, largely in cities: what the father of the "Megalopolis" concept, the geographer Jean Gottmann (1990) used to call the "spiraling mass of bits of information." What many people interpret to be a post-turban shift might actually be a transition from traditional, core-dominated, monocentric cities toward complex, extended, and polycentric city-regions made up of a multitude of superimposed clusters, grids, and internal and external connections.

This is an important argument, which leads us to stress four points. First, growing flows of electronic information may require *more* face-to-face contact to make sense of it all as the Bristol geographer, Nigel Thrift, has shown with his work on City of London electronic traders. Second, much of the electronic exchange on networks such as the Internet actually represent cities as places to visit, consume, travel to, or live within, as the many tourist and municipal and urban services sites on the Web demonstrate. In the United States, the fastest-growing Web sites are those that try to integrate the Internet at the level of the metropolitan region, simply because this has most salience to Net users. Private operators of integrating city-level Web sites in the United States have grown massively recently, attracted by the increasing maturity of the Web as a diffused medium and by their calculations that "80 percent of purchases are made within a 20 mile radius of the home" (McElvogue, 1997, page 2).

Third, it is easy, given the hyperbole about globalization, to underestimate radically the degree to which tele-mediated flows operate to sustain very local relations. The vast bulk of electronic exchanges, for example, are very local indeed: 60 percent of all phone calls and e-mails move within single buildings (Graham and Marvin, 1996). And, finally, even when stories are apparently about decentralization and substitution, essentially urban dynamics are usually at play. Most teleworking, for instance, is done for part of the week in the zones within and around the large cities that allow people to go to the office on one or two days a week for face-to-face meetings. When IT does support so-called "disintermediation," directly linking consumers and producers across distance—as is the case with many call centers delivering routine services online—their destinations tend not to be rural spaces but smaller, provincial, cities or, in sectors such as online computer programming, far-off cities such as Bangalore in India.

Urban Cultures/Cybercultures

STEPHEN GRAHAM AND SIMON MARVIN

Thirdly, the centers of many of our larger cities are experiencing renewed growth as interlinked centers of growing cultural industries (arts, theater, dance, music, publishing, fashion, media, graphic design, photography, architecture, leisure, sport, and so on). The importance of city centers has recently been reemphasized, based on the widening assertion that such cultural industries may, with appropriate policies, interlace positively within a framework of public space to support the emergence of "creative cities" (Landry and Bianchini, 1995). The central idea driving such policies is that cities can thrive only when strategies recognize that: "the defining characteristics of cities are high density, mixed use, stimulus, transactions and above all diversity" (Montgomery, 1995). But how do urban cultures interrelate with much-vaunted "cybercultures" at a time when *electronic* cultural interactions are exploding, fueled by digital technologies and the blurring of boundaries between computing, media, and telecommunications industries and technologies?

It is clear, at the level of large organizations, that large cities *already tend to dominate* the sectors that are blurring together with the emergence of multimedia: TV, publishing, art and design, film, and media and telecommunications. Such firms continue to rely on large cities for all the reasons stated above. But the prospects for creative synergies between urban and cybercultures seem extremely strong at the much more dynamic level of small and microfirms. In an apparently paradoxical twist, the continuous innovation in the Internet, digital media, and multimedia content industries, so often hailed by media and industry pundits as supporting the "death of distance," is being fueled by intensely local networks based on face-to-face interaction in selected urban districts.

In fact, as the value-added in IT industries shifts from the zones dominated by hardware production to places that can sustain innovation in software and content, so the focus of the industries may actually be shifting from Silicon-Valley-like Research and Development campuses to central, old-city locations. In the cultural industries, the creative small firms that dominate Internet software, digital design, and World Wide Web services, far from scattering toward rural idylls, seem in fact to be concentrating into a small number of gentrifying metropolitan information districts such as Soho and Tribeca in New York, Shoreditch in London, and Temple Bar in Dublin. As well as having good broadband telecom connections and tailored, Internet-ready office spaces, such districts are thriving through processes that are arguably analogous to those that spawned the first industrial districts in nineteenth-century cities. In a detailed study of Soho and Tribeca in Manhattan, for example, Dan Hill found that the raw material for such industries is the sort of informal networks, high levels of creativity and skill, tacit knowledge, and intense and continuous innovation processes that become possible in an intensely localized culture based on ongoing, face-to-face contacts supported by rich, dense, and interdependent combinations of meeting places and public spaces. Clustering in certain "information districts" may thus support the informal and ongoing innovation networks and serendipitous contacts that seem central to the success of small and micro digital arts and creative firms (Hill, 1997).

Most important here, the Internet, with its "spiraling mass" of information, communication, transactions, and specialized media flows, is now weaving into fashion every aspect of urban functioning in contemporary city-regions. Such trends are most advanced in the United States, which demonstrates the strong metropolitan bias of both the production and consumption sides of the Internet. On the *production* side, for example, downtown New York's Silicon Alley has emerged, along with districts in downtown San Francisco and other large cities, as a remarkable concentration of small and microfirms, based on digital art and design, Web production, and digital and multimedia services. These draw on the city's unparalleled arts, cultural industries, and literary traditions. One of the main motors of the recent economic renaissance in Manhattan, Silicon Alley encompasses more than seven hundred new media firms that rely on intense, informal, local contacts to sustain continuing innovation and interaction (Hill, 1997). Interestingly, urban planning and policy are beginning to find ways of supporting this new information district, as we shall see in the next section. It must be stressed however, that currently only a relatively small number of urban districts are being redeveloped in this way. Moreover, these "organic" spaces are very difficult to develop "artificially"—that is, in the absence of existing appropriate, high-skill levels, contact networks, supportive services, and local entrepreneurial culture.

On the *consumption* side, it seems that the metropolitan dominance of the Internet might actually grow rather than decline, as it becomes massively diffused and accepted, and gradually weaves into all aspects of urban life. This is certainly the recent experience of the world's most mature Internet market, the United States (Moss and Townsend, 1997). The top fifteen metropolitan core regions in the United States in Internet domains accounted for just 4.3 percent of national population in 1996. By, 1996 this had risen to almost 20 percent, as the Internet became a massively diffused and corporately rich system. As Moss and Townsend (1997) suggest, "the highly disproportionate share of Internet growth in these cities demonstrates that Internet growth is not weakening the role of information-intensive cities. In fact, the activities of information-producing cities have been driving the growth of the Internet in the last three years." Manhattan now has twice the domain density (that is, concentration of Internet hosts) of the next most "Internet-rich" U.S. city—San Francisco—and six times the U.S. average (Moss and Townsend, 1997).

In such a context, there are many opportunities for weaving "access points"—Internet and service kiosks—into the fine-grained fabric of cities to animate, enliven, and inform what goes on in the public and private realms of cities and metropolitan regions. Whilst there are many problems here to do with the high costs of technologies, highly uneven social access and skill levels, and dangers of oppressive surveillance, a growing range of initiatives at the urban level are currently experimenting with new media solutions to support the improved delivery of public services, support community networking, and enhance local economic, social, and cultural development.

But such public initiatives are far outweighed by the sheer *economic* logic of the Internet. Already, private Internet providers are themselves starting to develop integrating Web sites at the urban level. These aim to support coherent and legible relationships between the many services on the Web that fall within a particular city and the population of that city. The need for urban Internet guides is especially powerful in the larger, global cities that dominate Internet innovation and use. New York, for example, now has more than ten dedicated "virtual city" Web sites that aim to draw together various portfolios of local Internet-based services (Graham and Aurigi, 1997).

Urban Communities/Virtual Communities

Finally, all aspects of the social use of telecommunications remain highly dominated by, and bound up with, the lives and social worlds of urban populations and communities. It is in our metropolitan regions that the most rapid diffusion of mobile phones, cable systems, and the Internet has developed, and where the rich communicational and transactional fabric of cities is increasingly supported by complex tapestries of telecommunications networks. One only has to witness the recent explosion of the use of mobile phones on our city streets to understand this. Thus, for example, the many virtual communities on the Internet are made up of both globally stretched Usenet groups, and Multi-User Dungeons (MUDs), and so on, and a growing range of community networks at the local level in towns and cities, aimed at feeding back positively onto the social dynamics of individuals cities (Graham and Aurigi, 1997).

Some writers have even suggested that local urban community networks such as the Cleveland Freenet, Santa Monica Public Electronic Network and Seattle Community Network, as well as the more recent "virtual" or "digital city" movement, represent hope for truly interactive, democratic, media systems that might help revive, enliven, and inform the public realm of their host cities (see Schuler, 1996). The hope here is that local IT systems that support interactive community debates, will help to bring together the diverse social, cultural, and geographical fragments of extending city regions, adding important coherence and legibility to a city's "electronic realm" in the process. In the long run, computer networks "grounded" in particular local communities might be more sustainable, effective, and meaningful than those that rely purely on IT-based exchange across global distance. Wakeford (1996) argues that grounded community IT networks can often support higher degrees of trust (with "persistent" rather than "transient" identities). They can also relate more effectively to real problem-solving and can interrelate with training centers and face-to-face contact, supporting reciprocal, frequent, and supportive interactions that relate strongly with the wider public realm. Finally, these advantages can often allow them to draw in wider cross sections of people than can global Internet newsgroups.

But such assertions and rhetoric need to be tempered by the realization that profoundly deep social divisions in access to all communications technologies are woven into the fabric of our cities (see, for example, Demos Collection, 1997). Whilst elite groups are superconnected to phone and IT networks at home, school, in their cars, and at work, even the humble telephone is an expensive luxury in many more marginalized urban neighborhoods. One neighborhood in inner Newcastle, for example, had only 27 percent of its households connected to the telephone in the late, 1980s (Graham and Marvin, 1996, Chapter 5). Home access to the Internet, with its prerequisites of skills, electricity, space, hardware, software, telephone, modem, Internet account, and cash for online and phone charges, is unlikely to be a priority for the large proportion of socioeconomic groups facing poverty, debt, and problems paying for essential bills. This places a premium on supporting access to community IT networks and Internet-based systems in the public spaces of cities.

One of the key policy issues for the tele-mediated city, therefore, is how to address deep social segmentations based on access to, and exclusion from, the new communications media and the growing ranges of information, resources, and transactional and working opportunities offered over them (see Schön, et al., 1998). As more and more IT-based systems become the norm—for example with growing reliance on home and mobile telephones, home IT systems, and electronic cash—so it becomes more and more disadvantageous to experience "network poverty" beyond the reach of such systems. But this is not to assert that systems like the Internet can act as a silver bullet to head complex problems of social exclusion, in the manner of the U.S. politician Newt Gingrich's absurd, utopian, and patronizing "laptops to the ghettos" rallying cry in 1995. Rather, it is to stress that new community-based electronic networks are required that, as a matter of course, work to enroll the broadest possible range of users and voices. Such experiments must be seen as attempts to explore the fullest potential of the new media, as realms for social communications at the most meaningful geographical level to most people—that of the metropolitan region.

EMERGING TELECOMMUNICATIONS-ORIENTED URBAN PLANNING STRATEGIES

Clearly, it is no longer adequate to consider policies for cities and those for telecommunications and new media entirely separately. The above imperatives suggest that only through addressing the complex interactions between cities and telecommunications will the potential of the technology be realized. This realization is currently leading to a wide range of policy experiments that aim positively to shape how the new media relate to specific cities or parts of cities. Early examples can be drawn from a bricollage of evidence drawn from cities in the United States, Canada, Malaysia, Europe, the United Kingdom, and elsewhere around the world. These examples have not yet coalesced around a coherent new paradigm of urban policy. Many can be criticized as technologically determinist, environmentally problematic, or socially exclusionary.

But we would argue that together they point to a new style of planning and urban policy. Such urban strategies try to shape face-to-face interactions in place (and the transport flows that sustain these) in parallel with electronically mediated ones across distance. Currently, we can identify three emerging styles of such "urban telecommunications planning": integrated transport and telecommunications strategies, city-level new media strategies, and so-called "information districts" and "urban televillages."

Integrated Transport and Telecommunications Strategies

The first set of initiatives attempts to shape and manage the relations between physical movement and mobility through the application of new media combined within particular forms of urban physical development. Each embodies a particular conception of the relations between different forms of communication and their role in the development of the city.

Urban and Regional Teleworking Initiatives
First, there are urban and regional teleworking initiatives. There is a growing set of initiatives, especially in the United States, that are attempting to grapple with the problems of developing a metropolitan-region approach to teleworking to make a positive contribution to environmental improvement—particularly in reducing vehicle emissions. For example, Telecommunications for Clean Air is a two-year program funded by the Californian South Coast Air Quality Management District to use telecommunications to meet rigorous air quality standards. The main aims of the program are to identify cost-effective solutions to air quality and congestion, to contribute to economic growth, and to develop a regional approach to problem-solving.

The Telework Facilities Exchange is designed to expand telecommuting participation in local government by providing low-cost, flexibly located facilities and marketing these practices to other organizations joining the exchange (Telecommunications for Clean Air, 1994). A public sector employee would normally commute 35 miles each way to his or her office. Instead, employees commuted to a vacant office a few miles from their home to use a workstation connected to their office. Those workers participating in the program reduced their normal vehicle miles traveled by 88 percent. As a result, if 30 percent of the region's 484,000 local-government employees each worked one day a week at the exchange, nearly 500,000,000 vehicle miles could be saved each year (Telecommunications for Clean Air, 1994).

These findings have to be treated with caution, because studies indicate that teleworking can generate "rebound effects." Although commute trips and time can be saved, additional recreational and shopping trips may be generated. Telecommuters may also decide to live farther from the city, so increasing the length of remaining commutes. And the space freed on highways is quickly filled with new commuters (see Mokhtarian, 1990; Department of Energy, 1994). But these tensions could be managed at a metropolitan level, as teleworking is coordinated within the context of wider transport and land-use strategies. The U.S. initiatives are particularly interesting because of the high degree of organizational innovation in the delivery mechanisms for teleworking and the much stronger links to mainstream transport, air quality, and land-use planning policies than tend to exist in Europe.

Assessments of the environmental potential of teleworking in the United Kingdom have remained largely at the level of national aggregate assessments (British Telecom, 1992; CEED, 1992). Overall, the conclusions are that the beneficial impact of telecommunications may be limited. Even assuming that teleworking continued to grow at a fast rate, the Royal Commission on Environmental Pollution concluded that it would have only a small role to play in the reduction of emissions. But although the national environmental benefits may be small, there could be potential in large conurbations in the United Kingdom to develop initiatives within a wider environmental policy framework. A recent study by a Cambridge-based consultant, for example, argued that 1.25 million miles per year could be saved if two thousand office-based staff at Cambridge Council were to telecommute (*Environment*, 1997). Further development work is necessary, perhaps drawing critically on the U.S. experience. For instance, BT provides limited guidance for local authorities attempting to integrate telecommunications into urban environmental and sustainability strategies. And the Association of County Councils has started to consider how IT and telecommunications could be linked with the green agenda (British Telecom, 1997; Association of County Councils, 1996). The key issue is the need to integrate carefully teleworking within the context of wider transportation and land-use plans.

Communication Corridors
Second, there are new forms of communication corridor strategies that attempt to shape how telecommunications, transport, and land use interplay within broader urban commuting corridors. Those based on existing rail/transit networks attempt to manage travel demand on both the road and the rail network through the provision of teleworking centers and incentives to travel off-peak. The Metro Net initiative in Los Angeles, for example, involves retrofitting a high capacity fiber-optic network alongside the 300-mile regional Metro Rail and Link network (Siembab, 1992). The proposals are designed to achieve three objectives: to generate revenue through leasing capacity, to develop services to enhance ridership of the system, and to improve regional mobility through developing station-based employment and service centers. The mobility strategy has been designed to fit in with the objectives of a series of wider regional communications and land-use strategies. More specially, it is hoped that the strategy will contribute toward the implementation of the Air Quality Management Plan, the Development Plan, the Regional Congestion Management Program, and the promotion of regional economic growth. The proposals

would develop telecommunications facilities at or near stations for conferences, education, and job training, to make the metro system a destination in itself.

Further development would link both the metro and telecoms networks to targeted parcels of adjacent land in order to attract new employers whilst maximizing public transport usage. These ideas mirror proposals in the United Kingdom to set up telecommuting offices along the Folkestone-to-Waterloo rail line in order to reduce the number of rush-hour commuters and enable a Channel tunnel link to run on existing tracks (Roarke Associates, 1994). A more recent proposal suggested building a ring of teleworking centers around the M25 motorway to deal with predicted car traffic growth. The architects, Roarke Associates, argued that the teleworking centers would cost £450 million, whereas road-widening would cost £1450 billion—a saving of £1 billion (*London Times*, 1997). Both these initiatives are at the proposal stage and have not been implemented. However, they illustrate some interesting ideas about how communications planning could integrate telecoms and transport, and start to make wider links to land-use strategies. Yet, at an institutional level, there is still considerable uncertainty as to which organizations could take the lead with such complex initiatives involving so many different dimensions of planning.

Road Transport Informatics

The third type of initiative focuses on the development of Road Transport Informatics (RTI). Citywide initiatives are rapidly emerging here, concerned with the use of RTI systems to manage transport networks more effectively. There are major initiatives in Europe, the United States, and Japan, and the National Economic Development Council estimates that the global IT and traffic-management market will be worth £29 billion in 2010. However, objectives of RTI are often poorly defined and are often not closely linked with land-use and work patterns. These initiatives are more often characterized by a form of technical fix dominated by strong producer-led interests. RTI strategies have assumed importance in the context of European Union (EU) funding programs where the technologies are seen as making a major contribution to sustainable development (CEC, 1995).

There have been a large number of feasibility schemes evaluating the potential of various forms of RTI and electronic tolling in the United Kingdom. But again, there has been a failure to link such debates within the context of wider urban management, regeneration, and land-use strategies. These issues are being considered more widely in North America. The Highway 407 that is currently being built in Toronto is billing itself as "Tolls but No Jams" (*Toronto Star* July 29, 1996, pages A6–A7). Located in one of the most congested highway corridors in North America, a $1-billion-dollar, 36 kilometer highway will eventually connect the airport to downtown Toronto. The scheme is being developed by Canadian Highways International Corporation, a private consortium of four companies that will be funded by the receipts from electronic tolls. In return for the higher charges, users will benefit from higher road speeds than the current limit, and no traffic jams. If demand increases, the highway can be expanded to ten lanes, and tolls can be raised to reduce peak travel volumes. The scheme is being marketed to those firms operating just-in-time production methods and that require high degrees of certainty in travel times for the movement of goods and services. There is now major development interest in highway land involving commercial, retail, leisure and recreation, and housing use adjacent to the new road. This initiative is an interesting example of the combined planning of electronic, transport, and land-use infrastructure designed to develop a congestion-free, higher-speed, and lower travel-time corridor through the congested region. But this new development trajectory is extremely socially exclusionary. It is very much designed to meet the needs of large international corporations and elite users prepared to pay the premium for increased certainty.

Other RTI initiatives focus on the development of local and regional initiatives in driver information and control systems. These initiatives are based on proposals to carry more traffic by making better use of the existing road network, through pretrip planning, route guidance, traffic management and control, and network management applications. It is hoped that the provision of information to drivers on road conditions can increase the efficiency of the network to minimize delays, unreliability, and environmental damage. For instance, it is estimated that driver information could increase the capacity of the road network by 1 percent and provide a 10 percent savings in journey times and a 6 percent reduction in mileage. The Scottish consultative document argues that the region is well placed to use these technologies because 80 percent of the population live within a relatively self-contained belt across the country (Scottish Office, 1993).

There are a number of problems with the emerging set of urban communications strategies in the United Kingdom. They tend to remain largely disconnected from mainstream urban strategies and have poorly developed links with land-use planning. They also tend narrowly to represent a limited and technologically determinist view of urban futures based around notions of a producer-led "technical fix" to the problems of urban mobility. These initiatives begin to provide examples of an emerging style of planning that attempt to integrate telecommunications within mobility and environmental stategies.

City-Level New Media and IT Strategies

The second broad, emerging policy area is citywide new media strategies. IT strategies for community networking, local economic development, and public service delivery have been underway in many U.K., European, and American cities for a decade or more. Following the American experience, community networks such as Freenets, the Manchester, Kirklees, and Nottingham Hosts, and the Newcastle NewNet system, based on the Internet, have emerged that try and use computer communications to support grassroots, local economic, and voluntary activities (see Graham and Marvin, 1996). Many local authorities are also experimenting with videotex systems, electronic kiosks, and smart-cards systems to deliver information on public services, and aim to improve the services themselves. In the United Kingom, the new government report, *The New Library: The People's Network* (see *http://www.ukoln.ac.uk/services/lic/new library/*), proposes to wire up both schools and libraries as places where IT networks can be made widely available for local communities.

Local services have developed patchily on the new urban cable networks developing across the United Kingdom. And virtually all major U.K. cities now have a presence on the Internet, where so-called "virtual cities" range from simple tourist promotion and local databases, to sophisticated spaces that attempt to add coherence to all local activities on the Internet, to widen local access and skills, to open up interactive services for local debates, and to develop information and communications services that feed back positively onto the development of the home city (Graham and Aurigi, 1997). Interestingly, the most innovative virtual cities use the analogies of city "spaces," "squares," and "districts," so that the many services they offer relate directly to their counterparts in physical urban space. The most sophisticated of these in the United Kingdom is currently Virtual Bristol, supported by a partnership of the City Council, universities, and Hewlett-Packard and launched in April, 1997. Not to be left out, BT is exploring the concept of "urban intranets"—Internet services that are accessible only to specified local communities.

This disparate range of local new media initiatives has two problems, however. First, these initiatives have tended to be fragmented, local, "IT islands," largely ignoring each other. And second, they have usually been developed with little or no attention to how they relate to the physical urban realm or to the broader development dynamics and geographies of their subject cities. Thus, the challenge for U.K. cities is to shape coherent partnership-based strategies aimed at harnessing all types of new media applications—Internet, cable, kiosks, telephone, infrastructure—to their economic, social, and cultural development needs. Such issues need to begin with social, geographical, and institutional issues and policy needs and move on to how new technologies might meet these needs—rather than the other way round. Institutional solutions need to be found that harness the entrepreneurial energies of the new media industries and their growing interest in market-based local initiatives (like the booming commercial metropolitan Internet sites in the United States), while linking creatively and positively to the fragmented sets of agencies involved, in the broadest sense, in the governance of U.K. cities (local authorities, development agencies, health, education and information institutions, firms, schools, the community and voluntary sector, and so on). Clearly, urban media master plans will be impossible; what is needed are strategic frameworks so that the innumerable local media investments and initiatives emerge to be more than the sum of their parts.

Finally, and most important, from the point of view of this analysis, there needs to be a much more thoroughgoing attempt to link urban media strategies to the development of cities themselves, so ensuring that, wherever possible, synergies can be developed between media and place-based exchanges. Progress is being made here, however, at both the urban and regional levels. At the city level, strategic planners in cities such as Amsterdam and Lille have already attempted to integrate new media into the future urban visions. In dozens of cities across the world, teleports and telezones have been designated in particular urban districts blending advanced office and business space and sophisticated telecommunications facilities. In the United States, ambitious new "smart city" media strategies are tentatively starting to consider land-use planning and urban policy issues—as our discussions of strategic urban corridors and information districts demonstrate. Already, in some highly affluent communities such as Palo Alto and Blacksburg, Virginia, very high levels of Internet and e-mail access and use have begun to transform the communicational fabric of urban areas as these new media become woven into the fabric of urban life (see Graham and Marvin, 1996). Predictably, in a private-sector-led planning process, the consultancies engaged in "smart community" planning argue that "cities unprepared for these [new media-based] changes risk being consigned to geopolitical obsolescence before they even know what hit them" (International Center for Communications, 1997).

In the United Kingdom, the packaging of IT infrastructure with individual land-use developments—business parks, telecottages, wired villages, and so on—is increasingly common. But efforts are also starting to link broader urban media strategies with urbanwide development strategies. After a period when grant, training, and technological support was sprinkled through the city, Manchester is increasingly gearing its broad telecoms and IT initiatives to specific urban redevelopment and reuse projects and to strategic discussions about combating social exclusion in the city. A widening range of new, physical, IT-oriented projects has emerged linked into the network services on offer: the Electronic Village Halls (linked to community centers and initiatives through the city), existing managed workspaces in New Mount Street and proposed ones in the "Northern Media Quarter," and a center for multimedia development and applications in Hulme (Carter, 1996). A similarly broad-based IT and new media strategy, known as the GEMESIS project, is underway in adjacent Salford, backed by a broad partnership between the cable company, IT firms, local universities, and training providers. In partnership with its university sector, Manchester/Salford, like German cities such as Berlin and Bochum, is also building a new, broadband, Metropolitan Area Network (MAN) infrastructure ring in the city that will spur efforts to regenerate the inner city through research and development and scientific innovation.

Europewide, cities at the vanguard of new media strategies are cooperating through the Telecities network to exchange experience, develop lessons for best practice, support pilot initiatives, and lobby the EU for further support. Telecities also links into Europe's efforts to support the emergence of what it terms a "regional information society" through its broadly based Inter-Regional Information Society Initiative (IRISI). This supports integrated packages of ICT-based pilot projects in designated regions in sectors as diverse as education, health, social services, transport and logistics, media, and public services. But again, there exist few links between the way the EU is considering information and communications technologies (ICT) applications, services, and infrastructure, and broader considerations about spatial development in the future (CEC, 1997).

Information Districts and Urban Televillages

The final area where new media policy is becoming directly linked with policies for particular urban spaces is the emergence of information districts and urban televillages. Building on the debates about urban villages in Europe, and the New Urbanism movement in the United States, interest is growing rapidly in how media infrastructure and services can be designed and managed, geared to sustaining and feeding back on particular urban districts. In California, the concept of the televillage—an integrated urban place supported by a whole suite of ICT infrastructures and services—is gaining support. The Blue Line Televillage, a two-square-mile area on one of the new public transit corridors in Los Angeles, is based on a holistic strategy to manage land use, transport trips, and electronic communications so that synergies emerge between the three, creating a "liveable" community with reduced automobile use, higher community-based activities, and higher urban densities than in the usual LA suburbs (Siembab, 1992).

Physical places for supporting IT training and services—community centers, computer centers, telework centers, IT links in schools, hospitals, transport facilities and libraries, and electronic kiosks in public and semipublic spaces—are integral to the plan that is backed up by a broad, public-private-community partnership and an extensive array of online public services. In partnership with the public transport operators in the LA region, a new fibre-optic network is being developed to link together whole constellations of televillages across the region. Different packages of IT and telecoms infrastructure and services are being offered for different land uses; "distributed" organizations are being encouraged; and attempts are being made to include more marginalized social groups. The philosophy is that IT-based retrofitting in existing U.S. urban areas will mean that many urban problems might be addressed "with very little new physical construction and no dramatic changes in density" (Siembab, 1992).

The other emerging example of combining new media and urban regeneration at district level is the concept of the "information district." Here, the emphasis is on creating urban "milieux" that sustain economic growth in new cultural and "symbolic" industries, where informal face-to-face contact is essential, while also providing high-capacity online linkages to the wider world. Such strategies are inspired by the emergence of information districts described above. Most often, information district strategies emerge organically, as in the cases considered above—New York's Silicon Alley, Dublin's Temple Bar, and Manchester's Northern Quarter—where clusters of such industries emerge spontaneously in inner urban districts. Then the challenge is to intervene to further support the growth of small and microfirms in the relevant sectors, while also ensuring that appropriate property is available and that broader efforts are made to improve the wider urban realm and the contribution of the industries to the economic and social revitalization of the city as a whole (Hill, 1997). Thus both New York and Los Angeles have offered grant schemes and tax exemptions to small and microfirms in the new media sectors. Backed by the powerful New York New Media Association (NYNMA), specialized multimedia

88

centers offering managed workspaces and high-level telecoms bandwidth have also started to emerge in Silicon Alley, as have dedicated venture-capital funds and orchestrated events and programs designed to encourage local face-to-face networking. Elsewhere in the United States, the city of Spokane in Washington State has wired up much of its downtown to attract multimedia firms.

In Europe, strategies at the neighborhood and district level have begun to look to coherent interventions in the urban realm, new media. At the institutional level, to try to sustain, develop, or encourage local clusters of multimedia firms, Manchester has explicitly adopted the Silicon Alley model to support its Northern Media Quarter on the edge of the city center. Sheffield's well known Cultural Industries Quarter (CIQ) strategy, aimed at clustering the broadest possible range of media, design, music, film, and cultural industry firms in one part of the city center, is now backed up by a widening range of online services financed by a public private partnership called NEO (Hill, 1997). Dublin's Temple Bar district is backing up its physical regeneration efforts, weaving a parallel infrastructure for electronic multimedia exchange.

In London's Soho media core, meanwhile, a specialized telecommunications network was recently constructed by a consortium of film companies called Sohonet. This system links the tight concentration of film and media headquarters in the district directly to Hollywood film studios, allowing online film transmission and editing over international scales via highly capable, digital, broadband connections. The network is seen as a critical boost to the broader global ambitions of the U.K. film and cultural industries.

CONCLUSION:
INTEGRATING TELECOMMUNICATIONS INTO URBAN PLANNING

In this chapter we have attempted to demonstrate that new information technologies actually resonate with, and are bound up within, the active construction of urban places, rather than making them somehow redundant. Urban places and electronic spaces are increasingly being produced together. The power to function economically and link socially increasingly relies on constructed, material places that are intimately woven into complex media infrastructures linking them to other places and spaces. "Today's institutions" argues William Mitchell (1995, page 126), "are supported not only by buildings but by telecommunications and computer software." Thus the articulation between widely stretched media and telecommunications systems and produced material places becomes the norm. It is, indeed, a defining feature of contemporary urbanism. "Constructed spaces," continues Mitchell, "will increasingly be seen as electronically serviced sites where bits meet the body— where digital information is translated into visual, auditory, tactile or otherwise sensorily perceptible form, and vice versa. Displays and sensors for presenting and capturing information will be as essential as doors" (Mitchell, 1995). As cities extend into polycentric metropolitan regions, the spaces of the city are being constructed within broader and more complex urban fields, networked together by more sophisticated, integrative, technological networks.

With the above examples, we have started to map the emergence of a potentially significant shift in urban strategies based around the idea of trying to shape how built spaces and electronically mediated interactions work in parallel. Reviewing a set of innovative initiatives, it is apparent that planning initiatives are proliferating that try actively to shape the articulations between the development and use of new media and communications technologies and urban places. Such initiatives are supported by the widening efforts of planners, urban development agencies, transport bodies, and media firms to understand the complexities through which electronically mediated communications interact with land use, the urban realm, transport, and face-to-face contact. Moreover, it is clear that the initiatives reviewed above are only the start. Virtually every Western city worth its salt now seems to uses "cyber" and "silicon" as obligatory prefixes in its urban marketing campaigns. Many beyond those discussed above are also exploring how they can address places and IT networks in parallel.

We would argue that the current growth of explicitly urban telecoms strategies and initiatives is broadly to be welcomed. This is for three reasons. First, it is acknowledged that city-telecoms interactions are intrinsically bound up with contemporary metropolitan life. Second, these policies are based on much more sophisticated understandings of the complex and subtle relations between new media and urban life than those "death of distance" or "End of Cities" ideas generally implied by dominant "information society" debates. And third, these proliferating policies suggest that the articulations between urban spaces and new media technologies are open to innovative, local, and planned interventions that can bring benefits that neither untrammelled market forces nor distant central state hierarchies can deliver.

But what might these nascent policies mean for urban planning and urban development more broadly? Obviously, speculation is difficult in such an embryonic policy arena. In these conclusions we would therefore only like to address two key questions. First, are urban telecommunications initiatives likely to be able to succeed in shaping positive synergies between place-based interactions and development and electronically mediated interactions and development? Or are they merely stylistic and symbolic, aimed at adding value and high-tech kudos to prestigious real estate developments? Second, what might these initiatives mean for broader notions of the city and for ideas of integrated metropolitanwide planning? More particularly, are these initiatives likely to reinforce and recreate new forms of socioeconomic exclusion and environmental damage, or might they genuinely emerge as useful attempts to develop a more inclusive and sustainable urban futures?

90

Turning to the first question, we must first sound some notes of caution. For, despite the widening range of initiatives, we remain highly cautious about their current usefulness in terms of both their magnitude and direction. In terms of their magnitude, we must raise serious warnings against *overstating* the potential role of telecommunications and information technology in urban strategies. Whilst most approaches to urban strategies are still grappling with new ways of planning for transportation girds and urban places in parallel, it is still the case that electronic interconnections and networks are most often still hidden and taken for granted.

In terms of direction, it is clear that even when land use, transport, and telecoms are considered in parallel, real progress will come only when two further problems are addressed. First, policy-makers will need to fight actively against prevailing assumptions (which are actually deeply embedded within Western culture as a whole) that new technologies can somehow be rolled out as technical quick-fix solutions to complex urban problems. In a context where most urban policy-makers and planners lack knowledge and experience of the telecommunications sector, there is the danger that urban strategies could uncritically embrace the transformational rhetoric that characterizes contemporary notions of technology "impacts" upon the city that we touched on at the start of this chapter. New telecommunications initiatives are still often intimately connected with utopian and deterministic ideas of technology's beneficial and linear impacts upon the social, environmental, and spatial development of cities. Developing more nuanced and sophisticated concepts of the potential roles of telecommunications in urban strategy will require policy-makers to look more critically at the role of technology in contemporary urban strategies.

Achieving this, however, is difficult for another reason. Powerful media and technology firms are exploiting the hyperbolic rhetoric of cyberspace, the information superhighway, and the global information society to enroll poorly informed urban public policy-makers into making local "partnerships" to develop new information districts, communications corridors, and high-tech economic development zones of various sorts. Growing interurban competition, and the tendency for urban policy-makers to jump on the latest policy bandwagon, are being exploited by a wide range of consultants and media conglomerates. Such organizations are keen to add value and symbolic kudos to their own efforts to build up demand for new configurations of real estate, developed spaces, and all the associated technological hardware and services embedded in them. Public subsidies, discounted land deals, infrastructural assistance, credibility, and the sheer marketing weight of public policy-makers can do much to raise the profile of new, planned "high-tech" spaces (and, therefore, developer profits).

But the real benefits of such initiatives to localities may be dubious or massively overblown because they remain inappropriate to real local needs. Thus, planners and local policy-makers need to educate themselves as quickly as possible about the burgeoning worlds of new media technologies. They need to be wary of being seduced into expensive partnerships of dubious real local benefit by the lustrous promises of information-age hyperbole. It is here that critical local debate about the real communicational needs of urban places, and the policy models that derive from these, is necessary.

Above all, planners must be sensitive to the important *symbolic* power of information and new media technologies as signifiers of high-tech modernity. They must also be attentive to whose interests this symbolic power serves, and how. Arguably, this symbolic power (which, by its very nature is very visible), is as significant, perhaps more significant in some cases, than real new applications or telecommunications infrastructures (which often remain unknown or hidden). Labeling a place "cyber" this, "silicon" that, or "tele" something else is an affirmation that it is switched onto global circuits of economic, cultural, or social exchange via electronic networks. It is a potent, symbolic attempt to lure in mobile capital, people, and investment, which adds value to fixed infrastructure, land, and real estate even when they are clearly in tension with highly dynamic and mobile flows of services, media, information, and money over telecommunications grids.

Such symbolism can take extreme forms. At one stage, for example, Edinburgh City Council considered building an artificial satellite dish on its Maybury business park because BT argued that there was no technological need for there to be one in the city, which has world-class satellite facilities accessible from other places (Graham, 1999). Of course, if local policy-makers willingly embrace this symbolic power and use it creatively to their own advantage, through place-marketing strategies and the like, all well and good. But they must be careful not to be duped by it, and not to believe uncritically all the promises of corporate and media firms that this new (publicly subsidized) media or IT network will miraculously solve all local problems of traffic congestion, social polarization, economic development, environmental sustainability, and so on.

Which brings us on to our second question: What might these initiatives mean for broader notions of the "city" and for ideas of integrated metropolitanwide planning? Here, too, there is cause for concern. In the light of the above discussion, we clearly need to unpack the social assumptions and biases built into current urban telecommunications initiatives. We need to ask how urban telecommunications initiatives might link to wider urban debates around social equity, the public realm and culture, economic development, and environmental improvement. With such a strong supply push from powerful media and real estate interests, there are clearly dangers that urban telecommunications strategies are being configured in highly biased ways that might perpetuate and reinforce widespread existing trends toward social and spatial polarization in urban areas.

The danger is that the foci of initiatives will center overwhelmingly on configuring new media technologies according to the needs and geographies of affluent, privileged nodes, spaces, and corridors in metropolitan regions whilst ignoring and excluding marginalized zones. The former, of course, are already at the vanguard of IT applications and are the hot spots of demand for all forms of telecommunications and media applications and services (Graham and Marvin, 1996). In the context of liberalizing telecommunications regimes, the risk is that market forces will encourage both corporate and media interests and urban policy-makers to invest their efforts in communications corridors for the highly mobile, information districts for the information elites, and media consumption spaces for affluent professionals with high disposable incomes. In short, urban telecommunications strategies may work simply to extend the existing relational privileges of powerful zones, spaces, and interests in the city.

Such fragmented policy packages, superimposed as patchworks across the urban landscape, reflect wider trends within urban governance toward the collapse of the notion of coordinated, metropolitanwide planning (Graham and Marvin, 1999). Complex patchworks of special-interest zones and public-private governance initiatives are tending to replace systematic, metropolitanwide public planning (Boyer, 1996). As Bosma and Hellinga (1997, page 16) argue, in contemporary planning practices, "the primary matter of importance is no longer an integral approach, but the cheerful acceptance of regions as an archipelago of enclaves."

Urban telecommunications initiatives are clearly contributing to such an "archipelago of enclaves." The worrying thing about the urban telecommunications initiatives reviewed above may both reflect and sustain wider social polarization trends. Thus, within cities, smart transport corridors and "wired" enclaves might support forms of "telematics superinclusion" (Thrift, 1996) for elite groups, allowing these elite groups to live in cocooned (often sometimes walled) enclosures while still accessing personal and corporate transport and telematics networks. Meanwhile, however, a short distance away, in the interstitial urban zones, there are likely to be "off-line" spaces (Graham and Aurigi, 1997), or "lag-time places" (Boyer, 1996; 20). In these often-forgotten places, access to the new technologies will remain highly problematic. Time and space will remain profoundly real, perhaps increasing constraints on social life because of welfare and labor market restructuring and the withdrawal of banking and public transport services.

But perhaps we are being too negative here. For we must also stress the positive potential of urban telecommunications initiatives as well as the need to be wary of their symbolic power and cautious about the possibilities that such initiatives may reinforce urban social and spatial polarization. Progressive, inclusionary telecommunications and IT policies, integrated into particular urban strategies and designed to tie cities together rather than split them apart, might have important, positive roles in shaping the articulation between place-based and electronically mediated realms. They might help, quite literally, to ground the globally integrating world of new media interactions, making them more meaningful in real places, real communities, real lives. Such initiatives may help to embed new technological innovations in particular places, rather than just supporting an ever-more momentous delocalization through market-driven forces of globalization in the economy, society, and culture. And, given enough stress on the needs of low-income communities, such initiatives might actively counter wider urban polarization trends (see Schön, et al., 1997).

Indeed, one might even argue that *without* active, progressive resistance to untrammeled globalization and the colonization of local spaces by global media markets, mobilized through the rubric of creative, place-based IT strategies, social need, the particularities of place, freedom of expression, and local cultural diversity may tend to be squeezed out of the corporate, commodifying logic of globalization. As Grossman (1995) puts it, "media conglomerates will not fill the vital educational, civic, and cultural needs" of real places and real cities. Strategies like the one in Manchester show that, just because privately inspired urban IT initiatives have followed a particular trajectory, this does not mean that these cannot be challenged by incorporating wider social and environmental concerns into policy development.

ACKNOWLEDGMENTS

We gratefully acknowledge the support of Demos and Comedia, particularly Ken Worpole, Bill Solsbury, and Liz Grenhalgh, who allowed us to undertake this research. Responsibility for contents, of course, rests with the authors.

REFERENCES

Association of County Councils. (1996). *Green Communications: Planning for Telematics, Teleworking and Telecounties*. London: Environment Committee.

Bosma, K. and Hellinga, H. (1997). "Mastering the City." In K. Bosma and H. Hellinga, eds. *Mastering the City*. Rotterdam: NAI Publishers.

Boyer, C. (1996). *Cybercities: Visual Perception in an Age of Electronic Communication*. Princeton, NJ: Princeton University Press.

British Telecom. (1992). "A Study of the Environmental Impact of Teleworking," report by BT Research Laboratories.

————. (1997). *Telecommunications Technologies and Sustainable Development—A Guide for Local Authorities*. London.

Carter, D. (1996). " 'Digital Democracy' or 'Information Aristocracy'? Economic Regeneration and the Information Economy." In B. Loader, ed. *The Governance of Cyberspace*. London: Routledge, 136–154.

Castells, M. (1996). *The Rise of the Network Society*. Oxford: Blackwell.

CEC. (1995). "Contributions of the Information Society to Sustainable Development." Brussels: CEC.

————. (1996). "Information and Communication Technologies for Sustainable Technical Development." Final report. Brussels: CEC.

————. (1997). *European Spatial Development Perspective*. Brussels: CEC.

CEED. (1992). *The Environmental Impact of Teleworking*. U.K. CEED Bulletin No 38, March–April: 10–11.

Demos Collection. (1997). *The Wealth and Poverty of Networks*. London: Demos.

Department of Energy. (1994). "Energy, Emissions and the Social Consequences of Telecommuting, Energy Efficiency in the U.S. Economy," Technical Report One, DOE/PO-0026. Washington, D.C.

Economist. (1995). "The Death of Distance." Telecommunications Survey, September 30–October 6.

Environment (1997). "Flexible Working Could Reduce Traffic." November 13.

Fitzpatrick, T. (1997). "A Tale of Tall Cities." *The Guardian On-Line* February 6: 9.

Gosling, P. (1997). *Government in the Digital Age*. London: Bowerdean Press.

Gottmann, J. (1990). "Urban Settlements and Telecommunications." In J. Gottman and R. Harper, eds. *Since Megalopolis: The Writings of J. Gottmann*. Baltimore: Johns Hopkins University Press, 192–205.

Graham, S. (1998). "The End of Geography or the Explosion of Space? Conceptualising Space, Place and Information Technology." *Progress in Human Geography*, 22; 2: 165–185.

———. (1999). "Satellite Dishes." In S. Pile and N. Thrift, eds. *City A-Z*. London: Wiley.

Graham, S. and A. Aurigi. (1997). "Virtual Cities, Social Polarization and the Crisis in Urban Public Space." *Journal of Urban Technology* 4(1): 19–52.

Graham, S. and P. Healey. (1998). "Relational Theories of Time and Space: Issues for Planning Theory and Practice," Paper submitted to European Planning Studies.

Graham, S. and S. Marvin. (1996). *Telecommunications and the City: Electronic Spaces, Urban Places*. London: Routledge.

———. (1999). *Splintering Networks/Fragmenting Cities: Urban Infrastructure in a Global-Local Age*. Routledge: London.

Grossman, L. (1995). "Maintaining Diversity in the Electronic Republic." *Technology Review* November/December: 23–26.

Hill, D. (1997). "Cultural Industries in the Digital City." Unpublished MA Dissertation, Manchester Metropolitan University.

Hill, S. (1988). *The Tragedy of Technology*. London: Pluto.

International Center for Communications. (1997). *Building Smart Communities*. Edinburgh: Guidebook, January.

Landry, C. and F. Bianchini. (1995). *Creative Cities*. London: Demos.

Lash, S. and J. Urry. (1994). *Economies of Signs and Space*. London: Sage.

McElvogue, L. (1997). "Bright Sites, Big City," *Guardian On-Line*, February 20: 2–3.

Martin, W. (1995). *The Global Information Society*. Aldershot: ASLIB.

Marvin, S. (1997). "Environmental Flows: Telecommunications and the Dematerialization of Cities," *Futures* Vol 29, No 1.

Mitchell, W. (1994). "Building the Bitsphere, or the Kneebone's Connected to the I-Bahn," *I.D.* November.

———. (1995). *City of Bits: Space, Place and the Infobahn*. Cambridge, MA: MIT Press.

Mokhtarian, P. (1990). "Relationships Between Telecommunications and Transportation." *Transportation Research*, Vol. 24A, No. 3: 231–242.

Montgomery, J. (1995). "Urban Vitality and the Culture of Cities." *Planning Practice and Research*, 10; 2: 101–109.

Moss, M. and A. Townshend. (1997). "Manhattan Leads the Net Nation." Available at http://www.nyu.edu/urban/ny_affairs/telecom.html.

Mulgan, G. (1991). "The Changing Shape of the City." In Stuart Hall and Martin Jacques, eds. *New Times*. London: Lawrence and Wishart.

Negroponte, N. (1995). *Being Digital*. London: Hodder and Stoughton.

Nilles, J. M., F. Carlson, P. Gray, and G. Hanneman. (1976). *The Telecommunications-Transport Trade Off*. Chichester: Wiley.

Nilles, J. M. (1988). Traffic Reduction by Telecommuting: A Status Review and Selected Bibliography. *Transportation Research* Vol. 22a No 4: 301–317.

Office of Technology Assessment. (1995). The Technological Reshaping of Metropolitan America. Washington: Congress of the United States.

Roarke Associates. (1994). Telecommuting Offices—A Proposal for Congestion Relief on London and S E England Rail Services. Roarke Associates.

Robins, K. (1995). "Cyberspace and the World We Live In." In Mike Featherstone and Roger Burrows, eds. *Cyberspace/Cyberbodies/Cyberpunk*. London: Sage, 135–156.

Schön, D., B. Sanyal, and W. Mitchell, eds. *High Technology and Low Income Communities*. Cambridge, MA: MIT Press.

Schuler, D. (1996). *New Community Networks: Wired for Change*. New York: Addison Wesley.

Scottish Office. (1993). "A National Driver Information and Control Strategy for Scotland." Consultation document. Los Angeles, CA.

Siembab, W. (1992). *Metro Net, Fiber Optics and Metro Rail: Strategies for Development.*

Telecommunications for Clean Air. (1994). *South Coast Air Basin.* Institute for Local Self Government.

Thrift, N. (1996). "New Urban Eras and Old Technological Fears: Reconfiguring the Goodwill of Electronic Things." *Urban Studies*, 33(8): 1463–1493.

Thrift, N. and K. Olds. (1996). "Refiguring the Economic in Economic Geography." *Progress in Human Geography* 20 (3): 311–337.

Times. (1997). "Teleworking Could Save a Billion." July 9: London.

Tuppen, C. G. (1992). "Energy and Telecommunications—An Environmental Impact Analysis." *Energy and Environment* Vol. 3, No. 2: 70–81.

Wakeford, N. (1996). "Developing Community Intranets: Key Social Issues and Solutions." Paper for British Telecom. London.

Warren, R. (1989). "Telematics and Urban Life." *Journal of Urban Affairs* 11(4): 339–346.

TELECOMMUNICATIONS INFRASTRUCTURE AND THE CITY

ADAPTING TO THE CONVERGENCE OF TECHNOLOGY AND POLICY

August E. Grant and Lon Berquist

INTRODUCTION

As the Telecommunications Act of 1996 sets the stage for broad national deregulation of telecommunications services, state and local governments are striving to implement and adapt to the procompetitive thrust of the Act. The trend toward communications industry deregulation and emergent market competition supplanting regulation has occurred concurrently with dramatic technological advances in the capability and efficiency of telecommunications networks. These technological enhancements are causing the distinctions between cable systems and telephone systems to blur, suggesting a technological convergence. Similarly, there has been a policy convergence among federal, state, and local governments in the sense that all have a stake in promoting competition and the proliferation of advanced telecommunications infrastructure touted by promoters of the Telecommunications Act.

Local governments, in particular, have a keen interest in the competition expected in the coming years, because the bulk of the technical infrastructure for both cable systems and telephone networks is situated geographically and operationally within the domain of cities. Because of this, the traditional two-tiered structure of federal and state regulation of telecommunications is rapidly evolving into a three-tiered regulatory structure as municipalities firmly assert control over their physical rights-of-way used by the telecommunications industry.

This chapter will explore the initiatives of local municipalities to ensure that development of advanced telecommunications infrastructure is available to their citizens, businesses, and institutions. Case studies of telecommunications infrastructure developments for a number of American cities will be presented.

In addition to discussing the competing regulatory frames, the analysis will explore the potential impact of the next-generation networks on the cities themselves. The analysis will include attention to the impact of increased opportunities for telecommuting on the urban infrastructure, the role of advanced telecommunications networks in economic development, and predictions of the impact of network implementation on urban quality of life (environment, education, and universal access).

BACKGROUND

The information revolution that began with the widespread diffusion of personal computer technology is taking on a new dimension through the rapid diffusion of networking technology. These network technologies offer a significant increase in the power and capabilities of computer technology, as each computer has become an element in a much larger and more complex system.

The earliest networking technologies, local area networks (LANs) connected computers within a single building or complex. Wide area networks (WANs) quickly followed, allowing connectivity among computers without regards to physical or geographical limitations. Ultimately, the Internet has enabled virtually any computer to be connected to virtually any other computer in the world.

But in order for these connections to be made, physical networks must be constructed. As the demands for connectivity increase, the demands upon these networks are increasing at a phenomenal rate, necessitating the construction of newer and more powerful networks. This chapter explores a range of issues surrounding the networking revolution, including the manner in which the physical construction of these networks impacts cities, as well as the potential impacts of the networks upon cities. Before discussing these impacts, it is important to examine how the Telecommunications Act helped to define the role that municipal governments must play in the implementation of advanced networks in their jurisdiction.

LOCAL GOVERNMENT AND THE TELECOMMUNICATIONS ACT OF 1996

The Telecommunications Act of 1996 preempts local regulation that might prohibit a business from providing telecommunication services, but affirms the authority of local government to manage its public rights-of-way and to charge telecommunications companies fair and reasonable compensation for the use of those rights-of-way (League of Cities, 1996).

Under the Act, municipalities may continue to renew cable franchises, collect franchise fees, require PEG (Public, Educational, and Government) access channels and institutional networks, and include facility and equipment requirements as part of the franchising process (League of Cities, 1996). Telephone companies wanting to enter the cable business must gain local franchises, but only for the cable television portion of their service. On the other hand, municipalities are restricted from regulating the telecommunications (voice) services provided by a cable television system. The Act allows a telecommunications provider to become a Federal Communications Commission (FCC) certified open video system (OVS), not requiring a local franchise, if the provider offers two thirds of the system's capacity to unaffiliated programmers. Perhaps most important for cities, electric utilities, previously forbidden from offering telecommunications services, are allowed to compete with LECs (Local Exchange Carriers — the local telephone companies) and cable television systems under the Act.

In addition to promoting competition, the, 1996 Act charges the FCC with reforming universal service. To accomplish this, the Federal-State Joint Board on Universal Service has made recommendations to replace the current subsidy system of universal service with a method that does not impede competition. The board calls for utilizing universal service funds to provide schools, libraries, and health care providers with substantial discounts on advanced telecommunications services (Federal-State Joint Board, 1997).

The Act has already led to jurisdictional battles within some states, with the telecommunications industry attempting to bypass local rights-of-way authority by dealing directly with state utility commissions (Estrella and Haugsted, 1996). Recognizing that the Telecommunications Act did not anticipate jurisdictional conflicts between city, state, and federal regulation, the FCC has created a State and Local Advisory Board to address issues of concern between states and cities (*Warren's Cable Regulation Monitor*, 1996).

Emerging Competition

Any advanced telecommunications network enters an increasingly competitive telecommunications market dominated by telephone and cable television companies. Telephone networks are rapidly being upgraded through fiber-optic deployment and computer-driven switching. At the same time, cable television systems are enhancing capacity by expanding fiber-optic backbones, allowing greater bandwidths and thus more programming channels. Moreover, the growing transition from analog to digital technologies is rapidly changing the utility of both cable and telephone networks, as they allow transmission of all sorts of information (voice, data, audio, video) as digitized bits.

The demand for digital communication links is not only spurring telephone and cable television companies to upgrade their networks, it is also encouraging other competitors to enter the fray. A host of new players may soon enter the market, including electric utilities (Rivkin, 1998) and specialized satellite networks (Bandy, 1996).

One of the most important driving forces behind the increasing competition in telecommunications networks is the Internet. Although the Internet has been in widespread use for less than a decade, it has already attracted 79 million users in North America (CommerceNet, 1998). The expectation of rapidly increasing demand for high-speed Internet access is one of the most important reasons for the push to deliver additional bandwidth to the home (Martin, 1996).

The rapid pace of technological development is not likely to slow any time soon. We should therefore expect even more new applications and services to emerge in the next twenty years, creating additional demand for telecommunications networks. The competitors of cable and telephone companies will need (and want!) to provide a full range of telephone, television, and data services. In the process, distinctions between telephone and cable industries will disappear.

Result: Significant Impact upon Urban Landscape

The impact of advanced telecommunications networks on global communication is more evident than the impact of these same networks upon the urban landscape, but the urban impacts of these networks may be equally profound, touching individuals more frequently (and perhaps more profoundly).

Many project that twenty-first-century economies will be built around information systems in the same manner that nineteenth- and twentieth-century technologies were built upon industrial systems (Bell, 1981). One implication of this projection is that advanced telecommunications networks will play the same role in the twenty-first century that streets and highways played in the twentieth century.

Following the highway analogy, the first set of impacts will be upon the structure of the cities themselves. These networks should be expected to become one of the most important centers of commerce for a city, but with an important difference. Whereas traditional centers of commerce, such as roads, rivers, ports, and so on, were geographically based, the information highways will allow connections among people and places without regard to geography.

The next impacts to consider relate to the industries themselves. Telecommunications companies will play an increasingly important role in the urban landscape, as virtually all industries will become increasingly dependent upon telecommunications services. Perhaps more importantly, the presence (or absence) of advanced telecommunications networks will affect decisions to build, relocate, or update industrial facilities. The cost savings that will result from the availability of advanced networks may become one of the most important components of economic development efforts.

The key to exploiting these networks is planning. The first cities to construct these networks may enjoy a number of important advantages over those that choose to delay or ignore these networks. On the other hand, pioneering cities may also have the burden of disproportionately high costs to support false starts and technology that is sure to drop in cost over time.

TRADITIONAL ROLES OF LOCAL GOVERNMENTS IN TELECOMMUNICATIONS REGULATION

Traditionally, the role of municipal governments in the telecommunications industry has been limited. Involvement in the telephone industry is typically limited to setting rates for franchises and pole attachments (when the electric utility is owned by the municipality). Local governments played a much more important role in the early regulation of cable television, but almost every dimension of that role was eliminated by the 1984 Cable Act.

The result was the emergence of a two-tier system of telecommunications regulation, with federal and state governments splitting authority. The complexity of issues surrounding the introduction of advanced networks, however, offers a multitude of opportunities for local governments in telecommunications regulation, resulting in a three-tier system of regulation.

Local government involvement in telecommunications regulation started with cities' need and desire to control their rights-of-way. Indeed, municipal governments were the only existing regulatory body for telephone networks prior the Communications Act of 1934 (Gabel, 1995). *Rights-of-way* refers to the physical premises or facilities used by both telecommunications and utility companies to deliver services from their buildings to the customer. These include the streets, poles, ducts, conduits, or any other property managed by the local government. Under federal and state law, municipalities have the authority to collect fees in return for the private use of public property.

The precedent provided by control over rights-of-way allowed cities to expand their role in local telecommunications regulation through the assessment of "franchise fees," taxes or "rent" paid by utilities such as telephone and cable companies for the privilege of using a city's right-of-way. One reason for the emergence of a role for municipal governments in telecommunications networks is the fact that local telephone, cable television, and other networks are geographically bounded, with service areas roughly coinciding with city limits.

CURRENT ROLES OF LOCAL GOVERNMENT IN TELECOMMUNICATIONS REGULATION

The new areas of local government involvement in telecommunications networks include the authority to grant franchises for the use of the public right-of-way, permits for the construction of networks, and zoning regulations governing the location of switching and other facilities. In addition to these jurisdictional matters, cities have a practical reason to become involved in the provision of telecommunications services because the city government is one of the largest single consumers of telecommunications services in any area.

Franchising

A franchise is a license, or contract, between municipalities and telecommunications providers for use of the public rights-of-way. Under federal law, municipalities award franchises to cable television systems; and, in many states, municipalities award franchises to incumbent local exchange carriers (LECs) and competitive local exchange carriers (CLECs).

Construction Permits and Street Cuts

One of the more mundane but more important roles played by cities in the construction or modernization of telecommunications networks is the power of cities to control the construction process. This control includes the letting of construction permits, control over street cuts, and, where the city owns the electric utility, access to utility poles. The ability to expedite or impede street cuts is perhaps the most important one, as it is all but impossible to build a telecommunications network of any type without burying some cable under or across city streets.

Environmental Considerations

Closely related to the permit process is the attention by city governments to any type of construction that has environmental impacts. In addition to the direct impact of construction, environmental impacts of telecommunications networks include the aesthetics of utility poles, outdoor equipment "pedestals," and network facilities. Advanced telecommunications networks are also seen by many as providing potential environmental benefits, including reducing the number of automobile trips (through telecommuting) and commercial vehicle use.

Zoning Location of Business and Industry

One of the most important powers of local government is zoning—the authority to regulate where a business can be located. The zoning process can also be used to expedite or impede the process of constructing network facilities. Furthermore, where zoning regulations prevent the expansion of industries in a particular location, advanced telecommunications networks can play a role in enabling the construction of new facilities at remote sites.

GOALS FOR MUNICIPAL TELECOMMUNICATIONS INFRASTRUCTURE

For many cities, promotion of advanced telecommunications infrastructure is part of a broad strategic investment. Like the "wired city" projects that began with Lyndon Johnson's Great Society program, today's advanced infrastructure projects are meant to revitalize or sustain urban environments and to offer advanced services that may not be offered by incumbent telecommunications providers.

Among the strategies advanced by cities are advocating telecommunications as an economic development tool, promoting advanced telecommunications services, encouraging universal service, leveraging existing telecommunications infrastructure, and maintaining the efficient management of city rights-of-way.

Economic Development

Telecommunications infrastructure development has long been considered a strategic tool for economic growth at the national and state level. Additionally, in ever increasing competition for economic growth between regions and cities, investment in telecommunications infrastructure is seen as a crucial strategy to attract and retain business (Graham and Marvin, 1996). Mitchell Moss's research on urban infrastructure and economic development has discovered that investment in information infrastructure has allowed a number of cities to develop as significant centers of commerce. According to Moss (1987, page 140), to some extent, "the size and importance of a city is determined by the amounts and kinds of information flowing into and out of it, and by the way it is interconnected with other cities in the national flow network."

Advanced Telecommunications Infrastructure

As demonstrated later, many cities desire the most technologically advanced networks: switched broadband digital networks that provide two-way voice, data, video, and interactive multimedia communications. The technology should ensure competition through:

Abundant Bandwidth—to allow capacity for all service providers.
Open Platform—allowing both interoperability (technical compatibility) with existing networks, as well as equal access to service providers ensuring multiple services competing simultaneously over a single network.

For some cities, an advanced telecommunications infrastructure is part of a broader strategy to become a high tech center (Williams, 1988).

Universal Availability

Like national policies for universal service of the telephone network, a goal of cities is for advanced telecommunications networks to reach every residence, business, and institution in the city. The Telecommunications Act of 1996, while maintaining universal service goals and promoting discounts to schools and libraries, does little to promote access to advanced telecommunications services for residences (Fidelman, 1997).

Leveraging Existing Telecommunications Infrastructure

Local governments often have existing telecommunications infrastructure in place for city-run telephony or data communication, as well as utility communications. This can be utilized for a portion of the backbone of a new network, reducing the costs of building a network. For cities owning their own power utilities, telecommunications services can be bundled with electric services for a more efficient city service.

Management of City Rights-of-Way (ROW)

Increasingly, as incumbent telecommunications providers (cable and telephone) upgrade their systems, and as competitive access providers (CAPS) and competitive local exchange carriers (CLECS) enter the market, the integrity of the public streets and poles are compromised. An advanced network, open to all, alleviates some of the ROW concerns.

MUNICIPAL TELECOMMUNICATIONS INITIATIVES

To meet the above goals, many cities have implemented initiatives to enhance the technical capability of their local telecommunications network. Some cities, particularly those that own their own utilities, have developed or are considering advanced telecommunications systems in direct competition with their local telephone company or cable system. These initiatives can be categorized as cities that are merely expanding their current infrastructure for connecting government buildings and public institutions; cities that submit requests for proposals (RFPs) to partner with private firms in developing broadband networks to serve institutions, residents, and businesses; and cities that intend to build and own their own telecommunications infrastructure.

CITIES BUILDING OR EXPANDING CURRENT TELECOMMUNICATIONS INFRASTRUCTURE

Eugene, Oregon

The Eugene Water & Electric Board plans to contract with a private company to install fiber-optic lines to municipal buildings, the University of Oregon, public schools, and other institutions (Robertson, 1997).

Lakeland, Florida

More than one hundred miles of fiber are being built in Lakeland to aid its utility efforts. Like Anaheim (see below), SpectraNet is the private partner on this project.

Palo Alto, California

The City of Palo Alto is spending $2 million to develop a 26-mile fiber-optic ring to serve the city's internal needs as well as to connect schools, libraries, and medical clinics. The city will lease capacity to private carriers such as Brooks Fiber Communications and DEC, which has opened the Digital Internet Exchange (McCabe, 1997).

Santa Clara, California

Santa Clara has earmarked $3 million to build a fiber-optic backbone for general government use. $1.4 million has been reserved to investigate and build an enterprise network to provide services to businesses and eventually residences.

CITIES EXPANDING TELECOMMUNICATIONS THROUGH RFP PROCESS

Anaheim, California

The City of Anaheim, with a municipally run electric utility and its own internal telephone system, received eighteen proposals in June 1995 to develop a public-private Universal Telecommunications System (UTS). The proposed networks would connect Anaheim's businesses, schools, residents, and government buildings, utilizing 50 miles of the Public Utility Department's (PUD) existing fiber-optic cable.

On January 9, 1996, the City Council authorized Anaheim's PUD to negotiate an agreement with SpectraNet International for the UTS. Construction of the system will be completed in two phases. The first phase, expected to take less than two years and cost $50 to $60 million, will connect commercial, industrial, and government buildings with fiber-optic cable. The second phase, to progress over five years, will extend to telecommunications systems to residential areas. The telecommunications system will be privately financed by SpectraNet, with the city receiving a one-time payment of $6 million and annual revenues of $1 million or 5 percent of gross revenues (whichever is greater) for its rights-of-way and existing fiber-optic infrastructure (City of Anaheim, 1995).

Austin, Texas

In June 1994, the City of Austin explored the possibility of building its own telecommunications network and issued a Request for Information (RFI) to measure the feasibility of such a network and the level of interest on the part of potential contractors, service providers, and citizens of Austin (City of Austin, 1994). A total of thirty-four responses was received from prospective users, incumbent telecommunications providers, competitive access providers, telecommunications consultants, product vendors, and prospective network providers.

The city altered its strategy in 1995 after the Texas Legislature passed a comprehensive telecommunications bill that prohibited municipal "direct or indirect" involvement in the provision of telecommunications services. In response to this legislation, the city issued a Request for Strategic Partners (RFSP) for a public-private partnership to implement an advanced telecommunications network (City of Austin, 1995).

Twelve firms responded in whole or in part to the RFSP and in April 1996, the City Council voted to negotiate a franchise with CSW Communications to build a hybrid fiber-coax (HFC) network to interconnect all homes, businesses, and institutions in the city (Grant and Berquist, 1996).

Los Angeles, California

Late in 1996, the City of Los Angeles issued an RFI to build a public-private telecommunication infrastructure. They expect to build an advanced fiber-optic network to serve internal city government needs as well as schools, businesses, and homes (McCann, 1998).

San Diego, California

San Diego issued an RFP through the San Diego Data Processing Corporation (SDDPC), a nonprofit consortium serving the city and regional agencies via the San Diego Network (SanNet). The SDDPC received eight proposals in January 1996 in response to its desire to build a "community-wide information infrastructure" (City of San Diego, 1995).

San Diego provided flexibility to respondents by allowing them either to develop a private virtual network (PVN) enhancing the telephony and data communication capabilities of the existing SanNet; or to build a more expansive telecommunications network (RTN) establishing a regional, open, switched, digital broadband network. Expectations were that the final project would be a private-public partnership, with the city becoming an equity partner in the enterprise. During their deliberations, however, the Telecommunications Act of 1996 passed, and the city reconsidered the entire RFP process. As in Seattle (see below), the process was abandoned with the hope that competition among private-sector telecommunications firms, touted by sponsors of the Act, would lead to the goals expressed in the original RFP.

Seattle, Washington

Seattle was one of the first cities formally to request proposals from firms to build a comprehensive broadband telecommunications system. In January 1994, the city issued an RFI seeking investors and developers interested in building an information highway in Seattle (City of Seattle, 1994). In October of 1994, Seattle received seventeen proposals in response to the RFP to build a privately financed telecommunications network.

Doubts about the financial viability of the proposed networks and concerns about the state of technology, particularly the availability and performance of digital customer premises equipment (CPE) and ATM switching equipment, caused the city to abandon the RFP deliberations. During this time, Viacom sold its Seattle cable franchise to TCI, and the city was able to leverage a major part of its stated goal—residential high-speed Internet access—in negotiations with TCI.

CITIES PROVIDING TELECOMMUNICATIONS SERVICES
Cedar Rapids, Iowa

Voters approved the City's utility telecommunications efforts in 1994. They have built a hybrid fiber-coax system that can provide video, voice, and data services to every resident and business in Cedar Falls (Colman, 1997).

Glasgow, Kentucky

Since 1990, the Glasgow Electric Plant Board has offered a combined service (4 Mbps Internet link and 52-channel cable television) over its coaxial cable system for $24.95 a month. Primarily built to service Glasgow's utility, the coax system was subsequently offered service to compete with the cable operator. The board plans to upgrade the entire backbone to fiber optics and has experimented with telephony (Manning, 1996).

Tacoma, Washington

City-owned Tacoma City Light has decided to spend $55 million to build a fiber-optics network throughout the city that will compete head-to-head with the existing cable operator and phone company. Services anticipated include high-speed data transport, electronic meter reading, and a 65-channel cable television system. Plans were approved by the Tacoma City Council in June 1997, after a Pierce County Superior Court Judge ruled that City Light can issue $35 million in internal bonds to begin the project (Nelson, 1997).

Springfield, Oregon

The Springfield Utility Board began work in the summer of 1997 on an initial $1.5 million-project to lay fiber-optic cable, with plans to spend $20 million to connect every home and business in town (Robertson, 1997).

POTENTIAL IMPACTS OF EMERGING ADVANCED NETWORKS ON CITIES

Analysis of the efforts by cities to attract advanced telecommunications networks indicates a number of important potential impacts of these networks upon the cities. Some of these are economic, including expanding opportunities for telecommuting and contributing to economic development efforts. But analysis of these cases suggests that a set of quality-of-life issues may be even more important, as these networks will impact education and the environment.

Economic Impacts

The economic impact of an advanced telecommunications network will vary depending upon the type of industry in an area, the type of network, and the manner in which the network is promoted.

Telecommuting

Telecommuting can be defined as the practice of using communication technology to allow a person to work at a location (such as home) other than his or her employer's facilities. At the simplest level, an ordinary telephone line can enable workers to stay in touch or connect a home computer with the office network. But in order to achieve maximum efficiency, a higher-speed connection such as an ISDN line is needed, allowing a telecommuter to enjoy the same level of computer network services enjoyed by those working at the office.

Telecommuting offers a number of advantages for both employers and workers. Employers can reduce their expenses for office space and related support functions, while the employees enjoy greater freedom over their work environment and schedules, freeing up the time that would otherwise be spent commuting. (It should be noted that there are also disadvantages associated with telecommuting, ranging from lack of institutional control over workers to lack of social interaction.)

Economic Development

The precise relation between telecommunications and economic development is not well understood (Wilson and Teske, 1990), however, at the very least, telecommunications can be best conceptualized as a necessary but not sufficient condition for economic development (Williams, 1991). The increase in and diversity of telecommunications systems are changing the nature of economic competition. How municipalities anticipate, analyze, and plan for this new environment may help determine the future economic health and environment of a community.

It is important to recognize that telecommunications can add value or impact the utilization of other infrastructures. Telecommuting, for example, has been promoted in many urban areas to displace traffic, saving energy and reducing pollution (Van Sell and Jacobs, 1994). Telecommunications infrastructure might also help manage traffic flow with networked traffic lights and traffic information technology (Graham and Marvin, 1996). Expectations are increasing for availability of consumer energy information systems that allow customer control over energy use and prices (Berquist and Grant, forthcoming).

Another aspect of telecommunications to consider is its impact on education. How might schools and colleges utilize advanced telecommunications networks? Opportunities for distance learning, instructional multimedia, teleconferences, and so on are enhanced with advanced telecommunications systems available within a community. Teleconferences as well as instructional learning and training via telecommunications may also be valuable for social service agencies and municipal departments.

Finally, government is often one of the largest users of telecommunications for internal communications and communications to the public. Many government services might be enhanced and provided to citizens via an advanced telecommunications network.

QUALITY-OF-LIFE IMPACTS

As important as advanced telecommunications networks will be in economic development, they should play an even more important role in raising the quality of life. These networks will impact the environment, the educational system, and the availability of a broad range of services.

108

Environment

As discussed earlier, the most obvious environmental impact of an advanced telecommunications network may be a reduction in automobile trips. Telecommuting, home shopping, and "virtual" meetings may reduce the demand for new streets and highways, as well as reducing air pollution from automobile exhaust. Data flows over advanced networks may similarly reduce the volume of traffic from commercial vehicles as well.

One less obvious environmental impact is a negative one—the construction of advanced telecommunications networks will cause major inconveniences, as well as many temporary (and perhaps a few permanent) eyesores. Installation of a network that will pass every residence, business, and institution in an area will surely cause a measure of inconvenience to every residence, business, and institution.

The final environmental impact is related to the use of an advanced network as a tool to attract new businesses to an area. Many industries that make the most extensive use of telecommunications networks are also "clean" industries, desired by communities because of their minimal impact upon the environment.

Education

The process of education may be revolutionized by advanced telecommunications networks. Schools will no longer be limited to the information stored in the on-site library or media center, but will be able to access an incomprehensibly larger amount of information available through electronic libraries and the Internet.

Access to these information resources reduces the amount of time spent finding information and increases the time available to synthesize and report information. However, in order for these networks to be used to their full effectiveness, teachers and other professionals must be trained in the use of networked resources, and schools must shift resources to acquire the technology needed to go online.

Extension of the advanced telecommunications networks to the home should play an even more important role in the educational process, as students would have ready access to the vast store of information available electronically. Home access would also serve better to connect parents and teachers, as well as reducing the role of the teacher as the gatekeeper of information and technology.

New Interactive Services and Universal Access

Quality of life will also be improved as advanced telecommunications networks enable a new array of services, including a broad range of communications services such as electronic mail, facsimile, news, and so on. In considering the opportunities of increased connectivity, the issue of universal access must be considered. Interactive technologies such as the telephone, fax, and e-mail are valuable to a user only if other users have access to the same services. Early adopters have little reason to use the service, but the more users who adopt an interactive technology, the more useful it becomes to all other current and potential users. The implication is that policy-makers at all levels should consider the need to provide incentives for adoption by all members of a community to ensure that any such service has the maximum value to all users. (For a detailed discussion of universal access and critical mass, see Markus, 1987.)

CONCLUSION

Emerging telecommunications networks will impact urban areas as much in the twenty-first century as the automobile did in the twentieth century. Indeed, it is possible that the structure of the cities themselves may be profoundly impacted by the freedom from geographical restraints provided by emerging telecommunications networks.

It is therefore incumbent upon urban planners to consider advanced telecommunications networks as long-range (and short-range) plans are drawn. The manner in which these networks are built and operated will impact virtually every area of business, education, and economic growth. As work continues on the municipal initiatives discussed in this paper, additional insight into the role of municipal governments and these emerging networks is available nearly every day. As more cities incorporate advanced telecommunications networks into their planning process, a body of good examples should emerge.

One additional lesson that can be drawn from this discussion is the need for greater attention across all fields to the full range of "networks" that tie our society together. A few short years ago, we never expected that, as communication scholars, we would be trying to share our work across such a broad range of disciplines. The lesson is that society is built upon a structure of networks, including personal, collegial, economic, and cultural networks as well as telecommunications networks. Greater attention to the manner in which all of these networks impact all fields of study can help to better tie together academic researchers from all disciplines.

REFERENCES

Bandy, E. (1996). "Very Small Aperture Terminals." In A. E. Grant, ed. *Communication Technology Update*. 5th ed., Boston: Focal Press.

Bell, D. (1981). "The Information Society." In T. Forester, ed. *The Microelectronics Revolution*. Cambridge, MA: MIT Press.

Berquist, L. and A. E. Grant. (forthcoming). "The Emerging Municipal Information Infrastructure: The Austin Experience." In D. Hurley, and J. Keller, eds. *The First 100 Feet: Options for Internet and Broadband Access*. Cambridge, MA: MIT Press.

City of Anaheim. (1995). "Universal Telecommunications System Partnership," Report to the City Manager/City Council from the Public Utilities General Manager, October 25.

City of Austin. (1994). "Request for Information: Telecommunications Infrastructure."

———. (1995). "Request for Strategic Partners for Telecommunications Infrastructure."

City of San Diego. (1995). "Request for Proposals to Provide Telecommunications Infrastructure."

City of Seattle. (1994). "Request for Proposals for an Information Highway."

Colman, P. (1997). "Utilities Power Up Telco Pressure." *Broadcasting & Cable* March 17: 82–83.

CommerceNet. (1998). *The CommerceNet/Nielsen Internet Demographic Survey*. Cupertino, CA: CommerceNet.

Estrella, J. and L. Haugsted. (1996). "Rights-of Way: Cities or States?" *Multichannel News* May 13: 6.

Federal-State Joint Board on Universal Service. (1997). "Report and Order: Universal Service Order." CC Docket No. 96–45. Washington, DC.

Fidelman, M. (1997). "The New Universal-Service Rules: Less than Meets the Eye." *Civic.com* 1(7): 30–33.

Gabel, D. (1995). "Federalism: An Historical Perspective." In P. Teske, ed. *American Regulatory Federalism and Telecommunications Infrastructure*. Hillsdale, NJ: Lawrence Erlbaum.

Graham, S. and S. Marvin. (1996). *Telecommunications and the City: Electronic Spaces, Urban Places*. London: Routledge.

Grant, A. E. and L. Berquist. (1996). "Fiber Antics: Practical Lessons in Building Municipal Fiber Optic Networks." *New Telecom Quarterly* 4 (4): 43–49.

League of Cities. (1996). *The Telecommunications Act of 1996: What It Means to Local Governments*. Washington, DC.

Manning, R. (1996). "Glasgow's Full Service Utility: Electricity, Cable, and the Internet." *Louisville Courier-Journal* October 19.

Markus, M. L. (1987). "Toward a 'Critical Mass' Theory of Interactive Media: Universal Access, Interdependence and Diffusion." *Communication Research* 14(5): 491–511.

Martin, D. (1996). "Cable Telephony and Data Services." In A. E. Grant, ed. *Communication Technology Update*. 5th ed. Boston: Focal Press.

McCabe, M. (1997). "Palo Alto Moves Fast to Center of Internet: Fiber Optic Ring Nears Completion." *San Francisco Chronicle* June 26: A17.

McCann, M. (1998). "Los Angeles Builds Strong IT Four Ways." *Government Computer News/ State & Local* 4(4): 6.

Moss, M. (1987). "Telecommunications and the Economic Development of Cities." In W. H. Dutton, J. G. Blumler, and K. L. Kraemer, eds. *Wired Cities: Shaping the Future of Communications*. Boston: G. K. Hall.

Nelson, R. (1997). "Tacoma Decides to Build Its Own Fiber-Optic Network." *Seattle Times* March 17.

Rivkin, S. (1998). "If Competition Won't Build the NII, Utility Partnerships Will." In J. Marsh and A. E. Grant, eds. *Blue Sky: New Horizons in Telecommunications*. New York: Nova Science.

Robertson, L. (1997). "Two Oregon Utilities Install Fiber Optics." *The Register-Guard* June 24.

Van Sell, M. and S. M. Jacobs (1994). "Telecommuting and Quality of Life: A Review of the Literature and a Model for Research." *Telematics and Informatics* 11(2): 81–95.

Warren's Cable Regulation Monitor. (1996). "FCC to Create Local Advisory Committee on Rights-Of-Way." December 23.

Williams, F. (1988). "Telecommunications as Strategic Investment." Research Report, Center for Research on Communication Technology and Society, the University of Texas at Austin.

———. (1991). *The New Telecommunications*. New York: Basic Books.

Wilson, R. H. and P. W. Teske. (1990). "Telecommunications and Economic Development: The State and Local Role." *Economic Development Quarterly* 4(2): 158–174.

8

GLOBALIZATION, LOCAL GOVERNANCE, AND THE UNITED STATES TELECOMMUNICATIONS ACT OF 1996

Stephen D. McDowell

INTRODUCTION

The relationship between economic, cultural, technical, and policy developments of different geographic scopes has puzzled numerous social science researchers and theorists, especially during the 1970s through the 1990s, typified by a process of "globalization" of a number of markets, and investment, political, and social institutions. The relationship between the global and the local has been represented either as a standardization of all experience resulting from an invincible process, the progressive elimination of local distinctions, a contest between unique places and indistinct spaces, or even a new configuration of local and world production networks called "glocalization."

Undertaking research on these questions is complicated in several ways related to space and time. First, while globalization may be a process in which common elements are manifest in different parts of the world, the conflicts, relationships, and institutions supporting global patterns are evidenced at a variety of local and regional sites and relations that are not abstract or general. "World city" is a term that illustrates the tensions in the construction of global patterns from local elements. Second, while the goals of some actors to build more global markets, property rights, and cultural practices may result in fundamental structural change over time, this process is actually an aggregate of more short-term conflicts and steps that both reflect and reinforce a longer term process of globalization.

This chapter looks at telecommunications policy issues being confronted by cities and counties in the United States. It deals with policy issues being confronted at the local level of government following the passage and implementation of the Telecommunications Act of 1996. These issues often entail a reworked or conflictual relationship with state and federal governments and with firms providing telecommunications services. The conflicts also have aspects that are more of a long-term and fundamental nature, especially regarding questions about the nature of the duties and property rights of local jurisdictions. Are the public rights-of-way a public trust to be held for open access and use of the public, which includes private companies? Or are the public rights-of-way the property of cities, who must act in the interests of all constituents, even if it means enhancing the revenue to be derived from use of those resources to the detriment of some users?

Although conflicts between different levels of government are long standing in the United States, these cases are especially important in light of the 1996 Telecommunications Act's goals of promoting competition in local services, encouraging new entrants into telecommunications markets, and stimulating the rapid deployment of new technologies. Additionally, these issues arise in the context of broader shifts in scope and form of telecommunications governance at the national and international level. These conflicts also reflect and have implications for the shifting role of cities in the spatial reorganization of production and culture on a global basis.

SELECTED CASES AND ISSUES IN CONTENTION

In February 1996, a reworking of the United States Communications Act of 1934 was signed into law as the Telecommunications Act of 1996 (United States, 1996). The stated goals of this legislation were to introduce competition in all parts of the communications industry, to allow for the more rapid introduction of new technologies and services, while at the same time preserving and enhancing the ability of all U.S. citizens to gain access to existing and new technologies. The Act promised to promote competition among existing industry players and easier entry for service providers using new technologies. Three changes were of special importance for the telecommunications industry, for local governments, and for the provision of services to the public: the Act's attempt to promote competition in the provision of local telecommunications services; changes in the amounts that long-distance carriers would pay to connect with local carriers to complete calls (access charges); and reorganization of the institutions and mechanisms that promote universal access to telecommunications services. Decisions and initiatives on each of these questions are interlinked, in that those made in one area will shape the resolution of other issues.

As has been true of federal government efforts in the past in the United States to introduce, widen, or enhance market exchanges, these actions had significant implications for state and local governments and were met with concern and resistance (Horwitz, 1989; Teske 1995). Particularly, some of the governing roles, decisions, and rules of city and county governments were presented by industry groups, even during the formation of the Act, as posing impediments to the promotion of competition in telecommunications. The introduction of new services would, in the context of the 1996 Act, disturb the formal institution and informal patterns of relationships among different levels of telecommunications governance. Overlapping rules now regulate communications service providers at a national, state, and local levels. For instance, the use of rights-of-way along streets are treated differently for cable companies and telephone companies. Municipalities set zoning laws, but their range of actions has been constrained by the new federal Act of 1996. The licensing of the radiomagnetic spectrum remains under sole federal jurisdiction. Taxation of seemingly similar communications services differs among various services and between municipalities. The discussion below of just a few reported cases demonstrates the extent to which the conflict between telecommunications companies and municipalities has been made manifest on a number of fronts.

The Huntington Park, California, incident arose as a result of a local ordinance that was designed to reduce illegal activities such as drug sales and calling card fraud, and sought to do so by making pay telephone usage more difficult. The ordinance prohibited pay telephones on private property unless they were located completely within an enclosed building and at least ten feet from any public door. The California Pay Telephone Association filed a petition on December 23, 1996, calling for the Federal Communications Commission (FCC) to preempt the local ordinance on the grounds that this restricted competition between different services. The FCC (1997b) considered the petition, and in a decision released July 17, 1997, declined to intervene in the case. It found that "the record did not support a violation of either section 253(a) or section 276 of the Communications Act, as amended."

The case of TCI Cablevision and Troy, Michigan, has also attracted much national attention. TCI had initially sought relief, preemption, and a declaratory ruling that the City of Troy had exceeded its authority by seeking commitments that new fiber optic cable installations would not be used to provide telecommunications services until TCI had received permits and licenses as required by federal, state, and local authorities. The FCC decision of September 18, 1997 (FCC, 1997a) was viewed as a partial victory for both sides in the dispute. The FCC did find that the city had exceeded its scope of local franchising authority "by placing a telecommunications condition on its grant of cable permits," although Congress "clearly intended to separate the functions of cable franchising from the regulation of telecommunications services." The FCC kept this decision narrow in most respects. It did not agree with TCI's claims that it had been required to obtain a franchise to provide telecommunications services, since TCI was not providing and did not intend to provide telecommunications services. The FCC found that "the City has not sought to restrict the discretion granted to TCI" to choose the transmission technology and subscriber equipment used in the cable system. While the FCC declined to issue a declaratory ruling regarding preemption of the entire ordinance, the memorandum, opinion, and order did state:

We are troubled by several aspects of the Troy Telecommunications Ordinance in the context of the effort to open local telecommunications markets to competition. While Congress mandated a role for the Commission and the states in the regulation of telecommunications carriers and services, we are concerned that Troy and other local governments may be creating an unnecessary "third tier" of telecommunications regulation that extends far beyond the statutorily protected municipal interests in managing the public rights-of way and protecting public safety and welfare. . . . In particular, we articulate our concern regarding how redundant and potentially inconsistent levels of regulation . . . may deter or discourage competition. (FCC, 1997a)

The Maitland, Florida, case involved a municipality, the Florida Public Service Commission, and the Florida House of Representatives. The issues in this case are instructive, in that they mirror in some respects those encountered with a federal division of governance. The case initially arose because the City of Maitland had included a provision in an ordinance that the telephone company provide the same level and quality of services, including advanced services, in Maitland that it was providing at any locations in its service area. The telephone company interpreted this as an infringement on its license to operate in the state, and sought a ruling by the Florida Public Service Commission (PSC) that the city was in violation of Florida statutes. The Florida PSC considered the case and, in the summer of 1997, decided not to overrule the city. The firm sought legislative assistance, and in late 1997, a bill was introduced in the Florida House of Representatives that sought to limit the ability of cities to place certain requirements on those making use of rights-of-ways (Florida, House of Representatives, 1997). The bill would have also limited the amount charged for franchise fees to the management costs incurred by the city. A hearing was held on January 6, 1998, but no further action was taken on the bill (Florida, House, Committee on Utilities, 1997).

These issues arose in part because of the goal of the supporters of the federal bill to encourage the rapid introduction of new technologies and services. While the radiomagnetic spectrum is public property and is regulated and its use allocated by the federal government in the United States, the streets and public rights-of-way are (for some) the property of city and county governments. The National Park Service also owns or manages much public property in rural areas. Communications firms that made use of wired networks in the past (telephony, cable) are now considering investments in new technologies that use both wired networks as well as the radiomagnetic spectrum (wireless telephony, wireless cable, or multipoint multichannel distribution systems). Hence, while the federal government is attempting to allow competition and new services, these decisions involve the use of public property that the federal government does not fully control.

The FCC quickly recognized that, consistent with a long tradition of federal-state struggles of communications regulation, the Telecommunications Act of 1996 would prompt contention with state and local governments. It set up a Local and State Government Advisory Committee to attempt to deal with some of these issues (FCC, 1997d). The advisory committee made numerous recommendations in 1997 regarding local rights-of-way and telecommunications service competition, and responsibilities to notify states and localities involved in FCC proceedings, among others. The FCC has also compiled a number of documents connected to state and local governance issues, including the Huntington Park case in California, wireless facilities siting policies, interconnection of networks and competition in local telephone services,

Table 8.1 Selected Local Telecommunications Cases

City, State, Issue (Source)
Amherst, New York, cable franchise fees (Lakamp, 1998)
Anchorage, Alaska, railway easement (Kowalski, 1998)
Atlanta, Georgia, access to private buildings for new entrants (*Communications Today*, 1997a)
Berkeley, California, local low power broadcasting (National Lawyers Guild, 1997)
Chattanooga, Tennessee, telecom franchise fee (Tabin, 1998)
Cleveland, Ohio, city-owned cable (Beauprez, 1998)
Coral Springs, Florida (Ezrol, 1997)
Deltona, Florida, prepayment for digging (Perotin, 1998, Shaw, 1997)
Denver, Colorado, telecom fees (Estrella, 1997b)
Fairfax, Virginia (Shear, 1998)
Farmington, Connecticut (California PUC, 1997, p. 8)
Hillsborough County, Florida (Gilpin, 1998)
Huntington Park, California, pay telephone siting (FCC, 1997b)
Maitland, Florida, investment and service requirements (Florida, House of Representatives, 1997)
Park Ridge, Illinois (Estrella, 1997a)
Peoria, Arizona, rights-of-way fees (Nelson, 1997)
Phoenix, Arizona, rights-of-way fees (Fiscus, 1997, Maerowitz, 1997)
Prince George's County, Maryland, local telecom taxes (Schwartz, 1998)
Rice Lake, Wisconsin (*Communications Today*, 1997)
Troy, Michigan, licensing requirements (Ilka, 1997; Van Bergh and Tabin, 1997)

open video systems, reception devices for broadcast distribution services, environmental effects of radiofrequency (RF) radiation, universal service, and area code changes.

The 1996 Act is seen by some representatives of local governments as a sweeping usurpation of local authority, since it reduces state and local government power by limiting zoning, taxing, and franchise fees for some new services. Questions at stake include the applicability of the franchise fees charged for use of municipal rights-of-way to various service providers, zoning authority over the siting of towers to provide wireless services, state and municipal taxation of communications services, the provision of telecommunications infrastructure and services by city governments, and the role of local institutions—such as schools, libraries, and hospitals—in efforts to promote access to advanced telecommunications services.

Franchise Fees and Rights-of-Way

What should be the appropriate level of the franchise fees charged for use of municipal rights-of-way to various service providers, and any other building permit or administrative requirements for the use of rights-of-ways? Rights-of-ways are publicly owned but are necessary for terrestrial networks and communications and other infrastructures in order to provide a number of services. These networks may include road and sidewalk access, water, sewer, storm drain, natural gas, electricity, telephone, and cable television. Subscribers' premises need to be physically connected to these networks to gain access to these services. Additionally, these networks are necessary to provide other public and private services, such as postal service, garbage collection and recycling, or emergency police, fire, or ambulance services.

Some transportation and utility networks are owned and operated by local government, even if they were initially built by private companies. Other networks are owned and operated by private companies, which pay fees to make use of the public rights-of-way. Arrangements for local infrastructure construction and management have developed slowly, often with the prodding of state and federal governments interested in speeding the pace of economic development or removing local barriers to commerce (Horwitz, 1989). Apart from periodic building booms and initial construction, the pace of construction of communication and other infrastructure networks was relatively slow and stable throughout much of the twentieth century. Today's enthusiasm for investment in new communication technologies and services is more akin to that of the late-nineteenth and early-twentieth century.

Are the public rights-of-way a "public trust" to be held for open access and use of the public, which includes private companies? Or are the public rights-of-way the property of cities, which must act in the interests of all constituents, even if this means enhancing the revenue to be derived from use of those resources by some? On the one hand, telecommunications companies now argue that rights-of-way should be seen as a public trust, open to use by all entrants in the private sector at a minimal cost. The price for use of rights-of-way should be based on the actual "cost" of management fees, rather than any sort of fair market value for this access. The "costs" of managing different services provided on the same network or using joint resources, however, would be difficult to determine.

Legislation was introduced in 1997 and 1998 in several states (Florida, Arizona, Indiana, and Washington) to attempt to enforce a management fee structure on cities and counties for use of rights-of-ways. The Indiana bill would have prohibited payments "by a public utility for the use of the public rights-of-way or the fees and costs of litigation relating to the interpretation of this section or an ordinance adopted under this section" (Indiana, 1998). The Florida Legislation would have reduced the ability of local governments to require permits for the use of the rights-of-way, as well as limiting the fees for use of the rights-of-way to 1 percent of gross revenues or the management costs associated with that specific use of the rights-of-way (Florida, House Committee on Utilities and Communications, 1997).

On the other hand, cities and counties take the view that rights-of-way are public property, and that fair rents or usage fees must be paid by those making use of those public rights-of-way. This will provide benefits to all members of the public, especially those who do not make use of a particular communications service. For instance, while communications companies claim that municipal charges will be passed onto the consumer and hence raise the cost of communications services, these costs will be passed on only to the consumers who choose to purchase a service. If only 67 percent of television households subscribe to cable television, or if only a small portion of businesses make use of the services of an alternative local exchange carrier, is it appropriate that these users bear the costs of using public rights-of-way? If not, the whole public will subsidize the use of advanced communications services by certain small subgroups, justified by the assumption that the use of these services provides either direct benefits to many or at least indirect aggregate benefits for all.

Zoning Authority and Tower Siting/Placement

The appropriate authority of local governments over the siting of towers to provide wireless services has been the most high-profile and hotly contested local political issue in communities across the country. The initial drafts of the Telecommunications Act of 1996 included strong provisions to preempt the power of local governments to limit the placement or installation of antenna towers to provide personal communications services (PCSs). Even while the 1996 Act was being debated in the U.S. Congress during 1995, representatives of local governments raised concerns about the infringement of local government authority that the bill contained. The National League of Cities worked to limit the authority to preempt the powers of local governments that was present in early drafts of the bill (National League of Cities, 1997). Since digital PCSs operate using lower power than conventional cellular service, they require higher towers and closer tower placement than for cellular telephones. Like the cellular system, however, PCSs require a network of terrestrial towers in order to achieve seamless coverage over a service area. And if service demand becomes greater, cells may be divided into smaller geographic areas, requiring even more towers (California PUC, 1997).

As with rights-of-way, as a result of concerns over the effects of the placement of towers on land use and planning, cities and counties were very active in opposing the strong version of the preemption of local power that appeared in early drafts of what became the 1996 Telecommunications Act. The final bill included language that limited the ability of the FCC or the states to preempt or override local authority without clear reasons. Many cities placed moratoria on new tower construction during 1997 and 1998. More recently, cities have been trying to work with telecommunication companies, encouraging them to use city land, to share towers with other companies, and to camouflage towers for aesthetic reasons. Telecommunications firms have also sought to have the FCC make a broad ruling on preemption, rather than have to fight out every case with local governments, and in April 1997 the FCC (1997c) did issue a notice of proposed rule-making to further explore the issue of a broad set of preemption rules.

Local Taxation of Communication Services and Firms

Although communications services are governed and regulated at the federal and state level, a number of municipal taxes are imposed on communications and other services, even beyond the charges for the use of rights-of-ways. This is in addition to the broader questions of taxation of electronic services or transactions (Fox and Murray, 1997; Griffin et al., 1998; Peha and Strauss, 1997).

In May 1996, the State of Florida initiated a Governor's Telecommunications Taxation Task Force (1997), which looked at the various taxation and fees by different levels of government imposed on different telecommunications services. Taxation had arisen as an issue in part because of concerns about the taxation of Internet services and 1–800 services based in the state. The task force was asked to study the effects of a number of issues and make recommendations to the Governor and Legislature on:

- Changes in communications technologies and services;
- State and federal regulatory changes in communications technology and services;
- A favorable tax climate for the development and promotion of communications technology and services and businesses;
- Compliance with tax requirements and administrative costs;
- The competitive environment in taxing in-state versus out-of-state providers of communications technology and services;
- The availability and affordability of communications technology and services; and
- Maintenance of state and local government tax revenues generated from taxation of communications technology and services (Florida Telcommunications, 1997, page 3).

The task force issued a report in February 1997 that recommended, among other things, a unified sales tax on electronic communications services to replace all state and local taxes and franchise fees. This would be administered at the state level, and the services covered would not be dependent on technology or mode of delivery. This revenue would be distributed to state agencies and local governments, and would seek "revenue neutrality" so that no local government would have less revenue after the taxation reorganization. However, several services would be exempt from the tax, including "Internet access, electronic mail, two-way game playing, computer exchange services and related online services" as well as network services and equipment (Ibid., pages 4–5).

Municipal governments were concerned about this review for a number of reasons. The report seemed to consider franchise fees and sales taxes as being the same thing; while the latter was a tax on a service purchase, the former was a payment for the use of public property. As well, the effect of the overall effort might be to reduce the funds available to local governments, but certainly to reduce the authority of local governments to make decisions about appropriate levels of taxation and fees for utilities. No further legislative action was taken on the recommendations of the task force during 1997 or 1998.

Universal Service Provision

Low and stable pricing of local services, a goal supported by state regulators, has been a key ingredient of a universal access strategy at the federal level in the United States throughout the past sixty years. Other mechanisms to promote universal access included the Universal Service Fund to offset operating expenses for high cost telecommunications companies, and Rural Electrification Administration program loans to telephone companies. These programs were more effective in addressing unequal access problems across geographic regions than in addressing access issues for disenfranchised populations. Poor subscribers living in urban areas were less able to take advantage of programs that supported telephone companies and lowered rates to achieve universal access and service than those in rural and remote regions.

The 1996 Telecommunications Act included sections that sought to preserve and promote universal access to telecommunications services. It did so by both setting objectives for households, as well as identifying schools, libraries, and rural hospitals as agencies that should also have access to advanced communications services. The 1996 Act also attempted to restructure the programs that have kept local telephone rates low and supported lower rates in high-cost regions. It tried to make subsidies more explicit, rather than being buried in the cost structure of local, enhanced, or long-distance services. States are allowed to set their own policies to promote universal service, as long as they do not run against the federal policy. As well, public institutions at the local level, rather than private households alone, are now supported by the universal service policy mechanisms.

The provision of telecommunications infrastructure and services by city governments and the role of local institutions—schools, libraries, and hospitals—will possibly increase in efforts to promote access to advanced telecommunications services. Hence state and local governments, which want to ensure the effective and efficient delivery of public services, will be key actors in the implementation of universal service support mechanisms aimed at increasing access of disadvantaged groups.

LOCAL EVENTS AND GLOBAL RESTRUCTURING

Although conflicts between different levels of government are long standing in the United States, the cases and issues discussed here are especially important in light of the 1996 Telecommunications Act's goals of promoting competition in local services, encouraging new entrants, and stimulating the rapid deployment of new technologies. Additionally, these issues arise in the context of broader shifts in scope and form of telecommunications governance at the national and international level, and the shifting role of cities in the spatial reorganization of economic production and culture on a global basis.

Overall Shifts in Telecommunications Governance

These conflicts can be seen as one reflection of broader shifts in the scope and form of telecommunications governance. They are often seen as arising from the regulatory changes at the national level resulting from the implementation of the U.S. Telecommunications Act of 1996. However, the constraints placed on the role of national governments as a result of their commitments in international agreements on trade in telecommunications services also have implications for the range of national governing authority, and hence for relations among national and subnational governance bodies.

These cases also illustrate changing modalities of governance in the relationships between local, state, and federal governing and regulatory agencies. A variety of relationships among these agencies are evident, including legislation, regulation, litigation, negotiation, and consultation. These issues arose as a direct result of measures in Telecommunications Act of 1996. Following this legislation, the regulator, the FCC, was assigned the task of implementing this new set of rules. However, under the U.S. system of quasi-judicial regulation, legislation and rule implementation are interpreted on a case-by-case basis and have less effect without a regulatory decision supported by specific reasoning. Litigation contesting regulatory decisions, originated by companies claiming that their ability to expand services or offer new services was limited, has provided the opportunity for the cities and counties to make the case for a very narrow and limited set of circumstances where the FCC should preempt local authority, despite the call by firms and trade associations for more widespread and declaratory rulings. Thus far, the FCC has been restrained in its use of whatever additional preemption authority given it by the 1996 Act, possibly seeking to avoid a prolonged cycle of appeals to federal courts by local governments and firms, as has happened with other FCC decisions implementing the 1996 Act.

The FCC State and Local Government Advisory Council has provided one ad hoc mechanism or forum for reviewing these issues, developing some clarification of the questions at stake, and providing advice to the FCC and to state and local governments in dealing with a number of these questions. Both FCC Chair William Kennard and Barbara Esbin (Associate Bureau Chief, Cable Services Bureau) have emphasized consultation and cooperation among different levels of government. William Kennard (1997), while speaking to the November 1997 Annual Convention of the National Association of Regulatory Utility Commissioners (NARUC), stated that the FCC would attempt to operate with common sense: "Common sense means writing rules that are clear and understandable and deal with real problems. It means finding practical solutions to problems. And it means forging a relationship between the FCC and the states that allows us to do that." Barbara Esbin (1998) spoke directly to the issue of land use and zoning policies in an April 1998 review of these issues in a speech for the National Conference of State Legislatures: ". . . the Commission's approach to the preemption issues in each of these actions [is] cautious, measured, and mindful of the shared obligations of federal, state and local governments under the Act." Further, "it is Chairman Kennard's stated intention to resolve wireless facilities siting problems by working together with state and local officials to find solutions to the problems . . . [and] the Commission is currently concentrating on facilitating discussion between industry organizations and the [Local and State Government Advisory Committee]." Esbin also noted that: "Considerable progress has occurred with respect to collaboration between industry and the LSGAC staff" on antennae and RF emission guidelines. While this emphasis in 1998 on consultation suggests an intensification of this process, it remains to be seen whether and in what ways the FCC retains the ability to use its formal regulatory powers to provide final resolution of these issues.

On the other hand, while the FCC and large telecommunications firms have central legal power and more concentrated resources and expertise than cities (which may have to hire outside experts or join collective cases to undertake telecommunications planning—see Armstrong, et al., 1997; Fidelman, 1997; Leibowitz and Associates; 1998), the huge absolute number of cities and counties would tax the institutional capacity of the FCC and courts to deal with all the cases that might arise. Additionally, the myriad of rules, permitting processes, licenses, and taxation and fee processes that local governments administer and can manipulate could result in numerous cases arising in each city if even some of the mathematical possibilities were to materialize. Hence there are strong incentives to use a consultative and cooperative processes as much as possible, even for the agency holding formal legislative authority.

One possible substantive change in the role of local governments that may arise from these consultations is that local governments may be seen only as service delivery vehicles, while overall policies will be set in the national and international forums or in consultation with national agencies (Bonnett, 1998; Christensen, 1997; Dinan, 1997). For instance, Brenda Trainor (1995), while defending the role of local governments in telecommunications, does so by referring to local government expertise and experience in service delivery:

> What does local government do best? Traditional powers of public safety, health, and welfare are well organized, and local governments provide direct service in these areas consistent with national policy. Local transportation and right-of-way management policies are implemented in concert with federal, state, interstate and regional coordination. Take garbage, for instance. Trash is collected under appropriate franchise or delegated powers of local government and hauled regionally to regulated trash sites under state and federal mandates. Why should telecommunications be any different?

However, by allowing all major policy and planning decisions to shift elsewhere, appropriate and legitimate roles for self-governance at the local level may be lost, and along with them, the ability of local government to serve as a unique and proximate public forum to discuss, deliberate, and respond to the variety of issues and problems that local places must deal with.

As noted above, there are risks to national telecommunication bodies of relegating local governments to a service delivery role. Universal access to communications has often been seen solely as the obligation of central nation-state governments to promote citizens' access to a set of services. Central policy and regulatory governing bodies have derived some legitimacy from their role in promoting social objectives such as access and universal service, rather than just setting the ground rules for fair market exchanges or leveling the playing field. A definition of services that should be provided universally includes the role of subnational governments and public bodies in defining service delivery programs in their jurisdiction would not only be less neat conceptually than a nationwide universality; if subnational governments are encouraged to take active efforts to promote access to communications services to encourage economic and social participation and development, this would also contribute to the decline of a common national experience of access to communication services.

New Technology Introduction and Shared Governance

These local conflicts encountered in a redefinition of national telecommunications governance also reflect a public policy commitment and industry objectives to introduce new technologies rapidly. New communications technologies and services—such as radio pagers, personal communications systems, video services offered by telephone companies, or direct broadcast satellite— integrate multimedia services and wired and wireless modes of delivery in new ways (Baldwin et al., 1996; Jameson, 1996). Over the twentieth century, separate and complex divisions of governance between federal, state, and local bodies have arisen for radio/wireless, telephone, broadcasting, and cable television services. For instance, while the FCC allocated the spectrum for use by broadcasters, it sought to achieve a goal of localism (Horwitz, 1989; McChesney, 1994). New services and technologies may disturb these governance arrangements, and face conflicting regulations from various levels of government.

The goal of the 1996 Act of promoting or allowing for the introduction of new technologies and services is also accompanied by other policy objectives that complicate the matter. Specifically, spectrum auctions have been introduced in the 1990s to allocate the spectrum for subscriber-based wireless services. The method of auctioning the use of a public resource to raise revenues and the spreading out of the period of payments mean that the FCC has assumed two new roles. Firstly, revenue generation has now been added to regulation in the public interest as a goal the FCC must try to meet (Butterfield and McDowell, 1998). The FCC has an incentive to maximize revenue, and hence to maintain the spectrum to be used by new technologies and services as a valuable resource. Secondly, given that the FCC seeks to increase the value of the spectrum, it is not a disinterested party in its dealings with local governments over tower siting issues. Pestle and Miles (1997) make the claim that: "The FCC is in a conflict of interest position because it has been directed by Congress to help balance the Federal budget by selling off airwaves for cellular service."

Firms also have some crosscutting interests on these questions. In the Troy case, the incumbent cable company sought to remove certain stipulations on its permits for construction of fiber optic cable networks. Although these services were limited to cable television for residences, there were also telecommunications services being offered for public institutions. In other cases, it is new firms that seek permits from cities and from private property owners to provide services that compete with those offered by incumbent carriers. In these cases, the incumbent carrier may be less aggressive in supporting the rapid provision of permits by cities. Firms seeking to offer competitive local telephone service have complained that the incumbent telephone companies are slow to meet their interconnection requirements, making use of stalling and lawsuits in a strategic fashion.

Cities and Reorganized Economic Production

These communications policy and governance questions can also be understood in the context of more fundamental and structural changes in globalization: the shifting spatial organization of production and consumption at a global and local level (Cox, 1987; Drache and Gertler, 1991; Harvey, 1990; Mosco, 1996), and the role of cities and regions in the global economy (Brunn and Leinbach, 1991; Graham and Marvin, 1996; Hershberg, 1996; Wallis, 1996). The regionalization and localization of production are occurring alongside global coordination (Civille and Gygi, 1995; Estabrooks and Lamarche, 1987). This transition has been labeled post-Fordist production, flexible accumulation or just-in-time production (Amin, 1994; Jones, 1997).

In this economic environment, typified by increasingly mobile global capital, it is argued that enhancing place-based characteristics of infrastructure, education, and lifestyle make up the few remaining goals that government may realistically undertake. However, national or state governments may not be the best positioned to advance these objectives, given the supposed aversion in the United States to industrial policy at the national level (Etzkowitz, 1997). This is despite the focus on national information infrastructure policies (Drake, 1995; Kahin and Wilson, 1997). Cities or regional governments may have a more appropriate role in providing communications, transportation and other physical infrastructures, educational, research and technology institutions (Amirahmadi and Wallace, 1995; Celeste, 1996; Coburn, et al., 1996; McClelland, 1998), and a lifestyle to attract a trained and capable workforce in order to draw and retain mobile global capital (see Fox, 1996). Cities and local governments have noted these developments in their planning (Barnes and Ledebur, 1994), and have promoted the use of telecommunications infrastructure as a locational advantage (Hepworth, 1990; Kellerman, 1993; Kasarda and Rondinelli, 1998; Peck, 1996) and the use of advanced telecommunications to enhance educational programs.

124 While this type of analysis assumes a rather instrumental use of public institutions and the population, there are also good reasons for enhancing the role of cities drawing more from democratic and critical analysis (Doheny-Farina and Herwick, 1997; Morley and Robins, 1995; Van Tassel, 1996). As global capital becomes more mobile and standardized in what Manuel Castells (1996) calls the "space of flows," the unique and immobile attributes of historical places may become more important for identities and culture. Similarly, if national governance institutions are becoming more attuned to the requirements of global trade and investment, local governance is seen by some as the site where democratic deliberation and the public sphere can be reinvigorated (Bird, et al., 1993).

By asserting a strong federal role and trying to standardize the conditions for competition across the country, is federal preemption moving telecommunications governance in directions absolutely the opposite of what emerging conditions may require? More flexibility and matching of telecommunications infrastructure and services to the attributes of the local economy may not be promoted through a standard set of rules that are set in the abstract yet applied and defined in concrete cases.

New network investment will not occur at the same time in all places. Given the extensive capital requirements for advanced network developments, some places will be first, and others will come later. Investment and infrastructure planning was part of the regulatory process in the past. Advanced communications networks built by private companies will now be planned to serve market demands. These companies also have significant international investment opportunities that were less open in the past. Hence, a more uneven topography of communications network capabilities is likely to emerge over time with the set of policies and conflicts outlined above.

State and local governments are already trying to address this dynamic so as not to be relegated to the second or third tranche of investment, whether through constructing their own networks or working cooperatively with telecommunications firms. However, state and local governments bidding competitively with others to attract advanced network investment may contribute to an uneven development process and may not necessarily pursue or support mechanisms to promote widespread access to communications services.

ACKNOWLEDGMENTS

The author would like to thank Emily Clark and Rhonda Blount for research assistance.

REFERENCES

Amin, Ash, ed. (1994). *Post-Fordism: A Reader*. Oxford, UK: Basil Blackwell.

Amirahmadi, Hooshang, and C. Wallace. (1995). "Information Technology, the Organization of Production, and Regional Development." *Environment and Planning* Vol. 10: 1745–1775.

Armstrong, Peter, Pat Miles, and John W. Pestle. (1997). "Memorandum Regarding FCC City of Troy Decision." Grand Rapids, MI: Varnum, Riddering, Schmidt and Howlett, October 13.

Baldwin, Thomas, D. Stevens McVoy, and Charles Steinfield. (1996). *Convergence: Integrating Media, Information, and Communication*. Newbury Park, CA: Sage.

Barnes, William, and Larry C. Ledebur. (1994). "Local Economies: The U.S. Common Market of Regional Economies." National League of Cities, Research Reports on America's Cities. Washington, DC.

Beauprez, Jennifer. (1998). "Cities Unite the Build Cable Council, Communication Networks." *Crain's Cleveland Business* January 19: 2.

Bird, Jon, et al., eds. (1993). *Mapping the Futures: Local Cultures, Global Change*. London: Routledge.

Bonnet, Thomas. (1997). *The Twenty-One Most Frequently Asked Questions about State Telecommunications Policy.* National Governors' Association Publications. Washington, DC.

——. (1998). "Is the New Global Economy Leaving State/Local Tax Structures Behind?" *Public Management* Vol. 80.

Brunn, Stanley D., and Thomas R. Leinbach, eds. (1991). *Collapsing Space and Time: Geographic Aspects of Communication and Information.* London: HarperCollins.

Butterfield, Katherine, and Stephen D. McDowell. (1998). "FCC Spectrum Auctions: Evaluating Public Policy Experiment." Paper presented to the International Communication Association 1999 annual meeting, San Francisco, California.

Burns, Nancy. (1994). *The Formation of American Local Governments: Private Values and Public Institutions.* New York: Oxford University Press.

California Public Utilities Commission. (1997). "Wireless Siting Issues—Roundtable Seminar," Santa Barbara, California, October 23, notes compiled by Allison Perez.

Castells, Manuel. (1996). *The Rise of the Network Society, The Information Age: Economy, Society and Culture.* Vol. 1. Cambridge, MA; Oxford, UK: Blackwell.

Celeste, Richard F. (1996). "Making Technology Count for America's Communities." *Forum for Applied Research and Public Policy* Vol. 11: 45–48.

Christensen, Sandra L. (1997). "The New Federalism: Implications for the Legitimacy of Corporate Political Activity." *Business Ethics Quarterly* July: 81–91.

Civille, Richard, and Kathleen Gygi. (1995). "Developing Four Corners Regional Telecommunications: Community and Economy." Conference Report. San Juan Forum, Durango, CO, January 9.

Coburn, Christopher, Dan Berglund, and Robert Usher. (1996). "Collaboration Key to Competitiveness." *Forum for Applied Research and Public Policy* Vol. 11: 7–74.

Cohen, Jodi B. (1998). "MEAG at Work on $35 Million Fiber-Optic Network." *The Bond Buyer* February 12: 48.

Communications Today. (1997a). "Competitors Suffering From Limited Access to Buildings, Rights-of-Way." November 5.

Communications Today. (1997b). "FCC Seeks Comment on Preemption Case in Wisconsin." October 22.

Communications Today. (1998). "Park Service Mull Right-of-Way Rules." January 30.

Cox, Robert W. (1987). *Production, Power, and World Order: Social Forces in the Making of History.* New York: Columbia.

Dinan, John. (1997). "State Government Influence in the National Policy Process: Lessons from the 104th Congress." *Publius* (Spring): 129–142.

Doheny-Farina, Stephen and Mark A. Herwick. (1997). "The Wired Neighborhood (book review)." *Journal of Urban Affairs* Vol. 19.

Drache, Daniel, and Meric S. Gertler, eds. (1991). *The New Era of Global Competition: State Power and Market Policy.* Kingston: McGill-Queen's.

Drake, William J., ed. (1995). *The New Information Infrastructure: Strategies for U.S. Policy.* New York: Twentieth Century Fund.

Esbin, Barbara S. (1998). "Panel Discussion: "Telecommunications Deregulation—A Threat to State and Local Land Use and Zoning Policies?" Presentation to the National Conference of State Legislatures, Commerce and Communications meeting, April 17.

Estabrooks, Maurice, and Rudolph Lamarche, eds. (1987). *Telecommunications: A Strategic Perspective on Regional Economic and Business Development.* Moncton: The Canadian Institute for Research on Regional Development.

Estrella, Joe. (1997a). "Ameritech Hits Franchise Roadblock." *Multichannel News.* December 8: 12.

——. (1997b). "Denver Preps 'Test Case' on Telecom Fees." *Multichannel News.* September 22: 10.

Etzkowitz, Henry. (1997). "From Zero-Sum and Value-Added Strategies: The Emergence of Knowledge-Based Industrial Policy in States of the United States." *Policy Studies Journal* Vol. 25: 412–424.

Ezrol, Kerry L. (1997). "Letter to the Honorable Julia Johnson, Chairman, Florida Public Service Commission, Re: City of Coral Springs — Ordinance No. 97–114 (Telecommunications)." July 3.

Federal Communications Commission. (1997a). "In the Matter of TCI Cablevision of Oakland County, Inc. CSR-4790, Petition for Declaratory Ruling, Preemption and Other Relief Pursuant to 47 U.S.C. 541, 544 (e), and 253, Memorandum Opinion and Order." Released September 19.

———. (1997b). "California Payphone Association Petition for Preemption of CCB Pol 96–26 Ordinance No. 576 NS of the City of Huntington Park, California Pursuant to Section 253 (d) of the Communications Act of 1996." FCC 97–251, Memorandum Opinion and Order, July 17.

———. (1997c). "In the Matter of Preemption of State and Local Zoning and Land Use Restrictions on the Siting, Placement and Constructions of Broadcast Station Transmission Facilities, Notice of Proposed Rulemaking." Adopted August 18.

———. (1997d). "FCC State and Local Advisory Committee Met Today: Discussed Impact of Telecom Act on State and Local Communities." Press Release. April 18.

Federal-State Joint Board on Universal Service. (1996). "Recommended Decision." CC Docket 96–45. Washington, DC: Federal Communications Commission, November 8.

Fidelman, Miles. (1997). *Telecommunications Strategies for Local Government: A Practical Guide*. Washington, DC: Government Technology Press.

Fiscus, Chris. (1997). "Phone, Cable Fee to Buy Desert; Telecommunications Firms Say Phoenix is Imposing Tax." *The Arizona Republic* December 16: A1.

Florida Telecommunications Taxation Task Force. (1997). *Report to the Governor and the Legislature*. Tallahassee: State of Florida, February.

Florida, House of Representatives. (1997). "Telecommunications Rights-of-Way Act, HB 3291."

Florida, House of Representatives, Committee on Utilities and Communications. (1997). "Bill Research and Economic Impact Statement, HB 3291, Telecommunications Rights-of Way." December 17.

Fox, Sharon E. (1996). "The Influence of Political Conditions on Foreign Firm Location Decisions in the American States (1974–1989)." *Political Research Quarterly* March: 51–75.

Fox, William F., and Matthew W. Murray. (1997). "The Sales Tax and Electronic Commerce: So What's New?" *National Tax Journal* Vol. 50: 573–592.

Gilpin, Francis. (1998). "County Wants Money in 2 Weeks." *The Tampa Tribune* February 14: 4.

Griffin, Ken, Paula D. Ladd, and Roy Whitehead. (1998). "Taxation of Internet Commerce," *The CPA Journal* Vol. 68: 42–45.

Graham, Stephen, and Simon Marvin. (1996). *Telecommunications and the City: Electronic Spaces, Urban Places*. London: Routledge.

Harasim, L., ed. (1993). *Global Networks: Computers and International Communication*. Cambridge, MA: MIT Press.

Harvey, David. (1990). *The Condition of Postmodernity: An Enquiry into the Origins of Cultural Change*. Cambridge, MA: Basil Blackwell.

Hearn, Ted. (1997). "Cable Looks to FCC for Relief on Fees; Cable Television Operators [seek] FCC's Help on Franchise-Fee Underpayments." *Multichannel News* November 24: 48.

Hepworth, Mark. (1990). *Geography of the Information Economy*. New York: Guilford Press.

Hershberg, Theodore. (1996). "Regional Cooperation: Strategies and Incentives for Global Competitiveness and Urban Reform." *National Civic Review* Vol. 85 (Spring/Summer): 25–30.

Horwitz, Robert Britt. (1989). *The Irony of Regulatory Reform: The Deregulation of American Telecommunications.* New York: Oxford University Press.

Ilka, Douglas. (1997). "In Oakland County: Troy, TCI Applaud Split Decision on Cable." *The Detroit News.* September 25: C5.

Indiana. (1998). "IN 1376" (www.state.in.us/bills/in/in1376.html) [cited by Michael Chui on telecomreg listserv]

Jameson, Justin. (1996). "New Media: The Likely Development Path and Future Regulatory Requirements." *Telecommunications Policy* Vol. 20, No. 6: 399–413.

Jones, M. R. (1997). "Spatial Selectivity of the State? The Regulationist Enigma and Local Struggles over Economic Governance." *Environment and Planning* Vol. 29 (May): 831–864.

Kahin, Brian, and Ernest J. Wilson III, eds. (1997). *National Information Infrastructure Initiatives: Vision and Policy Design.* Cambridge, MA: The MIT Press.

Kasarda, John D., Dennis A. Rondinelli. (1998). "Innovative Infrastructure for Agile Manufacturers." *Sloan Management Review* Vol. 39 (Winter): 73–83.

Kellerman, A. (1993). *Telecommunications and Geography.* London: Belhaven.

Kennard, William. (1997). "Speech of FCC Chairman William E. Kennard to the Annual Convention of the National Association of Regulatory Utility Commissioners." November 10. Boston, MA.

Kowalski, Robert. (1998). "Railroad Deal Questioned: Lawmakers Quiz Sheffield on Fiber-Optic Cable Easement." *Anchorage Daily News* February 7: 1C.

Lakamp, Patrick. (1998). "Town Board Rejects Increase in Cable TV Franchise Fee." *The Buffalo News* February 24: 4B.

Ledebur, Larry C., and William C. Barnes. (1993). "'All in it Together'—Cities, Suburbs and Local Economic Regions." National League of Cities, Research Reports on America's Cities. Washington, DC.

Leibowitz and Associates. (1998). Background Documents for Sixth Annual Telecommunications Seminar, January 14. Orlando, Florida.

Maerowitz, Marlene Pontrelli. (1997). "Hello Gilbert! Pass Proposed Telecom Rules." *Arizona Republic* December 13: EV10.

McChesney, Robert W. (1994). *Telecommunications, Mass Media, and Democracy.* New York: Oxford University Press.

McClelland, Stephen. (1998). "California Dreaming?" *Telecommunications* Vol. 32. No. 3: 66–68.

Morley, David, and Kevin Robins. (1995). *Spaces of Identity: Global Media, Electronic Landscapes and Cultural Boundaries.* London: Routledge.

Mosco, Vincent. (1996). *The Political Economy of Communication.* London: Sage.

National Lawyers Guild Committee on Democratic Communications. (1997). "Court Rejects FCC's Constitutional Catch 22." Press Release. December 25. Washington, DC.

National League of Cities. (N.D.). "The Telecommunications Act of 1996: What It Means to Local Governments." Washington, DC: National League of Cities.

———. (1994). *The Information Superhighway Game.* Washington, DC: National League of Cities.

———. (1997). "Issues Background." (mimeograph).

———. (1996). *1996 Municipal Policy: Transportation and Communication.* Washington, DC: National League of Cities.

Nelson, Jeffrey. (1997). "Fees OK'd for Rights of Way; Cable, Phone Firms to Pay Rent in Peoria." *The Arizona Republic* December 19: 1.

Osten, Neal. (1996). Director, Committee on Commerce and Communications, National Conference on State Legislatures, Testimony Regarding the Telecommunications Act of 1996, before the Joint Committee on Federal Relations, State of Maryland, June 25.

Peck, F. W. (1996). "Regional Development and the Production of Space: The Role of Infrastructure in the Attraction of New Inward Investment." *Environment and Planning* Vol. 28. February: 327–339.

Peha, Jon M., and Robert P. Strauss. (1997). "A Primer on Changing Information Technology and the Fiscal." *National Tax Journal* Vol. 50. September: 607–621.

Perotin, Maria M. (1998). "Laying Cable May Cost Companies, Deltona Leaders are Reviewing an Ordinance that Would Require Paying Up Before Digging." *The Orlando Sentinel* January 11: K2.

Pestle, John W., and Patrick Miles. (1997). "Memorandum Regarding Further FCC Preemption of Local Zoning—Cellular and Broadcast Towers." Grand Rapids, MI: Varnun, Riddering, Schmidt and Howlett, September 12.

Public Technology Inc. (1994). *Local Government Roles and Choices on the Information Superhighway: Tenants or Architects of the Telecommunications Future.* Washington, DC: PTI.

———. (1995a). *Answer Information Packet: Cellular Towers.* Washington, DC: PTI, August.

———. (1995b). *Surfing the Net: A Local Government Guide to Internet Connection.* Washington, DC: PTI, April.

Schwartz, Shelly. (1998). "Local Telecom Taxes Cause Uproar in Maryland." *Daily Record* (Baltimore, MD). February 18: 1.

Shaw, Gwyneth K. (1997). "Deltona Clears Up Cable Fees Spat." *The Orlando Sentinel.* December 17: D3.

Shear, Michael D. (1998). "Cable TV Upgrades Promised; Fairfax Expands Channels, Internet Ties." *The Washington Post* February 21: D1.

Tabin, Barrie. (1996). "FCC Starts New Rulemaking Process: Cities Need to Take Activist Role." *Nation's Cities Weekly* March 4: 5.

———. (1998). "Court Strikes Down Chattanooga's Telecom Franchise Fee." *Nation's Cities Weekly* January 12: 7.

Teske, Paul, ed. (1995). *American Regulatory Federalism and Telecommunications Infrastructure.* Hillsdale, NJ: Lawrence Erlbaum.

Trainor, Brenda J. (1995). "The Local Government Perspective: Can the Harmonica Play in the Symphony." Presentation to New York Law School Conference "Universal Service in Context: A Multidisciplinary Perspective." December 6.

United States. (1996). Telecommunications Act of 1996 (Public Law 104–104). February 8.

Van Bergh, Mark, and Barrie Tabin. (1997). "FCC Issues Ruling in City of Troy Case, Leaves Local Telecommunications Ordinance in Place." *Nation's Cities Weekly* September 29: 6.

Van Tassel, Joan. (1996). "Yakety-Yak, Do Talk Back!: PEN, the Nation's First Publicly Funded Electronic Network, Makes a Difference in Santa Monica." In Rob Kling, ed. *Computerization and Controversy: Value Conflicts and Social Choices,* 2nd ed. San Diego: Academic Press, 547–551.

Vermont, House of Representatives. (1998). Towers Preemption Resolution (J. R. H. 109).

Wallis, Allan D. (1996). "Regions in Action: Crafting Regional Governance Under the Challenge of Global Competitiveness." *National Civic Review* Vol. 85 (Spring/Summer): 15–24.

NOKIA AS A REGIONAL INFORMATION TECHNOLOGY FOUNTAINHEAD

Stanley D. Brunn and Thomas R. Leinbach

> The image of shopkeepers in Venice or accountants in El Paso clutching a phone made in the land of reindeer and saunas may seem wacky.
> —Kyle Pope, *Wall Street Journal*, August 19–20, 1994

> In the future, telecommunications will see to it that people live life differently.
> —From a Nokia publication, *Connecting People in a Changing World*

> The success of Nokia seems to be as interesting as the success of the national hockey team.
> —*Helsinki Sanomista* 1996

Michael Porter (1990) in his widely read treatise on *The Competitive Advantage of Nations* notes that for states and corporations to succeed in the worlds of global restructuring, there needs to be cooperation between governments and industries, the identification of niche markets, cutting-edge managerial and production strategies, and a culture of innovation.

These ingredients Porter identifies as being significant for traditional industries, such as chemicals, household appliances, and motor vehicles, but also for emerging industries tied to fashions, foods, and entertainment. We would add high-technology industries to Porter's list, and especially those associated with electronic commerce. In that category we would include a variety of information and communications technologies (ICTs), such as minicomputers, computer software, fax machines, and cellular telephones.

The demands for and production of these information and communications technologies are increasing worldwide, not only in slow-growing economies, but also in those that are experiencing rapid growth. The markets include corporations, governments, and consumers, including consumers from a wide age span. This is apparent in the sales of computers and computer software to large and small businesses, to elementary schools and universities, to libraries, and to households. Products are designed and produced for a variety of markets—youth and elderly, slow and fast learners, low- and high-tech consumers, and those with a variety of lifestyles. Advertising on television, in magazines and newspapers, on billboards, and on the Internet reveals the markets companies seek to identify. What these products say about a society is that it is mobile and wishes to be connected to places and people, and people who may be in various places, not necessarily in fixed locations.

Our chapter examines one company in the global ICT business (Amirahmadi and Wallace, 1995). Nokia is a Finnish company that since 1995 has become a global leader in the production of cellular telephones. We examine Nokia's rise to prominence in light of Porter's context of companies seeking competitive advantage to be successful in global markets. We introduce the term "regional fountainhead" as a useful concept that illustrates the source and spillover effects of an ICT firm both within Finland and elsewhere in Europe. Fountainheads are analogous and contemporary versions of lead firms, such as Boeing and Microsoft in the Seattle area (Erickson, 1972; Erickson, 1974).

In our examination of Nokia, we focus on four major themes. First, we provide a brief history of the company from its nineteenth century beginnings to its emergence in the electronics field in the 1960s. Second, we describe the present situation of the company in Finland's economy. Third, we discuss how and why this company has achieved national and international success as a major leader in cellular telephone production. We examine these successes in light of Porter's model for international competitiveness and the utility of that model as applied to high-tech firms such as Nokia. Fourth, we identify some of the challenges confronting Nokia's future, not only within Finland and Europe, but internationally. We conclude with a brief summary and posit some questions meriting further inquiry.

BRIEF HISTORY

Traditional images of Finnish industry are associated with timber, forest products, furniture, ships (especially icebreakers), and Valco (a government television picture tube company). The importance of the forest industry was evident in the slogan Nokia used during the 1970s, "Finland lives from its forests" (Väänänen, 1996, page 63). Nokia is an old Finnish industry; its origins are traced to 1865 when an engineer named Fredrik Idestam built a pulp mill on a river in southwest Finland to produce paper. A small town eventually grew up around this mill site, and a company formed and achieved success in the production of paper and cardboard products. Later, in 1912, a cable company was opened and during the 1930s it expanded to produce cables for the emerging telegraph and telephone networks. Still later the company entered into the rubber products business, producing tires, galoshes, rubber bands, raincoats, and toys. In 1966 Nokia entered the electronics field. Initially it employed only 460 people and it was the country's fourth largest employer in electronics; today it is the largest with nearly 40,000 employees. 1966 was also the year that Nokia's three industries—forest products, rubber, and cable—merged. Thus when Nokia entered the production of consumer electronics and later, mobile phones, it was already a familiar industrial name to Finns. Its products were purchased within Finland and also in the nearby former Soviet Union, Britain, France, and elsewhere in Europe.

Nokia's industrial profile and history during the 1960s to 1980s were not unlike that of other small industrial firms in Europe. It produced multiple products, including electronic cables, rubber and paper products, chemicals, and electronics products. Nokia was involved in eleven different industrial fields during the 1980s, which made it difficult for foreign investors to understand the corporation (Lovio, 1996, page 87). It experienced both upturns and downturns as it purchased unsuccessful companies and sought ways to grow and produce items for demand nationally and within Europe. Its position in peripheral Europe, near the Soviet Union, hampered its development within Europe and in particular with its large neighbor to the east and in East Europe.

The successes of Nokia early this century, and even recently, are attributed in large part to support from the government (Ylä-Anttila, 1996), which played a key role in industrial development within Finland, especially in promoting the electronics field during the 1960s, which were times of growth and optimism. This assistance not only spurred such companies as Nokia to develop national industries, for example, in television and cable connections, but also prevented Finnish companies from being absorbed by larger foreign competition.

Nokia benefited from government provision of R&D money to support new industrial incentives and also financial assistance to prevent takeover by foreign firms. Nokia's entry into the high-technology field began in the 1980s, when the CEO Kari Kairamo took the helm. As executive, he was an active and strong leader who saw Finland's future as closely tied to developments occurring on the continent. He favored an active foreign policy for Finland, and as early as 1987 supported the country's entry into the European Union, as well as greater commitments to higher education (Michelsen, 1996). His dynamic leadership was clearly an important factor, as the company became a leading producer of telephones, television sets, and satellite dishes. In an interview with *Soumem Kuvalehti* in 1986 he reported that: "Finland has so far been forgotten in the border of Lapland, in the periphery. Although the response to technology has been positive, not enough resources have been allocated to it. This can be seen from the fact that only in the past few years have we been members or financiers of large international research facilities. We have developed our co-operation, but we still often take the place of an onlooker" (Michelsen, 1996, page 44). As a result of more Europeanization, these and other changes in the Nokia community by Kairamo meant the company changed more in a decade than it had in the previous century. He started Nokia College, where talented young scientists could be trained in the country's universities and technical schools. Kairamo felt that some of the country's educational problems were due to structural limitations. He stated: "Our educational system is very stiff and full of bureaucracy. It hasn't been able to change along with the rapidly changing environment" (Michelsen, 1996, page 46). Kairamo also acquired firms in Sweden and Germany, but these successes were also marked by some economic failures. The result was that some of his dreams, including the college idea, were eventually discarded. But the internationalization dream was not. He wanted changes fast and had difficulty accepting business failures, which led to his committing suicide in 1988.

Kairamo was succeeded by a vice president whose economic and political policies, while not as ambitious as Kairamo's, also emphasized the electronics field. The current president and CEO of Nokia is Jorma Ollila, whose origins in Nokia are traced to the Nokia Mobile Phone Division. It is under his leadership that the company divested itself of various consumer electronics and invested in cellular fields. A *Fortune* reporter wrote that following a 1992 brainstorming meeting, Ollila emerged and "quickly scribbled the words telecommunication, global, focus, and value-added on a piece of paper. Although it may not be a literary masterpiece, this piece of writing has directed Nokia's strategy every since" (Jacob, 1996, page 87). The result was that the company attracted a group of new, young, and forward-thinking engineers and leaders, who see their country, industrial economies and politics in ways different from their predecessors.

During the 1970s and 1980s, Nokia pursued an active acquisition policy and sought to refashion itself in several ways. The company's strategy sought to develop a corporate structure modeled after General Electric, that is, one that was successful in producing a variety of electronics products. In the 1970s Nokia made several acquisition decisions, and one of these was the purchase of the Swedish television and electronics firm, Luxor. In 1988 Hollming, a German shipbuilding firm sold Salora, a Finnish electronics firm, to Nokia. The joint venture, Salora-Luxor, grew quickly and by 1985 it had produced 600,000 color television sets. However, Nokia, still seeking a lead role in consumer electronics, gradually bought other companies and became the third leading manufacturer of color televisions and decoders.

Europe experienced an economic downturn in 1988, and profits declined. Yet all facets of Nokia's business were profitable except consumer electronics. While the new management wanted to divest itself of unprofitable television products, it made still another acquisition, the Finnish television production firm, Finnlux. This was done largely to stave off acquisition by Asian electronics firms. Eventually Nokia sold its picture tube manufacturing to Panasonic and in 1994 ceased manufacturing VCRs. Finally, with poor profits on television products, Nokia ended the production of this product in 1996. In fact, other European companies made similar decisions at this time. While Nokia did not profit from this experience in consumer electronics, it did gain valuable knowledge that later would prove useful in the design and manufacture of cellular phone products.

DEVELOPMENT OF COMPETITIVENESS IN TELECOMMUNICATIONS

For a variety of reasons, telecommunications has always been a strong industry in Scandinavia. Nokia's particular success came as it acquired the technology for producing cellular phones from a joint venture that it initiated. The firm, Mobira, developed a solid reputation for cellular phone production in Scandinavia. International success finally came in 1984, when the Mobira Talkman, a portable cellular phone, came on the market and captured attention as a result of its innovativeness. Yet Nokia realized only small profits from cellular phone production in the early 1990s. Since this innovation was rather slow to take off, the parent firm pursued experimentation with designs and features so that when it made the decision to specialize, it gradually became successful (Singh, 1994).

Nokia has always faced competition from firms in Sweden, especially the giant Ericsson, which has a larger regional and continental market (Lemola and Lovio, 1996a). That firm had more employees in R&D (17,000) than Nokia (7000) and spent more money on R&D—(FIN 10 billion (U.S.$1.8 billion) versus FIN 3 billion (U.S.$540 million) in 1995. However, the two firms manufacture different products, so they are not true competitors. Ericsson emphasizes semiconductors and military technology products, which require more research than cellular phones. Among Nokia's competitive advantages are that its labor costs are significantly less than in Sweden. An opportunity for growth was seized, since many skilled engineers in Finland could not and did not work year-round in Finland's other industries, including timber and paper products. Thus there was an available skilled labor supply. Also Nokia was able to adapt more quickly to respond to emerging niche markets than could larger firms. A rapid response time has been shown to be an important ingredient in the company's successful production of a variety of cellular phone products for European and non-European markets within the past few years. An added competitive advantage is that its cellular products are cheaper and have a broader and deeper market potential than the more expensive products (for example, televisions and VCRs) of its competitors. Nokia's phones are lightweight, and streamlined in appearance, and are only moderately expensive. Management also saw its own small firm size, flexible management style, and cooperative work atmosphere as assets in the competitive cellular communications field in Scandinavia and Europe. In 1996 the British *Financial Times* and the Price Waterhouse Annual Report ranked Ericsson eleventh and Nokia nineteenth in telecommunication, but Nokia was ranked first in most efficient use of technology, while Ericsson ranked third (Lemola and Lovio, 1996b, page 7).

A CORPORATE PROFILE

According to Nokia's 1997 Annual Report, the company employs more than 37,000 persons (13 percent more than 1996) in Finland and 45 other countries. It has added more than 20,000 employees in the last three years alone. The company's network includes thirty-six R&D centers, which employ more than 10,000 persons. Nokia spent five times more on R&D in 1997 than in 1991. Seventy-six percent, or 28,000, of Nokia's employees reside in Europe, followed by 4700 in the Americas and 3950 in the Asia-Pacific region. The company's corporate headquarters is in the Helsinki amenity suburb of Espoo. About 6000 Nokia employees live in the Helsinki area. Nokia's major research office is in Salo, near Turku, and there are R&D operations scattered throughout the country.

Nokia production operations are divided into two large areas: Europe and

Americas and the Asia-Pacific region. In the Asia-Pacific region, the head offices are Sydney, New Delhi, Tokyo, Beijing, Tehran, Dubai, Jakarta, Seoul, and Singapore. In the Americas there are offices in Ajax, Ontario; Mexico City, São Paulo, and Buenos Aires; Irving-Fort Worth and Westlake, Texas; Boston, Tampa, and Sausalito. The company has twenty-seven production plants in twelve countries, including Finland. The R&D operations are in eleven countries, including the United States, United Kingdom, Hungary, Japan, and China.

The company's sales in 1997 were FIN 52.6 billion (US$9.8 billion). This figure represents a 34-percent increase over 1996. Nokia's success was reflected in the 97-percent increase in earnings per share. Rapid growth is attributed to the increased market in mobile communications, deregulated markets, and growth in data communications. Dramatic regional shifts in sales have occurred during the past decade. In 1987 sales, which were less than one third of those in 1997, were in Finland (40 percent), followed by the rest of Europe (45 percent), and other regions (15 percent). Major sales by region in 1997 were in Europe (59 percent), followed by Asia-Pacific (23 percent), and the Americas (18 percent). Nokia's largest markets in 1997 were in the United States, United Kingdom, and China, each which had sales in excess of FIN 6 billion (US$1.14 billion). Next were Germany and then five other European countries, including Finland. Australia, also in the top ten, had sales roughly equal to that of Sweden. The top ten countries account for 66 percent of total sales in aggregate.

The sales by major business group in 1997 are mobile phones (51 percent), telecommunications (35 percent), and multimedia network terminals and industrial electronics (14 percent). Nokia is Europe's largest and the world's second largest (after Motorola) producer of mobile telephones. According to industry estimates, there were about 201 million mobile phone users worldwide at the end of 1997, an increase from 135 million the year before. In 1997 there were 66 million new subscribers who purchased 101 new phone sets. Nokia's share of the global market is estimated to be 21 percent, with 21.3 million phones sold in 1997. Nokia estimates that its penetration of cellular markets in 1996 was 25 to 30 percent in Scandinavia, 17 percent in the United States, 13 percent in Japan, and in single-digits percentages in Germany and France.

The key areas of growth are in wireless/voiceless telecommunications; R&D programs in audiovisual signal/data processing and communications; third-generation voiceless systems; and integrated multiservice network solutions. Nokia continues to be a pioneer in mobile technology and a leading supplier of digital cellular networks. It is also a major producer of advanced transmission systems and access networks, multimedia equipment, satellite and cable receivers, and other telecommunications products. At the end of 1996, Nokia declared it was the global market leader in digital cellular phones, one of the two largest suppliers of GSM (Global System of Mobile Communications) networks and the world's largest supplier of DCS 1800 systems. The company listed that year as its accomplishments three new digital products, three new analog phones, an Asian-language interface, a HATIS (Hearing Aid Telephone Interconnect Systems) adapter, and the Nokia digital data/fax card.

The company continues to grow and expand outside Europe with new products. During 1997 it developed thirty-one new phone designs, ten new wireless products, and new phone colors for its Asia-Pacific markets. One of its newest products is the Nokia 9000 Communicator, which is the first full-ranged GSM phone, with fax, e-mail, short message server, address book, calendar, and Internet connection. The product was sold in more than thirty countries in 1996. Nokia produces a wide range of mobile phones in all standards, including analog phones and digital phones for GSM, TDMA, PCS/DCS, and Japanese digital standards. It was the first manufacturer to introduce various products for Asian language users, including Chinese, Thai, and Indonesian. It produces infrastructure equipment for both mobile and fixed networks. In the multimedia area, Nokia produces network terminals and a variety of industrial products for workstation monitors and mobile phone accessories.

Publicity is increasing the name recognition and products of the company, which advertises in a variety of consumer products outlets, including newspapers and magazines, radio and television, outdoor advertising, and on the Internet. The company won an international marketing competition, and part of its campaign included the free 1994 concert by the Leningrad Cowboys in Berlin (Lemola and Lovio, 1996a, page 7). Its Nokia 9000 Communicator has appeared in the spy thriller *The Saint*. Other Nokia products were in TV shows including *Seinfeld*, *Mission Impossible*, and *Friends*. Now there is the Nokia Sugar Bowl on New Year's Day from New Orleans. Television ads in Europe and America portray multiple uses and users of Nokia products. The company has also received a number of editorial awards for advertising displays, including in *Byte Magazine*, *PC World*, *Windows* magazine, and *Family PC* magazine.

THE INGREDIENTS OF SUCCESSFUL COMPETITIVE ADVANTAGE

The Nokia story has been the subject of research by Finnish social scientists, economists, and industrial historians (Lemola and Lovio, 1996b). Their research, along with publications by the company, aid in unraveling the multiple reasons why this historically small company in peripheral Europe has become a world leader in mobile cellular communications.

We identify eight reasons for the company's success as the world leader in cellular phone technology and production. First, the company has a history in Finland as a producer of consumer electronics. This history, as noted above, is tied to television picture and cable connection production. This background assisted the company in its acquisition during the 1970s and 1980s of other electronics firms that were also producing consumer products for Scandinavia and Europe. But it was Nokia's decision to invest in digital and wireless technologies that sparked the early success in the cellular field. The first digital transmission systems were developed in 1969. Nokia delivered Europe's first digital switch in 1982 and the world's first digital GSM network in 1991. These successes were marked by other introductions that included new mobile phone generators and base stations and state-of-the-art solutions that facilitated wireless data traffic. With its Nokia 9000 Communicator, whose demand will increase over time, Nokia became the first company to offer cellular connection to the Internet.

Second, Nokia was able to emerge and succeed as a leader in electronics products and in cellular phone technology by cooperating with and assistance from the government. Nokia has always cultivated good relations with the government, but especially during the past several decades. More recently, the government encouraged many government offices and systems to use Nokia products, including defense and postal services. Financial support was also forthcoming from TEKES, a provider of high-tech research in Finland. These investments provided assistance in the form of technical training in Finnish universities for engineers. But the government ministries also recognized and supported changes occurring in the 1990s that would help diversify the country's economy and exports. A specific decision that benefited Nokia and other Finnish firms was the decision to join the European Union. This, coupled with the lessening of economic and political tensions in Europe that accompanied the end of the Cold War, was significant. It also merits mention, as the quote at the beginning of this paper states, that Nokia has much support from the people themselves. A 1996 newspaper article in *Talouselama* reported that "Nokia's return to stardom is also craved by the people of Finland (at last the group that has already swallowed their envy). The world championship in ice hockey and Nokia's success are cornerstones in the modern Finnish national self-image" (Lemola and Lovio, 1996, page 8). The corporate base has remained in Finland even though most of its sales are outside the country; that loyalty factor is an important contributor to its success. Also, its decision to produce items for mass consumption, not luxury products for the elite, has contributed to its popularity and produced a sense of pride among Finns. The Finns are currently the world's heaviest Internet users and probably have the highest adoption rates of cellular phones.

Third, the company was led by creative and imaginative leaders, in particular Kairamo, who during the, 1980s saw that the electronics field was changing rapidly. It was Kairamo who had the vision that Nokia could not compete with regional rival Ericsson, which had a larger R&D budget, more employees, and a strong European market, by producing the same products. Nokia needed to carve new investment niches that would be successful. Today Nokia spends more on R&D than any other Finnish company. In 1996 it spent FIN 3 billion (U.S.$570 million). Nokia accounts for roughly one fifth of all R&D Finnmarks spent in Finland. The executive leadership has persuasively argued that Nokia could produce, with its small budget, flexible production policies, and strong ties to national engineering and technical schools, a product that was in demand in the communications field. Strong, creative, and dynamic leadership that was able to identify new markets and follow world trends in consumer electronics has been a trademark of management decisions and the company's success in the 1990s.

Fourth, there are also "coincidence" factors. Nokia's decision in the 1980s to acquire Hollming (a German company) and Salora proved to be important to the company's efforts to develop a focus on cellular phone communications. Another factor is the fortuitous change following the end of the Cold War. Finland has moved from being a "peripheral" state to a "gateway" state, with emerging markets in former East Europe and Russia as well as investment in electronics, communications, and data services in new states. Geopolitics changes the ways countries look at regions and the way firms in market economies look at the world. These changes on the regional political map brought about ventures unheard of a decade ago.

Fifth, the firm was able to identify a niche and exploit it with a highly skilled labor force whose costs were lower than similar industrial firms elsewhere in northern and central Europe. While the company was not the inventor of cellular phone technology, it is a very good example of a "fast second strategy," that is, it learns and adapts quickly to potential market demands in product designs and costs for multiple markets in Europe and elsewhere (Lemola, 1996, page 154–155). This feature has been a key to its success. It was also the first cellular communications company to build small cellular networks and support systems, not huge ones like Motorola. Also Nokia uses Intel, while other companies rely on their own computers and programming languages.

Sixth, there are several distinct features of the Finnish labor force that are critically important in the company's success. Finns place a high value on continued education and are among the world's most literate populations. The government, with the support of industries, has a well-developed, highly integrated, and technologically equipped set of universities and technical institutes. These, as noted above, benefit Nokia and other firms. The Finns are a highly disciplined work force with a strong and loyal work ethic. Lemola and Lovio (1996, page 12) note that the ethics of Nokia leaders are very Finnish; this includes hard work and a Lutheran work ethic. The Finns are recognized in Europe for their high quality training and innovations in architecture, furniture design, and electronics, and skills in industrial design and engineering, especially icebreakers, ship engines, and forest product machinery. The study of foreign languages is compulsory in the schools. Knowledge of English, which is widespread in Finland and is also the language of the Internet and electronic commerce, is essential in companies engaged in international marketing.

Seventh, the company has spawned other industries, especially in data communications, benefitting Nokia and other companies in Finland. It helped create a "telecluster," that is, a concentration of industries specializing in electronics, data processing, and related knowledge services (Markusen, 1996; Porter, 1996). Nokia became the "fountainhead" of this advanced set of industries and without its leadership, it is unlikely that the cluster would exist. The government has been supportive of these industries and clusters. As noted above, Nokia already has strong ties with institutes of higher learning, especially the University of Oulu, the Technical Institute of Tampere, and others elsewhere in Finland.

Eighth, and finally, the company has used its successes in Finland and Europe to expand its operations to North America and most recently Asia. A crucial question for these emerging markets is the cellular phone technology

138

that will develop. The United States uses cdma (closed like Apple) and tdma (open like PC). Cdma is becoming popular in the United States Asians like GSM technology and are making up by concentrating on cdma. Nokia builds cdma supporting phones, not the networks. The major question about cellular phone technology is what the global norm will be. If Japan, Europe, and the United States all develop different technologies, then Asia will become the battleground for the cellular technology. Nokia envisions opportunities for sales to companies and individuals in urban and rural areas that are becoming more computer-oriented and literate, and connected to the Internet. At the same time, the company's R&D operations are designing a host of related products that might accompany the purchase of a cellular telephone. These include recording data on phone and fax numbers, low- and high-level mathematical problems, games, and Internet connections. These products are designed for people of all ages. Some look like toys, others have a more sophisticated appearance. The company's marketing director, Kari-Pekka Wilska, has said about the shape of Nokia phones: "The phone has to feel good, and after that comes everything else" (Pulkkinen, 1996, page 112). The company also foresees its entry into the promising data communications field where it seeks to become a world leader.

THE FUTURE

While Nokia is admittedly a world leader in the production of cellular telephones, retaining that position will not happen without continued investment, innovative engineering, creative marketing, and social and geopolitical forethought. The company sees its futures in two main areas: (1) voice will become wireless; and (2) the great impacts the Internet will have on our daily lives. The innovations in 1997, and those anticipated in developing Internet capabilities and personal multimedia, illustrate the directions in which the firm is moving. The multimedia futures are in videotelephony, infotainment, media, and inter/intranet.

Yet a number of uncertainties exist. Will Nokia be able to remain flexible enough in its production to be able to identify and focus on potential and emerging niche markets in Europe and elsewhere? Will Nokia continue to be the world leader in cellular telephones, or will it also become a leader in the production of other telecommunications technologies, for example, communications technologies in passenger vehicles, the workplace, and homes? In regard to the labor force, will Finland be able to train enough engineers, marketing staff, and advertisers, or will the company come to rely more on non-Finnish labor forces from other continents? (The answer is that Nokia will have to rely on engineers trained elsewhere as not enough can and will be trained within Finland.) The data communications fields will also be important in twenty-first century economies; Finland sees Sweden and Japan as healthy competitors. Can Finland become a major player in this field? And, finally, what kinds of government support can the company expect from Finland and other countries where it establishes branches? And what will

Nokia's international strategy be? What kinds of benefits will countries attempting to lure Nokia R&D offer to the company and workers? With new and vast markets opening for Nokia products in South and East Asia, as well as Africa, the geopolitics of industrial location will become crucial in the twenty-first century.

SUMMARY

STANLEY D. BRUNN AND THOMAS R. LEINBACH

Nokia represents a very good example of a firm that fits Porter's recipe for success in the international arena. It has a history of industrial production and name recognition within its own country and region. It has experienced cyclical behavior throughout its history, an experience not unknown to firms that have made transitions from producer to consumer items in Europe and North America during the past fifty years. Strong leadership has been an additional hallmark of its success and in particular for identifying a niche that was "waiting to be filled" by the "right company coming along at the right time with the right product." All these, as well as close ties to the state, historically and more recently, were important in assisting the company in carving out its place in the region (Amirahmadi and Wallace, 1995).

Our own research into Nokia in the future will focus on five major questions. First, we want to examine more closely international production strategies; that is, how, when, where, and why the expansion outside Europe has occurred? We will seek to test this firm's experience against the existing theoretical literature. Related to this question is our interest in knowing the locational criteria Nokia considered in making decisions about production overseas. Second, we want to analyze the role Nokia is playing in Finland's foreign policies. These policies are crucial not only within the European Union, but also in efforts to develop production facilities and markets in the Americas, Asia-Pacific, and Africa. Third, we wish to investigate the niche markets that Nokia has created, and examine how they were defined. What specific cultural, social, and political attributes are operating in these niche markets? Fourth, we believe it is important to measure the impact of ICT production on cities and regions, especially outside the home country (Amirahmadi and Wallace, 1995). It is useful to examine how these impacts relate to competition from other foreign firms, especially from Asia, and their economic, cultural, and political impacts. Returning to Porter's model, it is worth examining the corporate structures and production linkages of domestic and foreign firms (Simmie, 1997; Feng, 1995). Whether there are indeed different models for domestic and foreign companies producing information and communications technology is a question worthy of study. Certainly the issues of government deregulation and international competition in the service economies are different from when Porter wrote his treatise. Fifth, and finally, we want to study the images (words and languages in workplace, home, leisure settings, and so on) Nokia uses in introducing and promoting its products in various cultures using different media. To answer this question we will examine advertising by the company on television, in airline, business, and tourist magazines, on outdoor advertising, and in newspapers.

These questions are important in studying Nokia because what it is selling is a product that has multiple uses for multiple markets. For those who are unfamiliar with Nokia's playful advertisements, they are high-tech, colorful, and replete with images, not words.

ACKNOWLEDGMENTS

We gratefully acknowledge the assistance of the following individuals: from Nokia, Ms. Marianne Holmlund and Mr. Jouni Meriluoto, who provided copies of annual reports and answered questions about the company; Mr. Sam Sorsa, a student from Finland studying at the University of Kentucky, who translated the Lemola and Lovio volume about Nokia for us, and geography professors and friends in Finland, Harri Andersson, Kai Husso, and Markku Löytönen, who also answered questions we had about Nokia and Finland.

REFERENCES

Amirahmadi, H and C. Wallace. (1995). "Information Technology, the Organization of Production, and Regional Development." *Environment and Planning A* Vol. 27: 1745–1775.

Erickson, Rodney A. (1972). "The Lead Firm Concept: An Analysis of Theoretical Elements." *Tijdschrift voor Economische en Sociale Geografie*. November–December: 426–437.

Erickson, Rodney A. (1974). "The Regional Impact of Growth Firms: The Case of Boeing, 1963–1968." *Land Economics* Vol. 50: 127–36.

Feng, Li. (1995). *The Geography of Business Information*. London: Wiley.

Holmlund, Marianne. (1998). Communications Manager, Nokia Corporate Communications, personal communication. January 26.

Jacob, Rahul. (1996). "Nokia Fumbles, but Don't Count It Out." *Fortune* Vol. 133, No. 3, February 19: 86–88.

Lemola, Tarmo. (1996). "Riitaako kolme miljardia markka?" ("Will Three Billion Finnmark Be Enough?"). In Tarmo Lemola and Raimo Lovio, eds. *Miksi Nokia, Finland* (Why Nokia, Finland?) Helsinki: Werner Söderström Osakeyhtiö (in Finnish), 144–173.

Lemola, Tarmo and Lovio, Raimo, eds. (1996). *Miksi Nokia, Finland* (*Why Nokia, Finland?*). Helsinki: Werner Söderström Osakeyhtiö (ten articles in Finnish)

———. (1996). "Nokia ja suomalainen identiteetti" ("Nokia and the Finnish Identity"). In Tarmo Lemola and Raimo Lovio, eds. *Miksi Nokia, Finland* (*Why Nokia, Finland?*). Helsinki: Werner Söderström Osakeyhtiö (in Finnish): 7–15.

Leinbach, Thomas R. and Brunn, Stanley D. (N.D.). "Cities, Firms, and Regions in the Worlds of Electronic Commerce: Does Geography Matter in Competitive Advantage." Unpublished manuscript.

Lovio, Raimo. (1996). "Yhtymien moudonmuutokset ja liiketoimintojen kiertokulku" ("Corporate Transformations and the Circulation of Business Transactions"). In Tarmo Lemola and Raimo Lovio, eds., *Miksi Nokia, Finland* (Why Nokia, Finland?). Helsinki: Werner Söderström Osakeyhtiö (in Finnish), 80–101.

Markusen, Ann. (1995). "Sticky Places in Slippery Space: A Typology of Industrial Districts." *Economic Geography* Vol. 71: 293–313.

———. (1996). "Interaction Between Regional and Industrial Policies: Evidence from Four Countries." *International Regional Science Review* Vol. 19: 49–77.

Michelsen, Karl-Erik. (1996). "Kari Kairamon unelma: eurooppalainen Soumi"

("Kari Kairamo's Dream: European Finland"). In Tarmo Lemola and Raimo Lovio, eds. *Miksi Nokia, Finland* (Why Nokia, Finland?). Helsinki: Werner Söderström Osakeyhtiö (in Finnish), 36–61.

Nokia. (1996). Annual Report.

———. (1997a). Nokia in Europe.

———. (1997b). Nokia in the Americas.

———. (1997c). Nokia in India.

———. (1997d). Nokia in Asia-Pacific.

———. (1997e). Towards Telecommunications.

———. (N.D.). Telecommunications Systems for a Changing World.

———. (1997). *Discovery. Nokia's Telecommunications Magazine* Vol. 45, Third Quarter.

———. (1998). Press Release. February 12.

Nokia on the Web (*www.nokia.com*).

Pope, Kyle. (1994). "How Oy Nokia Turned Its Smokestack Blues into Cellular Stardom," *Wall Street Journal* August 19–20: 1 and 8.

Porter, Michael. (1990). *The Competitive Advantage of Nations.* New York: Free Press.

———. (1996). "Competitive Advantage, Agglomeration Economies, and Regional Policy." *International Regional Science Review* Vol. 19: 85–91.

Pulkkinen, Matti. (1996). "Miten jättiläisää horjutetaan?" ("How To Stagger the Giants?"). In Tarmo Lemola and Raimo Lovio, eds. *Miksi Nokia, Finland* (*Why Nokia, Finland?*). Helsinki: Werner Söderström Osakeyhtiö (in Finnish), 102–121.

Simmie, James, ed. (1997). *Innovation, Networks and Learning Regions?* London: Regional Studies and Jessica Kingsley.

Singh, Ajit. "Global Economic Change, Skills, and International Competitiveness." *International Labour Review* Vol. 133: 167–183.

Väänänen, Teemu. (1996). "Yhtymäjohtamisen ja kansallisen kehikon muutos" ("Corporate Leadership and the Change in the National Framework"). In Tarmo Lemola and Raimo Lovio, eds. *Miksi Nokia, Finland* (*Why Nokia, Finland?*). Helsinki: Werner Sönderström Osakehytiö (in Finnish), 62–78.

Ylä-Anttila, Pekka. (1996). "Teollisuuspolitiikan ikuisuusongelman ratkaisu?" ("The Solution for Industrial Politics' Eternal Problems"). In Tarmo Lemola and Raimo Lovio, eds. *Miksi Nokia, Finland* (*Why Nokia, Finland?*). Helsinki: Werner Sönderström Osakehytiö (in Finnish), 174–191.

FROM DIRT ROAD TO INFORMATION SUPERHIGHWAY

ADVANCED INFORMATION TECHNOLOGY (AIT) AND THE FUTURE OF THE URBAN POOR

Bishwapriya Sanyal

INTRODUCTION

Two starkly opposite social trends mark the last decade of the "American Century."[1] On the one hand, there is widespread excitement about the actual achievements and as-yet unachieved potential of advanced information technology (AIT).[2] On the other hand, there is a pervasive sense of social hopelessness about the state of the nation's urban poor.[3] All evidence point in the same direction: there have been steady increases in income and wealth inequality during the last twenty years, and the problem of urban poverty has hardened over the years, trapping millions of Americans in inner-city areas without employment, health care, schools, decent housing, or safe neighborhoods.[4]

Will the progress in advanced information technology help or further hurt the poor? Some technology enthusiasts argue that the trends are crystal clear: the new technology holds the key to a radical transformation of social relations, one that would bypass conventional channels of political expressions controlled by the elite.[5] For others, the future looks less rosy. They point out that there are computer haves and computer have-nots: the inner-city blacks and Hispanics have much lower computer use than suburban, white, and young Americans.[6] Although some of this difference in computer use might be leveled off through progress and widespread dissemination of AIT—as with telephone and television usage—other differences in technological endowments may be accentuated over time because, paradoxically, AIT produces effects in opposite directions simultaneously, as a great leveler of opportunity while being an amplifier of inequity too.[7]

How should planners and policy-makers respond to AIT's potential for, as well as threats, to the urban poor? That is the question I discuss in this chapter. My discussion draws on a colloquium organized by the Department of Urban Studies and Planning at MIT in the fall of 1995.[8] At the time we planned the colloquium, we were aware that there are no "technological fixes" for the problem of urban poverty. We were also aware that social engineering has its limits, and social policies are rarely crafted solely for the poor's benefit. Yet we thought that we could provoke new analyses of the leading question by bringing together academics and activists engaged in understanding AIT from different perspectives. The academic's view would offer a view from "the top," rooted in an analysis of global socio-technological-economic trends hinged on AIT's rise, and an equally global assessment of the likely effects of these trends on the urban poor. In contrast, the community activists would provide a view from "the bottom," rich in details about individuals and communities, the many constraints they face daily, and how these constraints shape AIT's influence on their lives. The view from the bottom was to complement the view from the top; and such a synthesis, we had hoped, would generate innovative answers to the question motivating the colloquium.

What follows is my interpretation of the key issues raised in the colloquium.[9] First, I describe the somewhat counterintuitive finding that community activists who in the past shunned technological progress are now eager to learn about AIT's intricacies. Second, I discuss why universal access to AIT is essential and why the market, left to itself, will not provide such access. Third, I analyze, briefly, current government policies regarding AIT and find them inadequate for ensuring universal access. I conclude the analysis with some suggestions for policies necessary to channel AIT's benefits to the urban poor.

THE TECHNO-ENTHUSIASM OF SOCIAL ACTIVISTS

In the 1960s, social activists who worked in poor neighborhoods used to be deeply skeptical as to whether technological innovations could ever lead to socially progressive outcomes.[10] They associated all technological progress then with America's effort to win the Vietnam War. Surprisingly, in the 1990s, social activists are eager to learn about AIT's intricacies, hoping to capture some of the new technological power of rapid communication for the benefit of their communities.[11] What explains this striking change in attitude?

One plausible hypothesis is that in the 1960s ordinary citizens viewed technology as a centralizing and controlling social force serving the interests of large corporations and faceless bureaucracies. AIT does not fit this image. Its interactive potential and decentralizing nature make it appear democratic and people-friendly.[12] Although this hypothesis may have some merit, it does not fully explain the level of enthusiasm among social activists that we noticed at the colloquium.

A second and more accurate hypothesis is that the social activists' change in attitude is largely due to changing times. The 1990s are marked by two trends, both very important for social activists. First, a significant decline in government spending for urban poverty since the 1980s has created immense pressure on community leaders to acquire up-to-date information on resource availability.[13] These leaders are anxious that, lacking electronic access to resource announcements, they will be severely disadvantaged to compete for scarce resources. The activists are right to assume that, as the pressure on government mounts to reduce social spending and streamline bureaucratic operations, government agencies responsible for resource disbursement will increasingly shift to the electronic communication mode to reduce operating cost. Hence it is crucial for community activists to be plugged into the electronic network.

Yet another reason, which is also unique to the 1990s, is that now social activists are increasingly unable to build a critical threshold of support for their efforts by relying only on the spatial community to which they belong. The single most important factor that hurts community solidarity in low-income areas now is social and cultural heterogeneity among the urban poor.[14] Spatial proximity alone does not create community solidarity any longer because of the increasing differentiation, primarily by race, which is the result of immigration over the last thirty years. This differentiation poses a particular challenge for the social activists who, to claim social resources, must demonstrate they represent a significant size of constituency. AIT provides the opportunity for community leaders to build a critical mass of constituency by drawing support from across the country without having to assemble everyone at the same time and place.

A third reason—and one which is also a particular characteristic of the 1990s—is the popular perception that the poverty alleviation efforts initiated in the 1960s and continued for some thirty years have not been successful.[15] Community activists confront this popular prejudice daily in every encounter with government officials, private philanthropists, and public foundation representatives. Consequently, to seek resources for poverty alleviation in the 1990s, one must convince a prospective funder, be that government, private firms, or nongovernmental organizations, that one has conceived a new approach to poverty alleviation no longer tied to the social welfare policies of the kind which encouraged dependency and socially irresponsible behavior. In reality, however, there is no strikingly different approach to poverty alleviation, even considering the new welfare-to-work policies. The current problems of urban poverty which have, in fact, hardened over the last thirty years, require very similar efforts as before, to be pursued with even more vigor: the urban poor still need employment, a living wage, affordable housing, convenient transportation, safe neighborhoods, and so on.[16] There is no new magic solution to these problems. Community activists, however, cannot tell this simple and unpleasant truth while seeking resources; they have to invent "something innovative," something in line with the current thinking, to draw attention to themselves.

Being connected to the electronic communication mode creates the image that community activists are up-to-date in poverty alleviation efforts. Conversely, community activists not integrated into the electronic loop are viewed as being stuck in the old mode of community organizing which, as mentioned above, is popularly perceived to have been ineffective. The pressure to have an e-mail address and, preferably, a Web page of its own is very real for a community organization, and is one that activists can ignore at their own peril. Hence community activists devise "new ways" of doing old things: they continue to provide social services, but now with electronic information on employment possibilities for welfare recipients, for examples. It is not my intention to dismiss all such new efforts as a new gloss on an old problem: I am simply struck by how much of the current effort to upgrade community development efforts technologically is driven not by new insights about social problems but by old fears that if one is perceived as technologically backward, one becomes severely disadvantaged in advocating social progress.[17]

MARKET PROVISION OF UNIVERSAL ACCESS?

Despite my skepticism about the new techno-enthusiasm among social activists, I acknowledge that AIT offers the urban poor a new set of opportunities. But in order to benefit from AIT, the poor must be connected to the digital world.

AIT's potential benefits are many.[18] Unlike television and radio, AIT offers the opportunity for interaction between the computer and its users, creating the conditions necessary for learning, confidence-building, and self-empowerment. Also, AIT's decentralizing nature offers the poor an opportunity to be entrepreneurial in its use. Unlike earlier waves of technological innovation, such as the Industrial Revolution, AIT lends itself to multiple, local variations and to the exercises of multiple forms of local control. With the World Wide Web, every user has the potential of becoming a broadcaster. And the new network technology opens up hitherto unrealized potentials for communication. Every individual has the potential for discovering and making connections with other individuals of like interest and mind. Add to that the endless possibilities for customization, opened up by the technologies of the Net and the computer. Together these possibilities offer a new opportunity for grassroots communication among individuals and groups striving to create strong communities.

To capture AIT's potential for the benefit of the poor requires that they be connected to the digital world.[19] Hence the key policy issue is one of access to this world. Access, however, requires more than personal computers; it requires provision of infrastructure, affordable hardware, user-friendly software, and the will and motivation to employ them.[20] Not surprisingly, access to AIT is unequally distributed between the well-to-do and the poor.[21] Indeed, the world is comprised of computer haves and have-nots. The objective of public policy should be to bridge this gap, if the market fails to do so.

At this stage, market signals in the provision of AIT are somewhat mixed. On the one hand, the costs of hardware, as well as software, are on a downward spiral.[22] This creates the possibility that, as with the telephone and television, AIT may eventually become part of the daily life of everyone, including the poor. Two trends in the digital world make this a distinct possibility. First, there is a growing technological convergence whereby telephone, cable, and computer services can be provided together efficiently and at reasonable cost to the consumer. The set-top box, which turns the living room television into a computer monitor, is an example of this. The second trend, which complements the first, is a convergence in the industry structure, as firms that once provided telephones, cable, or computer-related services increasingly seek to move into one another's territories[23]—a trend that has been facilitated by the deregulation of the telecommunications industry since 1996. Under ideal circumstances, these two trends could lead to a higher level of efficiency in the production and delivery of services, which in turn could lower the marginal cost to provide these services to low-income areas.

On the downside, a number of trends suggest that the market alone cannot provide the poor with access to the digital world, and even if access is provided, it is questionable whether such access would be enough to integrate them into the nation's mainstream economic, political, and social life. First, technological convergence is not inevitable. Without some government support, private firms may be reluctant to invest in technological innovations with property rights that cannot be controlled. Second, the convergence in industry structure may not lead to cost reduction. On the contrary, it may reduce competition and increase the price of telecommunications services. After all, the deregulation of the telecommunications industry did not reduce the price for local cable services! And if the price of telecommunications services increases without a concomitant increase in real income of the poor, private firms may be reluctant to cater to poor communities.[24] This makes the danger of "digital redlining" quite real.

There are additional reasons to be concerned as to whether market mechanisms will eventually provide the poor with access to the digital world. Unlike in the earlier stages of the digital revolution, when technological innovations emerged from a relatively open system with many small innovators, in recent years only a few large firms have generated the major innovations. One reason for this change from the "blooming of a thousand flowers" to the dominance of a few is that innovations in AIT now require a large amount of finance capital as well as extensive social capital.[25] This prohibits entrepreneurship at the bottom and discourages innovations geared to the specific needs of the poor.

Lack of Social Infrastructure

Another obstacle to universal access may be the lack of social infrastructure. Unlike electronic infrastructure, which has received some attention from policy-makers, social infrastructure, or lack thereof, has received relatively little attention in policy discourse. But provision of adequate social infrastructure, is a key prerequisite for capturing AIT's benefits for the poor. By social infrastructure I mean good schools, well-equipped community centers, and, most important, educated and technology-receptive individuals, both children and adults who are capable of fully exploiting AIT's interactive potential. Without such social infrastructure in place, no amount of electronic infrastructure and affordable hardware and software can ensure that the benefits of universal access will trickle down to the poor. For example, in the absence of good teachers, who can educate the students how to use AIT for confidence-building, learning, and self-empowerment? And in the absence of good teachers, it is quite likely that mere connection to the Internet will encourage poor children to become "consumers of technology," spending time and money on electronic games.[26] In contrast, children who attend good schools in upper-income communities will learn to utilize the same technology to organize their knowledge, create data banks, and search them. This will challenge their minds and build self-confidence. The key issue for our purposes is: Can schools in low-income communities afford to employ an adequate number of good teachers to guide the students to utilize AIT in a productive way? I remain skeptical that, under the current system of funding public schools, which relies heavily on property taxes from the area residents, schools in poor areas will ever be able to provide the kind of education necessary to tap AIT's full potential.[27]

To ensure the poor's access to the digital world, one must not only upgrade the electronic and social infrastructure of schools, but other facilities as well. Efforts must be made to connect community centers, public libraries, and ultimately individual households to telecommunications infrastructure. This, too, will require more than the provision of computers. At the household level, low-income families are unlikely to make a quick transition to the electronic communication mode even if the benefits appear to be significant. Ironically, what would be required to make the transition is traditional, door-to-door campaigning by community activists who must patiently explain how to utilize personal computers and demonstrate how they provide access to information vital to the well-being of the poor families. Likewise, community centers and libraries would also require assistance to switch to the new communication mode. These public facilities would need resources not only to acquire computers and user-friendly software, but also to employ an adequate number of trainers who are willing and able to help the users make the transition.[28] And this kind of support cannot be in the form of one-time assistance only. With rapid technological advancement, old computer programs are likely to become obsolete soon; hence new programs must be installed periodically to reflect technological advances. Similarly, old computers have to be replaced with new computers with more capabilities. Without such regular improvements and maintenance of computer facilities, community centers and libraries in low-income communities are not likely to be of much use to area residents even if they are equipped with computers.

THE INADEQUACY OF CURRENT GOVERNMENT POLICIES

What has the government's response been to the challenges posed by the digital revolution? At the federal level, government policy has gradually evolved from Vice President Al Gore's 1993 proposal for an information superhighway to President Bill Clinton's proclamation in 1998 to connect all schools to the Net by the year 2000.[29] This policy evolution from preoccupation with the information superhighway to attention to schools was accompanied by two congressional efforts to address AIT-related issues: first, the National Information Infrastructure Advisory Council (NIIAC) was created in 1995; and, second, both the Telecommunications Act and the Communications Decency Act were passed in 1996.

At first glance, the NIIAC reports may appear to address the concerns of poor families in inner-city areas.[30] The Kick Start Initiative, for example, states that all schools, community centers, and other local institutions should be connected to the Internet to provide a new channel for civic participation. It does not, however, recommend any bold steps by the federal government to achieve this outcome; the initiative merely advises communities that they should make individual efforts toward this objective, given the success stories of such efforts at the local level. But as not all cities and towns are equipped with the same level of financial and human resources, how likely is it that, without significant support from either the state or federal government, disadvantaged communities will achieve this goal? And as mentioned above, access to the Internet may be a necessary but definitely not sufficient condition for educational improvement or civic participation. Schools as well as neighborhoods need teachers and activists who can use the new technology to turn the students and residents from being simply consumers to being producers of knowledge.

According to Mitchell Kapor, an original member of the NIIA and a participant in our colloquium, the main purpose of the NIIAC and its reports was not to address how to wire schools and community centers. Instead, NIIAC's central objective was to respond to the concerns of the intellectual property interests in Hollywood that pushed for copyright laws to protect against loss of revenue, not to draw the nation's attention to obstacles that low-income communities must overcome to participate equally in the new technological revolution.[31] Consequently, because the NIIAC did not address the key issue of how to achieve universal coverage, it missed an opportunity to take advantage of the technological and industry convergence that was taking place to devise new and effective public policies.

The sponsors of the Telecommunications Act of 1996 were equally oblivious to the needs of the poor. The Act opened up competition in various sectors such as local telephone and cable television, which may eventually lead to price reductions for all consumers; but in the main, the Act's proponents were not motivated by a concern for the disadvantaged. As Kapor argued persuasively in the colloquium, the Act was primarily "a business deal" among the major players in the telecommunications industry who wanted to expand into one another's market territory. Nothing in this Act improves or guarantees the poor's access to telecommunications services. On the contrary, with deregulation, universal service is likely to be even more difficult to enforce without large-scale subsidies, which are politically unpopular these days. As a result, it is quite plausible that low-income communities will be underserved or, worse, not served at all.

Policy-makers have not totally ignored the possibility that the digital revolution may bypass low-income communities. So far, however, the efforts to rectify the situation have been rather limited compared to the scope of the problem. For example, at the local level, a few cities participate regularly in the annual "Net Day celebration" by wiring some public schools to the Internet. Such efforts depend primarily on voluntary support in cash and kind. To generate voluntary support, cities have relied on local universities, well-established private firms, and wealthy philanthropists. The federal and state governments have applauded this sort of effort by cities because it fits in well with the current national mood to shift fiscal and other responsibilities from the federal to the state and local levels. Not surprisingly, the impact of the locally sponsored Net Days has been spotty and somewhat regressive because local authorities have been reluctant to take on the difficult task of providing upgraded technology to the most backward schools with the fewest resources.[32]

In sum, federal government policies regarding AIT have been motivated largely by business interests, with some concern that the new technology should not further accentuate the existing inequality in educational opportunities among children. The federal government has been most concerned, however, about the morality of its citizens. The enactment of the Communications Decency Act is an example of the federal government's deep concern that AIT may have a serious adverse effect on the morality of teenagers who may gain access to "immoral material" via the Internet and the Web. Similar concern for universal coverage of all citizens is, however, missing at the moment.

One reason why government has not actively ensured universal access is because policy-makers have not fully comprehended AIT's likely impact on relative distribution of life chances among all citizens. To date, the government's approach to AIT has been conditioned by the assumption that the adaptation of digital technology is crucial for business productivity; its impact on the poor has not been of particular concern because of the pervasive belief that none of the immediate problems of urban poverty can be addressed by AIT.[33] Policy-makers continue to believe that the glaring problems of urban poverty—drug use, badly maintained public housing, welfare dependency, out-of-wedlock births, and so on—cannot be addressed by ensuring universal access to AIT. The current national understanding is that these problems require better policing, more prisons, stringent laws against "deadbeat dads," and a new welfare system that would force the poor to earn a living.[34] Under these circumstances, President Clinton's call to connect all schools to the Internet by the year 2000 is the only sign that the government may have finally begun to comprehend the significance of the digital revolution.

UNIVERSAL ACCESS: THE KEY POLICY OBJECTIVE

It is apparent that the key objective of public policy should be to ensure universal access to AIT. To ensure access, policy-makers need to consider five elements: provision of social and electronic infrastructure; affordable hardware; user-friendly software; the ability on the part of the poor to use software; and periodic upgrading of hardware and software to keep pace with technological changes. Left to itself, the market may respond positively to one or two of the five elements—such as reducing the price of hardware and software—but it will not ensure all five. Furthermore, if these five elements are not met, market provided traditional services may be withdrawn from low-income areas. For example, as private banks upgrade their technology and replace traditional bank branch offices with electronic teller machines and home banking, low-income areas without electronic infrastructure may be bypassed unless services to such areas are required by the government.[35]

How to Ensure Access?

Public policies to ensure access should be built on the premise that much of the prevailing telecommunications infrastructure has been developed by private firms, and the government needs to build off that infrastructure to provide universal coverage. To do so, the federal government should first provide incentives to private firms but, lacking results, the government should stipulate that private service providers must offer a certain minimum level of services to low-income areas. This is not a radical proposal; governments have pursued a similar approach for years to ensure the availability of adequate housing for low-income families by providing various incentives to real estate developers who otherwise would not build low-profit-yielding buildings. Similarly, many local authorities have required cable companies to provide facilities for local channels accessible to low-income consumers. The level of subsidies may vary from case to case, but the principle is the same: without nudging by government, private firms are usually unwilling to provide services to low-profit areas. In the case of AIT, however, the nature of government prodding must be somewhat different from, say, in the provision of low-income housing. The government cannot subsidize the construction of infrastructure for universal service, because this would require a large volume of resources that for financial and political reasons the government cannot muster. Instead, the government should strategize how to achieve universal coverage incrementally, encouraging technological innovations that can facilitate the convergence of telephone, cable, and computer technologies. Such convergences are likely to reduce the service provision cost, ensuring universal coverage.

PUBLIC EDUCATION AND ACCESS TO AIT

There seems to be a consensus among policy-makers, particularly at the federal level, that to retain the nation's high productivity, children and youth, who comprise the country's future workforce, must be computer literate. Hence the federal government has begun to allocate some resources for schools in economically lagging regions to be connected to the Net.[36] The amount of support, however, is rather small considering the magnitude of the need at hand, and it reflects the federal government's understanding that the bulk of the necessary resources must be mustered locally by state and local governments.

It is apparent that public schools in low-income areas will not be able to raise the necessary resources locally. Even though some poor localities have managed to muster resources from private technology firms and wealthy philanthropists, such generosity cannot provide for the needs of all public schools. A second option is to raise property taxes. But the property tax base in low-income areas is not adequate for this purpose. Moreover, low-income families may not be able and willing to pay higher taxes. Hence the initiative will have to come from either state or federal government and may require some form of legislation like the Community Reinvestment Act, which directs private businesses such as banks to reinvest a fraction of their profit to revitalize economically lagging communities.

One plausible target for such a policy may be insurance companies, particularly companies providing health and car insurance, which charge relatively high premiums to provide services in low-income areas. Another possibility is for state governments to encourage partnerships between private firms and low-income communities. For example, in San Francisco a "community technology fund" was created in 1996 by Pacific Telesis and more than one hundred community organizations. The goal is to ensure that California's neediest residents will have access to telecommunication services after Pacific Telesis's merger with SBC Communications. Policy-makers everywhere can learn from this example: they need to understand business trends within the telecommunication firms located in their areas and help these firms benefit from such trends on the condition that firms would reinvest in low-income areas. The firms will appreciate this strategy for more than one reason: in addition to increasing their profits, this may provide them access to new markets. Note the following comment by Phil Quigley, chairman of Pacific Telesis: "These are emerging markets of California, and we believe it makes good business sense to serve them."[37]

Beyond Connection to the Net

At present, public schools in low-income areas lack basic necessities, such as classroom space and books and other educational materials. If these basic needs are not met, the quality of education is not likely to improve even if these schools are connected to the Net. Moreover, initial resistance to using the computer is likely, particularly if the teachers are untrained and cannot perceive AIT's benefit as a new educational technology.

The best way to introduce AIT to public schools is to demonstrate to the teachers and administrators how AIT can help them address some of the basic problems they have been confronting for years. For example, public schools in low-income areas usually suffer from a lack of parental participation. If AIT could be used creatively to enhance parents' participation, it is more likely to be adopted by these schools. Similarly, teachers and administrators might adopt AIT quickly if it can be shown to enhance the students' interest in learning science and mathematics.

As an educational technology, AIT is most likely to be effective where educational computers play the role of mediators, bridging between the students' hands-on, bodily knowledge, and the symbolic representations of knowledge usually favored in school.[38] In a mediating role, the educational computer enables descriptions to function as commands—descriptions making themselves real—so that a student can perceive what her or his description does. Often the effect is one of surprise, leading the student to questions that make it possible to arrive at a new understanding of the phenomenon. This, however, is not likely to happen quickly to students in poor communities who, lacking prior training, find it difficult to learn from the day-to-day experience. This failure to learn creates low self-esteem that makes these students feel that they have no useful, valid knowledge to offer. As a result, computers and AIT can have an intimidating effect on those students, creating the impression that machines know more than them.[39] Under these circumstances, the poor, even if provided access to AIT, are unlikely to transform themselves from consumers to producers of knowledge.

AIT and Community Development

AIT has opened up new possibilities for generating, processing, and storing fine-grained data, which can strengthen state-society relationships by creating transparency, trust, and accountability on both sides. For example, the 1996 welfare reforms requiring welfare recipients to find employment have created a new urgency for information on job openings, availability of rental housing, and access to public transportation. At the community level, area residents are anxious to know how efforts at fiscal federalism are likely to affect resource allocation for low-income areas.[40] On the government's side, too, there is a new urgency to know more about low-income area residents, so that the impact of welfare policy reforms can be monitored. Moreover, as the burden of responsibility is shifted from the federal to state and local levels to encourage devolution of power, there is a new need for fine-grained data at lower levels of government regarding demographic trends, land-use patterns, and so on.

Who should gather and disseminate these data was not a policy issue until very recently, as AIT reduced significantly the cost of data gathering, storing, and dissemination. The lower cost has created an incentive for private firms to provide these services. As a result, a debate is ongoing regarding the appropriate role of government in data generation and dissemination.[41] So far, the government has been efficient in collecting meteorological data, for example, but technological innovations in data collection and delivery do not usually emerge from government control of the process. On the other hand, certain types of information with large positive externalities may not be provided by private firms. This suggests that the government must be involved in gathering some basic information about all cities. Private firms may build on that basic information (which is expensive to collect and requires standardization that only the government can ensure) by collecting additional, detailed, disaggregated data that may be of interest to individuals, communities, and public institutions.

Data Needs of Poor Communities

If the Federal Geographic Data Committee (FGDC) accepts this division of labor, what should the government do to ensure that the data needs of low-income communities are met? To begin, someone has to decide what kind of data are important for the residents of low-income communities—for example, data on job openings and job-related training; the availability of various government programs designed specifically for urban, low-income areas; local area banks' lending practices, comparative insurance rates for cars, buildings, and health, and so on. More important, who should be collecting this data? And how are these data to be processed and stored, so that low-income households can access and utilize them easily for making informed judgments about jobs, investment, and spending plans—the kind of issues that are also important to suburban, middle-class families? Perhaps before the government decides to collect these data for equity reasons, it may be appropriate to inquire whether locally based entrepreneurs might want to respond to this market niche, even though the rate of return for providing this service may not be very high in the short run.

Even if local entrepreneurs respond to the communities' specialized data needs, government—particularly local government—must gather some basic data not only about low-income communities but also about the entire city. In storing these data and making them available for use, government must make sure that the programs used are compatible with the programs used by low-income residents.[42] Put another way, in storing information, government must not forget that even if universal coverage is achieved, upper- and lower-income area residents may be using different programs and different types of computers. This differential capacity to access and manipulate information between low- and high-income area residents is not likely to be bridged because new technological innovation will always be utilized first by high-income groups. Hence governments must be willing to support the minimum-threshold data needs of low-income communities, leaving the more advanced needs, perhaps, to private firms.

AIT and the Poor's Privacy

One issue rarely addressed by policy-makers is how low-income households should guard against the possible violation of one of their basic civil rights: privacy. As mentioned earlier, AIT's rapid development has drastically reduced the cost of data collection and dissemination, thereby encouraging large-scale data gathering on virtually every aspect of the social, economic, and political lives of citizens.[43] In some instances—such as data on medical records—the benefits of this new capability are significant. But as George Orwell warned long ago, a line must be drawn between public and private knowledge. The separation between the two spheres, private and public, are socially produced, and like other social decisions, this too is influenced not by poor citizens but by those who are relatively better off. As a result, inner-city residents searching for employment could face a situation where prospective employers or service providers may know more about their lives than necessary. With national concern rising over the crime rate, "deadbeat dads," unwed mothers, "welfare queens," abortion, and so on, a lucrative new market for data provision may flourish. In some instances this may lead to the violation of civil rights of citizens unless the government takes a strong stand against such disclosure.[44]

On a related issue, the federal government should closely monitor the impact of fine-grained data on household income and expenditures, which can now be collected and distributed cheaply. On one hand, officials can use this kind of rich data to fine-tune public policy, but on the other hand, market institutions may use the same data more precisely to redline certain areas. This may be particularly true for the provision of telecommunications' infrastructure, which will be needed most by families who can least afford it—that is, the unemployed engaged in job searches, the aged and disabled needing special services, and other such groups. Vulnerable and needy citizens like these must be protected against redlining. The government's record on stopping redlining in mortgage provision indicates that, although it is impossible totally to stop this practice, publicity of a few demonstrative cases may discourage it.

CONCLUSION

I started the chapter by identifying two starkly contrasting trends marking the end of the twentieth century in North America. On the one hand, we are witnessing the rise of AIT, a broad-gauged sociotechnological system analogous to earlier systems such as those associated with the Industrial Revolution. On the other hand, we are also witnessing a hardening of the problems of urban poverty and a sense of social hopelessness that America might have lost the war on poverty launched some thirty years ago by President Lyndon Johnson. Neither trends can be ignored by policy-makers.

We as a society and as individuals can choose how we shall think and act in relation to these dual and contradictory trends. But one thing is clear: to profit from the immense potentials opened by AIT, the poor must participate in it. This, of course, is, easier said than done. The poor are increasingly excluded from the nation's mainstream economic and political lives and are socially marginalized to the extent that they have become almost invisible. The rise of AIT offers opportunities and creates constraints to relink the poor to the mainstream. As a society, we need to think hard about how to capture AIT's benefits by overcoming the constraints. This analysis provides some suggestions in that direction. Needless to say, more remains to be done to transform the poor's dirt road into the information superhighway.

NOTES

1. For an elaboration of the term "American Century," see D. White (1996), *The American Century: The Rise and Decline of the U.S. as World Power.* New Haven: Yale University Press.
2. W. J. Mitchell (1995), *City of Bits: Space, Place, and the Infobohm.* Cambridge, MA: MIT Press.
3. C. Jencks and P. E. Peterson (1991), *The Urban Underclass.* Washington, DC: Brooking's Institute Press.
4. S. Danziger and P. Gottschalk, eds. (1998), *Uneven Tides: Rising Inequality in America.* New York: Russell Sage.
5. N. Negroponte (1995), *Being Digital,* Rydalmere, N.S.W.: Hodder and Stoughton.
6. U.S. Department of Commerce (1995), *Falling Through the Net: A Survey of the Have Nots in Rural and Urban America,* Washington, DC.
7. D.E. Sichal (1996), *The Computer Revolution: An Economic Perspective,* Washington, DC: Brookings Institute Press.
8. In the fall of 1985, the Department of Urban Studies and Planning at the Massachusetts Institute of Technology in Cambridge, Massachusetts, organized a

semester-long colloquium on the topic of "Information Technology and the Urban Poor." This effort was partially funded by the Kellogg Foundation. The papers presented at the colloquium are being published as a book, edited by D. Schön, B. Sanyal, and W. J. Mitchell, titled, *High Technology and Low Income Communities: Prospects for the Positive Use of Advanced Information Technology*, Cambridge, MA: MIT Press, 1998.

9. This paper draws on the forthcoming book's concluding chapter, titled "Information Technology and Urban Poverty: The Role of Public Policy," coauthored by B. Sanyal and D. Schön.

10. L. Winner (1978), *Autonomous Technology: Technics Out of Control as a Theme in Political Thought*, Cambridge, MA: MIT Press.

11. Nearly thirty community activists participated in the colloquium, attending weekly meetings. The activists comprised fellows, recruited from all across the nation, who had joined MIT's Community Fellows Program for a year, and locally based community activists with regional work experience in community organizing. For a list of names of community activists, see the preface to *High Technology and Low-Income Communities*.

12. G. Bender and T. Druckrey (1994), *Culture on the Brink: Ideologies of Technology*, Seattle: Bay Press.

13. M. B. Katz (1989), *The Undeserving Poor: From the War on Poverty to the War on Welfare*, New York: Pantheon Books.

14. E. Anderson (1996), *Street Wise: Race, Class, and Change in an Urban Community*, Chicago: University of Chicago Press.

15. This populist view is best described in C. Murray (1984), *Losing Ground: American Social Policy 1950–1980*, Basic Books. For a critique, see F. Blocks, et al., eds. (1987), *The Mean Season: The Attack on Welfare State*, New York: Pantheon Books.

16. See W. J. Wilson (1996), *When Work Disappears: The World of the New Urban Poor*, Knopf; and C. Jencks (1992), *Rethinking Social Policy: Race, Poverty and the Underclass*, Cambridge, MA: Harvard University Press.

17. T. Roszak (1994), *The Cult of Information*, Cambridge, UK: Lutterworth.

18. Much has been written already about this issue. For a good synthesis, see S. Graham and S. Marvin (1996), *Telecommunications and the City: Electronic Spaces, Urban Places*, London and New York: Routledge.

19. This is not a new insight but one that was reinforced by the colloquium. For a good overview, see R. Krieg (1995), "Information Technology and Low-Income Inner City Communities," *The Journal of Urban Technology* Vol. 3, No. 1.

20. For an elaboration, see W. J. Mitchell (1998), "Equitable Access to the Online World," in D. Schön, B. Sanyal, and W. J. Mitchell, eds., *High Technology and Low-Income Communities*.

21. Susan Goslee (1998), *Losing Ground Bit by Bit: Low-Income Communities in the Information Age*, Washington, DC: Benton Foundation, 1–9.

22. R. H. Anderson, et al. (1995), *Universal Access to E-mail: Feasibility and Societal Implications*, Santa Monica, CA: Rand Corporation.

23. Mitchell Kapor, the ex-Head of the Lotus Corporation, noted this point during the colloquium session in October 1996.

24. A. Long-Scott (1995), "Access Denied," in *Outlook*, Vol. 8, No. 1.

25. A. H. Amsden and J. C. Clark (1998), "Software Entrepreneurship Among the Urban Poor: Could Bill Gates Have Succeeded if He Were Black? . . . Or, Impoverished," in *High Technology and Low-Income Communities*.

26. B. Tardieu (1998), "Computer as Community Memory: How People in Very Poor

Neighborhoods Made a Computer Their Own," in *High Technology and Low-Income Communities*.

27. This is documented well in "For Computer Have-Nots: A Web of School Problems," *Washington Post*, March 11, 1998.

28. A. Beamish (1998), "Approaches to Community Computing: Bringing Technology to Low-Income Groups," in *High Technology and Low-Income Communities*.

29. "Clinton Advocates Technology Literacy and Access," Commencement Speech delivered by President Clinton at MIT on June 5, 1998, *MIT Tech Talk*, June 10, 1998, p. 6.

30. National Information Infrastructure Advisory Council (1996) *Kickstart Initiative: Connecting America's Communities to the Information Superhighway*, National Information Infrastructure Advisory Council, Washington, DC; National Information Infrastructure Advisory Council (1996) *A Nation of Opportunity: Realizing the Promise of the Information Superhighway*, National Information Infrastructure Advisory Council, Washington, DC.

31. Mitchell Kapor resigned from the National Information Infrastructure Advisory Council (NIIAC) to protest what he interpreted as NIIAC's hidden agenda.

32. D. Nakamura, "For Computer Have-Nots, A Web of School Problems," *Washington Post*, March 11, 1998.

33. L. Alvarez, "Internet Is New Pet Issue in Congress. Voters Lead and Lawmakers Fellow, Making the Most of a Theme," *New York Times*, June 28, 1998.

34. C. Jencks (1992), *Rethinking Social Policy: Race, Poverty, and the Underclass*, Cambridge, MA: Harvard University Press.

35. A. J. Fishbein (1998), "Bank Technology May Make Access Difficult For Some," Center for Urban Policy Research Report, Rutgers—The State University of New Jersey, Vol. 9, No. 1.

36. "Clinton Advocates Technology Literacy and Access," *MIT Tech Talk*, June 10, 1998.

37. E-mail announcement by *Business Wise*, October 15, 1996, p. 2.

38. B. For an elaboration, see J. Bamberger (1998), "Action Knowledge and Symbolic Knowledge: The Computer as Mediator" in D. Schön, et al., eds., *High Technology and Low-Income Communities*.

39. Tardieu (1998), "Computer as Community Memory."

40. L. Mishel, J. Bernstein, and J. Schmitt (1997), *The State of Working America 1996–97*, Economic Policy Institute, Washington, DC.

41. J. Ferreira, Jr. (1998) "Information Technologies that Change Relationships between Low-Income Communities and the Public and Non-Profit Agencies that Serve Them," in D. Schön, et al., eds., *High Technology and Low-Income Communities*.

42. For elaboration, see J. Ferreira, Jr. (1998), "Information Technologies that Change Relationships."

43. D. Lyon (1993), *The Electronic Eye: The Rise of Surveillance Society*, Cambridge, UK: Polity Press.

44. M. Winckler (1991), "Walking Prisons: The Developing Technology of Electronic Controls," *The Futurist*, July–August, pp. 34–36.

PART IV.

Impacts of

Telecommunications

CYBERSPACE OR HUMAN SPACE

WITHER CITIES IN THE AGE
OF TELECOMMUNICATIONS?

William B. Beyers

INTRODUCTION

We are in an era in which the nature of work—as measured by the industrial or occupational structure of economies—is changing dramatically, and in which the sources of income and wealth to those who create demand are shifting. Changes in economic systems are being fueled by the development of networks of communication, but these are not just the electronic networks of telephonic-based interaction systems. The steady and continued evolution of less expensive ways of moving humans and documents around our planet is also having major impacts upon the global economy. We have continued to push the envelope on the "time-space convergence" model articulated thirty years ago by Donald Janelle, and are witnessing the latest spatial adaptations to these continuously changing new opportunities for realignments in the structure of production, trade, and the spatial organization of settlement systems (Janelle, 1969).

In this chapter I argue that the evolving pattern of trade in advanced economies is based to a growing extent on knowledge-based service industries. Business enterprises producing this new economic base for regions challenge existing paradigms for the evolution of settlements. Will they be dominated by the impersonality of cyberspace or defined by the preferences of people in "human space?" In this chapter I argue that human space wins—we remake the settlement system based on new production factors and new industries, which reflect the ongoing social division of labor (Beyers and Lindahl, 1998).

A consequence of this pattern of structural change in the U.S. economy in the 1990s has been a change in the geography of growth in our nation. Some of the most successful metropolitan areas over the last several decades have stumbled in the early 1990s (such as Los Angeles), while some newer communities have boomed (such as Las Vegas). The shift from regional growth led by high-tech manufacturing to growth also driven by producer and consumer services and the demand for multimedia experiences has been one trend. Another has been the turnaround in rural America, where after the downturns of the 1980s we find faster growth than in metropolitan areas through the first half of the 1990s (Fuguitt and Beale, 1996).

To understand these new trends, we must unravel what is fueling trade in what many have called the New Economy—an economy dominated by growth in the production of information-related sectors. In work undertaken with David Lindahl, I have argued that this growth in demand is due to an expanding need for information which is not tied to the explicit movement of goods through the channel of distribution to consumers; rather it is due to a growing demand for specialized expertise needed by businesses, governments, and citizens in a host of circumstances (Beyers and Lindahl, 1996a). The suppliers of this newly demanded knowledge are found not only within companies and governments, but to a growing extent in freestanding "information merchants"—businesses purveying work that involves the production of information rather than goods and is not primarily related to the distribution of goods. These businesses include not only producer services, but also health, entertainment, and other services with consumer markets. In addition, people working in occupations that grant them considerable locational freedom should be considered in this group, such as airline pilots, entertainers, drilling-rig specialists, and so on, who are not only working for firms but also working as proprietors. Within this growing cadre of suppliers of work that is broadly informatic are many who can serve clients not located near them, thereby bringing revenue into regional economies from outside. In this respect, these enterprises, which Lindahl and I have dubbed "Lone Eagles"[1] and "High Fliers" are emerging as leaders in this new economy (Beyers and Lindahl, 1996b). These information-oriented businesses are, to a growing extent, forming the economic base of regions. For example, Lindahl and I have recently estimated that 73 percent of the growth of employment in Washington State between 1963 and 1987 was due to the growth in exports of services (Beyers and Lindahl, 1998).[2]

Based on hundreds of interviews, enterprises in the New Economy are evolving in the following manner. The continually growing specialized niche-oriented producer service and other service businesses, along with proprietors or employees with locational freedom, are to an increasing extent able to situate themselves *distant from their clients*. This has most often been read as a trend that means decentralization—movement to edge cities and rural areas (Garreau, 1992; Rasker and Glick, 1994). However, I do not see it as playing out this way. Rather, what I see is the possibility for individuals making these decisions—whether they be firms or proprietors—to make choices on a spatially more contingent basis within the settlement system. This leads immediately to the issue I raised in the title to this chapter: Wither cities in the age of telecommunications? Not only are many businesses in the information society strongly tied to localized markets (maybe about half of business volume),[3] but it is also in cities that most people working in these sectors *want* to live, for reasons related to consumption and tastes, and dictated by spousal relationships and other social relationships.

Modes of interaction in the New Economy are therefore more contingent than has traditionally been the case in the production of goods and in the distribution of goods, but the use of these new modes has not dramatically reshaped the location of supporting segments, traditionally referred to as the indirect and induced sectors. I think that Michael Storper's notion of untraded interdependencies becomes increasingly relevant when we consider these support dimensions (Storper, 1997). In the march forward into this information age we have, of course, assumed that it will proceed unabated to cause new forms of technology that will inevitably reduce costs in existing industries and grant them more and more spatial freedom. We must be suspicious of this assumption, due to the unpredictable nature of technological change. Thus the current revitalization of rural communities may be a "flash in the pan," or it may be the harbinger of a much more balanced settlement pattern.

A SNAPSHOT OF THE EVOLVING ECONOMY

Employment in the U.S. economy has been dominated by services since the 1920s, and the share of employment accounted for by services has continued to rise, today accounting for over three quarters of all jobs. However, the service economy is composed of a changing mixture of industries and occupations. Responding to the need for functionally useful classifications of these service industries, Browning and Singlemann developed a taxonomy based primarily on differences between intermediate and final demands, and the nature of the final demand for the service (Browning and Singlemann, 1975). Various studies of the recent history of the U.S. economy using the Browning-Singlemann classification have documented the relative growth of the producer, financial, and not-for-profit services, and the decline in the relative importance of distributive and mainly consumer services (Noyelle and Stanback, 1984; Beyers, 1991; Beyers and Lindahl, forthcoming, Chapter 2).

The rapid overall growth of services employment has taken place at a time when employment in the goods producing sector has stagnated. Since 1970, employment in primary, construction, and manufacturing sectors has been stable, at approximately 27 million jobs. Over the same time period, the U.S. economy has added more than 45 million service jobs. While this pattern of job change has been characterized as "deindustrialization" by some (Bell, 1975), it should be noted that in real terms the value in Gross Domestic Product (GDP) from primary, construction, and manufacturing sectors has never been higher (Bureau of Economic Analysis; monthly surveys). Yet the expansion of millions of relatively low-paying service jobs in retailing and sectors such as temporary help has fueled concern about the quality of jobs being created in the New Economy (Reich, 1992; Thurow, 1996). Moreover, some scholars have even forecast that technological change will reverse this long history of service employment expansion—that the network economy will eliminate much of this service employment (Harmon, 1996; Tapscott, 1996; Rifkin, 1995).

Industry-based measures of change in the U.S. economy obscure changes

163

in the types of jobs being created, and have led many scholars to examine change in the structure of occupations. In the four-year period from June 1992 to July 1996, 5.4 million of the 9.7 million new jobs in the United States were executive or professional occupations—generally high-skill jobs. Most of the rest of the jobs were created in sales and other service occupations. A recent study by Carnevalle and Rose has documented the rise of office work and high-skilled services, which they estimate to account for 58 percent of total employment in 1995, up from 41 percent in 1959. Thus the aggregate profile of job growth is associated with work related to information processing and decision-making, filled by highly educated workers (Carnevalle and Rose, 1998).

Where is this growth occurring in the New Economy? The metropolitan areas with the fastest growth over the 1985 to 1993 time period were Las Vegas, Seattle, Atlanta, Orlando, and St. Petersburg, while the nations largest cities— Los Angeles, New York, and Chicago—all experienced slow growth or employment losses (Beyers and Lindahl, forthcoming, chapter 2).[4] However, nonmetropolitan areas grew faster than metropolitan areas over this same time period (20.9 percent versus 16.4 percent respectively); manufacturing declined by 10.5 percent in metro areas while gaining 6.8 percent in nonmetro areas, and producer services grew almost as fast in nonmetro areas (34 percent) as they grew in metropolitan areas (35 percent). We have documented the fact that most of the growth in the information-oriented producer services has occurred in small, new establishments. While there are global corporations in the producer services, most growth is in new establishments. This pattern of relatively rapid nonmetropolitan growth has continued in the 1990s (Fuguitt and Beale, 1996; Cromartie and Nord, 1996). Between 1982 and 1992 in the business, engineering, and management sector in the United States, 55 percent of employment growth was associated with new firms (Beyers and Lindahl, forthcoming, Chapter 3).

This section documents that the geographical pattern of growth in the New Economy is different from the conception of scholars who emphasize megacities, global cities, and other visions of development constructed around the dominance of a few giant places. We are, in fact, experiencing a more decentralized pattern of development built around job growth and trade in a variety of types of regional economic specialties and capabilities, a point made recently by Storper in his treatise on the role of regional economies and the globalization thesis (Storper, 1997).

TRADE IN THE NEW ECONOMY

The preceding section documented the growing importance of information-oriented work in the New Economy and the strength of growth rates in rural communities and smaller metropolitan areas. Now I address the issue of trade in the New Economy, capitalizing upon information gathered in a recent study of producer service businesses. This section documents the continuing importance of face-to-face interaction in the age of telecommunications, while simultaneously demonstrating the development of greater levels of interaction—

expansion of the "space of flows" and "the edge of forever," to use Castells's terms — in the rapidly growing producer services sector (Castells, 1996).

Information Merchants, Lone Eagles, and High Fliers:
The Emergence of People and Businesses Trading Knowledge in Global to Local Channels

The vision of interaction in the global economy that is underscored in Castells's recent work is rooted in a production system built around manufacturing, and the trade in manufactured commodities (Castells, 1996). The Berkeley and California schools of industrial economics and geography have emphasized these relations in the development of "new industrial spaces." This view has been useful but possibly oversold in terms of its generic applicability to places (Markusen, 1996; Markusen, 1998; Storper, 1997).

While the industrial-district paradigm serves reasonably well to describe the development of some of the service economy, it does not cover all current forces. The bases for demand for the producer and other information-oriented services in Carnevalle and Rose's office and high-skilled service sector have been documented to be economy-wide, and include a significant consumer and government basis of demand (Beyers, 1991). For example, legal services firms may be exclusively focused on intellectual property issues. Computer software may be aimed at such diverse fields as epidemiology or art. Management consulting firms may specialize in assisting universities find key staff such as presidents or provosts. These few examples indicate specializations or "niches" that are quite independent of goods producing sectors.

We have recently documented the market locations for hundreds of producer service businesses, and find that the geographic pattern is bifurcated into two groups: (1) a group with strong, nonlocal markets, and (2) a group with predominantly localized markets. We refer to the export-oriented businesses as "Lone Eagles" and "High Fliers" — with Lone Eagles defined as proprietors having strong nonlocal markets, and High Fliers being businesses with more than one employee (Beyers and Lindahl, 1996b). The criterion used to classify an establishment as a Lone Eagle or a High Flier was for the establishment to sell 40 percent or more of its service externally, a cut point slightly higher than the overall average for nonlocal sales (36 percent). In both urban and rural areas, we find that about 40 percent of the proprietorships and businesses with employees fall into the Lone Eagle and High Flier categories. The other 60 percent of these businesses are strongly tied to local markets, suggesting a bifurcated population of businesses as measured by geographic market orientation in the New Economy. Table 11.1 provides summary information from these interviews.

The evidence presented in Table 11.1 shows a clear division in market location between the Lone Eagles and High Fliers, and the balance of the producer service establishments. We need additional survey evidence of this type to determine whether this bifurcated pattern of market orientation is characteristic of other sectors in the New Economy. Table 11.1 also makes it clear that

Table 11.1 Market Characteristics

Category	Export %	Sample Size
Proprietors		
Lone Eagles	81.5%	26
Local-Market Proprietors	7.0%	56
All Proprietors	31.0%	82
Small Establishments (2–10 employees)		
High Fliers	72.7%	130
Local Market Establishments	10.1%	241
All Small Establishments	32.0%	371
Medium-Sized Establishments (11–25 employees)		
High Fliers	73.7%	49
Local-Market Establishments	13.4%	52
All Medium-Sized Establishments	43.0%	10
Large Establishments (More than 25 employees)		
High Fliers	75.1%	55
Local Market Establishments	16.6%	70
All Large Establishments	42.0%	125
All Establishments	36.0%	687

as firm size progresses there is some tendency for external market orientation to increase, as even businesses in the localized market group have some increase in export market as size increases, but these shares still remain low in comparison to the High Fliers.

In the previous section it was documented that employment growth has been strong in the producer services, and we have established the fact that most of this growth is associated with an expansion in the number of establishments, not with increasing average size of existing businesses (Beyers and Lindahl, forthcoming, Chapter 3). How has the share of firms in the Lone Eagle/High Flier category changed over time? Using data from a sample of 381 establishments interviewed in 1993 who were also in business five years previously, we determined that 116 of these establishments fell into the Lone Eagle/High Flier group, while 265 had localized markets. Between 1988 and 1993, five establishments which met the Lone Eagle/High Flier criterion in 1988 had growth in local markets which moved them into the localized firm category. In contrast, 21 firms which were in the localized group in 1988 shifted to the Lone Eagle/High Flier category by 1993. Figure 11.1 shows a scattergram of changing local market shares for firms classified as Lone Eagles and High Fliers in 1993, and this figure documents the tendency not only for many firms to be moving into the Lone Eagle/High Flier category over time, but also for a number of those already in this group to be increasing their nonlocal market share. Thus, within a given cohort of establishments, over time more firms become Lone Eagles and High Fliers, and the cohort discussed here were firms that had been in business for at least five years when they were interviewed. Of the

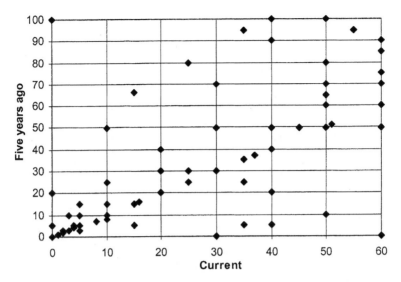

Figure 11.1 Lone Eagles and High Fliers: Change in Local Market Share
Note: Cases that lie above the principal diagonal represent increases in export shares.

cohort of establishments we interviewed who were in business for less than five years, some 31 percent fell into the Lone Eagle and High Flier category, documenting the fact that many young firms are also able to penetrate nonlocal markets.[5]

Why do these businesses develop stronger external markets; why do localized firms become Lone Eagles and High Fliers? Here are some comments from people that we interviewed that shed light on this process. "Want to expand area of market." "Trend is toward nationwide (market), don't have to be located by clients." "Becoming a West Coast firm. Geography is broadening substantially." "Work elsewhere includes Rhode Island, New York City — Public Interest Research Groups (PIRG). Working on getting job in Mexico. Geographic expansion due to increased reputation." As Lindahl and I have reported elsewhere, firms pursuing strategies aimed at geographic market expansion have payoffs, as measured by firm growth rates and relatively high sales per employee (Beyers and Lindahl, 1997).

Doing the Job: Getting Work Done and Delivering It to Clients in the New Economy

Clearly, both localized producer service businesses and Lone Eagles and High Fliers are trading their services, selling them to their clients. How do they do this in the age of telecommunications? We have explored this question by asking firms to indicate the importance of various means of producing and delivering their services to clients. We have also documented changes in the importance of these means of delivery over time (Beyers and Lindahl, forthcoming Chapter 7). Tables 11.2 though 11.4 present information on these means of production and trade. Table 11.2 documents the percentage of businesses in different categories that rely upon various means of producing and delivering their services, while Table 11.3 describes changes in the importance of these factors. Table 11.4 documents information similar to that contained in Table 11.2, but presents industry-specific detail.

Table 11.2 documents the fact that the typical producer service firm uses a multiplicity of modes of delivery and production for its services; about three means of production and delivery were considered highly important in the service production and delivery process by the typical firm. Table 11.2 indicates that some 87 percent of the businesses we interviewed found face-to-face meetings were highly important to production and delivery of their services, and 64 percent engage in highly important face-to-face meetings with written or graphical documents. The importance of face-to-face meetings in the producer services—a core sector in the New Economy—is not a surprise. Architects and their clients need to talk about design options and client preferences, review preliminary drawings, and so on. Security brokers need to help clients decide on the character of investment programs by talking with clients about their aspirations for the use of their financial resources. Accountants need to give advice to companies on how strategically to manage financial resources in the face of stronger government regulations or reporting requirements, even in this era of

Table 11.2 Percentage of Establishments Considering Factors to be Highly Important as a Means of Producing and Delivering Their Services

	Lone Eagles	High Fliers	Other Proprietors	Other Firms	Entire Sample
Face-to-Face Conversations at Clients' Offices	56.5%	38.9%	56.4%	38.5%	40.8%
Face-to-face Conversations at Establishment Office	26.1%	32.3%	36.4%	57.8%	46.2%
Telephone Conversations	52.2%	46.7%	41.8%	47.80	47.1%
Video Conferencing	0.0%	0.0%	0.0%	0.0%,	0.0%
Computer File Transfer:					
via modem direct	13.0%	14.8%	10.9%	9.8%	11.7%
via e-mail, Internet	8.7%	7.9%	3.6%	6.4%	6.8%
via LAN	0.0%	1.7%	0.0%	3.6%	2.6%
via WAN	0.0%	1.7%	0.0%	0.3%	0.8%
via mail/courier	21.7%	14.0%	14.5%	7.0%	10.5%
Written/Graphical Documents:					
face-to-face @ client	52.2%	34.9%	43.6%	34.6%	36.1%
face-to-face @ estab.	21.7%	17.9%	20.0%	36.6%	28.3%
mail/courier	26.1%	40.6%	30.9%	40.2%	39.1%
fax	39.1%	44.1%	25.5%	38.50%	39.4%
Other: satellite uplinks	8.7%	0.4%	0.0%	0.3%	0.6%
other	4.3%	4.4%	3.6%	2.0%	3.0%
Number of Highly Important Citations/Businesses	3.30	3.01	2.87	3.23	3.13
Sample Size	n=23	n=229	n=55	n=358	n=665

more automated financial record-keeping. Management consultants have to go to their clients' offices to define the issues needing consulting advice, learn about the operations of clients, and help forge solutions to issues requiring outside expertise.

While it is necessary for most producer service firms to interact in a face-to-face environment in the production process, Table 11.2 makes it clear that other means of interaction are also used. Telephone conversations, fax machines, and the shipment of computer files or documents are also important modes of interaction. Differences in the number of these modes of interaction do not vary much among the groups of businesses defined in Table 11.2, but there are differences in the mix of modes used depending upon status. Export-oriented Lone Eagles and High Fliers meet clients at their offices much less frequently than the locally oriented establishments, while they are more reliant on various means of computer file transfer and fax machines. Given that more than 75 percent of the typical Lone Eagle and High Flier establishments business is located outside their local area, this means that most of those engaged in these businesses must travel *interregionally* to their clients' locations, most likely by air, or clients must travel to the service specialist.

How are these means of interaction and delivery changing over time? Our interviews suggest that hardly any means of production and delivery are becom-

Table 11.3 Percentage Citing Changes in Importance of the Information Technology Factor

	Increase in Importance					Decrease
	Lone Eagles	High Fliers	Other Proprietors	Other Firms	Entire Sample	Entire Sample
Face-to-Face Conversations at Clients' Offices	0.0%	0.4%	0.0%	0.8%	0.6%	2.0%
Face-to-Face Conversations at Establishment Office	0.0%	1.7%	1.8%	2.2%	2.0%	2.7%
Telephone Conversations	0.0%	2.6%	0.0%	3.1%	2.6%	0.7%
Video Conferencing	0.0%	2.6%	0.0%	1.4%	1.1%	0.5%
Computer File Transfer:						
via modem direct	17.4%	14.0%	7.3%	15.4%	14.3%	0.4%
via e-mail, Internet	8.7%	10.9%	1.8%	10.6%	9.9%	0.0%
via LAN	4.3%	1.7%	0.0%	4.5%	3.2%	0.0%
via WAN	4.3%	1.3%	0.0%	0.6%	0.5%	0.0%
via mail/courier	0.0%	14.4%	10.9%	10.9%	11.7%	0.4%
Written/Graphical Documents:						
face to face @ client	0.0%	1.3%	0.0%	1.4%	1.2%	1.0%
face to face @ estab.	0.0%	0.4%	0.0%	0.6%	0.5%	1.6%
mail/courier	4.3%	1.3%	0.0%	2.0%	1.7%	0.7%
fax	8.7%	22.3%	12.7%	28.2%	24.2%	0.0%
Other: satellite uplinks	4.3%	2.2%	0.0%	0.3%	1.1%	0.0%
other	0.0%	1.7%	0.0%	0.8%	1.1%	0.0%
Cumulative % Change	52.2%	77.3%	34.5%	83.8%	76.4%	10.0%
Sample Size	23	229	55	358	665	665

169

ing less important, and most important, *there is no significant evidence that face-to-face meetings are becoming less important in the production process in the producer services.* Table 11.3 documents the proportion of establishments citing increases and decreases in the importance of ways of producing and delivering their services. Here we see that various means of computer file transfer and the shipment of written or graphical documents have become more important, and techniques not used much at all at the time the survey was conducted (1993 and 1994) are expected to become important (such as video conferencing and satellite uplinks). It appears that these changes are occurring in all groups of producer service businesses in Table 11.3. The last column of Table 11.3 indicates the proportion of our sample indicating that particular ways of producing and delivering their services had become less important. Collectively, these are weak in magnitude compared to the citations of increased importance, and while they are centered on shifts in the importance of face-to-face meetings, the percentages are very small compared to the importance of face-to-face meetings documented in Table 11.2. Thus the evidence in this table suggests that there are increases in the intensity of modes of interaction used to produce and deliver producer services, but that face-to-face meetings remain at the core of the way in which business is conducted in this rapidly growing segment of the American economy.

Table 11.4 presents more detail on the current use of information technologies by industry. The database used for this table is somewhat more limited than that used in Tables 11.2 and 11.3; therefore there are some differences

Table 11.4 Current Uses of Information Technologies to Deliver Service

	Non-depository Financial Institutions	Security Brokerages	Insurance Agents and Carriers	Temporary Help	Computer Services
1A. Face-to-Face Conversations at Clients' Offices	68.8%	65.4%	66.7%	43.8%	56.5%
1B. Face-to-Face Conversations at Establishment Office	62.5%	65.4%	53.3%	31.3%	13.0%
2. Telephone Conversations	37.5%	53.8%	60.0%	50.0%	41.3%
3. Video Conferencing					
4. Computer File Transfer:					
4A. modem	6.3%	7.7%	26.7%	0.0%	30.4%
4B. Internet	18.8%	7.7%	40.0%	0.0%	8.7%
4C. LAN	0.0%	3.8%	13.3%	0.0%	10.9%
4D. WAN	0.0%	0.0%	13.3%	0.0%	0.0%
5. Written/Graphical Documents:					
5A. at Clients' Office	0.0%	7.7%	53.3%	12.5%	13.0%
5B. at Establishment Office	0.0%	7.7%	26.7%	6.3%	4.3%
5C. via Mail/Courier	25.0%	15.4%	60.0%	25.0%	8.7%
5D. via FAX	25.0%	11.5%	40.0%	31.3%	8.7%
6A. Satellite Uplinks	0.0%	0.0%	0.0%	0.0%	0.0%
6B. Telex	0.0%	0.0%	0.0%	0.0%	0.0%
6C. Other	0.0%	0.0%	6.7%	31.3%	6.5%
Aggregate of Methods	250.0%	246.2%	466.7%	250.0%	217.4%

in the percentages related to use and change. However, Table 11.4 reveals important variations within the producer services in modes used to produce and deliver these services. Some such as legal services, depend upon clients primarily coming to their offices, while others primarily travel to their clients' offices, such as in management consulting and public relations. Some are prolific users of many information technologies, such as lawyers, while other sectors are somewhat less diversified in the ways they relate to clients.

The conclusion that may be drawn from these data is that we are increasing the intensity of our connectivity through the use of a wider variety of interaction technologies. In the producer services, businesses do not appear to be abandoning meetings of people. Rather, enterprises are supplementing these meetings with additional ways of producing and delivering services. How can we reconcile visions of the Transactional City developed years ago by Gottman with new insights, such as those developed by Castells, and visions of futurists such as Thurow and Rifkin who predict diminished opportunities for work due to advancements in the use of information technologies (Gottmann, 1983; Castells, 1996; Thurow, 1996; Rifkin, 1995)? Some thoughts on this question are presented in section IV.

The Intensification of Interaction in the New Economy

The hypothesis that I would like to advance, based on the interviews with the companies we have studied, is that there should be macro evidence of *increased*

Table 11.4 (continued)

Misc. Business Services	Legal Services	Architectural and Engineering Services	Accounting	Research and Testing Services	Management Consulting and Public Relations Services	Entire Sample
30.0%	19.0%	36.2%	50.9%	33.3%	63.5%	44.4%
12.0%	72.4%	18.8%	57.9%	19.0%	40.4%	38.1%
26.0%	75.9%	20.3%	35.1%	28.6%	44.2%	40.8%
10.0%	32.8%	2.9%	5.3%	4.8%	11.5%	13.5%
2.0%	29.3%	2.9%	0.0%	0.0%	7.7%	9.2%
0.0%	10.3%	0.0%	0.0%	0.0%	5.8%	3.8%
0.0%	0.0%	0.0%	1.8%	0.0%	0.0%	0.9%
30.0%	48.3%	78.3%	43.9%	23.8%	59.6%	40.8%
8.0%	36.2%	36.2%	31.6%	9.5%	7.7%	21.3%
18.0%	74.1%	42.0%	57.9%	71.4%	46.2%	40.8%
24.0%	82.8%	26.1%	33.3%	33.3%	48.1%	35.0%
2.0%	0.0%	1.4%	1.8%	0.0%	1.9%	0.9%
0.0%	0.0%	0.0%	0.0%	0.0%	1.9%	0.2%
8.0%	0.0%	1.4%	0.0%	4.8%	7.7%	4.5%
170.0%	486.2%	285.5%	329.8%	247.6%	367.3%	307.0%

levels of human-to-human interaction. An alternative hypothesis is implicit in Castells's view of society, and that of many futurists: that the network society will be leading us into a new space of flows that is not dominated by personal interaction. Evidence of my hypothesis should be supported through two major factors: (1) structural shifts in the economy that are pushing the relative development of sectors that favor human interaction, and (2) shifts in the way in which information-oriented businesses produce and deliver the information their clients demand. I have already documented evidence on both points. On point number 1, the relative growth of information-related sectors was documented earlier, and this chapter has also documented the growing proportion of businesses that are engaged in long-distance services trade, which would position them to be engaged in complex spatial processes of client-supplier interaction. On point number 2, businesses are increasing the number of ways in which they communicate with clients and produce their services, as the data presented in the preceding paragraphs of the chapter of this paper demonstrate. The proliferation of fax machines must have created huge demand for new telephone lines. The growth in e-mail and the Internet must be reflected in increased use of telephone lines as measured by connection time. The growth in the use of courier services and the ongoing shift toward the information services or the "office sector" should be reflected in relatively rapid growth rates in air travel and air freight. In short, the survey evidence just presented should be mirrored by statistics from the industries providing the means to produce and deliver these services.

In an attempt to document whether our survey evidence is corroborated by aggregate statistics, I have developed some indices related to interaction that I will argue are relevant to the New Economy. Figures 11.2 and 11.3 place this

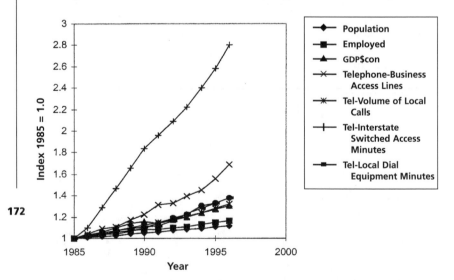

Figure 11.2 Interaction Measures—Telephone

Source: Statistical Abstract of the United States; Federal Communications Commission, Statistics of Communications Commons Carriers.

evidence on the table. These figures build on categories of information presented in Tables 11.2 through 11.4, without a perfect match of categories. The data in Figures 11.2 and 11.3 are indexed against levels in the year 1985, with background magnitudes for population, employment, and constant dollar measures of GDP. The trends in these figures are unmistakable: *Every index measure outstrips the background measures.* This result means that there has been a relative increase in the intensity of interaction compared to the growth of population, employment, and the GDP as measured in constant dollars. In Figure 11.2 we see explosive growth in the volume of long-distance telephone access minutes, and strong growth in the other measures of telephone use and capacity. The strong increase in the number of business access lines may be related to the development of network capabilities with equipment such as fax machines and computer networks, but it may also be related the structural change in the economy toward information services that have strong reliance on telephone lines for a variety of communication media and purposes.

Figure 11.3 presents interaction measures for air and mail, and the trend is similar to Figure 11.2. Strong growth in air freight is observed, which includes package courier services as well as other air freight. I was unable to obtain aggregate measures of the ton-miles or number of packages moved by air courier carriers such as Airborne Express, FedEx, or UPS over time. Therefore this index should be considered with caution. The relatively rapid growth in the volume of domestic air passenger traffic may again be related to structural shifts in the economy toward the information-oriented services that require face-to-face meetings by a growing cohort of Lone Eagle and High Flier businesses. Mail flows have increased relative to population and employment, tracking roughly with the expansion of real GDP.

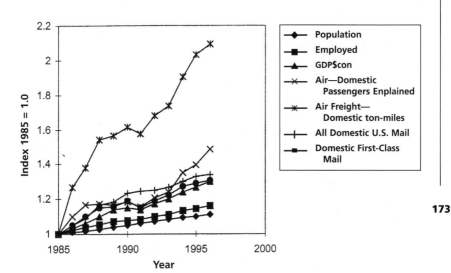

Figure 11.3 Interaction Measures—Air and Mail

Source: Statistical Abstract of the United States; Air Transport Association of America, Air Transport; U.S. Postal Service, Annual Report of the Postmaster General.

I regard the data in Figures 11.2 and 11.3 to be a "smoking gun" from a variety of perspectives. First, these data backstop our interviews, and support the argument that there has been an increase in the volume of interaction by more diversified modes. Second, these data support the argument that human-to-human interaction not only has remained important but, with the structural shift to the services, has not diminished in importance; *and*, with the likely increase in the proportion of enterprises in the Lone Eagle and High Flier category, that these trends are related to the strong relative growth in air passenger travel. I was unable to find data on the temporal trend of business air travel, but it appears to be about 48 percent of total air travel, according to Air Transport Association of America's home page.[6]

Third, these data raise the question of whether these measures of increase in interaction are a product of fundamental changes in the economy, or if they are rather a price response of the classic nature to reduced real costs of interaction. If telecommunications, mail, courier, and air travel costs have decreased in real prices, then elementary economic principles could also explain the trends just presented. Frankly, I have not developed data series as of this writing, which confront this third possibility, but it is a principle that is at the heart of Janelle's classic model of space-time convergence (Janelle, 1969).

IMPLICATIONS FOR CITIES AND THE SETTLEMENT SYSTEM

In approaching this chapter I wanted not only to consider evidence from a recent d National Science Foundation (NSF) project, but also to look beyond it to the themes of this volume and Professor Castells's brilliant conceptions related to the development of urban settlements and the information economy. In this final section of the chapter I'll be somewhat speculative.

The New Bases for Locational Choice: Freedom Exercised in a Richer Variety of Spatial Outcomes

If we have a growing cohort of workers in our society in the Lone Eagle and High Flier categories, and they have clients that are spatially dispersed, then this immediately raises the issue of where these people and companies have chosen to be located and why they have selected these locations. Our research indicates some important differences between those operating their businesses in urban and rural communities, and between localized firms and the export-oriented Lone Eagles and High Fliers.

Table 11.5 summarizes reasons considered to be highly important for location by 666 producer service businesses. These data are taken from two samples. The NSF sample is dominantly urban businesses, while the Economic Research Services (ERS) sample was conducted in rural counties located in 44 states. These two samples document the fact that most respondents had more than one factor that they considered as highly important in their location decision. Among the localized establishments, it is significant that proximity to their clients ranks as *less* important than proximity to the founder/owner/manager

Table 11.5 Factors Considered Highly Important in the Location Decision

	NSF	NSF	ERS	ERS
	Lone Eagles and High Fliers	Localized Establishments	Lone Eagles and High Fliers	Localized Establishments
Other Factors	47.6%	31.5%	41.8%	48.1%
Proximity to Major Clients	21.0%	30.4%	24.5%	25.2%
Owner/Founder/Manager's Residence Is Nearby	42.7%	33.0%	58.2%	62.2%
Lower Land/Energy/ Occupancy Costs	18.9%	20.0%	3.1%	0.0%
Prestige Location/ High-Quality Space	10.5%	15.2%	1.0%	2.2%
Presence of Complementary Firm Whose Services Assist You	6.3%	14.4%	4.1%	0.7%
High Quality of Life	11.2%	9.3%	65.3%	44.4%
Presence of Complementary Firm Whose Goods Assist You	1.4%	3.0%	0.0%	0.0%
Presence of Educated/Skilled Labor Force	4.2%	0.7%	3.1%	0.7%
Low Cost of Living	1.4%	2.2%	7.1%	3.7%
Lower Local Taxes	1.4%	0.7%	1.0%	0.0%
Government Assistance	0.0%	0.7%	0.0%	0.7%
Presence of Low-Cost Labor Force	0.7%	0.4%	2.0%	0.0%
Sum	167.1%	161.5%	211.2%	188.1%
(n)	143	270	98	135

residence and the "other" category. For the rural establishments, there is a clear emphasis on quality of life and proximity to the founder/owner/manager residence by all establishments. Analyses of the text related to answers that fall into the "other" category reveal the following: for the urban sample, space needs and specific building purchases were important, and for the Lone Eagles and High Fliers, convenient access to the transportation system was frequently cited as an important factor: "close to airport," "lab space plus office space together/airport access," "across the street from airport," "near to train," "transport convenience." For the rural establishments, the "other" factor was dominated by comments surrounding social considerations: "husband's home town," "family reputation in area," "hometown," "family grew up here," "wife from here." These socially linked comments are as common for the Lone Eagles and High Fliers as for the localized rural establishments.

The pattern of responses documented in Table 11.5 *does not* support a cost-minimizing location strategy for either the Lone Eagles or High Fliers or the localized establishments. Why? Elsewhere Lindahl and this author have demonstrated that the basis of demand for many of these companies is built around niche-market business concepts and forces of demand not rooted in cost, but rather linked to the demand for specialized information where cost is not a significant consideration or plays a minor role (Beyers and Lindahl, 1996a).

We have also documented that on the supply side these businesses position themselves in their marketplace to construct competitive advantage through projection of factors related to the *quality* of the information they can produce and the capacities inherent within their enterprise that cannot be duplicated by their clients. They tend to be pursuing differentiation strategies with more complex dimensions than those associated with Porter's generic strategies (Lindahl and Beyers, 1999). And we have documented motivations of founders who have started most of these enterprises, and find that they are drawn into their businesses because they want to be in charge of their lives and perceive business opportunities (Beyers and Lindahl, 1996a). These traits on demand, supply, and entrepreneurial dimensions, combined with responses reported in Table 11.5 with regard to location, imply flexibility in space. They suggest that businesses in this rapidly growing part of our economy may choose to a great extent where to establish their enterprise. If the market environment is favoring the explosion of establishments reported above in this chapter, then it may well be that there is not a tight pull to specific geographic locations for entrepreneurs wishing to start and operate organizations with localized markets or caught up in the interregional market place supplied by Lone Eagles and High Fliers.

I argue that these data point to an ability for many players in the New Economy to choose to be in the locations *they* want to be, whether they are firm owners, proprietors, or employees of High Fliers or localized businesses. I will assert that this is also the case for the labor force in establishments that are new as well as old, and in single-establishment organizations as well as global corporations with networks of offices spanning the planet. The culmination of these individual decisions of employees and employers is the evolving geographical pattern of employment in the New Economy. Today this growth is being shared between urban and rural communities, and within urban areas it is not dominated by excess growth at the top of the old urban hierarchy, but rather is being located in a host of smaller communities where people are exercising their preferences to live.

Agglomerations and Agglomerations!!

In the New Economy, meetings are clearly needed on a face-to-face basis, even as we expand the use of other modes of interaction.[7] Thus, we have agglomerations on a short-term, project-by-project basis between clients and suppliers, which may be just two people together for a short time or possibly for extended and repeated exchanges. Or such meetings may involve teams on both the client and supplier sides, and they could take place in the facilities of either or on some other terrain—at hotels and convention centers, in airport lobbies, at the beach, or in restaurants, and so on. The locational possibilities for these meetings are endless, as are the numbers of people on both the demand and supply sides, and the degree of real-time versus before/after work done by client and supplier.

The simultaneity of these interactions creates the need for institutions to support this work—institutions that are essentially the infrastructure undergirding the production process in the New Economy. They include not only the modes of interaction documented above, but also the spaces needed to feed and house the work force engaged in this production process. Here again the organizational possibilities are numerous and full of contingencies that I will not try to fully develop in this chapter. However, they include for localized firms as well as Lone Eagles and High Fliers, the homes of the labor force where computer-based work related to "the job" is undertaken to a growing extent. And for the Lone Eagles and High Fliers, they include the air travel, document courier, and telephone-based fax, file, Inter- and intranets that zap information around, as well as the associated transportation/housing/eating and drinking/entertainment/garment sectors, and the supports to office work—the Kinkos, the Manpower Americas, the taxicabs and bike couriers, and so on, that directly glue together at the local to the global level this flow of people and the fruits of their work.

The locational preferences for those establishments that are the drivers of business activity in this New Economy—those whose business is traded inter-regionally to constitute the evolving economic base—have produced the bases for the agglomerations of our era. Will these cities wither in the locational freedom implicit for more and more of the players in the New Economy? I do not think so, given the interviews that underpin this chapter. Notwithstanding the rapid growth of rural and smaller metro areas in the 1990s, there are powerful forces helping to maintain the position of the global cities, even if their relative position may be somewhat diminished (Lindahl, 1997). Daniels has recently spoken to these forces in the context of the growth and development of new centers of producer services in Asia—a vision developed before the current crises in Asian economies (Daniels). It is my view that most businesses in the New Economy will still select urban locations, and forecasts of change in the American economy anticipates these sectors will be the leading agents in the future development of jobs in these economies (U.S. Dept. of Labor, 1996). Yet a fraction of those involved in this evolving system *can* put down their roots outside major cities, and are doing so, given our survey evidence and secondary data. So the trend would appear to be this: greater locational freedom for establishments and firms in the New Economy, but the selection for most enterprises of an urban setting while a growing undercurrent of businesses seek out sites in exurban locations. The consequences of these leading agents' locational choices structure, to a growing extent, the production systems that are supported by them—the balance of the settlement system.

The Contingent Impact of Traditional Sectors

The leading New Economy sectors produce demands on the balance of the industrial system. We have traditionally viewed these sectors through a lens of input-output relationships of the indirect and induced effects mode. However, Michael Storper has recently produced an extended vision of the role of such impacts and relationships that describes them in broader terms, which recognizes the importance of the capacities inherent in these support sectors to create regional advantage, to create side effects or forces similar to economic advantages as classically associated with the cost impacts produced by agglomeration economies (Storper, 1997).

I would argue that the localized firms in the producer services are a key part of this system of untraded interdependencies in the New Economy. In contrast to the Lone Eagles and High Fliers, who have considerable flexibility in their location, these enterprises are embedded in their community for their markets. *However, they and the export-oriented segments of the New Economy go on to support an array of other players, who are the* real *creators of agglomerations and the hierarchy of settlements.* They supply the input factors, directly and indirectly, to the production system focused on enterprises in the New Economy, producing everything from paper to energy. Simultaneously, workers in sectors directly involved in the New Economy and supported by those linked to it in the public and private sectors, spend income and induce the creation of output in other sectors. In regions where this demand is unbalanced and leads to new capital outlays, there is an accelerator effect related to these demands.

If this scenario sounds old-fashioned, it is.

I argue that the economic geography driving the current development of the New Economy is structured just as it was in earlier eras where the key agents of development were goods. The structural logic has not changed, but the industries driving the economic system have changed, and there is evolution in the mix of supporting sectors. The way in which players in the New Economy work with each other has changed from the way in which players in the old economy did their work: they talk, meet, and communicate in a much more spatially-extensive network. Castells's space of Flows is occurring, but it is occurring with many people, not just bits and managerial elites. It is not just occurring for a few, but for a growing cohort of workers in advanced and advancing economies. As we find ways to economize on the production of knowledge in this evolving melange of information needs, we create new reasons for expanding the milieu within which we produce and consume it. What has changed is where people can position themselves in this industrial system as workers and entrepreneurs. To a growing extent they are defining its geography around noncost or noneconomic factors, and for the most unstandardized components of the New Economy, which have significant market power, there is little reason to expect these flexibilities to diminish.

We need to spend more time figuring out how production is taking place in this New Economy, in this new space of flows and timeless time to use Castells's terms, but also we need to figure out how this emerging system plays out in localities. In this chapter I have provided modest evidence that speaks to some of these factors surrounding growth and development of cities in this age of telecommunications.

178

ACKNOWLEDGMENTS

The support of the National Science Foundation for the measurement of some of the data presented in this chatper is gratefully acknowledged, through grant number SES–9224515, and the U.S. Economic Research Service, through cooperative study agreement number 43–3AEN–3090149. The comments of Peter B. Nelson and Jeffrey Garneau, graduate students in geography at the University of Washington, on drafts of this chapter are also acknowledged, as are those of Professor J. W. Harrington.

NOTES

1. The term Lone Eagle was coined by Phil Burgess, president of the Center for the New West in reference to telecommunications-related proprietors. See their Web site at *http://www.newwest.org*.

2. The balance of the employment growth was due to increased exports of manufactured goods and primary products.

3. We have recently estimated the weighted percentage of traded service sales to be about 55 percent; a simple average yields a lower estimate (about 35 percent). There are complex issues surrounding sampling and weighting related to refinement of these percentages, which should be regarded as bounding the likely level of trade in producer services from a metropolitan or a rural regional economy.

4. Our analysis finds growth rates over the 1985 to 1993 time period of 13 percent in core metro counties with populations over one million; but growth over 20 percent in smaller metro areas.

5. This percentage is the same as found for the Lone Eagle/High Flier sample for 1988 referred to in Table 3.1 and is slightly below the proportion of Lone Eagles and High Fliers in the overall sample (40 percent). The differing percentages are related to the fact that some establishments did not report 1988 sales patterns, but did supply these data for 1993, so the sample sizes and compositions vary somewhat between the overall sample and the sample used to calculate changes in market location reported above.

6. See *http://www.air-transport.org/data/execsum.html*.

7. See *The New York Times Magazine*, March 8, 1998, for an interesting profile of the "business class."

REFERENCES

Bell, D. (1973). *The Coming of the Post-Industrial Society.* New York: Basic Books.

Beyers, W. (1991). "Trends in the Producer Services in the U.S.: The Last Decade." In P. W. Daniels, ed. *Services and Metropolitan Development: International Perspectives.* London: Routledge, 146–172.

Beyers, W. and D. Lindahl. (1996a). "Explaining the Demand for Producer Services: Is Cost-Driven Externalization The Major Force." *Papers in Regional Science* Vol. 75: 351–74.

———. (1996b). "Lone Eagles and High Fliers in the Rural Producer Services," *Rural Development Perspectives* Vol. 11, No. 3: 2–10.

———. (1997). "Strategic Behavior and Development Sequences in Producer Service Businesses." *Environment and Planning* A Vol. 29: 887–912.

———. (1998). "Services and the New Economic Landscape." A paper for the 1998 European Regional Science Meetings, Vienna.

———. (forthcoming). Book manuscript in process for Guilford Press; tentatively entitled *Information Merchants: Leaders in the New Economy.*

Browning, H. and J. Singelmann. (1975). *The Emergence of a Service Society: Demographic and Sociological Aspects of the Sectoral Transformation of the Labor Force of the U.S.A.* Springfield, VA: National Technical Information Service.

Bureau of Economic Analysis. (monthly). *Survey of Current Business.*

Carnevalle A. and S. Rose. (1998). *Education for What? The New Office Economy.* Washington DC: Educational Testing Service.

Castells, M. (1996). *The Information Age: Economy, Society and Culture. Volume I The Rise of the Network Society.* Malden, MA: Blackwell.

Cromartie, J. and M. Nord. (1996). "Migration and Economic Restructuring in Nonmetro America, 1989–1994." *Economic Research Service Staff Paper* No. 9615.

Daniels, P. (1998). "Producer Services and the Asia-Pacific Region in a Global Context." *Asia Pacific Viewpoint* Vol. 39: 145–159.

Fuguitt, G. and C. Beale (1996). "Recent Trends in Nonmetropolitan Migration: Toward a New Turnaround?" *Growth and Change* Vol. 27: 156–174.

Garreau, J. (1992). *Edge City: Life on The New Frontier.* New York: Anchor Books.

Gottmann, J. (1983). *The Coming of the Transactional City.* College Park, MD: University of Maryland Institute for Urban Studies.

Harmon, R. L. (1996). *Reinventing the Business. Preparing Today's Enterprise for Tomorrow's Technology.* New York: The Free Press.

Janelle, D. (1969). "Spatial Reorganization: A Model and A Concept." *Annals of the Association of American Geographers* Vol. 59: 348–364.

Lindahl, D. (1997). *New Frontiers of Capital, A Geography of Commercial Real Estate Finance.* Unpublished doctoral dissertation, University of Washington.

Lindahl, D. and W. Beyers. (1999). "The Creation of Competitive Advantage by Producer Service Establishments." *Economic Geography.*

Markusen, A. (1996). "Sticky Places in Slippery Space: A Typology of Industrial Districts." *Economic Geography* Vol. 72: 293–313.

———. (1998). "Fuzzy Concepts, Scanty Evidence, Wimpy Policy: The Case for Rigor and Policy Relevance in Critical Regional Studies." Paper presented at the Association of American Geographers Annual Meeting, Boston, MA.

Noyelle, T. and T. M. Stanbach. (1984). *The Economic Transformation of American Cities.* Totowa, NJ: Roman and Allanheld.

Rasker. R. and D. Glick. (1994). "Footloose Entrepreneurs: Pioneers of the New West?" *Illahee* Vol. 10: 34–43.

Reich, R. (1992). *The Work of Nations.* New York: Random House.

Rifkin, J. (1995). *The End of Work. The Decline of the Global Labor Force and the Dawn of the Post-Market Era.* New York: G. P. Putnam's Sons.

Storper, M. (1997). *The Regional World. Territorial Development in a Global Economy.* New York: Guilford Press.

Tapscott, D. (1996). *The Digital Economy. Promise and Peril in the Age of Networked Intelligence.* New York: McGraw-Hill.

Thurow, L. (1996). *The Future of Capitalism. How Today's Economic Forces Shape Tomorrow's World.* New York: William Morrow & Co.

U.S. Department of Labor (1996). *Outlook 2005.*

THE TELECOMMUNICATIONS REVOLUTION AND THE GEOGRAPHY OF INNOVATION

David B. Audretsch and Maryann P. Feldman

INTRODUCTION

The telecommunications revolution has triggered a spatial revolution in terms of the geography of economic activity. In particular, the telecommunications revolution has rendered the marginal cost of transmitting information across geographic space to virtually zero. As a result, many policy-makers expect that the importance of geography and local proximity is being diminished. For example, *The Economist* recently declared: "The death of distance as a determinant of the cost of communications will probably be the single most economic force shaping society in the first half of the next century. It will alter, in ways that are only dimly imaginable, decisions about where people live and work; concepts of national borders; patterns of international trade. The death of distance will mean that any activity that relies on a screen or a telephone can be carried out anywhere in the world."[1]

While the telecommunications revolution may have triggered "the death of distance," for much of economic activity, innovative activity has become less associated with footloose multinational corporations and more associated with high-tech innovative regional clusters, such as Silicon Valley, Research Triangle, and Route 128. Only a few years ago, the conventional wisdom predicted that globalization would cause the demise of the region as a meaningful unit of economic analysis. Yet the obsession of policy-makers around the globe to "create the next Silicon Valley" reveals the increased importance of geographic proximity and regional agglomerations. The purpose of this article is to explain why and how geography matters for innovative activity, even as telecommunications has revolutionized the economics of spatial relationships.[2]

KNOWLEDGE SPILLOVERS

In the most prevalent model found in the literature of technological change, the model of the *knowledge production function* (Griliches, 1979), firms exist exogenously and then engage in the pursuit of new economic knowledge as an input into the process of generating innovative activity. The most decisive input in the knowledge production function is new economic knowledge. The greatest source generating new economic knowledge is generally considered to be R&D.

The recent wave of studies revealing small enterprises to be the engine of innovative activity in certain industries, despite an obvious lack of formal R&D activities, raises the question: *Where do new and small firms get the innovation producing inputs, that is the knowledge?* The answer proposed by Audretsch (1995) is: from other, third-party firms or research institutions such as universities. Economic knowledge may *spill over* from the firm or research institution creating it for application by other firms.

That knowledge spills over is barely disputed (Wheeler and Mitchelson, 1991). However, the geographic range of such knowledge spillovers is greatly contested. In disputing the importance of knowledge externalities in explaining the geographic concentration of economic activity, Krugman (1991a) and others do not question the existence or importance of such knowledge spillovers.[3] In fact, they argue that such knowledge externalities are so important and forceful that there is no compelling reason for a geographic boundary to limit the spatial extent of the spillover. According to this line of thinking, the concern is not that knowledge does not spill over but that it should stop spilling over, just because it hits a geographic border, such as a city limit, state line, or national boundary.

A recent body of empirical evidence clearly suggests that R&D and other sources of knowledge generate externalities, but studies by Audretsch and Feldman (1996), Jaffe (1989), Audretsch and Stephan (1996), Feldman (1994a and 1994b), and Jaffe, Trajtenberg, and Henderson (1993) suggest that such knowledge spillovers tend to be geographically bounded within the region where the new economic knowledge was created. That is, new economic knowledge may spill over, but the geographic extent of such knowledge spillovers is limited.

EVIDENCE FROM STATE-LEVEL DATA

Krugman (1991a, page 53) has argued that economists should abandon any attempts at measuring knowledge spillovers because ". . . knowledge flows are invisible, they leave no paper trail by which they may be measured and tracked." But as Jaffe, Trajtenberg, and Henderson (1993, page 578) point out, "knowledge flows do sometimes leave a paper trail"—in particular in the form of patented inventions and new product introductions.

In this chapter we rely upon a direct measure of innovative output, rather than on a measure of intermediate output such as patented inventions. The United States Small Business Administration's Innovation Data Base (SBIDB) is the primary source of data for this article. The database consists of new product introductions compiled from the new product announcement sections of more than one hundred technology, engineering, and trade journals spanning every industry in manufacturing. From the sections in each trade journal listing innovations and new products, a database consisting of the innovations by four-digit standard industrial classification (SIC) industries was formed. An innovation is defined in the database as "a process that begins with an invention, proceeds with the development of the invention, and results in introduction of a new product, process or service to the marketplace" (Edwards and Gordon, 1984, page 1). These innovation data have been implemented by Audretsch (1995) to analyze the relationship between industry dynamics and technological change.

There are several important qualifications that should be made concerning the SBIDB. The trade journals report relatively few process, service, and management innovations and tend to capture mainly product innovations. The most likely effect of this bias is to underestimate the number of innovations emanating from large firms, since larger enterprises tend to produce more process innovations than do their smaller counterparts. However, because it was found that the large-firm innovations are more likely to be reported in the trade journals than are small-firm innovations, the biases are perhaps somewhat offsetting.

Another potential concern might be that the significance and "quality" of the innovations vary considerably. In fact, each innovation was classified according to one of the following levels of significance: (1) the innovation established an entirely new category of product; (2) the innovation is the first of its type on the market in a product category already in existence; (3) the innovation represents a significant improvement in existing technology; and (4) the innovation is a modest improvement designed to update an existing product. Audretsch (1995) shows that about 87 percent of the innovations were in this fourth category, and most of the remaining innovations were classified in the third category.

An important strength of the database is that the innovating *establishment* is identified as well as the innovating *enterprise*. While this distinction is trivial for single-plant manufacturing firms, it becomes important in multiplant firms. This is because some innovations are made by subsidiaries or divisions of companies with headquarters in other states. Even though the headquarters may announce new product innovations made by the company, the database still identifies the individual establishment actually making the innovation.

Table 12.1 indicates that California is the state in which the greatest number of innovations was registered, followed by New York, New Jersey, and Massachusetts. A particularly striking feature shown in Table 12.1 is that the bulk of innovative activity in the United States occurs on the coasts, and especially in California and in New England. By contrast, no innovative activity is registered in certain Midwestern states such as North Dakota, South Dakota, and Wyoming. Of course, simply comparing the absolute amount of innovative activity across states ignores the fact that the manufacturing base of some states is larger than others. Thus the number of innovations generated per billions of dollars of value-added in manufacturing is also compared in order to control for the size of the geographic region. After controlling for the size of the manufacturing base, Massachusetts emerges as the most innovative state, registering more than twenty-two innovations per billion dollars of value-added, while New Jersey is the second most innovative state, with more than eighteen innovations per billion dollars of value-added. Even after controlling for the size of

Table 12.1 Innovative Activity in States

State	Number of Innovations	Value-Added ($ millions)	Innovations per Value-Added ($ billions)
Massachusetts	360	16,349	22.02
New Jersey	426	22,853	18.64
California	974	54,862	17.75
New Hampshire	33	2,175	15.17
Arizona	41	3,333	12.30
Connecticut	132	10,934	12.07
Minnesota	110	9,605	11.45
New York	456	44,290	10.30
Delaware	15	1,596	9.40
Colorado	42	4,472	9.39
Rhode Island	24	2,7373	8.77
United States	4,200	585,166	7.18
Florida	66	9,255	7.13
Pennsylvania	245	36,017	6.80
Illinois	231	40,279	5.73
Vermont	6	1,050	5.71
Washington	48	8,955	5.36
Oregon	32	6,138	5.21
Wisconsin	86	16,606	5.18
Texas	169	33,150	5.10
Ohio	188	43,055	4.37
Oklahoma	20	4,662	4.29
Georgia	53	12,549	4.22
Idaho	6	1,430	4.20
New Mexico	3	734	4.09
Maryland	28	7,116	3.93
Virginia	38	10,882	3.49
Utah	11	3,333	3.30
D.C.	2	610	3.28
Nebraska	9	2,867	3.14
Michigan	112	37,566	2.98
Kansas	15	5,338	2.81
Missouri	36	13,042	2.76
Iowa	20	8,684	2.30
South Carolina	18	8,186	2.20
Indiana	49	22,718	2.16
North Carolina	38	18,231	2.08
Nevada	1	495	2.02
Maine	4	2,343	1.71
Tennessee	20	12,663	1.58
Hawaii	1	786	1.27
West Virginia	4	3,880	1.03
Arkansas	5	4,882	1.02
Kentucky	9	9,546	0.94
Mississippi	4	5,619	0.71
Alabama	5	8,406	0.59
Louisiana	5	9,418	0.53

the geographic region, the result is that the bulk of the innovative activity in the United States occurs on the coasts and not in the Midwest.

While Table 12.1 indicates the geographic distribution of innovative activity in the United States, it obscures the propensity for innovative activity to spatially cluster by aggregating innovative activity across all industries. Thus the distribution of innovative activity for the seven most innovative four-digit SIC industries is shown in Table 12.2. A striking result is that the spatial concentration of innovative activity in particular industries is considerably greater than for all of manufacturing. For example, in the computer industry, 342 of the 821 innovations recorded, or 41.7 percent, are in California. And an additional almost 10 percent are recorded in Massachusetts. Thus, two states alone account for more than one half of all of the innovations in the computer industry. At the same time, the last column indicates that innovations in the computer industry accounted for slightly more than one third of all of the innovations in California and a little more than one fifth of all innovations in Massachusetts.

Similarly, nearly 40 percent of the 127 innovations in the drug industry (pharmaceuticals) were recorded in New Jersey, while an additional 14 percent were made in New York. Thus more than one half of pharmaceutical innovations were recorded in the New Jersey-New York area. At the same time, pharmaceutical innovations accounted for more than one tenth of all innovations registered in New Jersey.

Studies identifying the extent of knowledge spillovers are based on the knowledge production function. As introduced by Zvi Griliches (1979), the knowledge production function links inputs in the innovation process to innovative outputs. Griliches pointed out that the most decisive innovative input is new economic knowledge, and the greatest source that generates new economic knowledge is generally considered to be R&D. Jaffe (1989), Audretsch and Feldman (1996), and Feldman (1994a and 1994b) modified the knowledge production function approach to a model specified for spatial and product dimensions:

$$I_{si} = IRD^{\beta 1} \cdot UR_{si}^{\beta 1} \cdot (UR_{si} \cdot GC_{si}^{\beta 3}) \cdot \mathcal{E}_{si} \qquad \text{Eq. 12.1}$$

where I is innovative output, IRD is private corporate expenditures on R&D, UR is the research expenditures undertaken at universities, and GC measures the geographic coincidence of university and corporate research. The unit of observation for estimation was at the spatial level, s, a state, and industry level, i. Estimation of equation 12.1 essentially shifted the knowledge production function from the unit of observation of a firm to that of a geographic unit.

INNOVATIVE CLUSTERS

While there is considerable evidence supporting the existence of knowledge spillovers, neither Jaffe (1989), Jaffe, Trajtenberg, and Henderson (1993), nor Feldman (1994a and 1994b) actually examined the propensity for innovative

Table 12.2 Geographic Distribution of Innovative Activity for Most Innovative Industries

SIC	Industry	State	Number of Innovations	State Share of Industry Innovations	Industry Share of State Innovations
3573	Computers (n = 821)	California	342	41.7	35.1
		Massachusetts	78	9.5	21.7
		New York	58	7.1	12.7
		Texas	39	4.8	23.1
		New Jersey	38	4.6	8.9
		Illinois	28	3.4	12.1
3823	Process Control Instruments (n = 464)	California	80	17.2	8.2
		Massachusetts	61	13.1	16.9
		New York	45	9.7	9.9
		Pennsylvania	40	8.6	16.5
		Illinois	32	6.9	13.9
3662	Radio and TV Communication Equipment (n = 339)	California	105	31.0	10.8
		New York	40	11.8	8.8
		Massachusetts	32	9.4	8.9
3674	Semiconductors (n = 172)	California	84	48.8	8.6
		Massachusetts	17	9.9	4.7
		Texas	13	7.6	7.7
3842	Surgical Appliances (n = 152)	New Jersey	43	28.3	10.1
		California	17	I 1.2	1.7
		Pennsylvania	10	7.9	4.1
2834.	Pharmaceuticals (n = 127)	New Jersey	50	39.4	11.7
		New York	18	14.2	3.9
		Pennsylvania	10	7.9	4.1
		Michigan	8	6.3	7.1
3825	Measuring instruments for Electricity (n = 115)	California	37	32.2	3.8
		Massachusetts	22	19.1	16.9
		New York	13	11.3	2.9

Source: Feldman (1994).

activity to cluster spatially. But implicitly contained within the knowledge production function model is the assumption that innovative activity should take place in those regions, s, where the direct knowledge-generating inputs are the greatest, and where knowledge spillovers are the most prevalent. In our 1996a paper, we link the propensity for innovative activity to cluster together to industry-specific characteristics, most notably the relative importance of knowledge spillovers.

To measure the extent to which innovative activity in a specific four-digit SIC (standard industrial classification) industry is concentrated within a geographic region, we follow Paul Krugman's (1991b) example and calculate gini coefficients for the geographic concentration of innovative activity. The gini coefficients are weighted by the relative share of economic activity located in each state. Computation of weighted gini coefficients enables us to control for size differences across states. The gini coefficients are based on the share of activity in a state and industry relative to the state share of the national activity for the industry. Cases in which state or industry data have been suppressed have been omitted from the analysis. Table 12.3 ranks the gini coefficients of the number of innovations across the forty-eight continental states (excluding Hawaii and Alaska) for those four-digit SIC industries exhibiting the highest propensity to cluster spatially, as well as the corresponding values of the gini coefficients based on manufacturing value-added and employment. Thus innovative activity in the electronic components industry tended to be the most geographically concentrated, followed closely by switchgear apparatus and telephones.

Of course, as Jaffe, Trajtenberg, and Henderson (1993) point out, one obvious explanation of why innovative activity in some industries tends to cluster geographically more than in other industries is that the location of production is more concentrated spatially. Thus in explaining why the propensity for innovative activity to cluster geographically varies across industries, we need first to explain, and then control for, the geographic concentration of the location of production. Corresponding gini coefficients for the location of manufacturing (value-added) are also included in Table 12.3.

There are three important tendencies emerging in Table 12.3. First, there is no obvious simple relationship between the gini coefficients for production and innovation. Second, the gini coefficient of the number of innovations exceeds that of value-added and employment in those industries exhibiting the greatest propensity for innovative activity to cluster spatially. By contrast, the gini coefficients of innovative activity for most industries is less than that for value-added and employment.

Third, those industries exhibiting the greatest propensity for innovative activity to cluster are high-technology industries. There are, however, several notable exceptions. For example, in motor vehicle bodies, which is certainly not considered to be a high-technology industry, the geographic concentration of production of innovative activity is the seventh greatest in Table 12.3. One reason may be the high degree of geographic concentration of production, as evidenced by gini coefficients for value-added (0.9241) and employment (0.8089) that actually exceed that of innovative activity (0.6923). This points to the importance of controlling for the geographic concentration of production in explaining the propensity for innovative activity to cluster spatially. And finally, the gini coefficient for value-added exceeds that for employment in virtually every industry.

In our 1996 paper we measure three different types of new economic knowledge—industry R&D, university R&D, and skilled labor. A key assumption we make in examining the link between knowledge spillovers in an industry and the propensity for innovative activity to cluster is that knowledge externalities are more prevalent in industries where new economic knowledge plays a greater role.

One obvious complication in testing for this link is that innovative activity will be more geographically concentrated in industries where production is also geographically concentrated, simply because the bulk of firms are located

Table 12.3 Geographic Concentration of Production for Industries with Highest Propensity for Innovative Activity to Cluster

		Gini Coefficients		
		Innovation	Value-Added	Employment
3679	Electronic Components	0.7740	0.5889	0.5854
3613	Switchboard Apparatus	0.7420	0.7791	0.4951
3661	Telephones	0.7242	0.7576	0.6076
3621	Motors & Generators	0.7143	0.6480	0.4468
2511	Wood Household Furniture	0.7085	0.6288	0.5588
3711	Motor Vehicle Bodies	0.6923	0.9241	0.8089
2834	Pharmaceuticals	0.6916	0.7816	0.6771
3537	Industrial Trucks	0.6862	0.6384	0.4459
2824	Organic Fibers	0.6856	0.7617	0.7086
3612	Transformers	0.6376	0.7362	0.3841
2641	Paper Coating	0.6374	0.6023	0.3847
3563	Air & Gas Compressors	0.6349	0.6010	0.3937
3824	Fluid Meters & Devices	0.6295	0.7463	0.5463
3648	Lighting Equipment	0.6282	0.5828	0.6793
3576	Scales & Balances	0.6256	0.6591	0.6950
2038	Frozen Specialties	0.6231	0.6236	0.7076
3822	Environmental Controls	0.5904	0.7447	0.4423
2751	Commercial Printing	0.5822	0.5585	0.5621
2821	Plastics Materials & Resins	0.5792	0.8368	0.7645
3569	General Industrial Machines	0.5736	0.4869	0.6446
3494	Valves & Pipe Fitting	0.5685	0.4831	0.5062
2522	Metal Office Furniture	0.5569	0.6993	0.7785
2648	Stationery products	0.5443	0.6829	0.5712
2851	Paints	0.5434	0.5433	0.3414
3469	Metal Stampings	0.5431	0.5970	0.4238
3356	Nonferrous Rolling & Drawing	0.5420	0.6661	0.7281
2086	Bottled & Canned Soft Drinks	0.5385	0.6454	0.6465
3535	Conveyors & Related Equipment	0.5366	0.5727	0.5702
3583	Refrigeration Equipment	0.5363	0.5928	0.5941
2521	Wood Office Furniture	0.5347	0.7641	0.4293
3728	Aircraft Equipment	0.5333	0.8654	0.7384
3629	Electrical Apparatus	0.5328	0.5712	0.6708
3442	Metal Doors	0.5318	0.3131	0.2653
2542	Metal Partitions	0.5309	0.3576	0.3636
3799	Transportation Equipment	0.5290	0.6417	0.5419
3732	Boat Building	0.5268	0.7241	0.5252
3552	Textile Machinery	0.5219	0.7217	0.5769
2992	Lubricating Oils	0.5196	0.8637	0.5495
3589	Service Industry Machinery	0.5107	0.6376	0.7307
3079	Plastics Product	0.5107	0.4298	0.3703
2865	Cyclic Crudes & Intermediates	0.5041	0.8355	0.8256
3069	Fabricated Rubber Products	0.5012	0.6910	0.6472
3851	Ophthalmic Goods	0.5004	0.8221	0.5660
3499	Fabricated Metal Products	0.4902	0.4426	0.4070
3549	Metalworking Machines	0.4893	0.5834	0.6148
2034	Dehydrated Fruits	0.4878	0.8282	0.7784
3312	Blast Furnaces	0.4848	0.8167	0.7032
3559	Special Industry Machinery	0.4770	0.4873	0.6147
3647	Semiconductors/related	0.4731	0.8527	0.7134

Source: Audretsch & Feldman (1996a).

within close proximity. Even more problematic, though, is the hypothesis that new economic knowledge will tend to shape the spatial distribution of production as well as that of innovation. Indeed, we found that a key determinant of the extent to which the location of production is geographically concentrated is the relative importance of new economic knowledge in the industry. But even after controlling for the geographic concentration of production, the results suggest that industries in which knowledge spillovers are more pervasive—that is where industry R&D, university research, and skilled labor are the most important—have a greater propensity for innovative activity to cluster than industries where knowledge externalities are less important.

A growing literature suggests that *who* innovates and *how much* innovative activity is undertaken are closely linked to the phase of the industry life cycle. In our 1996b paper we suggest an additional key aspect to the evolution of innovative activity over the industry life cycle—*where* that innovative activity takes place. The theory of knowledge spillovers, derived from the knowledge production function, suggests that the propensity for innovative activity to cluster spatially will tend to be the greatest in industries where *tacit knowledge* plays an important role, because tacit knowledge, as opposed to *information*, can be transmitted only informally and typically demands direct and repeated contact. The role of tacit knowledge in generating innovative activity is presumably the greatest during the early stages of the industry life cycle, before product standards have been established and before a dominant design has emerged.

The stage of an industry life cycle has been typically measured by tracking the evolution of an industry starting with its incipiency, based on a wave of product innovations. But the measures, documented in the previous section, of geographic concentration and dispersion, for both innovation and the location of production, are available for only one point of time. That is, these measures provide a snapshot at a single point in time for each industry. Thus the life cycle stage of each industry at this point in time needs to be measured. More specifically, industries that are highly innovative and where that innovative activity tends to come from small firms are better characterized as being in the introduction stage of the life cycle. Industries that are highly innovative and where the large firms tend to generate that innovative activity are better characterized by the growth stage of the life cycle. Industries that have low innovation and where large firms have a higher propensity to innovate are better characterized by the mature stage of the life cycle. And finally, industries that have low innovation and where small firms have a higher propensity to innovate are best characterized by the declining stage of the life cycle. The higher propensity to innovate of small enterprises vis-à-vis their larger counterparts may reflect the seeds of the introductory phase of the life cycle of new products emerging in what would otherwise be a declining industry.

This framework was used to classify 210 four-digit SIC industries into these four stages of the life cycle. Highly innovative industries were rather arbitrarily defined as those industries exhibiting innovative activity in excess of the mean. Industries of low innovation were similarly defined as those industries with innovation rates less than the mean. The innovation rate is defined as the number of innovations divided by the number of employees in the industry (measured in thousands). The innovation rate is used, rather than the absolute number of innovations, in order to control for the size of the industry. That is, if two industries exhibit the same number of innovations but one industry is twice as large as the other, it will have an innovation rate one half as large as the other industry. To measure the relative innovative advantage of large and small firms, the small-firm innovation rate is compared to the large-firm innovation rate, where the small-firm innovation rate is defined as the number of innovations made by firms with fewer than five hundred employees divided by small-firm employment, and the large-firm innovation rate is defined as the number of innovations made by firms with at least five hundred employees divided by large-firm employment.

Using this classification system, sixty-two of the industries were classified as being in the introductory stage of the life cycle (defined as highly innovative with the small firms having the innovative advantage), thirty-two industries were classified as being in the growth stage of the life cycle (defined as highly innovative with the large firms having the innovative advantage), sixty-four industries were defined in the mature stage of the life cycle (defined as of low innovation with the large firms having the innovative advantage), and fifty-two were defined in the declining stage of the life cycle (defined as of low innovation with the small firms having the innovative advantage).

The results provide considerable evidence suggesting that the propensity for innovative activity to cluster spatially is shaped by the stage of the industry life cycle. On the one hand, new economic knowledge embodied in skilled workers tends to raise the propensity for innovative activity to cluster spatially throughout all phases of the industry life cycle. On the other hand, certain other sources of new economic knowledge, such as university research, tend to elevate the propensity for innovative activity to cluster during the introduction stage of the life cycle but not during the growth stage, but then again during the stage of decline.

Perhaps most striking is the finding that greater geographic concentration of production actually leads to more, and not less, dispersion of innovative activity. Apparently innovative activity is promoted by knowledge spillovers that occur within a distinct geographic region, particularly in the early stages of the industry life cycle, but as the industry evolves toward maturity and decline, may be dispersed by additional increases in concentration of production that have been built up within that same region. That is, the evidence suggests that what may serve as an *agglomerating influence* in triggering innovative activity to cluster spatially during the introduction and growth stages of the industry life cycle, may later result in a *congestion effect*, leading to greater dispersion in innovative activity. In any case, the results of this chapter suggest that the propensity for an innovative cluster to cluster spatially is certainly shaped by the stage of the industry life cycle.

Despite the general consensus that has now emerged in the literature that knowledge spillovers within a given location stimulate technological advance, there is little consensus as to exactly how this occurs. The contribution of the knowledge production function approach was simply to shift the unit of observation away from firms to a geographic region. But does it make a difference how economic activity is organized within the black box of geographic space? Political scientists and sociologists have long argued that the differences in the culture of a region may contribute to differences in innovative performance across regions, even holding knowledge inputs such as R&D and human capital constant. For example, Saxenian (1994) argues that a culture of greater interdependence and exchange among individuals in the Silicon Valley region has contributed to a superior innovative performance than is found around Boston's Route 128, where firms and individuals tend to be more isolated and less interdependent. Castells (1996) argues that such regional networks are a key source driving innovative activity

In studying the networks in California's Silicon Valley, Saxenian (1990, pages 96–97) emphasizes that it is the communication between individuals that facilitates the transmission of knowledge across agents, firms, and even industries, and not just a high endowment of human capital and knowledge in the region:

> It is not simply the concentration of skilled labor, suppliers and information that distinguish the region. A variety of regional institutions — including Stanford University, several trade associations and local business organizations, and a myriad of specialized consulting, market research, public relations and venture capital firms — provide technical, financial, and networking services which the region's enterprises often cannot afford individually. These networks defy sectoral barriers: individuals move easily from semiconductor to disk drive firms or from computer to network makers. They move from established firms to startups (or vice versa) and even to market research or consulting firms, and from consulting firms back into startups. And they continue to meet at trade shows, industry conferences, and the scores of seminars, talks and social activities organized by local business organizations and trade associations. In these forums, relationships are easily formed and maintained, technical and market information is exchanged, business contacts are established, and new enterprises are conceived. . . . This decentralized and fluid environment also promotes the diffusion of intangible technological capabilities and understandings.[4]

While many social scientists tend to avoid attributing differences in economic performance to cultural differences (Castells and Hall, 1994), there has been a series of theoretical arguments suggesting that differences in the underlying structure between regions may account for differences in rates of growth and technological change. In fact, a heated debate has emerged in the literature about the manner in which the underlying economic structure within a geographic unit of observation might effect economic performance. One view, which Glaeser, Kallal, Scheinkman, and Shleifer (1992) attribute to the *Marshall-Arrow-Romer* externality, suggests that an increased concentration of a particular industry within a specific geographic region facilitates knowledge spillovers across firms. This model formalizes the insight that the concentration of an industry within a city promotes knowledge spillovers between firms and therefore facilitates innovative activity. An important assumption of the model is that knowledge externalities with respect to firms exist, but only for firms within the same industry. Thus the relevant unit of observation is extended from the firm to the region in the tradition of the Marshall-Arrow-Romer model, and in subsequent empirical studies, but spillovers are limited to occurring within the relevant industry.

By contrast, restricting knowledge externalities to those occurring only within the industry may ignore an important source of new economic knowledge—interindustry knowledge spillovers. Jacobs (1969) argues that the most important source of knowledge spillovers is external to the industry in which the firm operates and that cities are the source of considerable innovation because the diversity of these knowledge sources is greatest in cities. According to Jacobs, it is the exchange of complementary knowledge across diverse firms and economic agents that yields a greater return on new economic knowledge. She develops a theory that emphasizes that the variety of industries within a geographic region promotes knowledge externalities and ultimately, innovative activity and economic growth.

The extent of regional specialization versus regional diversity in promoting knowledge spillovers is not the only dimension over which there has been a theoretical debate. A second controversy involves the degree of competition prevalent in the region, or the extent of local monopoly. The Marshall-Arrow-Romer model predicts that local monopoly is superior to local competition because it maximizes the ability of firms to appropriate the economic value accruing from their innovative activity. By contrast, Jacobs (1969) and Porter (1990) argue that competition is more conducive to knowledge externalities than is local monopoly.[5] It should be emphasized that by local competition Jacobs does not mean competition within product markets, as has traditionally been envisioned within the industrial organization literature. Rather, Jacobs is referring to the competition for the new ideas embodied in economic agents. Not only does an increased number of firms provide greater competition for new ideas, but in addition, greater competition across firms facilitates the entry of a new firm specializing in some particular and new product niche. This is because the necessary complementary inputs and services are likely to be available from small, specialist, niche firms but not necessarily from large, vertically integrated producers.

The first important test of the specialization versus diversity theories to date has focused not on the gains in terms of innovative activity, but rather in terms of employment growth. Glaeser, Kallal, Scheinkman, and Schleifer (1992) employ a data set on the growth of large industries in 170 cities between 1956 and 1987 in order to identify the relative importance of the degree of regional specialization, diversity, and local competition in influencing industry growth rates. The authors find evidence that contradicts the Marshall-Arrow-Romer model but is consistent with the theories of Jacobs. However, their study provides no direct evidence as to whether diversity is more important than specialization in generating innovation.

Feldman and Audretsch (1999) identify the extent to which the organization of economic activity either is concentrated, or alternatively consists of diverse but complementary economic activities, and how this composition influences innovative output. We ask the question: *Does the specific type of economic activity undertaken within any particular geographic concentration matter?* To consider this question, we link the innovative output of product categories within a specific city to the extent to which the economic activity of that city is concentrated in that industry, or conversely, diversified in terms of complementary industries sharing a common science base.

To identify systematically the degree to which specific industries share a common underlying science and technology base, we rely upon a deductive approach that links products estimated from their closeness in technological space. We use the responses of industrial R&D managers to a survey by Levin, Klevorick, Nelson, and Winter (1987). To measure the significance of a scientific discipline to an industry, the question was asked: "How relevant were the basic sciences to technical progress in this line of business over the past 10 to 15 years?" The survey uses a Likert scale of 1 to 7, from least important to most important, to assess the relevance of basic scientific research in biology, chemistry, computer science, physics, math, medicine, geology, mechanical engineering, and electrical engineering. Any academic discipline with a rating greater than 5 is assumed to be relevant for a product category. For example, basic scientific research in medicine, chemistry and chemical engineering is found to be relevant for product innovation in drugs (SIC 2834).

We then used cluster analysis to identify six groups of industries that rely on similar rankings for the importance of different academic disciplines. These six groups reflect distinct underlying common scientific bases. Table 12.4 lists these six science-based groupings, along with the most important critical underlying scientific disciplines, the mean rating for the importance of that scientific discipline, and the most innovative industries included in the cluster.

It should be emphasized that Table 12.4 identifies innovative groups in terms of clustering around the same underlying scientific bases, but not in terms of geographic space or even product space. For example, there are fifteen distinct industries included in what we term the Biomedical group. On average, each industry contributed 3.22 innovations. Their shared underlying knowledge base consists of chemistry (with a mean ranking on the Likert scale of 5.53), medical science, computer science, and material science. Surgical Appliances (SIC 3842), Surgical and Medical Instruments (SIC 3841), and Pharmaceuticals (SIC 2834) are three of the fifteen industries heavily dependent on this common underlying scientific knowledge base. There are twenty-one industries included in the Agra-Business group, thirty-four industries included in the Chemical Engineering group, seven industries in the Office Machinery group, and eleven industries included in the Industrial Machinery group. The largest science-based group is what we term High-Tech Computing, which includes eighty industries.

Table 12.5 presents the prominent cities within each science-based industrial cluster. Again, the listing of prominent cities recalls the well-known association between cities and industries. For example, Atlanta was a promi-

Table 12.4 The Common Science Bases of Industry Clusters

Cluster	Critical Academic Departments*	Most Innovative Industries
Agro-Business	Chemistry (6.06)	SIC 2013: Sausages
	Agricultural Science (4.65)	SIC 2038: Frozen Specialties
	Computer Science (4.18)	SIC 2087: Flavoring Extracts
	Biology (4.09)	SIC 2092: Packaged Foods
Chemical Engineering	Materials Science (5.32)	SIC 3861: Photographic Equipment
	Chemistry (4.80)	SIC 3443: Fabricated Plate Work
	Computer Science (4.50)	SIC 2821: Plastic Materials
	Physics (4.12)	SIC 3559: Special Ind. Machinery
Office Machinery	Computer Science (6.75)	SIC 3576: Scales and Balances
	Medical Science (5.75)	SIC 3579: Office Machinery
	Math (5.49)	SIC 3535: Conveyors
	Applied Math (4.64)	SIC 2751: Commercial Printing
Industrial Machinery	Materials Science (5.03)	SIC 355I: Food Processing Equipment
	Computer Science (4.76)	SIC 3523: Machinery
	Physics (3.94)	SIC 3546: Hand Tools
	Chemistry (3.88)	SIC 3629: Industrial Apparatus
High-Tech Computing	Materials Science (5.92)	SIC 3573: Computing Machinery
	Computer Science (5.63)	SIC 3662: Radio/TV Equipment
	Physics (5.45)	SIC 3823: Process Control Instruments
	Math (4.76)	SIC 3674: Semiconductors
Biomedical	Chemistry (5.53)	SIC 3842: Surgical Appliances
	Medical Science (5.47)	SIC 3841: Medical Instruments
	Computer Science (5.32)	SIC 2834: Pharmaceuticals
	Materials Science (5.02)	SIC 3811: Scientific Instruments

Source: Feldman & Audretsch (1999).

* The "Critical Academic Department" in Table 12.4 is based on the basic scientific research classifications used in the Levin, et al. (1987) study described above.

nent center for innovation that used the common science base of agra-business. While the national innovation rate was 20.34 innovations per 100,000 manufacturing workers, agra-business in Atlanta was almost five times as innovative. A Chi-Squared test of the independence of location of city and science-based industrial activity reveals that neither the distribution of employment nor the distribution of innovation is random. Industries that rely on a common science base exhibit a tendency to cluster together geographically with regard to the location of employment and the location of innovation. We conclude that the distribution of innovation within science-based clusters and cities appears to reflect the existence of science-related expertise.

To test the hypothesis that the degree of specialization or, alternatively, diversity, as well as the extent of local competition within a city, shapes the innovative output of an industry, we estimate a model where the dependent variable is the number of innovations attributed to a specific four-digit SIC industry in a particular city. To reflect the extent to which economic activity within

Table 12.5 Innovation in Science-Based Industry Clusters

Cluster	Prominent Cities	Mean Industry Innovations per 100,000 workers
Agro-Business	Atlanta	92.40
	Dallas	41.15
	Chicago	33.03
	St. Louis	91.74
Chemical Engineering	Dallas	38.09
	Minneapolis	66.67
	San Francisco	43.89
	Wilmington	85.47
Office Machinery	Anaheim-Santa Ana	92.59
	Minneapolis	31.86
	Rochester	72.20
	Stamford	68.40
Industrial Machinery	Anaheim-Santa Ana	54.95
	Cincinnati	66.01
	Cleveland	141.51
	Passaic, NJ	90.90
High-Tech Computing	Boston	73.89
	Houston	62.08
	San Jose	44.88
	Minneapolis	181.74
Biomedical	Boston	38.71
	Cleveland	68.76
	Dallas	35.22
	New York	188.07

Source: Feldman & Audretsch (1995).

a city is specialized, we include as an explanatory variable a measure of industry specialization that was used by Glaeser, Kallal, Scheinkman, and Shleifer (1992) and is defined as the 1982 share of total employment in the city accounted for by industry employment in the city, divided by the share of United States employment accounted by that particular industry. This variable reflects the degree to which a city is specialized in a particular industry relative to the degree of economic activity in that industry that would occur if employment in the industry were randomly distributed across the United States. A higher value of this measure indicates a greater degree of specialization of the industry in that particular city. Thus a positive coefficient would indicate that increased specialization within a city is conducive to greater innovative output and would support the Marshall-Arrow-Romer thesis. A negative coefficient would indicate that greater specialization within a city impedes innovative output and would support Jacobs's theory that diversity of economic activity is more conducive to innovation than is specialization of economic activity.

To identify the impact of an increased presence of economic activity in complementary industries sharing a common science base on the innovative activity of a particular industry within a specific city, a measure of the presence of science-based related industries is included. This measure is constructed analogously to the index of industry specialization, and is defined as the share of total city employment accounted for by employment in the city in industries sharing the science base, divided by the share of total United States employment accounted for by employment in that same science base. This variable measures the presence of complementary industries relative to what the presence would be if those related industries were distributed across the United States. A positive coefficient of the presence of science-based related industries would indicate that a greater presence of complementary industries is conducive to greater innovative output and would lend support for the diversity thesis. By contrast, a negative coefficient would suggest that a greater presence of related industries sharing the same science base impedes innovation and would argue against Jacobs's diversity thesis.

The usual concept of product market competition in the industrial organization literature is typically measured in terms of the size-distribution of firms. By contrast, Jacobs's concept of *localized competition* emphasizes instead the extent of competition for the ideas embodied in individuals. The greater the degree of competition among firms, the greater will be the extent of specialization among those firms and the easier it will be for individuals to pursue and implement new ideas. Thus the metric relevant to reflect the degree of localized competition is not the size of the firms in the region relative to their number (because, after all, many if not most manufacturing product markets are national or at least interregional in nature), but rather the number of firms relative to the number of workers. In measuring the extent of localized competition, we again adopt a measure used by Glaeser, Kallal, Scheinkman, and Shleifer (1992), that is defined as the number of firms per worker in the industry in the city relative to the number of firms per worker in the same industry in the United States. A higher value of this index of localized competition suggests that the industry has a greater number of firms per worker relative to its size in the particular city than it does elsewhere in the United States. Thus if the index of localized competition exceeds 1 then the city is locally less competitive than in other American cities.

In Feldman and Audretsch (1998) the regression model is estimated based on the 5,946 city-industry observations for which data could be collected. The Poisson regression estimation method is used because the dependent variable is a limited dependent variable with a highly skewed distribution. By focusing on innovative activity for particular industries at specific locations, we find compelling evidence that specialization of economic activity does not promote innovative output. Rather, the results indicate that diversity across complementary economic activities sharing a common science base is more conducive to innovation than is specialization. In addition, the results indicate that the degree of local competition for new ideas within a city is more conducive to innovative activity than is local monopoly.

CONCLUSION

The telecommunications revolution has drastically reduced the cost of transporting information across geographic space. High wages are increasingly incompatible with information-based economic activity, which can be easily transferred to a lower cost location. By contrast, the creation of new ideas based on tacit knowledge cannot easily be transferred across distance. Thus the comparative advantage of the high-cost countries of North American and Western Europe is increasingly based on knowledge-driven innovative activity. The spillover of knowledge from the firm or university creating that knowledge to a third-party firm is essential to innovative activity. Such knowledge spillovers tend to be spatially restricted. Thus an irony of the telecommunications revolution is that, even as the relevant geographic market for most goods and services becomes increasingly global, the increased importance of innovative activity in the leading developed countries has triggered a resurgence in the importance of local regions as a key source of comparative advantage.

The empirical evidence presented in this chapter suggests that R&D spillovers exist, and that they are geographically bounded. The extent to which such knowledge externalities exist as well as the cost of transmitting such spillovers across geographic space is not the same across industries and clearly contributes to the propensity for innovative activity to cluster more in some industries than in others. Apparently the stage of the industry life cycle, which presumably reflects the relative importance of tacit knowledge versus information, plays an important role in determining the importance of both R&D spillovers as well as their spatial dimension.

Increasingly scholars of technological change realize that external sources of knowledge are critical to innovation. The new learning on knowledge spillovers and the geography of innovation suggests that the boundaries of the firm are but one means to organize and harness knowledge. An analogous means of organizing economic activity is spatially defined boundaries. Geographic location may provide another useful set of boundaries within which to organize innovation. Geography may provide a platform upon which knowledge may be effectively organized.

ACKNOWLEDGMENTS

An earlier version of this paper was presented at the conference on *Telecommunications and the City*, organized by Yuko Aoyama, Barney Warf, and James O. Wheeler, University of Georgia, March 21–23, 1998. We are grateful to the useful comments and suggestions of the participants as well as the specific comments by Jim Wheeler and Yuko Aoyama.

NOTES

1. "The Death of Distance," *The Economist*, 30 September, 1995.
2. For earlier work on the geography of innovation, see Malecki (1985 and 1986).
3. Malecki (1996) points out that these views are not original with Krugman (1991).

4. Saxenian (1990, pages 97–98) claims that even the language and vocabulary used by technical specialists is specific to a region: ". . . a distinct language has evolved in the region and certain technical terms used by semiconductor production engineers in Silicon Valley would not even be understood by their counterparts in Boston's Route 128."

5. Porter (1990) provides examples of Italian ceramics and gold jewelry industries in which numerous firms are located within a bounded geographic region and compete intensively in terms of product innovation rather than focusing on simple price competition.

REFERENCES

Audretsch, David B. (1995). *Innovation and Industry Evolution*. Cambridge, MA: MIT Press.

———. (1998). "Agglomeration and the Location of Innovative Activity," *Oxford Review of Economic Policy* 14(2).

Audretsch, David B. and Maryann P. Feldman (1996a). "R&D Spillovers and the Geography of Innovation and Production," *American Economic Review*, 86(3), June: 630–640.

———. (1996b). "Innovative Clusters and the Industry Life Cycle." *Review of Industrial Organization*, 11(2), April: 253–273.

Audretsch, David B. and Paula E. Stephan. (1996). "Company-Scientist Locational Links: The Case of Biotechnology." *American Economic Review*, 86(3), June: 641–652.

Castells, Manuel. (1996). *The Rise of the Network Society*. Malden: Blackwell Publishers.

Castells, Manuel and Peter Hall. (1994). *Technopoles of the World: Making of 21st Century Industrial Complexes*. New York: Routledge.

Edwards, Keith L. and Theodore J. Gordon. (1984). "Characterization of Innovations Introduced on the U.S. Market in 1982." The Futures Group, prepared for the United States Small Business Administration under Contract No. SBA–6050–0A–82, March.

Feldman, Maryann P. (1994a). "Knowledge Complementarity and Innovation," *Small Business Economics* 6: 363–372.

———. (1994b). *The Geography of Innovation*. Boston: Kluwer Academic Publishers.

Feldman, Maryann P. and David B. Audretsch. (1998). "Innovation in Cities: Science-Based Diversity, Specialization and Localized Competition." *European Economic Review*, 43: 409–429.

Fuchs, Victor R. (1962). *Change in the Location of Manufacturing in the United States Since 1929*. New Haven: Yale University Press.

Glaeser, Edward L, Hedi D. Kallal, Jose A. Scheinkman, and Andrei Shleifer. (1992). "Growth of Cities." *Journal of Political Economy* 100: 1126–1152.

Griliches, Zvi. (1979). "Issues in Assessing the Contribution of R&D to Productivity Growth." *Bell Journal of Economics* 10(1), 92–116.

———. (1992). "The Search for R&D Spill-Overs." *Scandinavian Journal of Economics* 94(S): 29–47.

Jacobs, Jane. (1969). *The Economy of Cities*. New York: Random House.

Jaffe, Adam B. (1989). "Real Effects of Academic Research." *American Economic Review* 79: 957–970.

Jaffe, Adam B., Manuel Trajtenberg, and Rebecca Henderson. (1993). "Geographic

Localization of Knowledge Spillovers as Evidenced by Patent Citations." *Quarterly Journal of Economics* 63: 577–598.

Krugman, Paul. (1991a). "Increasing Returns and Economic Geography." *Journal of Political Economy*, 99(3): 483–499.

———. (1991b). *Geography and Trade*. Cambridge, MA: MIT Press.

———. (1991c). "History and Industry Location: The Case of the Manufacturing Belt." *American Economic Review* 81: 80–83.

Levin, R. C., A. K. Klevorick, R. R. Nelson, and S. G. Winter. (1987). "Appropriating the Returns from Industrial Research and Development." *Brookings Papers on Economic Activity*, 783–820.

Lösch, A. (1954). *The Economics of Location*. New Haven: Yale University Press.

Malecki, Edward J. (1985). "Industrial Location and Corporate Organization in High Technology Industries. *Economic Geography* 61, October: 345–369.

———. (1986). "Innovation and Changes in Regional Structure." *Handbook of Regional and Urban Economics* Vol. 1. Amsterdam: Elsevier, 629–645.

———. (1996). "Development, Geography, and Economic Theory." *Geographical Review* 86(4), October: 643–646.

Markusen, Anne, Peter Hall, and Amy Glasmeier. (1986). *High Tech America: The What, How, Where and Why of Sunrise Industries*. Boston: Allen & Unwin.

Porter, M. P. (1990). *The Comparative Advantage of Nations*. New York: The Free Press.

Saxenian, Annalee. (1990). "Regional Networks and the Resurgence of Silicon Valley." *California Management Review* 33(1): 89–111.

———. (1994). *Regional Advantage*. Boston: Harvard University Press.

Scherer, F. M. (1984). *Innovation and Growth: Schumpeterian Perspectives*. Cambridge, MA: MIT Press.

Thompson, Wilbur R. (1962). "Locational Differences in Inventive Effort and Their Determinants." In Richard R. Nelson, ed. *The Rate and Direction of Inventive Activity*. Princeton, NJ: Princeton University Press.

Warf, Barney. (1995). "Telecommunications and the Changing Geographies of Knowledge Transmission in the Late 20th Century." *Urban Studies* 32(2), March: 361–378.

Wheeler, James O. and Ronald L. Mitchelson. (1991). "The Information Empire." *American Demograpics* 13(3), March: 40–42.

INDUSTRIAL LOCATION IN THE INFORMATION AGE

AN ANALYSIS OF INFORMATION-TECHNOLOGY-INTENSIVE INDUSTRY

Darrene Hackler

INTRODUCTION

To understand and explain the decentralization of firms from the central cities to the suburbs, various disciplines have noted that more factors are involved than people and jobs. Firm location is often posited to be a function of the preferences of employers and employees, local fiscal incentives, price differentials, concentration of industry, labor pool, and other amenities. While the regional economic literature has analyzed the decentralization of firms from such a model, many authors have speculated that information technology (IT) has enabled a trend of "footloose" firms.[1] With the onset of the information age, firm and industry location patterns may be better understood if a firm or industry is considered to be IT-intensive in the production of goods or services. As Markusen, Hall, and Glasmeier mention, "a theory of location for high technology industry does not exist. Fragments must be culled from disparate parts of location theory and other scholarship on innovation in order to begin to build a satisfactory set of explanations."[2]

This study delves further into IT's effect on industry location with an empirical study of IT-intensive manufacturing industries at the county level. While similar analyses have been conducted, this study utilizes data on high-IT-intensive industrial location in counties and states and updates the empirical work completed on industrial location during the 1970s and 1980s.

In addition, this study analyzes whether IT intensity serves to reduce traditional locational constraints on industry. As explained by Hepworth, computer networks and other general IT innovations enhance the economies of scale and scope for firms, allowing them to share information and IT facilities. Thus, firms can extend their degree of geographical dispersal and have a higher level of locational flexibility.[3] Castells also notes the "low sensitivity of the industry to traditional factors influencing location, such as transportation costs or access to bulky raw materials."[4] Consequently, the study will determine if high IT-intensive industry is not only footloose in dispersion but also decentralizing from traditional urban centers.

In order to analyze this phenomenon, IT intensity will be defined on an industry basis *ex ante*. The definition will be applied to all manufacturing industries at the four-digit standard industrial classification (SIC) code in order to select a population of high-IT-intensive industries. The change in location patterns of high-IT-intensive manufacturing industries is analyzed for the United States, four states (Arizona, California, Minnesota, and New York), and a set of counties surrounding the metropolitan areas of Los Angeles, California, New York City, New York, Phoenix, Arizona, and Minneapolis-St. Paul, Minnesota for 1987, 1992, and 1994. The geographic and SIC code analysis provides a general indication of whether IT intensity has increased the degree of footlooseness and decentralization in IT-intensive manufacturing industries.

BACKGROUND

Decentralization and Location Theory

While the impact of IT on urban form and regions has been a recent focus among geographers, regional economists, and policy-makers, the majority of studies focus on the general decentralization of employment and population from the central business districts (CBDs) and central cities in metropolitan areas to suburbs and nonmetropolitan areas. Mieszkowski and Mills assert that the decentralization of residential activities was followed by the decentralization of employment, when firms followed the population to the suburbs with the adoption of truck transport.[5] Ascertaining IT's role in this decentralization trend would provide further understanding of geographical employment, population, and industrial location patterns.

The locational preferences of firms are a logical point of departure. The roots of location theory rely on three basic locational forces first identified by Alfred Weber: transport cost differentials, labor cost differentials, and agglomeration economies.[6] While the former two are essential, the final one shines the most light on firm location. Hoover classified agglomeration factors into three categories:

1. large-scale economies within the firm, consequent upon enlargement of the firm's scale of production;
2. localization economies for all firms in a single industry at a single location, consequent upon the enlargement of the total output of that industry at that location; and
3. urbanization economies for all industries at a single location, consequent upon the enlargement of the total economic size ([of the] population, income, output, or wealth [of an area]).[7]

This classification provides the essential underpinnings to understanding where firms locate. The concentration of automakers in Detroit, Michigan demonstrates localization economies. Urbanization economies include benefits related to urban scale as well as access to larger labor pools and other essential inputs.

Trade-offs of the cost of high-rise development, such as congestion, and the prospective benefits of urban areas, such as agglomeration, are under the greatest impact from IT:

> High-rise, concentrated settlement is costly and only worthwhile if transport or communications costs are high; yet, these have been falling for many years and will continue to fall steeply in the age of telecommunications. . . . Major innovations in transportation and communications have made the benefits of agglomeration available over ever larger areas, allowing many of the costs of congestion to be avoided."[8]

The data support this statement. The cross-sectional data from the Wharton Decentralization Project showed that most job growth, regardless of economic sector, is in the outer suburbs. In the 1980s, CBD job growth was either negligible or negative, with CBDs in the top ten cities growing at just over 1 percent per year during the period 1980 to 1986.[9] Finally, the work of Gordon, Richardson, and Yu suggests that there is "across-the-board relative (and often absolute) decline" in CBDs.[10]

Due to IT's invisible and hard-to-measure nature, traditional theories of economics and development are unable to assess IT's full impact on the location patterns of industry, employment, and population. Castells states that "traditional location theory fails to deal with the novel technological and economic conditions of the new industrialization process."[11] His analysis of the literature concludes that IT is restructuring industrial location through the spatial differentiation of distinct production functions. In general, technological innovation is centralized, while application of such innovations is decentralized.[12] The "tendency toward decentralization of production takes place in a context in which flexibility is the most important requirement in the relationship between the industry and its spatial location."[13]

Various studies have attempted to analyze quantitatively the distinct IT industrial spatial pattern that Castells describes. Most studies of IT industries in the 1970s and early 1980s focused on manufacturing employment as a proxy for firm location instead of on establishments in states and metropolitan statistical areas (MSAs) for the United States.[14] IT industry (often referred to as high-tech) was found to have a distinct tendency to disperse across localities and states.[15] Markusen, Hall, and Glasmeier's analysis of high-tech employment and plants concluded that:

> Much of [the dispersion] consists of an outward movement from a few high tech core states into neighboring states (California to Arizona and Nevada; Massachusetts to Vermont and New Hampshire), and also shorter-distance movement from a few dominant high tech metropolitan areas into neighboring SMSAs [Standard Metropolitan Statistical Area] (Los Angeles to Anaheim-Santa Ana-Garden Grove; San Francisco to San Jose; Boston to Worcester). In other words, it is relatively short-distance dispersal . . . much of

the benefit goes to states and areas that have not traditionally been industrial centers.[16]

Given that some degree of decentralization is found, does the trend continue with more current data and in specific metropolitan areas? Do IT-intensive industries decentralize from the center and grow in outer areas, whether this be a relocation, expansion, or start-up?

DATA, MEASURES, AND METHODOLOGY

Crucial to this study is the definition of IT intensity and the selection of appropriate industries for the analysis of high and low IT intensity. Various definitions have been utilized to define high-technology industry. Most often these are based on the use of higher skilled labor as a means for IT-intensive production. The working definition of high-IT-intensive industry for this study is based on the proportion of technical occupations in the industry's total labor force.[17] Glasmeier believes this nonstatic definition is appropriate because of IT's constantly changing nature. From this definition, IT-intensive industries are those in which the proportion of engineers, engineering technicians, computer scientists, mathematicians, and life scientists exceeds the national manufacturing average.[18]

The four-digit SIC codes defined as high-IT-intensive are from Glasmeier's work.[19] The data utilized for this analysis are the County Business Patterns series for the years 1987, 1992, and 1994.[20] The County Business Patterns series provides data on industrial location patterns for all manufacturing industries at the national, state, and county level. In order to capture the high-IT-intensive firm location pattern, firm establishments and employment data are analyzed for each four-digit SIC code of all manufacturing industries.[21] A national percentage of high-IT-intensive manufacturing establishments is calculated as the total number of high-IT-intensive manufacturing establishments to the total number of manufacturing establishments. In order to identify if the national percentage is exceeded and to show any patterns supporting greater locational variation of high-IT intensity industries, this percentage is compared with the percentage calculated in each county defined below.

For the national comparison, four geographical regions were purposively selected. Two are traditional large cities and their surrounding areas (Los Angeles, California, and New York City, New York), and two are second-tier cities and their surrounding areas (Phoenix, Arizona and Minneapolis-St. Paul, Minnesota).[22] These four cities were considered the core of their respective metropolitan areas and associated with surrounding counties by a freeway distance measure that varies for each region.[23]

Given the West's great expanses of land and freeways, a greater geographic area is encompassed such that the counties associated with Los Angeles and Phoenix are within a 50-mile freeway radius. Five counties in the Los Angeles metropolitan area are captured (Los Angeles, Orange, Riverside, San Bernardino, and Ventura). Three counties are associated with Phoenix (Maricopa, Pinal, and Yavapai). The East's economic and geographical character is more concentrated, and thus the counties selected for New York City's analysis are within a 10-mile radius. Data from five counties in New York (Bronx, Kings, New York, Queens, and Richmond) and three in New Jersey (Bergen, Essex, and Hudson) are collected. The Minneapolis-St. Paul region falls somewhere in between these two extremes, so all counties within a 20-mile radius are included (Anoka, Carver, Dakota, Hennepin, Ramsey, Scott, and Washington). The selected counties are exhibited in the maps in Figures 13.1 to 13.4.

The selected methodology is employed for several reasons. Understanding aggregate county location of IT-intensive industry with more recent data than past studies will enable a clearer picture of cities that are attracting and losing IT-intensive industry in the information age. The county as the unit of analysis is adequate for such an overarching examination. A comparison of high-IT-intensive percentages between central and outer counties will allow a general analysis of intrametropolitan location and serve as evidence for whether decentralization of high-IT-intensive manufacturing firms from the central county is a predominant pattern for each geographical region.[24]

The data utilized in this study are also advantageous. Not only does the use of establishments data provide a more direct measure of actual firm location, but also the data are not suppressed as often as employment data. "Summary records at the county level are not shown for any industry with fewer than 50 employees."[25] These industries report zero employment, but total establishments and establishment-sized designations are reported. Thus a study on high-IT-intensive industry is fully reliant on the fact that establishment data are analyzed.

Above all, social scientists are interested in policy implications. This study's presumption of high-IT-intensive dispersion, decentralization from the central county, and growth in outer counties may transfer additional power to locations in terms of economic development policy.

Expectations

While agglomeration and locational-specific patterns are often attributed to manufacturing and even to IT-intensive manufacturing, various findings in the literature indicate that other trends may be occurring: "The geographical concentration of manufacturing industries has fallen significantly over the past 15 years, perhaps reflecting the decreased importance of fixed costs and transport costs."[26] Since the major contention of this chapter is that IT is one of the major factors contributing to this deconcentration of industries in cities, footloose IT-intensive industries may be sponsoring this trend.

Other research indicates that agglomeration may not be as important to IT-intensive industries. The extent of diversity in manufacturing industries "matters in attracting 'new' or high-tech industries (such as scientific instruments and electronic components) and in permitting those new industries to flourish."[27] Directly related to IT industries, Schneider and Kim actually find that distance from the central city was positively related to growth of high-tech

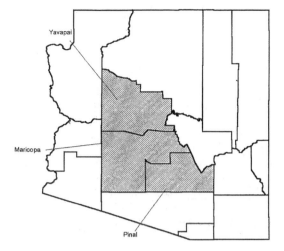

Figure 13.1 Arizona and Counties

Figure 13.2 California and Counties

industry, suggesting that high-tech is not as reliant on a central market for labor and goods as manufacturing as a whole.[28] Thus these industry studies are not exclusively suggesting the prevalent locational bias.

Castells, Hepworth, Markusen, Hall, and Glasmeier, and others also note that the variation in industrial location is greater for high-IT-intensive manufacturing industries. In the presence of IT, traditional variables such as transportation become less consequential to influencing location. Furthermore, high-IT-intensive manufacturing often involves various phases of production

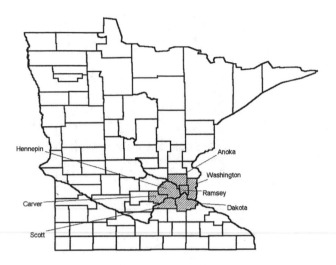

Figure 13.3 Minnesota and Counties

Figure 13.4 New York and New Jersey Counties

that are able to be easily decentralized. Consequently, these findings suggest that a certain degree of decentralization from central counties and growth in outer counties is to be expected.

RESULTS AND FINDINGS

National percentages of high-IT-intensive establishments and employment were calculated for 1987, 1992, and 1994. Employment in high-IT-intensive industries declined steadily from 9.01 percent in 1987, to 8.42 percent in 1992, and finally to 7.97 percent at the end of the year 1994. The national percentage of high-IT-intensive establishments decreased from 5.08 percent in 1987 to 4.98 percent in 1992 but increased to 5.04 percent in 1994; there was an overall decrease in establishments. Distinct trend differences exist between each year in the employment and establishments data. The findings reinforce the need to analyze the number of firms, not just employment, in high-IT-intensive industries. From the baseline average for employment and establishments, a comparison of the national average to the states of Arizona, California, Minnesota, and New York and to the associated counties is possible.

United States and Individual States

Table 13.1 compares the national, state, and county estimates for high- and low-IT-intensive employment and establishments in 1987, 1992, and 1994. With the national average for high-IT-intensive employment maintaining a steady decline, the most interesting state is Arizona, declining from 16.61 percent in 1987 to 8.01 percent in 1992, only to increase to 9.74 percent in 1994. With 1987's and 1994's percentages above the national average, this is by far the most dramatic variation in percentages. Also of interest is California's overall high average of high-IT-intensive employment as compared to the national and other state averages. California shows a similar pattern to that of Arizona with a decline in 1992 and increase in 1994.[29] New York's and Minnesota's patterns are distinct. New York increases between 1987 and 1992, only to decline in 1994, with only 1992 above the national average. Minnesota's high-IT-intensive employment increases for each year and is above the national average for 1992 and 1994.

As for high-IT-intensive establishments data, the data patterns are distinct from those of employment. As mentioned above, the national average decreased between 1987 and 1992 and increased between 1992 and 1994. California exhibits a slow decline in percent of establishments, but it still has a higher percentage of high-IT-intensive establishments than other states and is above the national average. Minnesota has a similar pattern to the United States, yet each year is above the national average. Overall, Minnesota is second in terms of percent of high-IT-intensive establishments for each year. Establishments show a clear ranking of states on the percent of establishments, with California first, Minnesota second, followed by Arizona and New York.

Arizona shows a slow increase in establishments, with 1987 equal to the national average and 1992 and 1994 above it. Taking California and Arizona together, the results support Markusen, Hall, and Glasmeier's finding of "outward movement from a few high-tech core states into neighboring states."[30] New York's high-IT-intensive establishments increase between 1987 and 1992, only to decrease to the initial percentage of 3.92 percent in 1994. However, unlike the other three states, each year for New York is below the national average. The state findings provide general trends and background for the county-level analysis of high-IT-intensive location patterns in the four metropolitan regions.

Table 13.1 1987–1994 IT-Intensive Manufacturing Industries Employment and Establishments Data
(Share of Total Employment and Establishments in Each Region)

	1987		1992		1994	
	Employment	Establishments	Employment	Establishments	Employment	Establishments
High IT-Intensive Manufacturing Estimates						
United States	9.01%	5.08%	8.42%	4.98%	7.97%	5.04%
Arizona*	16.61%	5.08%	8.01%	5.21%	9.74%	5.63%
Maricopa	11.54%	5.32%	9.86%	5.72%	3.32%	5.98%
Pinal	0.00%	4.35%	0.00%	3.56%	0.00%	3.02%
Yavapai	0.00%	3.92%	0.00%	3.63%	0.00%	2.31%
California	13.93%	5.96%	11.23%	5.88%	11.66%	5.80%
LA	10.51%	5.17%	10.04%	4.89%	8.59%	4.64%
Orange	16.00%	7.85%	10.49%	7.16%	11.31%	7.05%
Riverside	1.05%	4.84%	2.94%	4.85%	3.13%	5.22%
San Bernardino	1.33%	4.73%	1.90%	5.18%	2.17%	5.39%
Ventura	9.35%	9.42%	12.14%	8.87%	11.71%	9.52%
Minnesota*	8.88%	5.62%	8.94%	5.57%	9.36%	5.73%
Anoka	3.11%	6.82%	4.74%	6.70%	2.75%	6.92%
Carver	0.00%	6.37%	0.00%	5.29%	0.00%	6.52%
Dakota	1.76%	5.35%	1.51%	5.70%	2.23%	6.57%
Hennepin	9.47%	6.99%	9.12%	7.21%	9.13%	7.05%
Ramsey	2.84%	7.18%	2.11%	6.64%	2.88%	7.12%
Scott	0.00%	5.19%	0.00%	7.12%	0.00%	6.47%
Washington	0.00%	7.58%	0.00%	5.73%	8.20%	6.96%
New York	8.02%	3.92%	8.61%	3.97%	7.62%	3.92%
Bronx	0.37%	2.82%	0.12%	3.51%	0.32%	3.77%
Kings	1.37%	2.22%	0.61%	2.12%	0.81%	2.15%
New York	0.45%	1.02%	0.46%	1.08%	0.24%	1.00%
Queens	1.50%	3.42%	1.34%	2.98%	1.23%	2.75%
Richmond	0.00%	2.51%	0.00%	2.43%	0.00%	3.87%
Bergen	7.25%	6.66%	8.78%	7.23%	6.36%	6.60%
Essex	3.57%	6.33%	8.18%	6.18%	10.31%	5.88%
Hudson	0.87%	3.28%	2.29%	3.17%	2.21%	3.23%
Low IT-Intensive Manufacturing Estimates						
United States	91.64%	94.92%	91.42%	94.93%	92.03%	94.96%
Arizona*	80.55%	93.38%	91.99%	94.79%	90.26%	94.37%
Maricopa	88.46%	94.68%	90.14%	94.28%	96.68%	94.02%
Pinal	100.00%	95.65%	100.00%	96.44%	100.00%	96.98%
Yavapai	100.00%	96.08%	100.00%	96.37%	100.00%	97.69%
California	86.07%	94.04%	88.77%	94.12%	88.34%	94.20%
LA	89.49%	94.83%	89.96%	95.11%	91.41%	95.36%
Orange	84.00%	92.15%	89.51%	92.84%	88.69%	92.95%
Riverside	98.95%	95.16%	97.06%	95.15%	96.87%	94.78%
San Bernardino	98.67%	95.27%	98.10%	94.82%	97.83%	94.61%
Ventura	90.65%	90.58%	87.86%	91.13%	88.29%	90.48%
Minnesota*	91.12%	94.38%	91.06%	94.33%	91.69%	94.81%
Anoka	96.89%	93.34%	95.26%	93.30%	97.25%	93.08%
Carver	100.00%	93.63%	100.00%	94.71%	100.00%	93.48%
Dakota	98.24%	94.65%	98.49%	94.30%	97.77%	93.43%
Hennepin	90.53%	93.01%	90.88%	92.79%	90.87%	92.95%
Ramsey	97.63%	93.71%	97.89%	93.44%	97.12%	93.69%
Scott	100.00%	94.81%	100.00%	92.88%	100.00%	93.82%
Washington	100.00%	92.42%	100.00%	94.27%	91.80%	93.04%
New York	91.98%	96.08%	91.39%	96.03%	92.38%	96.08%
Bronx	99.63%	97.18%	99.88%	96.49%	99.68%	96.23%
Kings	98.63%	97.78%	99.39%	97.88%	99.19%	97.85%
New York	99.55%	98.98%	99.54%	98.92%	99.76%	99.00%
Queens	98.50%	96.58%	98.66%	97.02%	98.77%	97.25%
Richmond	100.00%	97.49%	100.00%	97.57%	100.00%	96.13%
Bergen	92.75%	93.34%	91.22%	92.77%	93.64%	93.40%
Essex	96.43%	93.67%	91.82%	93.60%	89.60%	93.86%
Hudson	99.13%	96.72%	97.71%	96.75%	97.79%	96.74%

* Percentages do not add up to 100 percent.

Arizona

Arizona's percentages for both high-IT-intensive employment and establishments are above the national averages and would seem to indicate higher averages for counties. In comparing the national and state percentages for Arizona to the three counties (Maricopa, Pinal, and Yavapai), evident gaps appear. Maricopa County includes the city and metropolitan area of Phoenix. Second-tier city Phoenix, and thus Maricopa County, have experienced recent growth.[31]

While high-IT-intensive employment is declining overall in the period from 1987 to 1994 (and with only 1987's percentage of 11.54 percent being greater than the national and state averages), high-IT-intensive establishments percentages increase each year, each above the national and state percentages. Establishments data, in particular, reinforce the general perception of Phoenix as a growing high-tech area.

However, both Pinal and Yavapai counties produce contrary results, with negligible high-IT-intensive employment in each county over the period. High IT-intensive establishments decrease over the period, and each year's percentage for each county is below the national average. Such results have large implications for analyzing intrametropolitan locational patterns. These will be discussed below in the section on implications.

California

Given the fact that the state of California has greater percentages than the national average for each year in both high-IT-intensive employment and establishments, California's counties should provide interesting patterns in comparison to those in other states. Los Angeles, Orange, and Ventura counties are all above the national average for high-IT-intensive employment for each year. Of these, Orange County's pattern of a decrease from 1987 to 1992 and an increase to 1994 is similar to California's overall state pattern but is below the state average for all but 1987. Los Angeles County is steadily decreasing and below the state average. Ventura County shows a large increase from 9.35 percent in 1987 to 12.14 percent in 1992, leveling off at 11.71 percent in 1994. Percentages for each of these counties, as well as the state average, suggest the impact of the recession in the early 1990s. For example, the Los Angeles metropolitan area's employment in the high-IT-intensive defense industry decreases greatly during this time period. Riverside and San Bernardino, while way below the state average and other counties, show a steady increase in high-IT-intensive employment, with Riverside showing the greatest growth in its percentages.

A different story plays out in high-IT-intensive establishments. Orange and Ventura counties are above the state and national averages but show different patterns. Ventura County decreases between 1987 and 1992 and increases between 1992 and 1994, while Orange County slowly declines over the entire period. Los Angeles County follows a pattern similar to Orange County, but only 1987's percentage is above the national average. Again, while below the

California averages, Riverside County and San Bernardino County experience a slow increase in high-IT-intensive establishments. Riverside County's 1994 percentage is above the national average, as is San Bernardino's 1992 and 1994 percentages. In total, high-IT-intensive establishments data are steadier throughout the time period, have less disparity among the counties, and corroborate the expectation of intrametropolitan decentralization.[32] Decreases in high-IT-intensive employment and establishments in Los Angeles and Orange, and somewhat in Ventura are paralleled by increases in Riverside and San Bernardino counties and indicate intrametropolitan decentralization.

Looking at the trends in high-IT-intensive employment and establishments over the entire period, Los Angeles County shows decreases for every year; Orange County shows decreases for all but one year; Ventura has both increases and decreases over the period; and finally Riverside and San Bernardino show increases across the board. If these five counties are analyzed from old to new or by proximity to the center of Los Angeles outward, direct parallels are evident indicating decentralization. Counties farthest from the center of the City of Los Angeles—Riverside and San Bernardino—are experiencing growth in both employment and establishments.

Minnesota

High IT-intensive employment and establishments in Minnesota are higher than the national averages for all except 1987's employment percentage. Minneapolis and St. Paul, located in Hennepin and Ramsey counties, are also considered second-tier cities, especially when both economies are combined into the Twin Cities. Hennepin County's high-IT-intensive employment decreases between 1987 and 1992 and levels off in 1994. Of the other six counties analyzed, three (Anoka, Dakota, and Ramsey) have some high-IT-intensive employment, but all are lower than the national and state averages. Scott and Carver have negligible high-IT-intensive employment. Interestingly, Washington County's growth to 8.2 percent in 1994 is above the national average. Washington County is the farthest from Hennepin County and borders Wisconsin. This increase, while supporting decentralization, is most likely not as great an increase as the percentage indicates. The data suppression of 1987 and 1992 employment figures for industries in the county that had fewer than fifty employees inflates the 1994 figure. In sum, Hennepin County accounts for the majority of Minnesota's high-IT-intensive employment percentages over the time period.

As for high-IT-intensive establishments, Minnesota's state averages are above the national percentages and mimic their pattern. High IT-intensive establishments in the seven counties are all above the national average and fall between 5.29 percent for Carver in 1992 and 7.58 percent for Washington County in 1987. Hennepin County has the highest percentages for 1992, second-highest for 1994, and third-highest for 1987.

Less disparity in the percentages of high-IT-intensive establishments than in employment is of interest, as is the fact that Anoka's, Hennepin's, and, to some degree, Ramsey's percentages are above Minnesota's average for the entire period. Anoka also displays some tendency of vertical disintegration, with employment in 1994 below 1987 but establishments showing growth overall. The data on high-IT-intensive establishments indicate that Minnesota and the counties surrounding the Twin Cities seem to have a high-IT-intensive advantage. The results for Minnesota in general and Hennepin County's growth do not emulate the decentralization trend found in California's counties. In fact the Twin Cities, like Phoenix, are attracting high-IT-intensive industry.

New York

The state of New York falls below the national average for high-IT-intensive employment and establishments in all except for 1992 employment. However, the inclusion of three New Jersey counties in the 10-mile radius of New York City yields interesting results. In fact, the two counties with the greatest high-IT-intensive employment are Bergen and Essex counties in New Jersey. Bergen County increases from 7.25 percent in 1987 to 8.78 percent in 1992 (above state and national averages) only to decline to 6.36 percent in 1994. Essex County increases dramatically over the entire period from 3.57 percent in 1987, to 8.18 percent in 1992, and finally to 10.31 percent in 1994, which is above the state and national average. The remaining county percentages of high-IT-intensive employment are below Hudson County's 2.29 percent for 1992, also in New Jersey. Thus growth in high-IT-intensive employment for the New York City metropolitan area occurs in another state, fueled by high-IT-intensive growth in New York City's New Jersey suburbs.

Of the four metropolitan areas analyzed, the high-IT-intensive establishments data from the eight counties analyzed for the New York metropolitan area show the greatest disparity in percentages. Bergen and Essex counties are above the national and state averages. Bergen County's high-IT-intensive establishments increase from 1987 to 1992 and decrease from 1992 to 1994. Essex slowly declines over the time period. While below both state and national averages, Bronx County in New York shows an increase from 1987's 2.82 percent to 3.77 percent in 1994. The remaining counties, besides Richmond County, have fairly level percentages for the time period. Richmond County's variation is greatest from 1992 to 1994, from 2.43 percent to 3.87 percent. The results from analyzing the high-IT-intensive establishments data are similar to that of the high-IT-intensive employment data. New Jersey's Bergen and Essex counties account for the majority of high-IT-intensive establishments, denoting intrametropolitan decentralization.

How Did Central and Outer Counties Fare?

Table 13.2 highlights the results of the locational analysis of high-IT-intensive industry for twenty-three counties in the metropolitan areas of Los Angeles, Phoenix, Minneapolis-St. Paul, and New York. The analysis accounts for five central counties containing each major city, and eighteen outer counties.

Table 13.2 Decentralization and Growth in Counties[33]

	Employment	Establishments
Central Counties: n = 5		
Decentralization over period 1 & 2*	2	1
Decentralization over period 1	2	2
Decentralization over period 2	1	1
Outer Counties: n = 18		
Growth over period 1 & 2	3	4
Growth over period 1	4	2
Growth over period 2	5	7

*Period 1 accounts for the years 1987–1992 while period 2 represents 1992–1994.

Given that the analysis is based on the argument that high-IT-intensive industry is better able to decentralize, an overall comparison of high-IT-intensive industry in each central and outer county is essential.

High IT-intensive manufacturing employment in four of five central counties experiences decentralization in either or both periods analyzed. Thus, the final percentages of high-IT-intensive employment in 1994 are found to be below that of 1987. The analysis of high-IT-intensive establishments reveals that only two of the four central counties (Los Angeles and New York counties) had overall decentralization. Hennepin and Ramsey counties (Twin Cities) experienced decentralization in period one in establisments and employment, respectively, but the growth in period two overwhelmed period one's results. Maricopa County (Phoenix) actually experiences growth in high-tech manufacturing establishments. This result reinforces another major finding of this paper—counties of second-tier cities are attracting high-IT-intensive industry while it is departing older cities such as Los Angeles and New York.

Overall, the expectation that outer counties should be experiencing growth in high-IT-intensive industry, is supported. Of the eighteen counties analyzed, twelve had experienced growth in high-IT-intensive employment in either period one, period two, or both periods. Seven of these displayed overall growth in employment such that a county's 1994 percentage was above that of 1987. While the other five counties had growth in employment during the first or second period, 1994 percentages were below that of 1987. For high-IT-intensive establishments, thirteen counties experienced growth. Nine of these exhibited overall growth in high-IT-intensive establishments, with the percentage in 1994 above that of 1987. Only four counties growing in either period one or two ended with the 1994 percentage below 1987.

The analysis provides general support for the decline of high-IT-intensive employment and establishments in central counties, but this finding is highly reliant on the age of the city within the county analyzed. Thus while decentralization of high-IT-intensive industry is presumed, a relevant variable to consider is the city's age—evident in the differences between Los Angeles/New York and Phoenix/Twin Cities. As second-tier cities, Phoenix and the Twin

Cities are the beneficiaries of the intermetropolitan decentralization of high-IT-intensive industry that Los Angeles and New York are experiencing.

A majority of outer counties are experiencing growth in high-IT-intensive employment and establishments. However, nearly half (7 of 18 in employment and 9 of 18 in establishments) displayed overall growth, with percentages of 1994 above those of 1987. Yet, of the remaining counties not showing overall growth, five counties in employment and four counties in establishments experienced growth in either period one or two. Thus the central-outer county analysis indicates that high-IT-intensive industries are able to leave traditional urban centers, with second-tier urban centers and outer counties (suburbs) proving notably attractive.

IMPLICATIONS AND CONCLUSIONS

The aggregate analysis of high-IT-intensive manufacturing establishments above brings several implications to light and suggests further refinements and steps to studying locational patterns of high-IT-intensive firms.

As for the direct data analysis, the states of California and Minnesota, as well as most of their counties, had the highest percentages of high-IT-intensive manufacturing establishments. Arizona and Maricopa County seemed to be increasing on a similar path. Also, while the state of New York and most of its counties were below the national average, the New Jersey counties of Bergen and Essex experienced increasing growth in high-IT-intensive manufacturing establishments. Case studies indicate that the growth was fueled by New York City's decentralization.[34]

A second implication of the data analyzed is that second-tier cities, such as Phoenix and the Twin Cities, seem to account for greater proportions of high-IT-intensive manufacturing establishments. The counties that contain Los Angeles and New York City seem to show decentralization of high-IT-intensive manufacturing establishments. Further analysis is needed to determine if second-tier cities truly have a high-IT-intensive advantage. Overall, the findings of intermetropolitan decentralization suggest that traditional manufacturing centers and older cities must pursue policies and means to recreate the city.

The data analysis also supports a trend of intrametropolitan decentralization from urban centers with growth in outer counties. Data from the New Jersey counties, several Minnesota counties, Ventura County, and, to a small degree, Riverside and San Bernardino counties imply that high-IT-intensive manufacturing establishments are locating outside of CBDs.[35] The implication of both intermetropolitan and intrametropolitan decentralization is that certain cities (outer counties and second-tier cities) are particularly advantaged and, therefore, may be more able to be proactive in attracting high-IT intensive industry.

One county exhibits a tendency of vertical integration in which the county experienced growth in high-IT-intensive employment but underwent a decline in high-IT-intensive establishments. In Essex County, New Jersey, high-IT-intensive employment grew from 3.57 percent in 1987 to 10.51 percent in 1994, more than doubling from 4,848 to 11,875 employees.[36] The number of high-IT-intensive establishments decreased from 6.33 percent in 1987 to 5.88

percent in 1994, which is a classic representation of vertical integration. Accord-ing to Hepworth, Storper and Christopherson, and Scott, vertical disintegration enhances localization and agglomeration at the local level because of the need for basic services.[37] Thus Essex's supposed vertical integration is perplexing.

While the findings are weaker, Bronx County in New York and Anoka County in Minnesota hint at some level of vertical disintegration. In Bronx, estab-lishments grew over the entire period while employment ended below its initial point. Anoka's results were less impressive, with establishments growing only in the second period for overall growth, and employment following Bronx's pattern. While not robust enough to draw concrete conclusions from, the results would seem to indicate some agglomeration in the outer counties of Bronx and Anoka.

Finally, high-IT-intensive manufacturing establishments data seem to explain locational patterns well and with less disparity among geographical areas than do employment data. Studies that attempt to capture locational patterns should consider establishments data over employment data to be able to obtain a better grasp on firm location decision-making, not to fall subject to the frequent suppression of employment data, as well as to capture vertical (dis)integration effects.

FUTURE RESEARCH

As indicated above, analysis of national, state, and county data provide a general understanding of high-IT-intensive industry location patterns. Given the sup-port for decentralization in central counties and growth in outer counties, regional economic development policies may be more successful in attract-ing high-IT-intensive firms. Entrepreneurial regions are likely to seek and attract high-IT-intensive firms with hope that such business growth will inspire further growth analogous to high-technology geographical centers such as Silicon Valley in California, Route 128 outside Boston, Massachusetts, and the Research Triangle in North Carolina. Further research on what economic development incentives are most significant in generating a change in loca-tion patterns of high-IT-intensive industries is needed for efficient and targeted policy at the local level.

ACKNOWLEDGMENTS

The following people were instrumental to the development of this article and the con-tinuing project: Arthur Denzau, Jacek Kugler, Thomas Horan, and Annette Steinacker for their insight and input; Grant McMurran for GIS expertise; Kara Serrano for edits and critique; and Chris Hoene for early data work, edits, and overall support. I am also grateful to the Digital Communities Initiative at Claremont Graduate University Research Institute for monies that assisted in funding the presentation of this analysis.

214

NOTES

1. The term "footloose" describes the ability and action of firms to relocate from tra-ditional economic centers. An entire firm or unit of a firm can be footloose.
2. Ann Markusen, Peter Hall, and Amy Glasmeier, *High Tech America: The What, How, Where, and Why of the Sunrise Industries* (Boston: Allen and Unwin, 1986).

3. Mark E. Hepworth, *Geography of the Information Economy* (London: Belhaven Press, 1989), 94.

4. Manuel Castells, *The Informational City: Information Technology, Economic Restructuring, and the Urban-Regional Process* (Cambridge, MA: Basil Blackwell, 1989), 74.

5. Peter Mieszkowski and Edwin S. Mills, "The Causes of Metropolitan Suburbanization," *Journal of Economic Perspectives* 7, No. 3 (Summer 1993): 135.

6. Alfred Weber, *Theory of the Location of Industry* (Chicago: University of Chicago Press, 1929).

7. E. Hoover, *The Location of Economic Activity* (New York: McGraw-Hill, 1948).

8. James E. Moore II, "Revised Statement Regarding Light Rail Funding: Exposition in Support of Testimony given July 12, 1995 before the Oregon House of Representative Light Rail Task Force." Available at *http://www.cascadepolicy.org/text/moorte.txt*, 3–4.

9. Top ten cities are New York, Los Angeles, Chicago, Philadelphia, Dallas, San Francisco, Boston, Detroit, Washington, DC, Houston. Anita A. Summers and Peter D. Linneman, "Patterns and Processes of Urban Employment Decentralization in the U.S. 1976–1986." Presented at the Comparisons of Urban Economic Development in the U.S. and Western Europe, Bellagio, Italy, July 9–13, 1990: 6.

10. Peter Gordon, Harry W. Richardson, and Gang Yu, "Settlement Patterns in the U.S.: Recent Evidence and Implications." Presented at the 36th Annual WRSA Meeting, Royal Waikolan Resort, Hawaii, February 23–27, 1997: 18.

11. Castells, 33.

12. Castells, 74.

13. Castells, 104.

14. Utilize employment data: Gordon, Richardson, and Yu (1997); Gordon Hanson, "Agglomeration, Dispersion, and the Pioneer Firm," *Journal of Urban Economics* 39 (1996): 255–281; Rodney Erickson and Michael Wasylenko, "Firm Relocation and Site Selection in Suburban Municipalities," *Journal of Urban Economics* 8 (1980): 69–85; J. Vernon Henderson, "Where Does an Industry Locate," *Journal of Urban Economics* 35 (1994): 83–104; Analyze manufacturing for the 1970s and 1980s: David Barkley, "The Decentralization of High-Technology Manufacturing to Nonmetropolitan Areas," *Growth and Change* (Winter 1988): 13–30; David Barkley and Sylvain Hinschberger, "Industrial Restructuring: Implications for the Decentralization of Manufacturing to Nonmetropolitan Areas," *Economic Development Quarterly* 6, No. 1 (February 1992): 64–79; Mark S. Henry, David L. Barkley, and Shuming Bao, "The Hinterland's Stake in Metropolitan Growth: Evidence from Selected Southern Regions," *Journal of Regional Science* 37, No. 3 (1997): 479–501; Donald Lyons, "Agglomeration Economies among High Technology Firms in Advanced Production Areas: The Case of Denver/Boulder," *Regional Studies* 29 No. 3 (1995): 265–278; Mitsuru Ota and Masahisa Fujita, "Communication Technologies and Spatial Organization of Multi-Unit Firms in Metropolitan Areas," *Regional Science and Urban Economics* 23 (1993): 695–729; Amy K. Glasmeier, "Innovative Manufacturing Industries: Spatial Incidence in the United States," in *High Technology, Space, and Society*, ed. Manuel Castells, (Beverly Hills, CA: Sage Publications, 1985); 55–79; Amy K. Glasmeier, *The High-Tech Potential: Economic Development in Rural America*, (New Brunswick, NJ: Center for Urban Policy Research, 1991); Breandán Ó hUallacháin, "The Location of U.S. Manufacturing: Some Empirical Evidence on Recent Geographical Shifts," 22 (1990): 1206–1222.

15. Markusen, et al., 172; Mark Schneider and Duckjoon Kim, "The Effects of Local Conditions on Economic Growth, 1977–1990: The Changing Location of High-Technology Activities," *Urban Affairs Review* 32, No. 2 (November 1996): 131–156.

16. Markusen, et al., 172.

17. Markusen, et al., Glasmeier (1985 and 1991), and Schneider and Kim also use this definition.

18. Life scientists include geologists, physicists, and chemists.

19. Glasmeier (1991), 20–22. Given that the 1980 occupational definition is used to select out high-IT-intensity manufacturing industries at the four-digit SIC code level, the 1987 reclassification of the SIC codes presented some difficulty to this analysis. The 1987 County Business Patterns series does not utilize the reclassified SIC system, and thus the data were sorted according to Glasmeier's original list of high-IT-intensive industries. For the years 1992 and 1994, the four-digit SIC codes were adjusted to correspond with the original high IT-intensive SIC codes.

20. U.S. Bureau of the Census, *County Business Patterns* (Washington, DC: U.S. Government Printing Office, 1987, 1992, 1994.)

21. The Census defines an establishment as "a single physical location at which business is conducted or where services or industrial operations are performed. It is not necessarily identical with a company or enterprise, which may consist of one establishment or more." Employment (mid-March employment) is paid employment consisting of full- and part-time employees, including salaried officers and executives of corporations, who were on the payroll in the pay period including March 12. U.S. Bureau of the Census, *County Business Patterns: General Explanation*, Online, Available at *http://www.census.gov/pub/epcd/cbp/download/genexpl.int.*

22. Second-tier cities are those attracting industry and jobs over the past ten to fifteen years.

23. Freeway distance data will be used from the U.S. Bureau of the Census' Tiger Database, a digital map database. A county is considered to be in the declared freeway mileage radius if more than 50 percent of the county's land is within the declared radius.

24. Los Angeles County contains the City of Los Angeles; New York County contains New York City; Maricopa County contains Phoenix; Hennepin County contains Minneapolis, and Ramsey County contains St. Paul.

25. U.S. Census Bureau's general explanation of the County Business Pattern data set is available at *http://www.census.gov/epcd/cbp/view/genexpl.int.*

26. Edward Glaeser, "Are Cities Dying," *Journal of Economic Perspectives* 12, No. 2 (Spring 1998): 144–145.

27. Vernon J. Henderson, A. Kuncuro, and M. Turner, "Industrial Development in Cities," *Journal of Political Economy* 103, No. 5 (1995): 1067–1090, cited in John M. Quigley, "Urban Diversity and Economic Growth," *Journal of Economic Perspectives* 12, No. 2 (Spring 1998): 136.

28. Schneider and Kim, 146.

29. For 1987, Arizona's figures for high- and low-IT-intensive firms did not equal 100 percent. Together high- and low-IT-intensive employment equaled 97.16 percent, and establishments equaled 98.46 percent. This result seems to indicate that high-IT-intensive employment and establishments are, if anything, underreported.

30. Markusen, et al., 172.

31. MSA containing Phoenix was fastest growing economy studied by Pollard and Storper, "almost doubling its total employment and recording absolute growth in all industry groups" from 1977 to 1987, with concentrated growth between 1977 to 1982. Jane Pollard and Michael Storper, "A Tale of Twelve Cities: Metropolitan

Employment Change in Dynamic Industries in the 1980s," *Economic Geography* 72, No. 1 (January 1996): 11.

32. Steinacker notes that "economic growth appears to have shifted away from cities, with suburbs the primary beneficiary and exurban areas becoming competitive as well." Annette Steinacker, "Economic Restructuring of Cities, Suburbs, and Non-Metropolitan Areas: 1977–1992," photocopied, 1998, 30.

33. For employment, results of six outer counties were not reported. Data for five of these had no IT-intensive employment, or data have been suppressed. One county, Queens in New York, experienced decentralization. For establishments, results for one central county and five outer counties were not reported. All displayed contrary results. Maricopa County, a central county, experienced growth, while the five outer counties experienced decentralization over both periods.

34. Office of Technology Assessment, *The Technological Reshaping of Metropolitan America* (Washington, DC: U.S. Government Printing Office, September 1995).

35. Further analysis on what attracts these firms and if any geographical limits exist is of great importance. For example, the results for Yavapai and Pinal Counties seem to indicate that the radius for Arizona needs to be decreased. The radius may be too great to capture decentralization that could be occurring out of the Phoenix area, if any.

36. Total employment actually decreased from 135,640 to 115,125 for the period.

37. Hepworth, 155; M. Storper and S. Christopherson, "Flexible Specialization and Regional Industrial Agglomerations: The Case of the US Motion Picture Industry," *Annals of the Association of American Geographers*, 77 (1987): 115; A. Scott, "Industrial Organization and Location: Division of Labor, the Firm and Spatial Process," *Economic Geography* 62 (1986): 220.

REFERENCES

Barkley, David. (1988). "The Decentralization of High-Technology Manufacturing to Nonmetropolitan Areas." *Growth and Change* (Winter): 13–30.

Barkley, David and Sylvain Hinschberger. (1992). "Industrial Restructuring: Implications for the Decentralization of Manufacturing to Nonmetropolitan Areas." *Economic Development Quarterly* 6 No. 1 (February): 64–79.

Castells, Manuel. (1989). *The Informational City: Information Technology, Economic Restructuring, and the Urban-Regional Process.* Cambridge, MA: Basil Blackwell.

Erickson, Rodney and Michael Wasylenko. (1980). "Firm Relocation and Site Selection in Suburban Municipalities." *Journal of Urban Economics* 8: 69–85.

Glaeser, Edward. (1998). "Are Cities Dying." *Journal of Economic Perspectives* 12, No. 2 (Spring): 139–160.

Glasmeier, Amy K. (1985). "Innovative Manufacturing Industries: Spatial Incidence in the United States." In Manuel Castells, ed., *High Technology, Space, and Society.* Beverly Hills, CA: Sage.

———. (1991). *The High-Tech Potential: Economic Development in Rural America.* New Brunswick, NJ: Center for Urban Policy Research.

Gordon, Peter, Harry W. Richardson, and Gang Yu. (1997). "Settlement Patterns in the U.S.: Recent Evidence and Implications." Presented at the 36th Annual WRSA Meeting, Royal Waikolan Resort, Hawaii. February 23–27.

Hanson, Gordon. (1996). "Agglomeration, Dispersion, and the Pioneer Firm." *Journal of Urban Economics* 39: 255–281.

Henderson, Vernon J. (1994). "Where Does an Industry Locate?" *Journal of Urban Economics* 35: 83–104.

Henderson, Vernon J., A. Kuncuro, and M. Turner. (1995). "Industrial Development in Cities." *Journal of Political Economy* 103, No. 5: 1067–1090.

Henry, Mark S., David Barkley, and Shuming Bao. (1997). "The Hinterland's Stake in Metropolitan Growth: Evidence from Selected Southern Regions." *Journal of Regional Science* 37, No. 3: 479–501.

Hepworth, Mark E. (1989). *Geography of the Information Economy*. London: Belhaven Press.

Hoover, E. (1948). *The Location of Economic Activity*. New York: McGraw-Hill.

Lyons, Donald. (1995). "Agglomeration Economies among High Technology Firms in Advanced Production Areas: The Case of Denver/Boulder." *Regional Studies* 29, No. 3: 265–278.

Markusen, Ann, Peter Hall, and Amy Glasmeier. (1986). *High Tech America: The What, How, Where, and Why of the Sunrise Industries*. Boston: Allen & Unwin.

Mieszkowski, Peter and Edwin S. Mills. (1993). "The Causes of Metropolitan Suburbanization." *Journal of Economic Perspectives* 7, No. 3 (Summer): 135.

Moore II, James E. (1995). "Revised Statement Regarding Light Rail Funding: Exposition in Support of Testimony Given July 12 before the Oregon House of Representatives Light Rail Task Force." Available at *http://www.cascadepolicy.org/text/moorte.txt*.

Pollard, Jane and Michael Storper. (1996). "A Tale of Twelve Cities: Metropolitan Employment Change in Dynamic Industries in the 1980s." *Economic Geography* 72, No. 1 (January 1996): 1–22.

Office of Technology Assessment. (1995). *The Technological Reshaping of Metropolitan America*. Washington, DC: U.S. Government Printing Office, September.

Ó hUallacháin, Breandán. (1990). "The Location of U.S. Manufacturing: Some Empirical Evidence on Recent Geographical Shifts." *Environment and Planning* A 22: 1206–1222.

Ota, Mitsuru and Masahisa Fujita. (1993). "Communication Technologies and Spatial Organization of Multi-Unit Firms in Metropolitan Areas." *Regional Science and Urban Economics* 23: 695–729.

Quigley, John M. (1998). "Urban Diversity and Economic Growth." *Journal of Economic Perspectives* 12, No. 2 (Spring): 127–138.

Schneider, Mark and Duckjoon Kim. (1996). "The Effects of Local Conditions on Economic Growth, 1977–1990: The Changing Location of High-Technology Activities," *Urban Affairs Review* 32, No. 2 (November): 131–156.

Scott, A. (1986). "Industrial Organization and Location: Division of Labor, the Firm and Spatial Process." *Economic Geography* 62: 215–231.

Steinacker, Annette. (1998). "Economic Restructuring of Cities, Suburbs, and Non-Metropolitan Areas: 1977–1992." Photocopied.

Storper, M. and S. Christopherson. (1987). "Flexible Specialization and Regional Industrial Agglomerations: The Case of the US Motion Picture Industry." *Annals of the Association of American Geographers* 77: 115.

Summers, Anita A. and Peter D. Linneman. (1990). "Patterns and Processes of Urban Employment Decentralization in the U.S. 1976–1986." Presented at the Comparisons of Urban Economic Development in the U.S. and Western Europe, Bellagio, Italy, July 9–13.

U.S. Bureau of the Census. *County Business Patterns*. (1987, 1992, 1994). Washington, DC: U.S. Government Printing Office.

Weber, Alfred. (1929). *Theory of the Location of Industry*. Chicago: University of Chicago Press.

MILIEU PREFERENCES AMONG HIGH-TECHNOLOGY COMPANIES

Robert Mugerauer

RESEARCH LITERATURE

The study utilized the substantial research literature both on the location of high-technology companies and on environmental perception and qualitative research methodology. The broad account of location theory is found in Markusen, Hall, and Glasmeier (1986), who establish at least five factors as important: (1) amenities (good climate, educational options, appropriate housing prices); (2) access features (airport and highway access); (3) agglomeration economics (presence of business services, location of headquarters of Fortune 500 corporations); (4) social-political factors (importance of defense spending, low percentage of blacks in the resident population); and (5) labor force factors.

Given the character of the subject matter, the previous and available data sets, and the interests of the researchers, most of the work in this area operates with and reports its results in statistically analytic terms (Castells, 1991; Hall and Markusen, 1985; Glasmeier, 1991, 1986; Malecki, 1980; cf. Mugerauer, 1996b). Surprisingly, there is not much substantial work on high-technology environments that also takes into account the extensive methodology or results of quantitative environmental-landscape-housing behavior, perception, and preference research (an exception is Brill, 1995–96; Brill and Parker, 1994). Providing a context for the study of high-technology at the local and site scales, this body of knowledge includes analysis of other subject areas at larger regional and metropolitan scales (Craik and Zube, 1976; Kaplan, 1987). Other helpful quantitative research includes the exemplary work on residential preferences and satisfaction by John B. Lansing, Robert W. Marans, and Robert B. Zehner (1970), the work on landscape preference and satisfaction by Rachel and Stephen Kaplan (1989), Craik and Zube (1976) and Robert Bechtel (1977). This tradition of research, of course, takes a statistical report form and normally relies on questionnaires or controlled simulations and responses.

Unfortunately, these valuable and accurate ways of assessing people's responses to environments do not finally exhibit the patterns of their direct, value-laden experiences, perceptions, and decision-action procedures that occur as part of their lifeworlds (Gold and Burgess, 1962; Mugerauer, 1990, 1991; Mugerauer and Branch, 1996). Obviously there is an important gap in the current research, to be filled by inquiry that proceeds by dialogue in which members of the high-technology community speak for themselves rather than passively responding to hypothetical alternatives laid out for them by researchers. In the area of qualitative study, there is background work that utilizes anthropological, sociological, and psychological methods, and an interesting body of work in managerial and organizational studies (Weiss and Delbecq, 1987; Delbecq and Weiss, 1988; Saxenian, 1990, 1991). What is needed next is to add research in environmental behavior and perception preferences through the use of qualitative, dialogical methods.

METHODOLOGY

As seen from the literature review, the current quantitative approach dominates research, and our area of interest would be well served by a complementary, qualitative approach, such as taken in phenomenology and critical ethnography. The study reported here developed the phenomenological and critical hermeneutical approach of open-ended listening. In contrast to the focused interview (Zeisel, 1984), the open-ended interview or discussion is used with variations by a range of theoretically different approaches: by Bellah, et al., (1985) as a form of sociological dialogue; by ethnographers (Spradley, 1979; Hammersley, 1992; Jackson, 1989; Rogers, 1983; Garfinkel, 1967); by phenomenologists (Psathas, 1989; Seamon, 1979); by hermeneutical researchers (Mugerauer, 1996a); and by critical theorists, especially those using Habermas's theory of communicative action (Habermas, 1984, 1987; Forester, 1992). Classically, the phenomenological investigations of Edmund Husserl (1970) and Martin Heidegger (1982) argue that only through description of the primary lifeworld can the subject matter or problem be located and specified as "question-worthy"—a process that explicitly brings forth to consciousness what the precise sciences subsequently conceptualize and then measure and test. More radically, educator Paulo Freire's dialogic community building approaches have been applied to participant-based research concerning the social impact of technology (Freire, 1968, 1973; Mugerauer, 1998).

What is distinctly phenomenological and critical-hermeneutical in this study is attention to how peoples' milieus are constituted by the interaction of their historical and personal meanings and values with their structural-historical social, natural, and built environments. The critical-phenomenological-hermeneutical approach describes and critically analyzes the multiple levels in these lifeworlds. Along with close observation and documentation of exterior and interior environments, attention to contextual social and business cultures, and a study of the historical-economic development of high-technology locations and sites, I carried out forty-two *exploratory* interviews. I (1) open-endedly asked high-technology CEOs and professional employees in Central Texas and California, concentrating on the Austin and San Jose areas, for their stories about where and how they had decided to locate their companies/themselves both in regard to general locations and specific sites; and (2) after explaining that specific factors (such as costs, local business culture, and amenities) have been considered important by previous researchers (as indicated in the Literature Review, above), I then candidly asked what factors seemed important in their cases. The goal was not to prove anything, but to *explore and discover* by means of dialogue: to listen to and hear what the respondents wanted to say about their milieus, lives, and value systems and procedures of action. The interviews ranged from fifteen minutes to one and a half hours, with an average of about forty minutes.

After completing the interviews, I analyzed the responses by using a critical-phenomenological-hermeneutical patterning technique that builds up constellations of similar and dissimilar statements, spatially juxtaposing relations in the forms of mental maps through alternative configurations (Mugerauer, 1994a, 1989). As a very brief example of the procedure: one interviewee (dressed in shorts and loose shirt) may indicate that his office space reflects the company's clean-desk policy, which requires all work be locked away at the end of the day, that his huge monitor (it is about two feet square) is compensation (with a laugh) for not having a window, that the dress code has been loosened because of difficulty recruiting and retaining professionals, and that he had been a team leader but now works more individually. A second interviewee may say that she is glad to be out of the overly hierarchical structure of her former Boston company and now enjoys the looser process of group decisions, and even though her office is smaller and plainer than the one in Boston, she doesn't care and is glad she came, which happened because of a visit with a friend to her friend's boyfriend in Austin. The reported tidy desk of the first person with no window would be joined visually (by a line or circling) with the smaller office of the second person, and a related join would be made about both of them having humble surroundings but not complaining. Another join would be made between the two cases of reported preference for the more casual work atmosphere they currently enjoy. The process continues with as many details of as many interviews being connected, building up larger and larger patterns with the connections and variations among them. The resulting overall patterns naturally have much more detail available than is summarized and reported below.

RESPONSES AND DISCOVERIES

Note that, for the summary of responses reported here, there is little numerical analysis beyond providing basic numbers for some responses in order to indicate a general magnitude of response or to make a basic comparison between the California and Texas participants. This is because the total sample of forty-two is *not* statistically significant and was not collected in a systematic manner lending itself to quantitative analysis (for example, this exploratory study did not try to have equal numbers of females and males, or CEOs and professionals, or people from large and small companies; and in any case, patterns were *not* different among CEOs and professionals, or males and females). And to reassert the project's goal, the intent was to discover and initially explore the issues that the participants themselves found important, not to measure or prove anything. To avoid the tedium of noting relatively meaningless small numbers in what follows, the study uses "most" to indicate 75 percent or more of the respondents and "many" to indicate between 40 percent and 74 percent. Following are the major *clusters* of responses:

1. Utilitarian Factors

Most of the respondents noted that the utilitarian dimensions were important in both work and outside-of-work lives, but *assumed* that these features would be provided for by their employment— based on their previous experiences, pay and status levels, and beliefs that they would not consider a move or location without the pragmatic aspects being more than adequately satisfied. They noted, for instance, the high cost of housing in California and how larger and better houses were available in Central Texas at a lower cost. Similarly, CEOs and higher-management executives cited the importance of low site and building costs (whether purchased or leased), a large, highly trained, and motivated pool of potential employees for recruitment and retention, and energy costs. Several company presidents and individuals mentioned an item we had not found discussed with the same high level of interest or intensity in the literature: concern for the speed, extent, and ease of connection to the electronic-communication infrastructure at the location site. The point is that roadways and airports, while important at one level, are not as important to all sectors of high-technology activity and likely will decrease in importance compared to available bandwidth and mode of systems available for telecommuting, inter-active communications such as teleconferencing, rapid data transfer via modem, and so on (Mugerauer, 1994b).

2. Social Factors: Interpersonal Relationships

Almost all of those interviewed (92 percent) asserted that the prospects for positive and fruitful interpersonal or social relationships, both at work and outside work, were of great importance in location decisions. The style of the company's decision-making process, of the region's information sharing patterns, of networking to solve problems and build up future product and employment possibilities were very important. CEOs and owners of smaller businesses tended to emphasize their relations with clients and providers, where their new activities, products, or services often resulted from what the others wanted or discovered they could do, or where they valued the regular occasions for meeting with colleagues and competitors to stay in touch with what was going on in the area. The proximity and access to decision-makers, especially in government agencies and the universities were important to many of the central Texas players. Individual employees valued the chance to learn of new prospects, of the ups and downs of companies' fortunes or about the character of work there, of support from people who were going through the same experiences as them. Naturally, the reported features of such interpersonal transactions varied dramatically, from dependable and trustworthy to predatory, from casual to lasting friendships that moved beyond business life.

The generally casual business dress code and the fairly democratic decision-making process of many smaller companies in central Texas were positively valued by many respondents, especially in contrast to their previous employers on the East Coast or with larger and more formalized companies. Several of those interviewed presented the opposite position, finding that the lack of professional dress and of hierarchical chain-of-command, even in some larger companies in Texas, was distressing to them and, they believed, boded ill for the companies. Of course, others worked in more formal and hierarchical contexts and found the latter to be fine. (This finding and its range supports those of Saxenian, 1990, 1991.)

As noted, areas of outside-of-work life came up, not systematically, but usually as part of the discussion of what the respondents did with whom in the line of business. For this report, we can separate several aspects. To use words from the interviews, the fact that "bright," "confident," "energetic," "hard-working," "future-oriented," and "entrepreneurial" people were around was important for business and outside-of-work social activity. More than half of the players went out of their way to explain that there was no clear line between work life and outside-of-work life; that what they did with whom was generally all part of one connected routine. Others noted that they left their work behind and kept it very separate from outside-of-work life.

Participants indicated that the characteristics of the natural and cultural environments were important. The availability of both cultural and outdoor recreational activity was valued. Central Texas respondents reported that the ability to ride motorcycles or sports cars on the winding roads of the hill country was a major draw; others said that a place where they could sail, hike, run, cycle, or play golf was a factor of satisfaction.

More than half said that climate was one of the reasons they located where they did: Californians noted their mild climate, and Texans pointed out that theirs was, variously, great or good for most of the year (except summer). Most of the comments concerning climate were put comparatively: the constantly nice conditions of California and generally nice climate of Texas were contrasted favorably with the upper Midwest and Northeast U.S. There were also considerable digs, by both Californians and Texans, at the weather at the other end of their axis: Californians touted their constant conditions, and Texans noted their appreciation for changing weather compared to California's boringly predictable niceness.

As to cultural milieu, the presence of a lively music scene and of cultural events was important to Texans. California respondents did not have much to say in this regard except concerning the San Jose Symphony Orchestra (these interviews took place before the San Jose High-Tech Museum was built). The image or sense of place was considered positive by many Texas respondents, especially as Austin has an image that is considered to be "cool," or "hot," or "on the move" because of the mix of high-tech, multimedia, and live music, and the composite dynamic/laid-back cachet.

The social character of San Jose's and Austin's surrounding communities was important to about half of those interviewed. Of these, about half expressed their preference for a homogeneous milieu, with a population "like we are." The other half explicitly mentioned that a tolerant, multicultural milieu, where people enjoyed being part of and working with a diverse population was important to them as individuals or to their companies. (An implication, which is being examined in subsequent research, is that there is a profound split between preference for suburban or urban milieus among high-technology CEOs and professional employees.)

About one third of those interviewed mentioned the importance of being "able to belong" and to contribute to California's or Central Texas' communities. The fact that Austin and San Jose were medium-sized with small communities nearby and open to newcomers seemed important, several noted, because it allowed them a chance to really contribute to the artistic, social, cultural, and business activities, and to the local educational systems at all levels.

Amenities

The appreciation of amenities was mentioned by all except the group who said utilitarian factors alone impacted their decisions. The latter pragmatic group comprised about 40 percent of the total, as noted; slightly more than one third of these, either deliberately or offhandedly, *after the formal interviews*, related that amenity factors did in fact matter. Many of the comments concerning outside-of-work or professional "quality of life" or amenity factors have already been mentioned above, in Section 2 on interpersonal relations. For business life, respondents found that important amenities included the prestige of address and niceness or luxury of buildings and interiors, and the positive economic images of the Silicon Valley and Central Texas regions (which, of course, *also* have utilitarian dimensions by connoting power, trustworthiness, and so on). Going beyond the aspects already discussed, the major features for outside-of-work life included the opportunity for a stimulating private life with other young and interesting adults, and the easy availability of the arts and music scenes, outdoor recreation, good restaurants and high-quality, even "exotic" foods, coffees, and wines. The ease with which one could exercise, find escape from long and intense work, and attend to being healthy was significant to about a sixth of the group. (These results seem to parallel the findings of Byers (1998) and Power (1996) that the personal satisfaction and qualitative factors are more important that the conventional, pragmatic ones.)

224

CONCLUSIONS

Several conclusions push themselves to the fore: first, that social and amenity factors do play a role in location and site decisions, along with utilitarian factors. Second, that these three aspects, while distinguishable for conceptual understanding, actually are not separate, since one activity or thing often has several of these sorts of meaning or value simultaneously. About 80 percent of those interviewed believed that high-technology companies and employees "assume" the presence of utilitarian factors. Of these respondents, a subset of half (that is, 43 percent of the total group) went on to say that because of the assumed satisfaction of pragmatic factors, the real location decisions were made on the basis of nonpragmatic social and amenity aspects of business or outside-of-work life. It should be noted, though, that this expectation is the result of intense preparation and continual cultivation. And in the formal role of "being interviewed," CEOs, managers, and professional employees likely will speak as "responsible business people," emphasizing, as expected, their concern for utilitarian, "bottom-line" features— as distinct from the more appropriate amenity orientations of their personal lives. An equal number held that in the end only the economic and utilitarian factors mattered.

As a result of the interviews, it is obvious that the respondents presented four major sorts of connected information, no matter how subtly classified and related, which provides a basic pattern for the next-generation instrument to be refined through one more pilot project before being used for the full-scale study. The four aspects relevant in making general location and specific site decisions for their companies or themselves are: (1) the character of the natural milieu and climate, (2) the utilitarian factors, (3) the social factors, (4) amenity aspects. Each of these plays a role for business and outside-of-work life-worlds that are sometimes distinct, but are very often complexly intertwined. In addition, it mainly appears that high-technology is a heterogeneous phenomena, in which differentiations need to be made among (a) manufacturing and nonmanufacturing, (b) the importance of differently sized settlements, especially the mid-sized city, (c) in respect to the (by now familiar) difference between individuals' and groups' preferences for suburban or urban milieus.

REFERENCES

Bechtel, Robert B. (1977). *Enclosing Behavior*. Strousburg, PA: Dowden, Hutchinson, & Ross.

Bellah, Robert, et al. (1985). *Habits of the Heart*. Berkeley: University of California Press.

Brill, Mike. (1995–1996). "Brill's Last Word." Monthly column in *Interiors*.

Brill, Mike and Cheryl Parker. (1994). *Now Offices, No Offices, ... Wild Times in the World of Office Work*. Toronto: Teknion.

Beyers, W. (1998). "Cyberspace or Human Space: Whither Cities in the Age of Telecommunications?" Paper presented at Telecommunications and the City, University of Georgia, Spring.

Castells, Manuel. (1991). *The Informational City*. Oxford: Blackwell.

Craik, Kenneth H. and Ervin H. Zube, eds. (1976). *Perceiving Environmental Quality: Research and Applications*. New York: Plenum.

Delbecq, A. and J. Weiss. (1988). "The Business Culture of Silicon Valley: Is It a Model for the Future?" In J. Weiss, ed. *Regional Cultures, Managerial Behavior, and Entrepreneurship: An International Perspective*. New York: Quorum.

Forester, John. (1992). "Critical Ethnography: On Fieldwork in a Habermasian Way." *Critical Management Studies*. London: Sage, 45–65.

Freire, Paulo. (1968). *Pedagogy of the Oppressed*. New York: Seabury Press.

———. (1973). *Education for Critical Consciousness*. New York: Seabury Press.

Garfinkel, Harold. (1967). *Studies in Ethnomethodology*. Englewood Cliffs, NJ: Prentice Hall.

Glasmeier, Amy K. (1986). *High-Tech America: The What, How, Where and Why of the Sunrise Industries*. Boston: Allen and Unwin.

———. (1991). *The High-Tech Potential*. New Brunswick, NJ: Center for Urban Policy Research.

Gold, John R. and Jacqueline Burgess, eds. (1962). *Valued Environments*. London: George Allen and Unwin.

Habermas, Jürgen. (1984, 1987). *Theory of Communicative Action*. 2 vols. Boston: Beacon Press.

Hall, Peter and A. Markusen, eds. (1985). *Silicon Landscapes*. Winchester, MA: Allen and Unwin.

Hammesley, Martyn. (1992). *What's Wrong With Ethnography?: Methodological Explorations*. New York: Routledge.

Heidegger, Martin. (1982). *The Basic Problems of Phenomenology*. Bloomington: Indiana University Press.

Husserl, Edmund. (1970). *The Crisis of European Sciences and Transcendental Phenomenology*. Evanston, IL: University of Northwestern Press.

Jackson, Michael. (1989). *Paths Toward a Clearing: Radical Empiricism and Ethnological Inquiry*. Bloomington: Indiana University Press.

Kaplan, Rachel. (1987). "Dominant and Variant Value in Environmental Perception." In A. S. Devlin and S. L. Taylor, eds. *Environmental Preferences and Land Preferences*. New London: Connecticut College.

Kaplan, Rachel and Stephen Kaplan. (1989). *The Experience of Nature: A Psychological Perspective*. New York: Cambridge University Press.

Lansing, John B., Robert W. Marans, and Robert B. Zehner. (1970). *Planned Residential Environments*. Ann Arbor, MI: UMI Research Press.

Malecki, E. J. (1980). "Dimensions of R&D Location in the U.S." In *Research Policy* 9: 2–22.

Markusen, Ann, Peter Hall, and Amy Glasmeier. (1986). *High-Tech America*. Boston: Allen and Unwin.

Mugerauer, Robert. (1989). "Images of Austin." Austin: University of Texas Community and Regional Planning Program, Working Paper Series. Paper 006.

———. (1990). "Midwestern Suburban Landscapes and Residents' Values." In R. Selby, et al., eds. *Coming of Age*. Urbana: University of Illinois.

———. (1991). "Post-Structural Planning Theory." Austin: University of Texas Community and Regional Planning Program. Working Paper Series. Paper 032.

———. (1994a). "Taking Responsibility for the Technological Landscape." In *Interpretations on Behalf of Place*. Albany: State University of New York Press.

———. (1994b). "Electronic Communication and the Physical Community." In *Electro-Comm 94*. Austin: Austin Software Council.

———. (1996a). *Interpreting Environments: Tradition, Deconstruction, Hermeneutics*. Austin: University of Texas Press.

———. (1996b). "Alternative Symbolic Analysts: Plugging into the Information Flow in Austin, Texas," In Dennis Crow, ed. *Geography and Identity: Exploring and Living the Geopolitics of Identity*. Washington, DC: Maisonneuve Press.

———. (1998). "Qualitative GIS: Disclosing Worlds, Not Representing Them." Paper presented at Varenius Specialist Meeting, Pacific Grove, California, November.

Mugerauer, Robert and Shelly Branch (1996). "High-Technology Landscapes & The Quality of Life." *Platform* (Spring): 4–5, 12.

Mugerauer, Robert and Lance Tatum. (1998). *High-Tech Downtown*. Austin, TX: School of Architecture.

Power, Thomas. (1996). *Lost Landscapes and Failed Economies: The Search for a Value of Place*. Washington, DC: Island Press.

Psathas, George. (1989). *Phenomenology and Sociology: Theory and Research*. Center for Advanced Research in Phenomenology. Washington, DC: University Press of America.

Rogers, Mary F. (1983). *Sociology, Ethnomethodology, and Experience: A Phenomenological Critique*. Cambridge: Cambridge University Press.

Saxenian, A. (1990). *Origins and Dynamics of Production Networks in Silicon Valley*. Working Paper No. 535. University of California at Berkeley, The Institute of Urban and Regional Development.

———. (1991). *Contrasting Patterns of Business Organization in Silicon Valley*. Working Paper No. 535. University of California at Berkeley, The Institute of Urban and Regional Development.

Scott, A. (1983). "Industrial Organization and the Logic of Intra-Metropolitan Location, II: A Case Study of the Printed Circuits Industry in Greater Los Angeles." *Economic Geography* Vol. 59, October: 343–367.

Seamon, David. (1979). *A Geography of the Lifeworld*. London: Croom Helm.

Spradley, James C. (1979). *The Ethnographic Interview*. New York: Holt, Reinhart, Winston.

Weiss, J. and A. Delbecq. (1987). "High-Technology Cultures and Management: Silicon Valley and Route 128." *Group and Organization Studies* Vol. 12, No. 1 (March): 39–54.

Zeisel, John. (1984). *Inquiry by Design: Tools for Environmental Behavior Research*. New York: Cambridge University Press.

TELEWORKING AND THE CITY

MYTHS OF WORKPLACE TRANSCENDENCE AND TRAVEL REDUCTION

Andrew Gillespie and Ronald Richardson

INTRODUCTION

The information revolution positively abounds with myths. The starting point for most of these myths is that of "a feverish belief in transcendence; a faith that, this time round, a new technology will finally and truly deliver us from the limitations and the frustrations of this imperfect world" (Robins, 1995). One of the most potent of such myths is that of the "end of geography," in which the constraints that bind us to places and that have imposed upon us a "tyranny of distance" are becoming, or are about to become, electronically transcended.

The theme of this volume—telecommunications and the city—has been a fertile breeding ground for variants of this myth (Graham, 1997). In this chapter, we attempt to debunk three interlinked myths concerning the implications of information and communications technologies for the future nature and form of the city. These might be categorized as "myths of disappearance through redundancy," in that in each case technological advance is assumed to transcend the need for an existing, and by implication outmoded, type of activity with its particular spatial expression. The myths are:

- the unnecessary workplace
- the unnecessary city
- the unnecessary need to travel

In the first half of the chapter, we reveal the false premises upon which the first two of these myths are constructed, and argue that neither the conventional workplace nor the physically bounded city are rendered redundant through the new technologies of virtuality. Rather we attempt to demonstrate that "places of work," in the sense both of individual workplaces and of the agglomeration of such workplaces into cities, are highly functional and effective forms of human organization, and as a result are likely to prove considerably more persistent and resilient than the technological futurists would have us believe.

In the second half of the chapter, we move from the conceptual level to a more empirically informed, though still speculative, consideration of the implications of "teleworking" — broadly defined, for the spatial form of the future city and for the travel patterns that are likely to be engendered. The forms of teleworking that we consider extend beyond home-based telecommuting to encompass other forms of working associated with communications technologies and also the new forms of tele-mediated service consumption with which they go hand in hand. Drawing upon an empirical investigation of recent trends in Britain, our objective is to demonstrate that, far from reducing the need to travel and contributing to more environmentally sustainable urban forms, the new communications technologies seem, conversely, to be associated with mobility-intensive and spatially dispersed activity patterns.

UNNECESSARY PLACES?

The "end of geography" line of argument rests on the assumption that the spatial ties that bind us into particular places will be relaxed to the point of severance through the space-transcending power of technology. The particular places that concern us here are the workplace and the city. Let us first consider why some have argued that the existence of these places will be rendered unnecessary as a result of the technological revolution, before challenging the assumptions that underpin these arguments.

With respect to the workplace, Hiltz (1984) first argued that the emergence of online communities would challenge the way in which we think of an office: "Usually, one thinks of it as a place, with desks and telephones and typewriters. In thinking about the office of the future, one must instead think of it as a communications space, created by the merger of computers and tele-communications" (Hiltz, 1984, page XV). A similar line of thinking was developed by Huws, Korte, and Robinson (1990, page 208), in suggesting that "the traditional concept of the workplace as a fixed geographical space will be replaced by more abstract notions of the working context as a set of relationships, a network, an intellectual space."

The idea of an established physical place becoming redundant and replaced by a more fluid and immaterial electronic space has also been applied to the city itself. Marshall McLuhan predicted that "with instant electric technology ... (the) very nature of the city as a form of major dimensions must inevitably dissolve like a fading shot in a movie" (McLuhan, 1964, page 366, quoted in Gold, 1991), while Berry (1973) used a similar metaphor in arguing that communications technologies would act as a "solvent which would dissolve the core-oriented city." The emergence of new communications networks such as the Internet and of cyberspace technologies that have the "ability to simulate environments within which humans can interact" (Featherstone and Burrows, 1995, page 5), has led to renewed questioning of the role, indeed the very legitimacy, of the city. According to William Mitchell (1995, page 107), "the very idea of the city is challenged and must eventually be reconceived," a task that he embarks upon through his vision of a "City of Bits":

This will be a city unrooted to any definite spot on the surface of the earth, shaped by connectivity and bandwidth constraints rather than by accessibility and land values, largely asynchronous in its operation, and inhabited by disembodied and fragmented subjects who exist as collections of aliases and agents. Its places will be constructed virtually by software instead of physically from stones and timbers, and they will be connected by logical linkages rather than by doors, passageways, and streets. (page 24)

The idea of the "loss of the city" through "the decline of physical presence in favour of an immaterial, phantom presence" (Virilio, 1996, page 45, quoted in Robins, 1996) is similar to the notion outlined above that the conventional work*place* will be displaced by the "elusive office" (Huws, et al., 1990) of shared electronic work*spaces*. The problem with both visions lies in their impoverished understanding of the rationale for, and benefits of, physical presence.

The Necessary Workplace

In the case of the workplace, the difficulties in establishing viable forms of teleworking reveal the significance of physical presence within the activity called "work." Recognizing that much work is difficult to detach from its broader working context, teleworking trials and experiments have tended to concentrate on particular kinds of work that appear to be most likely to be sustainable outside the conventional workplace (Gillespie and Li, 1994). Two broadly defined kinds of work have been identified as potentially suitable for teleworking from home: first, low level repetitive tasks such as data entry where the need for contact is assumed to be negligible; and, second, professional staff carrying out cognitive creative tasks (Kraut, 1989).

However, in practice it proves extremely difficult to identify tasks in either of these categories that are sufficiently self-contained to be sustainable in a telework environment. A survey in the United Kingdom of home-based teleworking in large and medium-sized enterprises, for example, found that "loss of face-to-face to contact" was by an overwhelming margin the most significant perceived problem with respect to the introduction of teleworking (National Computing Centre, 1992). This finding is consistent with other evaluations of teleworking trials and experiments, in which the difficulties associated with the lack of face-to-face contact are found to be the major barrier to the growth of teleworking, both from the perspective of the employees who are deprived of the social and networking aspects of work in a shared workplace, and from the perspective of managers who encounter problems of controlling, monitoring, and motivating teleworkers (Gray, et al., 1993).

The widely acknowledged skepticism of managers to teleworking is usually attributed to an out-moded conservatism (Huws, et al., 1990; Qvortrup, 1992). Yet the desire of managers to maintain face-to-face contact through direct physical presence simply acknowledges the importance of informal communications in the workplace in providing "the basis of supervision, socialization, social support, on-the-job learning by doing, and of the reproduction of corporate know-how and culture" (Kraut, 1989, page 26). Not to recognize this is to completely misunderstand the nature of what managers do, for as Boden and Molotch (1994) point out, managers spend more than half of their workday in copresence with others.

Even those jobs that are perceived to be self-contained and strongly individual, such as certain creative tasks, are found to be difficult to maintain in a teleworking environment, where the opportunity provided by the workplace for "bouncing ideas off other people" is denied or restricted (Stanworth and Stanworth, 1991). Similar findings have been established by Christiansen, Jacobsen, and Kalsdottir (1996), based on in-depth interviews with highly qualified professionals in the United States and Denmark with long-standing experience of telework. Their research stresses the importance of physical presence in much of the work that professionals do, such that frequent presence in the workplace is regarded as a necessity for viable, sustainable teleworking; they conclude that for professionals, teleworking more than two days a week seems problematic.

For "teleservices"—services where face-to-face communication with the business or consumer customer is replaced or complemented by telephone-based communications—the opportunities for the dispersal of work beyond traditional shared workplaces to the home would, from the purely technical point of view, appear to be an option (Richardson, 1997); the expertise embedded in the software often means that levels of worker expertise need not be high, while the control mechanisms in the software allow real-time monitoring by supervisors, in terms of immediately available statistical data and the ability to listen in to calls and to record conversations. Yet the dominant tendency in teleservices is to organize work into (often very) large, highly "industrialized" automated, tailorized workplaces, known as "call centers" (Richardson, 1994; Richardson and Marshall, 1996).

There are a number of reasons for this. First, the technology is generally designed on the basis that teleservice tasks will continue to be performed in call centers; that is to say, suppliers are conservative in how they design and advertise products (though most of the major suppliers of call-center technology have now developed small-office/home-office call-center technologies). Second, it may not make economic sense for a company to distribute calls to workers' homes; the cost of transmitting both voice and data traffic to a large number of workers' homes as opposed to a single central site, requiring at minimum ISDN lines, is unlikely to be cost-effective unless levels of flexibility or productivity are increased very significantly. Furthermore, investing in call-center technology for a large number of home-based agents may not make economic sense; the technology can be used only by one agent, whereas in a call-center it may be used by three or more agents covering a number of shifts, in, say, an 18 to 24-hour-per-day operation; and staff turnover (in the United Kingdom) is estimated to average around 20 to 30 percent per annum and thus there is no guarantee of a return on capital investment.

Third, and crucially, although the work is routinized and in theory subject to control through output targets, as in other industries managers prefer to have their workforce in one (or a few) places. Call-center managers interviewed in the United Kingdom by the authors and asked about call-center working from home generally greeted the question with incredulity—the process of management is seen as complex enough without introducing another layer of complexity. Why develop new training and motivational strategies for home-based workers, and spend time ensuring they don't feel marginalized and isolated, when managers have a call-center to run? In addition, managers suggested that there are definite benefits of the call-center environment, which would be hard to replicate in the home, the key benefit being teamworking, around which most call-centers are organized and performance pay calculated. There was also skepticism as to whether the kind of people who work from home would be well suited for teleservice work, the assumption being that more gregarious, outgoing people are best suited for call-center work, and that these are likely to prefer an office environment where socialization is possible.

We would conclude that for both professional and more routinized home-based teleworking, many of the problems in implementation are due to a failure to understand the significance of the workplace or the activities that take place within it. The flawed conception that underlies much of the discussion around the potential of teleworking from home is to see the workplace primarily as a physical location to which workers travel in order to undertake the individual work tasks assigned to them (Gillespie and Li, 1994). What these approaches fail to recognize is that the workplace is a highly functional device for facilitating the activities of collaborative work *groups*, which is how nearly all work is accomplished (the excessive individualism of conventional academia notwithstanding!). From this perspective:

> (p)erhaps the attainment of "the elusive office" will remain just that, elusive, and the work*place* will prove resistant to being substituted by a virtual work-s*pace*. Perhaps, for a little while longer at least, the obstinacy of the workplace in the face of its imminent demise will ensure that location independence remains an unrealised goal. (Gillespie and Li, 1994, page 270)

The Necessary City

The reasons why the electronic dissolution of the city is not imminent are similar to, and at least as compelling, as the reasons for the persistence of the workplace. Indeed, far from undermining the role of the city, as many earlier predicted, the emerging consensus is now that telecommunications and information technologies are contributing to a *strengthening* of the role of major cities within a global "space of flows" (Castells, 1989 and 1996; Graham and Marvin, 1996).

One reason why the electronic redundancy of the city has not come about lies in the mutually reinforcing interaction between concentrations of demand for specialized telecommunications services, and the supply of those services.

Far from equalizing the supply of telecommunications services across the globe, the combination of rapid technological advance, the increasing specialization of customer demand and the liberalization of telecommunications supply has led to an increasingly differentiated geography of telecommunications provision (Gillespie and Robins, 1991). As Mitch Moss first pointed out, these developments are leading to "the creation of a new telecommunications infrastructure designed to serve the information-intensive activities of large metropolitan regions" (Moss, 1987, page 536).

Taking the example of the United Kingdom, which has one of the most liberal telecommunications regimes in the world, the "landscape" of telecommunications provision has become highly differentiated, with cities the clear beneficiaries. In the City of London, firms benefit from a host of competing suppliers (including British Telecom, Mercury, City of London Telecommunications, MFS Telecommunications, Worldcom, and Energis; see Ireland, 1994) and the most advanced service offerings. In the central business districts (CBDs) of other major cities, and in business parks and other concentrations of business activity, firms have a range of potential suppliers and access to most advanced services. In the remaining urban areas, firms have a more restricted choice of supplier, with direct connection usually available only from British Telecom (BT) and, where infrastructures have been built, from the local cable operator. In many small towns and rural areas, customers are confronted with a *de facto* monopoly supplier, while some rural customers do not even have direct access to digital exchanges capable of providing services such as basic-rate ISDN (Gillespie et al., 1994). The general pattern, then, is one of metropolitan "hot spots" of intense competition and investment, surrounded by "warm haloes" of duopolistic competition in the urban areas, giving way in turn to "cold shadows" of *de facto* monopoly in rural Britain (Gillespie and Cornford, 1995).

A second and still more significant explanation for why electronic technologies have not undermined the rationale for the city lies in the continued, indeed increasing, need for copresence in human affairs. According to Boden and Molotch (1994, page 258), "(a)lthough in some instances communication is best done by more impersonal means, modernity implies no dilution in the degree that face-to-face—or, more precisely, 'copresent'—interaction is both preferred and necessary across a wide range of tasks," leading to what they term the "compulsion of proximity." It is the enduring nature of this compulsion that continues to provide the rationale for cities. As Tony Fitzpatrick (1997, page 9, quoted in Amin and Graham, 1997, page 413), the Director of Ove Arup, puts it as follows:

> Cities reflect the economic realities of the twenty-first century. Remote working from self-sufficient farmsteads via the Internet cannot replace the powerhouses of personal interaction which drives teamwork and creativity. These are the cornerstones of how professional people add value to their work. Besides, you cannot look into someone's eyes and see that they are trustworthy over the Internet.

Indeed, it can be convincingly argued that trends such as globalization, and the increasing velocity and volatility of the economy that is attendant upon it, are serving to accentuate the role of cities as interpreters of change and managers of risk (Mitchelson and Wheeler, 1994). Telecommunications networks, of course, have contributed greatly to the process of globalization and time-space compression, and hence are part of the explanation for the accentuated role for cities. Sassen (1991, page 5) points out that it is "precisely because of the territorial dispersal facilitated by telecommunications that agglomeration of certain centralizing activities has sharply increased," while Thrift's (1996) work on the City of London has demonstrated that the growth of information from new communications technologies has presented fundamental problems of interpretation for workers in the City that have forced greater rather than less face-to-face communication. The same point is made by Boden and Molotch (1994, page 274, original emphasis):

> The scattering made possible by the new technologies may indeed intensify the need for copresence among those who coordinate dispersed activities and interpret the information pouring in from far-flung settings. The more information produced by the new technologies, the higher the premium on copresence needed to design, interpret, and implement the knowledge gained. *In other words, the only way to deal effectively with the simple communication of high technology is with the medium of highest complexity—copresence.*

In this sense, of course, the city can be interpreted as the form of human settlement that has as its purpose the maximization of copresence. We can in consequence conclude that the anticipated (by some at least) demise of the city through technological redundancy not only been has exaggerated, it is has been completely misspecified, for the role of the city is actually being *enhanced* through global telecommunications networks. Such reflections have led Castells (1996) to predict that the dominant form of urbanization in the next millennium will be that of the "megacity," huge urban agglomerations forming the nodes of the global economy:

> in spite of all their social, urban and environmental problems, megacities will continue to grow, both in their size and in their attractiveness for the location of high-level functions and for people's choice. The ecological dream of small, quasi-rural communes will be pushed away to countercultural marginality by the historical tide of megacity development. (Ibid., page 409)

We began this chapter by suggesting that there were three "myths of disappearance" associated with information and communication technologies that we intended to debunk. Having now established the continued necessity of workplaces and of cities, in the remainder of the chapter we intend to concentrate on the third myth, which concerned the "unnecessary need to travel." This will require us to consider developments in urban spatial form, from which the need to travel is in part at least derived. Our focus will be to look at various types of "teleworking" in order to open a window onto the spatial structure and travel patterns of the future "informational city."

TELEWORKING AND THE NEED TO TRAVEL

Much of the rhetoric around teleworking, particularly in the United States, has concerned its potential to substitute for travel, specifically the journey to work. Although the implications for travel would therefore at first sight appear to be obvious, in reality the outcomes can be rather complicated. Mokhtarian (1990) reminds us that there are four possible interactions between tele-communications and travel:

(i)   substitution (i.e., telecommunications decreases travel);
(ii) enhancement (i.e., telecommunications directly stimulates travel);
(iii) operational efficiency (i.e., telecommunications improves travel by making the transportation system more efficient);
(iv) indirect, long-term impacts (e.g., telecommunications may affect locational and land use decisions, thereby affecting travel).

Based on an extensive review of the literature, Graham and Marvin (1994, page 269) conclude that:

> the relationship between telecommunications and the urban environment is not as simple as the substitutionist perspective would imply. Instead, electronic and physical transformation proceed in parallel, producing complex and often contradictory effects on urban flows and spaces.

As a means of illustrating the validity of this conclusion, this section will examine the travel implications of various types of teleworking, drawing upon a report undertaken for the U.K. Parliamentary Office of Science and Technology by the authors (Gillespie, Richardson, and Cornford, 1995). The findings concentrate on the U.K. and European experience and are necessarily speculative, for both the extent of teleworking and the amount of research that has been undertaken on it are very much less in the United Kingdom and (particularly) the rest of Europe when compared with the United States. Although there is well-developed U.S. literature on teleworking and its travel implications (see, for example, Nilles, 1988; Kitamura, et al., 1990; Mokhtarian, 1991; Niles, 1994; Mokhtarian, et al., 1995; Handy and Mokhtarian, 1996), the very different urban spatial contexts in the United States (particularly in California, where most of the research has been undertaken), means that little confidence could be attached to transferring U.S. results to U.K. and European urban contexts. In the absence of appropriate evidence, therefore, necessarily we will need to be speculative.

In the above-mentioned study (Gillespie, et al., 1995), we developed a five-fold classification of "telework" in the broader-than-usual sense of all forms of work organization that are based around information and communications (ICT) technologies:

1. *Electronic homework*—in which the worker undertakes paid employment from home (either as an employee or self-employed) supported by ICTs. It is this category of work that is, in the European context, usually con-

veyed by the term "telework" (in the United States it is more usually referred to as "telecommuting"), but in our analysis this was just one form of a broader category.

2. *Telecottages*—or shared facilities from which teleworking to other locations can take place. In the United Kingdom/European context, and in contrast to the United States where "neighborhood telework centres" have been established in a number of metropolitan areas, shared access teleworking facilities have been developed only in rural areas, hence our use of the term "telecottage."

3. *Nomadic or mobile workers*—these workers are mobile, use portable ICT equipment and work from a combination of locations, including home, cars/trains/planes, customers' premises and the central office (which is often reorganized and downsized to accommodate "hot-desking").

4. *Remote offices*—this category encompasses firms and organizations that have used ICTs to reorganize across space, both centralizing functions into (usually) fairly large, specialist offices, but often at the same time taking the opportunity presented by ICTs to site these offices at lower cost locations. Telephone call-centers for delivering teleservices are one particular form within the remote-office category.

5. *Group or team telework*—developments in ICTs are increasingly making possible geographically distributed teamwork, in which interconnected work tasks can be performed by workers operating from a number of locations using a shared virtual workspace.

Below we attempt to review and, given the limited empirical material to draw upon, to speculate upon the likely locational trends that will be associated with these forms of (broadly defined) teleworking and the likely travel patterns that will be associated with them. We ignore the telecottage category, as, in the U.K. context, rural shared facility centers have only a handful of teleworkers operating from them (Richardson and Gillespie, 1999).

Electronic Homeworking

From the evidence reviewed above (such as Christiansen, et al., 1996), we can surmise that the growth of electronic homeworking (EHW) will be relatively modest, and that it will in the main be part-time in nature, perhaps being undertaken for a day or two a week (this is certainly the case in the United States; see Lund and Mokhtarian, 1994). Its impact upon urban form and travel will be hardly revolutionary therefore, both because its incidence will be relatively limited and because most electronic homeworkers (except those who are self-employed) will still need to commute to their office for the majority of their working days.

Because of the latter feature, and because the incidence of electronic homeworking is higher in those professional occupations and service activities that are concentrated in cities, EHW in the United Kingdom is overrepresented in metropolitan regions, particularly London. Huws's (1993) survey of employers in the United Kingdom established that while London accounted for 16 percent of the country's total sample of employers, it accounted for 24 percent of employers with teleworkers. Although we do not yet have access to data on the residential location of teleworkers, we can assume that they are geographically constrained by the need to travel to their employer's premises and, frequently, to the premises of clients as well, for home-based teleworkers working for a single employer spend on average a quarter of their time on the employer's premises and a further quarter elsewhere (Huws, 1993). Even freelance teleworkers, who might be assumed to have the greatest degree of locational freedom and who are most usually associated with rurally based lifestyles, are often constrained by the need to be close to clients, and survey evidence reveals that more than half of such teleworkers live in the centers or suburbs of cities (Huws et al., 1996).

Even the limited impacts upon urban travel associated with the substitution of some journeys to work by electronic means need to be qualified by taking into account a number of further issues (Gillespie, et al., 1995):

- *The mode of travel of trips replaced by EHW* — the possibility arises that public transport or soft mode trips could be substituted, rather than car-driver trips, with the risk that the critical mass of commuters needed to support public transit or car pools could be reduced, leading in the longer term to greater car dependence (U.S. Department of Transportation, 1993). This risk is likely to be more significant in European cities than it would be in the already predominantly car-dependent American metropolises. Thus a study of telecommuting in the Netherlands (reported in Mokhtarian, et al., 1995) found that nearly all telecommuting occasions replaced public transport or bike trips rather than car trips. In the case of London, with many long-distance rail commuters, it has been suggested that part-time EHW may exacerbate the economic problems of rail transit if it is concentrated on certain days of the week (for instance, Fridays), reducing rail revenues on these days while the same amount of infrastructure is still needed to get people into Central London on the other days of the week (Department of Transport, 1993).
- *The impact of EHW on noncommute trips* — the incorporation of other journeys, such as dropping children at school or shopping, into the commute trip, a process of "trip chaining," could lead to additional journeys being generated (either by the teleworker or by other household members) if the commute trip is electronically substituted. Additionally, electronic homeworkers will generate substantial business travel, notably to meet clients.
- *The impact of EHW on the travel behavior of other household members* — it has been hypothesized that there may be additional trips generated by other household members. Although the limited evidence from the United States does not lend support to this hypothesis (Kitamura et al., 1990; Mokhtarian, et al., 1995), it may well be that in the United Kingdom, with much lower levels of household car ownership, journeys foregone by telecommuting will generate additional travel by making the car available for other household members (Lyons, no date).

- *The impact of improved traffic flow on latent demand* — one of the likely outcomes of EHW is to reduce peak-hour travel and hence ease road congestion. If this is so, however, then latent demand is likely to induce additional travel in much the same way that building new road capacity does. In the United States, it has been estimated that "perhaps half the potential reduction in vehicle miles traveled directly attributed to telecommuters will be replaced by new traffic, induced by lower levels of congestion and higher average speeds" (U.S. Department of Energy, 1994, page xi).
- *The longer-run impact on residential location and average commute distances* — it has been hypothesized that telecommuting will encourage residential relocation to sites further from workplaces, because longer commuting distances can be traded off for less-frequent work trips (Mokhtarian, et al., 1995). Limited U.S. evidence adds some support to this hypothesis, in that a survey of telecommuters in California who had relocated revealed that in 50 percent of the completed move cases the move was farther away from the central office, compared with 30 percent moving nearer (Nilles, 1991, cited in Lyons, undated).

So what can be concluded concerning the urban form and travel implications of EHW? First, we can conclude that the implications will be modest. Estimates derived primarily from U.S. experience suggest that with 5.8 percent of the workforce telecommuting for an average of 1.2 days per week, the associated net reduction in vehicle miles traveled in 1991 was 0.51 percent (Mokhtarian, et al., 1995). In the United Kingdom, with an appreciably lower incidence of EHW, with shorter journeys to work, and with a modal split less dominated by the private car, we can anticipate that the net substitution effect will be appreciably less than the 0.51 percent estimated for the United States. It will therefore be some appreciable time before any impacts of EHW on urban form or on urban travel patterns are likely to be discernible.

In the longer term, we might anticipate the impacts in the United Kingdom to be as follows: the main effect of any growth in EHW is likely to be the expansion of the functional metropolitan region centered on London, where most EHW is concentrated (Huws, et al., 1996). Given that the broader context of locational change in office employment in this region is that of deconcentration from central London, EHW will simply add further impetus to the process by which the nodality of the region in terms of work travel is reduced, with a more diffuse pattern of travel developing. Invariably, the new patterns of travel, both to work and to meetings, clients' premises, and so on, will be more car dependent than the centrally focused patterns of travel they replace.

238

Mobile Teleworking

Although there is agreement that nomadic or mobile teleworking is growing significantly, there are few reliable statistics on its incidence or rate of growth. Gray, Hodson, and Gordon (1993) estimate that there are more than 7 million nomadic desk jobs in the United States, and over 1.5 million in the United Kingdom, but the basis for their estimates is not stated. There has always been mobile work, of course, such as sales staff and field engineers; our interest is in the way some firms are starting to look strategically at how new technologies can be used to change working practices, with a view to reducing costs and improving customer service, and the locational and travel implications of such changes.

One example of a new working practice with potentially significant implications for the demand for office space, the location of office space, and the substitution/generation of travel is "hot-desking," introduced first in computer companies such as IBM and Digital, but now spreading more widely into firms with other mobile staff (Gillespie, et al., 1995). In the case of IBM, the stimulus for hot-desking was cost competition, coupled with a recognition that the was overprovided with expensive office space, given that many of the staff spent much of their working days out on the road or at customers" premises. The hot-desking scheme developed and introduced by IBM involved providing an average of one desk for two workers, with all of the desk space shared, and increasing in the amount of space for meetings. The new working practices have proved successful in terms of productivity, generating the following changes in employee time use (Young, 1992):

- travel time   −13%
- time with customer   + 36%
- time in office   −23%
- total space saved   −30%

A significant increase in nomadic working in conjunction with concepts such as hot-desking, if taken up widely, would have obvious implications for office space demand, with a significant reduction in the average space requirements of certain sectors. The increased emphasis on the mobility of the workforce is also likely to encourage firms to locate in out-of-town sites with easy access to the road network and with plentiful parking space rather than in city-center locations, thus reinforcing existing trends toward out-of-town developments.

To the authors' knowledge, no published studies have been carried out on the transport implications of this form of mobile teleworking, and there are a range of possible outcomes—some contradictory—if the practice continues to grow. Where workers have traditionally been mobile but are now being discouraged from traveling to their office base, the number of miles traveled per worker should fall, as in the IBM case reported above. However, as part of the rationale behind strategic changes in working practices such as hot-desking is to "get closer to the client," one would also expect that there would be more visits to each client than previously. If customers come to expect more site visits as a matter of course then more, rather than fewer, miles may be traveled. A further possibility is that if mobile working spreads to new areas of work, the overall travel could increase even though time traveled per worker falls (new groups of mobile workers could also have an impact on existing modal splits, with more workers having to take the car). Finally, new travel patterns may emerge as the classic commuting trip to the office declines and workers stay at home until it is time to visit the client. We can assume that these trips are likely to be less city-center-dominated than the classic commute trip, as well as being more car-dependent.

Group or Team Teleworking

Despite the existing technological limitations on the development of team teleworking (Gillespie, et al., 1994), there can be little doubt that new forms of work organization are pulling in this direction. An increasing business focus on quality and customer service, the need for flexibility to cope with turbulent markets, and an emphasis on innovation are leading to new structures within information-based organizations in which "task-focused teams," often crossing organizational boundaries, are becoming the new paradigm of work organization (see, for example, Opper and Fersko-Weiss, 1992). Of course, not all teamworking involves spatially distributed teams, but multiple pressures are pushing in this direction. The process of globalization, the increasing need for organizations flexibly to combine and recombine their spatially dispersed specialized human resources, and the requirement to forge strategic alliances with other organizations possessing complimentary assets are all leading to the construction of task-focused teams with geographically distributed participants.

As with the other forms of telework considered above, one might assume that team telework would cut down on demand for travel. As far as we are aware, however, no detailed studies have been carried out into this aspect of team telework, so we cannot make detailed comments on the travel patterns it generates. We would, however, make the following observations. Generally speaking, computer-supported team telework not only means more tele-mediated contact with groups across space; it also means tele-mediated contact with groups with whom contact has been limited or nonexistent, as firms or networks reorganize to take advantage of distributed resources (for example, skilled labor and laboratory facilities). These new contacts also generate new travel demands as groups find that technological and organizational capacity is not (for the moment, at least) sufficiently developed to take shared tasks from inception to fruition. So, for example, it is likely that distributed R&D teams will travel for face-to-face meetings across the world, whereas previously they may have worked only locally. Even for teams working within national boundaries, more travel can be generated by teamwork. In the case of IBM, for example, distributed teams focused on business sectors, so as to get "closer to the client," mean that teamworkers may be physically further away from both their clients and their fellow teamworkers. Despite the sophisticated supporting electronic networks, face-to-face meetings are still required, both with clients and with other team members, but now instead of popping next door to meet work colleagues, or traveling a few miles to meet clients, workers now have to travel up and down the motorway on a regular basis.

We would therefore anticipate that team teleworking, in expanding the geographical spread of participants in the virtual work activity space, is likely to lead to new demands for travel and to substantial increases in the distances over which business travel takes place.

Remote Offices—The Example of Call-Centers

The locational and travel implications of call-centers are particularly complex and interesting, due to two features; first, the work concerned frequently moves between cities as well as between different types of location within cities; and second, the travel implications extend beyond work travel to also encompass travel to consume.

In the case of telebanking in the United Kingdom, for example, there are two clear locational implications with respect to employment (Marshall and Richardson, 1996). First, the possibility of separating production and consumption is allowing the relocation of substantial parts of the production process to lower-cost parts of the country, with cities such as Leeds, Edinburgh, and Glasgow gaining appreciable numbers of telebanking jobs. To an extent, therefore, travel to work to a bank branch in say, London, or to a small town in the outer Southeast of England is being replaced by a journey to work to a call center in, say, Leeds (with an appreciable degree of job downsizing en route, due to the much higher levels of labor productivity associated with tele-mediated service delivery).

Second, "in contrast to most bank branches, nearly all telebanking operations are on business parks on the edge of cities, rather than in town or city centers. There is no need for an expensive city-centre location" (Ibid., page 1855). The two locational effects are usually compounded such that jobs are in effect moving from the center or suburban high street of one city to an out-of-town business park location in another city. The shift in the type of intra-urban location is inducing a clear modal shift in that out-of-town call centers tend to have a much higher car mode share than the jobs they are replacing (Arup Economics and Planning/CURDS, 1998). The modal shift due to locational change is exacerbated by the greater incidence of shift-working in telebanking operations, militating against the use of public transport.

These work travel changes induced by implicit shifts in the location of employment are matched by changes in travel to consume, though in this case the journey is not geographically displaced but rather is electronically substituted. In the example of a bank branch in a London high street, therefore, telebanking is leading to the disappearance of both journeys to work and journeys to bank, although a portion of the journey to work is reappearing in a very different guise on a business park in a city in the north of England. The complex interplay of these production and consumption elements in traditional and tele-mediated modes of service delivery, and their different implications for urban spatial structure and for patterns of work travel and travel to consume, require further empirical investigation.

CONCLUSION

What can we conclude about the implications of teleworking, broadly defined, for urban form and for travel patterns and travel behavior? First, it might be observed that it is remarkable that so much research effort has been expended on studying the locational and travel implications associated with a handful of electronic homeworkers, when so little has been expended on studying the locational and travel implications associated with a very much larger number of workers whose working practices are being radically changed by new ICTs (for a notable exception, at least with repect to locational trends, see Office of Technology Assessment, 1995).

Second, the notion that teleworking will lead to reduced travel, and hence to more environmentally sustainable cities, is, at the very least, open to question. Even with respect to EHW, where the most obvious potential for travel substitution is to be found, we have concluded that the most likely long-term effect in the United Kingdom is that the geographical extent of the London "daily urban system" will be expanded, and the nodality of the region in terms of travel patterns will be further reduced. When we consider the likely travel impacts of the growth of mobile working and of spatially dispersed teamworking, we are at once confounded by the almost complete absence of empirical research. However, both of these significant developments in working practices appear likely to expand the daily activity spaces of individual workers and to lead to significantly increased journey distances. It also seems likely that significant modal shifts in the direction of increased car dependency will be associated with these new ways of working. Finally, the location of teleservice employment in large call centers has, within the context of the particular planning regime in the United Kingdom over the last ten years, clearly been associated with a shift from city center and high-street locations to out-of-town/edge-of-town business park locations, and will have helped fuel the growth in car dependency in the journey to work.

The "reduced demand for travel" scenario, which is usually invoked with respect to teleworking may, then, be decidedly misleading in terms of its apparently positive contribution to building more sustainable cities. Not only are communications technologies expanding the "activity spaces" within which work takes place, leading to longer distances traveled, but in addition, journey patterns associated with new ways of working are becoming more diffuse and less nodal, and hence more difficult to accomplish by public transport. This effect is exacerbated by companies adjusting their premises stock to accommodate more effectively new ways of working, leading to a reduction in demand for conventional city-center offices and an increase in demand for office space in office park environments with high levels of accessibility to the motorway system. At the same time, the substitution of tele-mediated for face-to-face banking and other services risks further undermining the role of city centers and high streets, as branch offices are closed and customers are served from large teleservice centers, themselves usually located on business parks. Far from contributing to more sustainable urban ways of life and travel behavior, therefore, teleworking and teleservices seem to be developing hand in hand with lower-density, less nodal urban forms and with travel behavior that is more car-dependent than before. Teleworking and tele-activities are, then, perhaps best understood not as developments that suppress the demand for mobility but, rather, as forms of what might best be described as "hypermobility."

REFERENCES

Amin, A. and S. Graham. (1997). "The Ordinary City." *Transactions of the Institute of British Geographers* New Series 22, 4: 411–429.

Arup Economics and Planning and CURDS. (1998). "Changes in Working Practises in the Service Sector." Final Report to the U.K. Department of the Environment, Transport and the Regions, Arup Economics and Planning, London and CURDS, Newcastle.

Berry, B. J. L. (1973). *The Human Consequences of Urbanization.* New York: St. Martin's Press.

Boden, D. and H. L. Molotch. (1994). "The Compulsion of Proximity." In R. Friedland and D. Boden, eds. *No(w)here.* Berkeley: University of California Press.

Castells, M. (1989). *The Information City: Information Technology, Economic Restructuring, and the Urban-Regional Process.* Oxford: Blackwell.

———. (1996). *The Rise of the Network Society: Volume 1 of The Information Age: Economy, Society and Culture.* Oxford: Blackwell.

Christiansen, A. H., K. N. Jacobsen, and A. Kalsdottir (1996). "Her & Der: Master Thesis on Telework as It Is Applied in Professional Work." (*http://www.dk-online. dk/users/kaare_nordahl_jacobsen/#specialelink*).

Department of Transport. (1993). "Transport." In *Teleworking—The Government Views.* Proceedings of a seminar organized by the Teleworking Special Interest Group, mimeo.

Featherstone, M. and R. Burrows (1995). "Cultures of Technological Embodiment: An Introduction." In M. Featherstone and R. Burrows, eds. *Cyberspace, Cyberbodies and Cyberpunk: Cultures of Technological Embodiment.* London: Sage.

Fitzpatrick, T. (1997). "A Tale of Tall Cities." *The Guardian On-Line.* February 6: 9.

Gillespie, A., M. Coombes and S. Raybould (1994). "Contribution of Telecommunications to Rural Economic Development: Variations On a Theme?" *Entrepreneurship & Regional Development* 6: 201–217.

Gillespie, A. and J. Cornford (1995). "Network Diversity or Network Fragmentation? The Evolution of European Telecommunications in Competitive Environments." In Banister, D., R. Capello, and P. Nijkamp, eds. *European Transport and Communications Networks.* Chichester: John Wiley and Sons.

Gillespie, A. and F. Li Feng. (1994). "Teleworking, Work Organization and the Workplace." In R. Mansell, ed. *The Management of Information and Communication Technologies: Emerging Patterns of Control.* London: ASLIB.

Gillespie, A., R. Richardson, and J. Cornford. (1995). *Review of Telework in Britain: Implications for Public Policy.* Report prepared for the U.K. Parliamentary Office of Science and Technology. Newcastle upon Tyne: Centre for Urban and Regional Development Studies.

Gillespie, A. and K. Robins (1991). "Non-Universal Service? Political Economy and Communications Geography." In J. Brotchie, M. Batty, P. Hall, and P. Newton, eds. *Cities of the 21st Century: New Technologies and Spatial Systems.* Harlow: Longman.

Gold, J. R. (1991). "Fishing in Muddy Waters: Communications Media, Homeworking and the Electronic Cottage." In S. D. Brunn and T. R. Leinbach, eds. *Collapsing Space and Time: Geographic Aspects of Communication and Information*. London: Harper Collins Academic.

Graham, S. (1997). "Telecommunications and the Future of Cities: Debunking the Myths." *Cities* 14, 1: 21–29.

Graham, S. and S. Marvin. (1996). *Telecommunications and the City: Electronic Spaces, Urban Places*. London and New York: Routledge.

Gray, M., N. Hodson and G. Gordon. (1993). *Teleworking Explained*. Chichester: John Wiley and Sons.

Handy, S. and P. L. Mokhtarian. (1996). "Forecasting Telecommuting: An Exploration of Methodologies and Research Needs." *Transportation* 23: 163–190.

Hiltz, S. R. (1984). *Online Communities. A Case Study of the Office of the Future*. New Jersey: Ablex.

Huws, U. (1993). *Teleworking in Britain*. Employment Department Research Series No. 18. Sheffield: Employment Department.

Huws, U., S. Honey, and S. Morris. (1996). *Teleworking and Rural Development*. Rural Research Report No. 27, Rural Development Commission. London: Rural Development Commission.

Huws, U., W. B. Korte, and S. Robinson. (1990). *Telework: Towards the Elusive Office*. Chichester: John Wiley and Sons.

Ireland, J. (1994). "The Importance of Telecommunications to London as an International Financial Centre." Subject Report XVIII, The City Research Project, London Business School and Corporation of London.

Kitamura, R., J. Nilles, P. Conroy, and D. M. Fleming. (1990). "Telecommuting as a Transportation Planning Measure: Initial Results of California Pilot Project." *Transportation Research Record* 1285: 98–104.

Kraut, R. E. (1989). "Telecommuting: The Trade-Offs of Home Work." *Journal of Communications* 39: 19–47.

Lund, J. and Mokhtarian, P. (1994). "Telecommuting and Residential Location: Theory and Implications for Commute Travel in the Monocentric Metropolis." *Transportation Research Record* 1463: 10–14.

Lyons, G. D. (No Date). "Telecommunications-Transport Interaction: Teleworking and the Implications for Transport." Transportation Research Group, University of Southampton, mimeo.

McLuhan, H. M. (1964). *Understanding Media: The Extensions of Man*. London: Sphere Books.

Marshall, J. N. and R. Richardson. (1996). "The Impact of "Telemediated" Services on Corporate Structures: The Example of 'Branchless' Retail Banking in Britain." *Environment and Planning A* 28: 1843–1858.

Mitchelson, R. and J. Wheeler. (1994). "The Flow of Information in a Global Economy: The Role of the American Urban System in 1990." *Annals of the Association of American Geographers* 84, 1: 87–107.

Mitchell, W. (1995). *City of Bits: Space, Place and the Infobahn*. Cambridge, MA: MIT Press.

Mokhtarian, P. L. (1990). "A Typology of Relationships Between Telecommunications and Transportation." *Transportation Research* 24A(3): 231–242.

Mokhtarian, P. L. (1991). "Telecommuting and Travel: State of Practise, State of the Art." *Transportation* 18 (4): 319–342.

Mokhtarian, P. L., S. L. Handy, and I. Salomon. (1995). "Methodological Issues in the

Estimation of the Travel, Energy, and Air Quality Impacts of Telecommuting." *Transportation Research* 29A (4): 283–302.

Moss, M. L. (1987). "Telecommunications, World Cities and Urban Policy." *Urban Studies* 24: 534–546.

National Computing Centre. (1992). *Teleworking in the U.K.: An Analysis of the NCC Teleworking Surveys*. Manchester: National Computing Centre.

Niles, J. S. (1994). *Beyond Telecommuting: A New Paradigm for the Effect of Tele-communications on Travel*. Report to the U.S. Department of Energy by Global Telematics. (http://www.lbl.gov/ICDS/Niles/)

Niles, J. M. (1988). "Traffic Reduction by Telecommuting: A Status Review and Selected Bibliography." *Transportation Research* 22A(4): 301–317.

———. (1991). "Telecommuting and Urban Sprawl: Mitigator or Inciter." *Transportation* 18: 411–432.

Office of Technology Assessment of the U.S. Congress. (1995). *The Technological Reshaping of Metropolitan America*. OTA-ETI-643. Washington, DC: U.S. Government Printing Office.

Opper, S. and H. Fersko-Weiss. (1992). *Technology for Teams: Enhancing Productivity in Networked Organizations*. New York: Van Nostrand Rheinhold.

Qvortrup, L. (1992). "Telework: Visions, Definitions, Realities, Barriers." In OECD, ed. *Cities and New Technologies*. Paris: OECD.

Richardson, R. (1994). "Back-Officing Front Office Functions—Organisational and Locational Implications of New Telemediated Services." In R. Mansell, ed. *The Management of Information and Communication Technologies: Emerging Patterns of Control*. London: ASLIB.

———. (1997). "Network Technologies, Organisational Change and the Location of Employment." In A. Dumort and J. Dryden, eds. *The Economics of the Information Society*. Brussels: OECD/EU.

Richardson, R. and A. Gillespie. (1999 forthcoming). "The Economic Development of Peripheral Rural Places in the Information Age." In M. Wilson and K. Corey, eds. *Information Tectonics: Space, Place and Technology an Information Age*. Chichester: John Wiley and Sons.

Richardson, R. and J. N. Marshall. (1996). "The Growth of Telephone Call Centres in Peripheral Areas of Britain: Evidence from Tyne and Wear." *Area* 28(3): 308–317.

Robins, K. (1995). "Cyberspace and the World We Live In." *Body & Society* Vol. 1(3–4): 135–155.

———. (1996). "Foreclosing on the City? The Bad Idea of Virtual Urbanism." Mimeo, Centre for Urban and Regional Development Studies, University of Newcastle upon Tyne.

Sassen, S. (1991). *The Global City: New York, London, Tokyo*. Princeton, NJ: Princeton University Press.

Stanworth, J. and C. Stanworth (1991). *Telework: The Human Resource Implications*. London: Institute of Personnel Management.

Thrift, N. (1996). *Spatial Formations*. London: Sage.

U.S. Department of Energy. (1994). *Energy, Emissions and Social Consequences of Telecommuting*. U.S. Department of Energy, Office of Policy, Planning and Program Evaluation.

Virilio, P. (1996). *Cybermonde, la Politique du Pire*. Paris: Textuel.

Young, H. (1992). "Workplace Solutions." Paper presented to the Beacon Group Teleworking 92 Conference, September 15, Brighton.

PART V.

Case Studies of the Effect of Telecommuncations Technology on Urban Space

16

THE POLITICAL SALIENCE OF THE SPACE OF FLOWS

INFORMATION AND COMMUNICATION TECHNOLOGIES AND THE RESTRUCTURING CITY

Alan Southern

INTRODUCTION

One of the aims of this chapter is to consider the response of city policy-makers to the idea that new information and communication technologies (ICTs) provide a route to urban economic restructuring.[1] There is, I suggest, a political salience to this which is often marginalized in studies on ICTs and urban economies. This chapter looks at the political salience of what Castells (1996) terms the space of flows. It follows recent attempts made by local planners and policy-makers in Sunderland, a city in the northeast of England, to connect their place to the global electronic architecture spreading across the world. Sunderland, therefore represents a contemporary attempt in the United Kingdom to use ICTs in the restructuring of an urban economy and I use it as a case study here.

There are a number of logics to this restructuring process. The first is the way in which there is a shift taking place in the framework of society, of which city economies are obviously a part. By this I refer to the move toward an informational mode of development, another term suggested by Castells (1989; 1996). The restructuring of cities is taking place within this shift, and the role and potential of ICTs are highly relevant to urban areas because the source of economic activity is today driven by knowledge generation and ever intensified information processing. This is seen most markedly in the major cities of the world, such as London and New York, which act as the command points in the world economy (Sassen, 1991). The role of ICTs in the restructuring of places like Sunderland is little researched.

The second logic is associated with the set of ICT-based activities evident in many places, which are conscious attempts by city planners and policy-makers to connect the local with the global economy. ICT activities of this sort follow a typical path of economic restructuring that often draw on traditional government funding mechanisms and programs. Their focus will, in some way, be about infrastructure development, not only the physical laying of wires, cable, and satellite, but of the softer features of infrastructure development concerned with people. These are about the skills and education of the local labor force and their reproduction, as part of the shift toward a new mode of development. In this chapter, the City of Sunderland Telematics Strategy provides evidence of the strategic planning of ICT-based activities.

Not only are ICT projects an extension of the economic development activity of the city, they are legitimized through the social and economic rationales that underpin them. The third logic is about the scope and legitimacy of ICTs, which are in fact the key features of the local governance of ICTs. The local governance of ICTs is a new area of development, one which is as yet little understood, but which takes account of the partnerships and coalitions that are springing up to shape particular types of urban economic restructuring. In Sunderland, the work of the Sunderland Telematics Working Group (STWG) has taken on the local governance role. The STWG is a subgroup of the main regeneration body in the city, known as the City of Sunderland Partnership, and therefore draws on the knowledge and expertise of key local actors from private, public, and voluntary sectors. In the context of this book, I suggest that the local governance of ICTs is an attempt to impose a local logic to the space of flows, and this in effect is its political salience.

This chapter is structured in two main parts. First of all I consider the notion of a city restructuring for the informational mode of development. Briefly, an overview of what Castells (1996) refers to as the informational mode of development is given, and then I suggest what the shift toward this means for local economies. An introduction to the Sunderland Telematics Strategy is provided here, and two examples of ICT projects are outlined. These examples are provided from either end of the ICT activity spectrum, involving a community based initiative to recycle computers and a project that is part of a broader economic development package about the construction of an international business site to support efforts to diversify the Sunderland economy. The second part of this chapter raises issues associated with the political salience of the space of flows. The concept of the space of flows is about the actors who can shape the spatial logic of the informational mode of development (Castells, 1996), and I suggest here that the local governance of ICTs is an important feature of this. This part of the chapter takes into account the dynamics of ICTs in their local setting, and how the STWG has sought to shape the space of flows.

RESTRUCTURING CITY ECONOMIES FOR THE INFORMATIONAL MODE OF DEVELOPMENT

The Shift toward the Informational Mode of Development

In recent years there has been an emerging literature that has considered the role of information and communications technologies in economic restructuring. Commentators such as Batty (1990), Hall (1993), and Mitchell (1995) have concentrated on the effects of ICTs on the morphology of cities. There have been analyses of organizational and institutional restructuring and the effects of ICTs, such as in the retail sector (Ducatel, 1990), the telecommunications sector (Luthe, 1993) and in government (Andersen, 1998; Bellamy and Taylor, 1998). Others, such as Dabinett and Graham (1994), Gibbs and Tanner (1997), and Gillespie and Williams (1988) have paid particular attention to the integration of ICTs for the benefit of local economic development. While each of these areas overlap in some way, one of the most useful conceptual bases for this work that provides new analytical tools for urban studies has been the idea of a technological revolution currently converging with fundamental changes in the structure of capitalism (see for instance Graham, 1997; Graham and Marvin, 1996; Castells, 1989, 1996).

Castells (1996) has cited four areas where this convergence is most prominent. The first is the area of ICTs being harnessed to enhance the productivity of capital and labor; the second is how they support and deepen the capitalist logic of profit-seeking; third, how ICTs are playing a more significant role in creating new conditions for profit-making, specifically through the globalization of production, financial circulation, and markets; and the fourth area is about ICTs being used to marshall support for productivity gains in the interest of the competitiveness of national economies, often at the expense of social programs and protection. Convergence, and each of these areas, is most visible in the core activities of "advanced" economies—in particular, the growth in importance of service industries such as financial and business sectors, the decentralization of management functions in large organizations, the policy focus on small-sized indigenous firms such as from the European Commission Directorate General (DG23), which aims to provide coordination of small-firm policy across member states, the restructuring of the public sector, particularly institutions of governance, the types of skills in demand from employers, and so on, all of which increasingly interweave the functionality of ICTs. This represents a shift toward what Castells (1989) calls an informational mode of development, whereby the interaction between technology and social actors shapes local economic restructuring.

Before we can understand what this means for local economies, it is worth considering what Castells refers to when he speaks of a shift toward an informational mode of development. Castells (1989, 1996) is careful to distinguish between the mode of production and the mode of development. The former is about the societal framework in that local economies operate, such as capitalism or former-Soviet-Union-based communism (statism), while the latter is about the techniques of development which enable local economies to operate (Castells, 1996). Table 16.1 uses the concepts outlined by Castells (Ibid.) to map out in very simple manner a trajectory for the mode of development. Under an agrarian mode of development, the technical basis for productivity was based around quantitative increases in labor and in natural resources, and the main organizational principle was focused on land ownership and concentrated wealth. During the industrial mode of development, the introduction of new energy sources such as steam power and electricity provided an essential source of technical productivity decentralized throughout the production process, which peaked through the economies of scale achieved under Fordism (Aglietta, 1979). This was most marked in the twentieth century, and in the postwar period the technical source of productivity was an important

Table 16.1 The Trajectory of the Mode of Development

Mode of Development	Source of Productivity (Technical)	Principle of Organizational Structure
Agrarian	Quantitative increases in labor; Quantitative increases in natural resources (i.e., land)	Land ownership and concentrated wealth
Industrial	Introduction of new energy sources and the ability to decentralize the use of energy throughout production and circulation processes	Economic growth based on maximizing outputs, i.e., through economies of scale
Informational	Knowledge generation, information processing, and symbol communication	Technological development; toward the accumulation of knowledge and higher levels of complexity in information processing

Source: Castells, 1996, page 17.

part in the relationship between production and consumption, a relationship often regulated in some way by the state (Sayer, 1989). More recently—some commentators contrast the idea of post-Fordist period and the informational age (see Allen, 1992)—the informational mode of development has as its technical source for productivity knowledge generation, information, and symbol communication based on rapid information processing technologies.[2]

For the purpose of this chapter and to understand the restructuring processes that are taking place in contemporary cities, Table 16.1 provides a useful starting point to consider how economic development rests on the ability to harness new technologies, geared toward the accumulation of knowledge, in all industrial and commercial sectors. Of course, the reader must be wary of any attempt to suggest that the move toward the informational mode of development has taken place as a teleological process.

Local Economies and Information and Communication Technologies

Castells (Ibid.) sees the complexity involved in greater information processing as the new material and technological basis of economic activity today. We should note however, that the processes of economic restructuring and the rise of informationalism are distinct. We should also recognize how their convergence has resulted in a new techno-economic paradigm:

the two components of the paradigm are distinguishable only analytically, because while informationalism has now been decisively shaped by the restructuring process, restructuring could never have been accomplished, even in a contradictory manner, without the unleashing of the technological and organisational potential of informationalism. (Castells, 1989, page 29)

As Cooke (1989) has shown, the pressures to restructure in U.K. regional and local economies are severe, and it is significant, therefore, that urban economic development at this time is coinciding with the pervasive character and material basis of the informational mode of development. The relevance of this for city economies is that it places the use of ICTs firmly in the court of urban economic restructuring.

In the Northeast of England, planners are well aware of the potential of ICTs, but they have been reluctant to include them in their policies for restructuring for a number of reasons. Often, many other day-to-day operations are considered to be more important; then again, there is the intangible nature of the technology itself, particularly as physical infrastructure is mainly, but not always, seen to be outside the scope of most local governance agencies, who are strapped for funding (Southern, 1997). Even so, this has not prevented telecommunications from growing as an area of interest for social scientists and for urban planners (Graham and Marvin, 1996). The case of Sunderland indicates some degree of consciousness on the part of city planners of how they can shape their future using ICTs. Sunderland demonstrates an identifiable shift in the attitude of city planners and policy-makers toward ICTs, focused on basic local economic infrastructure development, attempts to attract new inward investment and to develop a program of reskilling for the city labor force, and how to employ the technology to improve the quality of life of the city's residents.

"'Connection" to the Informational Mode of Development

In this section I consider the mechanics of restructuring in Sunderland, where we find city policy-makers proactively seeking to assess the value of integrating ICTs into local economic development. They are trying to achieve the means by which they can connect their local economy to the informational mode of development, characterized by what we understand as the global economy. This is quite a substantive shift, because although Sunderland is the newest city in the United Kingdom (declared by Royal Charter in 1992) it has an industrial history steeped in the traditional work of deep coal mining and shipbuilding. Less than thirty years ago, these two sectors made up a third of male employment in Sunderland, amounting to some 40,000 jobs. Now there are no deep coal mines, and shipbuilding has ended. The mechanism to restructure Sunderland's economy has rested heavily on funding from European and central U.K. government to attract new inward investment and stimulate indigenous businesses.

On top of this, the arrival of Nissan on the outskirts of the city in the 1980s established a new set of manufacturing principles for the area. The importance of Nissan's decision to locate in Sunderland was highly significant, so much so that the leader of the City Council stated that without the Japanese car company the city would have been devastated jobwise. He argued

> Nissan was the catalyst that has enabled us to survive during the loss of our traditional industries and we've continued to grow because of Nissan.... [ICTs are] an important aspect of the development of the city; for job creation,

for information in society, for education, for every angle of life within the city, it's important we get in on this revolution. . . . [T]his is like the last century, when you had the railways expanding, if you got a railway station in the city, you where ahead of the game in what you could do. Telematics is exactly the same. (Interview with author, March 1997)

The need for change within the city was understood, and, as we see below, a number of the ICTs initiatives were actually fitted into existing policy programs. During efforts to restructure, city planners and policy-makers began to see how they could weave a strategic approach to development, one which would include the embryonic beginnings of an interface between the global informational economy and the Sunderland economy, based on ICTs. Attempts to coordinate this rested with the Sunderland Telematics Working Group (STWG), and its aims and objectives captured in the City of Sunderland Telematics Strategy.

The City of Sunderland Telematics Strategy

The core themes of the Telematics Strategy are outlined in Table 16.2; in effect, it is these that display the strategic vision for ICTs development in the city. The idea is to make them operational through a number of projects that follow a familiar model of economic restructuring. It is a requirement of the STWG that projects involving ICTs contribute to existing economic development programs, containing desired outputs in relation to training and job creation, and are subject at specific points in time to monitoring and evaluation. These are simply

Table 16.2 The Core Themes of the Sunderland Telematics Strategy

Core Theme	Aim of the Strategy
Infrastructure	By focusing on infrastructure, city leaders are looking to develop the physical electronic architecture and the soft infrastructure centered around people, both of which, they believe, have to be developed simultaneously to absorb the perceived growth in telematics activity.
New Inward Investment	To facilitate new inward investment, the city has to provide a workforce with skills to match the requirements of new telematics-related industries. Many companies that operate on a global basis and that seek to locate in areas of competitive advantage will find this attractive, argue city planners.
Lifelong Learning	This is an area focused on developing programs of training and learning to enable the updating and maintenance of relevant skills for the local labor force. City leaders believe it will provide employers with the skilled people needed and will support a lifelong learning system, which is relevant across time as well as industry sector.
Quality of Life	This theme is about the provision of better access to information services and to the decision-making processes that take place in the city, made by local authority officials. The aim is to make available more opportunities for training and work and to address many concerns about a polarized society of information haves and have nots.

Source: City of Sunderland Partnership, 1996.

the lessons city planners have learnt from the competitive funding mechanisms established for U.K. and European government funded programs.

By acting as an extension to the rest of the objectives for the city's economic restructuring, the themes achieve something of a legitimacy. Economic restructuring and development become their rationale. So moves toward establishing a number of Electronic Village Halls (EVHs) situated across the city to act as community-based telematics centers—providing hardware alongside other community services such as training and day care facilities—are aimed at tapping into the developed community enterprise sector that exists in Sunderland and to exploit fully funding raised through existing urban regeneration initiatives. In another project focused on encouraging local small firms to use ICTs, the aim is to draw on work already underway at the university, the local Business Innovation Center, and the Regional Technology Center, supported by the City Council and Training and Enterprise Center. Although time and space constraints prevent a thorough overview of all the projects contained in the Sunderland Telematics Strategy, an indication of the scope of ICTs initiatives and, importantly, the scope of their legitimacy, can be considered by briefly looking at two other disparate projects.

Communities and Connection

As Castells talks about the "search for new connectedness around shared, reconstructed identity" (1996, page 23) he begins a debate around the role of new social movements and ICTs. New social movements he suggests, will be significant in the way in which the space of flows will be used. For instance, they will emerge to create their own services and meet their own needs within the informational mode of development. This theoretical position needs to be more thoroughly analyzed, although one way in which we can associate new social movements with ICTs is through the way local communities seek to use electronic networks and shape developments in ICTs. At the very least, this is a defence of space through ICTs, and there is an emergent literature taking shape around community-based ICTs (see, for instance, Qvortrup, 1989; Walker, 1997). In Sunderland this has manifested in various ways to include community based organizations in the construction of the Telematics Strategy. One of the projects that is currently operational is the Computer Recycling Project, which aims to establish a large pool of redundant computer equipment to be recycled to provide low cost hardware for local voluntary and community agencies.

Interestingly enough, this project took on a life of its own prior to the launch of the telematics strategy, but was ultimately integrated into the efforts of STWG. Those involved in the voluntary sector initiated a recycling enterprise from the premises of Sunderland Community Furniture Services Ltd (SCFS). SCFS is a registered charity and a company limited by guarantee, and is mainly concerned with renovating furniture, such as bedding, living room furniture, and white goods, and recycling scrap aluminium, wastepaper, and textiles. SCFS also trains people who for one reason or another have been unable to complete their training and education in the more formal surroundings of a further education college or school. The project manager realised that there were very few organizations that recycled computers and recognized the extent of waste that exists as PC systems are updated. SCFS raised funding to employ two trainees to learn how to restore donated computers that the company obtains from regional private and public-sector organizations.

SCFS estimates that in the region of twenty machines are needed to allow one computer to be distributed. Many machines received for recycling have been previously stripped of important components by technicians from the donor company. It therefore becomes a labor-intensive process to test equipment and to build a cannibalized PC. Even so, the project manager of SCFS believes a case can be made for recycling, as he argued:

> virtually every voluntary organization in the region would be able to use a computer at some point. If we can supply them it would be wonderful, but we need the support of businesses, universities and colleges, and local authorityies to be able to do that. (Interview with the author, June 1997)

The extent to which this is a labor-intensive process raises questions about whether it can be maintained as a commercially viable part of Sunderland's ICTs program. At present it is being subsidized by other parts of SCFS, but it clearly requires further support in terms of finance and donor agencies.

There are two significant aspects to this project. The first is that the activity should take place as a community-based response to the informational mode of development, and the second is that it should be situated in a broader vision of telematics and economic restructuring for the city. The work of SCFS is aimed at the provision of low-cost connectivity, and this acts as a metaphor for the way attempts are being made in the city to integrate ICTs activities within the broader economy. It is a concrete attempt to spread levels of awareness of and access to ICTs for socioeconomic development targeted at particular groups. The fact that this is not carried out by a more commercially oriented company may reflect a lack of confidence in the business idea, particularly as it is not yet a commercially viable program. However, while it is useful to consider the way in which the informational mode of development is being dictated by powerful global organizations, in this ICTs project, the work has a strong community enterprise focus. This shows us, as Castells (1996) has noted, why there is a need to understand resistance to the forces shaping the space of flows, and why in some cases community-based responses and new social movements are part of that process.

256 Connection for the Future

A second initiative, one which resides at the opposite end of the spectrum from the recycling project, is the development taking place at Doxford International Business Park. This is an edge-of-town business site, similar to many such sites across the United Kingdom, which is part of a targeted attempt to bring in to the city new industries that are interested in contemporary office space and R&D and light industrial processing facilities, preferably new high-technology-based firms. The City Council is of the opinion that Doxford will act as an attractor for new major inward investment and will stimulate smaller, new, local businesses which are able to operate in the competitive conditions of a global economy. Early entrants onto Doxford include large information-processing centers, such as financial and insurance companies, call centers for services such as Barclays telephone banking operations, the energy provider London Electric, and the regional headquarters of Mercury One-to-One, Nike, and Camelot (the U.K. lottery operator). One important aspect of this is that the decision was taken between the developers and the council, influenced by the STWG, to establish part of the Doxford site as a named teleport.

Initially, the notion of a teleport in the context of Doxford is simply an enhancement of the image of the site and a plan to market in a more direct manner the future potential of the physical electronic hardware that has been installed. Even so, the electronic infrastructure provided at Doxford is by no means unique. It is provided by some of the main telecommunications companies that operate in the United Kingdom (specifically British Telecom and Mercury), and consists of fiber-optic and hybrid fiber-optic and coaxial cabling. Land-line cable is ducted into all the office space, allowing offices and call centers to develop appropriate digitized data and voice communications systems that support the importing, processing, and exporting of information-based on telecommunications. In addition, negotiations are currently under way to locate a satellite ground station at Doxford. It has been significant to the site that the decision was taken by central U.K. government to designate Doxford as an Enterprise Zone for a period of ten years from April 1990. This has meant that Sunderland has been able to secure a site with a very competitive business environment for potential inward investors.

According to the developers of Doxford, Akeler Developments, comparative uniform business rates (UBR) act as an important locational decision-making factor to new inward investors. Office space to equivalent to Doxford in the City of London would result in a UBR of £167 per square meter; in Birmingham a UBR of £86 per square meter; and in Manchester a UBR of £83 per square meter. Companies that decide to locate in Doxford have zero UBR costs until April 2000. It is little wonder then, that the provision of an up-to-date ICT infrastructure is impressive to prospective investors only as part of a bigger package of enticement—so much so that a Development Executive from Akeler provided an interesting perspective on inward investment into the city:

> we use it [ICTs] very much as a marketing tool because we hope they [potential inward investors] will recognize that certainly in the future this will be very important to them. In terms of their current operations, it isn't a vital criteria when choosing this site over others. (Interview with author, August 1997)

However, the positioning of Doxford is an integral part of the Sunderland Telematics Strategy, even if at present it is about representing a future business environment. The Doxford teleport idea is important therefore, and it is presently being moved forward around four major components.

The first component is the development of a Teleport Communications

Hub. City planners see this as offering a wide range of international communications facilities designed to attract companies looking for a U.K. base. Both the World Teleport Association and the British Space Agency have encouraged Sunderland to develop its communications hub to consist of land and satellite links, and city policy-makers take some pride in pointing out that only London can boast a bigger teleport facility in the United Kingdom. Second, a Global Teleport Training Centre is being developed to become a main U.K. center for teleport training for many types of business activity, from chief executive training to call center skills, including training aimed at small firms and for unemployed people on IT projects. The third component is the Teleport Business Start-Up Centre. This is targeted toward a business support infrastructure that includes managed workspace, business advice, and counselling and mentoring for new telematics-based businesses. These three components overlap to provide a critical mass of telematics-related activities on the site and, where appropriate, can involve other support agencies in the city, such as the Sunderland Business Innovation Centre. The fourth element is the International Teledemocracy Centre. This is slightly different in emphasis as it is about designing, testing, developing, and implementing applications relevant to governance and citizenship in the informational age, an area consistent with many policy debates emerging from central and European government.

The teleport idea has more to with the need for Sunderland to diversify its local economy rather than any moves toward ICTs integration. ICTs development at Doxford has an estimated cost in the region of £10 million (City of Sunderland Partnership, 1996). However, the site is marketed as a provider of high-quality office accommodation in an Enterprise Zone with good all-round communication links. Those businesses that have located on Doxford are contemporary information processing industries, such as financial institutions and service-based call centers. The notion of a teleport is not important to these businesses, and the provision of an electronic architecture is simply a requirement for their business today. The ICT potential of Doxford is about what connection to the informational mode of development today can mean for business preparedness tomorrow. So while the teleport may be symbolic for the STWG, it is only part of the creation of a local economy that contains a social mission in the form of a recycling project as well as other economic restructuring initiatives—a local economy that is fully connected to the global economy.

Much of what became evident in Sunderland has also been witnessed, in some form or other, in a number of other places in the Northeast of England (Southern, 1997). Furthermore, the pressures to restructure and the pervasive character of the informational mode of development are generic to many places across advanced economies. The next section considers the political salience of the space of flows, looking again at the process of legitimizing the ICTs activities that are often about the competitive nature of development and the issues of local governance that this entails. The following section therefore considers the role of the actors who became involved in shaping the Sunderland Telematics Strategy.

THE POLITICAL SALIENCE OF THE SPACE OF FLOWS

The Local Dynamics of the Space of Flows

The space of flows is providing a new spatial logic (Castells, 1996). The concept of the space of flows is distinct from the idea of the informational mode of development, in that it specifically refers to the sequences and interactions between actors in organizations and institutions whose behavior, strategy, and policy shape spatial logic through the practice and consciousness of society (Ibid.). At the level of the city, local policy-makers, planners, and urban gatekeepers have an important role to play in this. In the main, actors from these groups do not determine (other than in a few small-scale instances) the electronic architecture that provides a global ICT network and the placeless logic of this architecture. However, they do seek to influence how the space of flows will become the leading spatial manifestation of power and function in their locality, for as Castells (1996, page 378) suggests, such manifest consequences are currently displacing the influence of the space of places.

We should not see this as meaning that place has become a redundant concept. As we can see in Sunderland, locality and key actors concerned with place form part of an evolving informational mode of development whereby time and space is compressed (Harvey, 1989a) or distanciated (Giddens, 1990) as the local is connected to the global. But shaping the space of flows is more than connectivity, because connection to the global ICT architecture means that specific parts of the planet become interlinked, each place with a set of "well-defined social, cultural, physical, and functional characteristics" (Castells, 1996, page 413). This is in essence, a hub and spoke logical schematic seen in the design of information systems, a schema that is being applied to a globally defined geography.

For cities, it means that each place holds its own role and respective weight in the information-processing and wealth generating activities of the new mode of development. This can be a major source of contradiction, not least because the requirements of major companies and their leading managerial elite, who are responsible for delivering technological development and greater levels of information-processing activity, may not be consistent with the sustainable development of place. As a result there may be areas of ICT development that act as sites of contestation between the global company elite and representatives of the local state. It is for this reason that the local governance of ICTs has become a salient feature in economic development.

Graham (1997) has pointed to the low levels of interest in ICTs by local policy-makers and planners, and has suggested it is still relatively rare to find proactive ICT policies. Furthermore, he notes, if such policies exist, city policy-makers often find it difficult to control who benefits from an ICT infrastructure that cannot be constrained by traditional boundaries. However, as the evidence from Sunderland shows, as the space of flows unfolds, its political salience can be evaluated by the role of key political actors involved in ICT development within cities. In Sunderland, the Telematics Strategy is a concrete manifestation of the local political and economic dynamics that take place in the city, involving both public and private sectors. City policy-makers, in responding to the space of flows, are seeking to plan their local economic future in light of the impending effects and contradictions of the informational mode of development.

One of the most striking features of the local dynamics of the space of flows in Sunderland was the speed in which the Telematics Strategy was introduced. The levels of coordination and strategic outlook it now contains are an expression of ways to shape a new spatial logic, an outlook that is now firmly established within the consciousness of city planners.

Early Sunderland Responses to the Space of Flows

Just three years ago in 1995, during an overview of the Northeast regional ICTs development, a picture of Sunderland emerged that contrasts to the current image of a telematics city. Work that was taking place at this time was piecemeal and uncoordinated. To summarize, at this time the cable franchise had recently been obtained by Bell Cablemedia, although there was little actual cable laying taking place showing how far behind Sunderland actually was.[3] Apart from the infrastructure provided by British Telecom (BT) and, to a much lesser extent Mercury, one of the few pieces of hard ICT architecture had been installed during the development of Washington New Town. This is ironic because it consisted of a coaxial cable infrastructure to support communal TV and radio reception, a feature common to many New Towns built in the United Kingdom during the 1960s and early 1970s, but hardly representative of a new, dynamic, information-processing-based city. As in the case of many other U.K. urban areas, the work of the cable franchise company was considered by the City Council to be highly significant, although the main concerns at the time revolved around potential environmental damage as cable laying took place. Other developments in Sunderland included the European and U.K. government-funded CCTV system, developed in the city center to reduce crime and encourage shoppers to visit Sunderland, and some internal progress on the local authority information systems, which at some stage, it was then considered, would be linked to the provision of external electronic communication systems for the public; at the university there were some training courses being run on using the Internet for business.

However, this is only part of the picture. A number of regeneration initiatives taking place at the same time also came to be influential. A major development for the strategic view on Sunderland's future rested with the funding obtained via the SRB for establishing the City of Sunderland Partnership. The first round of the SRB Challenge Fund in 1995 provided Sunderland with the mechanisms for the strategic direction, operational implementation, monitoring, and day-to-day management of regeneration projects. The funding provided by the U.K. government, some £2.1 million in its first year and £10.9 million in total, secured the finance to form the City of Sunderland Partnership. Key players in this current alliance include high profile local business leaders, local university representatives, the chief executive of the City Council and the City Council leader, and representatives from local quangos, such as the Training and Enterprise Council and Business Link.[4] Community groups were given access to the partnership, including community-based activists and representatives from the voluntary sector. Not only did the partnership act as a catalyst for new programs of regeneration, but it acted as the genesis for the manifestation of the Telematics Strategy.

Shaping the Space of Flows:
The City of Sunderland Telematics Working Group

The partnership laid out the scope and legitimacy of a number of economic restructuring initiatives that came to involve ICTs. For instance, land reclamation projects allowed the university to build new facilities, including a new School for Information Systems. Partnership members recognized this as a strategic strength for the city, providing existing or potential local firms with the opportunity to tap into a pool of IT skilled graduates. Coinciding with this, city officials sought to encourage partnership member agencies to find funding from other quarters, particularly the European Commission (EC), identifying EC Structural Funds and Research and Technological Development programs as potential sources for financing the Telematics Strategy. As this work unfolded, it became very important that any attempts made to coordinate ICT activity won executive support from local city leaders. This was secured when the chair of the City of Sunderland Partnership, the managing director of a locally based major brewery, and the chief executive of the local authority gave their support. These and other city leaders became convinced of the potential for the local economy if ICT development could be shaped. Another member had convinced partnership leaders of the need for a coordinated approach following attendance at the annual conference of the World Teleport Association (interview with a member of STWG, April 1997).

Under the auspices of the City of Sunderland Partnership, what was in effect the inaugural meeting of the City of Sunderland Telematics Working Group took place. This was set up through the transfer of ideas gained from an international conference where many contributors from North America, Europe, and the Far East demonstrated their own telematics success stories. According to one member of the STWG, the meeting represented the "great significance to the city" that ICTs were seen to hold (interview with author, April 1997), and as we see above, the work of the group led to a new analysis of economic restructuring, such as the developments that took place at Doxford.

The structure of the STWG replicates the full partnership. It involves the vice chancellor, two pro-vice chancellors from the local university, and the chief executive of the City Council, who is supported by a city authority officer responsible for local economic policy and for identifying European funding opportunities. There are also representatives from the local TEC and Business Innovation Centre, the Sunderland-based Regional Technology Centre, and the voluntary sector, and a representative from community organizations active in the city. It is fair to say that each of the representatives holds an agenda specific to the aims of the organization he or she represents, and from the discussions I have had with the representatives, this provides the basis for conflict and contestation over the allocation of resources. Nevertheless, to a large extent there has been a political compromise achieved between STWG members to focus on how ICTs can be governed in a beneficial manner for the whole of the city. The City Council leader made a forceful point when he explained that "we all believe in this" and that there was "a common belief that this is beneficial" (interview with author, March 1997).

In its early days, while all members agreed to participate and contribute where possible, two figures emerged from STWG charged with taking the idea of telematics forward. A major objective was to establish the Telematics Strategy. Through a series of discussions over an eighteen-month period, key areas for ICT development were identified, each of which related to the aims and objectives of the agencies involved. These areas were pulled together, culminating in the launch of the Telematics Strategy in December 1996. Regular meetings of the STWG have established the plan of action based around the core themes shown in Table 16.2. This has shaped emergent ideas, along with the uncoordinated activity previously in place, into a single strategic ICT method for local economic development with the backing of the key citywide partnership body. The STWG, then, sought to capture many of the initiatives already being carried out or being planned, and importantly sought to provide leadership in terms of expenditure of the budgets already in place or being planned.

The early months of establishing the STWG and the Telematics Strategy were really focused on pooling existing knowledge, expertise, and experience, and providing an action plan that would convince each member agency to commit resources and deal with implementation. This has not been easy to achieve. Many of the aims in the Telematics Strategy are still without clear funding, although some have won additional finance. However, as the overview of Doxford and the recycling project shows, winning funding for ICT initiatives is not the key to coordinating a political response to the space of flows; rather, the key is the manner in which all activities are brought together under an umbrella vision for the city, creating as a whole something that has proven most significant.

During discussions with various members of the STWG, it was pointed out that the group and Telematics Strategy exist without funds. Yet for Bailey (1995), not having direct access to finance does not prevent a local partnership being formed based on:

> the mobilization of a coalition of interests drawn from more than one sector in order to prepare and oversee an agreed strategy for the regeneration of a defined area. (Bailey, 1995, page 27)

However, I would suggest that such a description is not analytically comprehensive enough for bodies that have emerged to shape the space of flows. While the process of mobilization in the case of Sunderland has been driven by a small number of individuals, and the range and balance of power within STWG is indeed contested, both situations being similar to other types of partnership, the area of coverage is about shaping the space of flows. In this sense, the local ICT partnership enables the kind of speculative activity around projects that become a focus of public and political attention (Harvey, 1989b). We might add further that the STWG acts as an entrepreneurial form of local governance, seeking to attract and develop production and consumption spending and to demonstrate advantages of its local place to other players in the global economy. The legitimacy of STWG is crucial, therefore, to this form of local governance, because at the very least it maintains levels of government support for local efforts to shape the space of flows, and at best it enables efficient and coordinated connection of the local economy to the global economy.

In the final section of this chapter I reflect on the evidence from the Sunderland case study and draw out some of the most notable points, which I suggest are typical of cities restructuring for the informational mode of development. While, as Castells suggests, we can identify the convergence of economic restructuring and the explosion in ICTs applications, for urban economies we can also identify some of the logics that underpin this. First there is the behavior of key political actors who believe their locale should engage with the informational mode of development and seek to connect the local with the global economy. Second there is the competitive nature of ICT development, which raises issues of local governance, and it is this area that gives rise to the political salience of the space of flows.

Summary: The Logics of City Restructuring in the Informational Age

I began this chapter by suggesting that the shift towards the informational mode of development is highly relevant to the restructuring of cities. This is because ICTs are being harnessed to provide new and favorable conditions for the continuation of capitalism, in terms of enhancing productivity, and creating new ways to seek out profit by means of globalizing production and by acting as a totem to marshall support for national economic activity (Castells, 1996). The structures of advanced economies are changing with more and more attention being paid to knowledge management in sectors such as finance and insurance and a greater recognition overall of how industry depends ever more on the rapid processing of information. This has coincided with organizational change in the structure of private sector firms and has resulted in systems of flexible management that increase control and authority over business processes. The public sector too, in all advanced nations, has gone through a period of major restructuring and is increasingly dependent on gathering data on the way governance is conducted. The restructuring of cities, therefore, is taking place within an overall rise in informational activities whereby the source of productivity is driven by knowledge generation and ever intensified information processing (Ibid.).

For local policy-makers, the shift toward an informational mode of development provides a new set of challenges. Connection to the informational age has indeed become part of the restructuring process for city planners and policy-makers. Conscious attempts can be seen at the local level to restructure urban economies by embracing the new demands of the informational mode of development and by recognising how the local economy needs to connect to the global economy. This involves locally based ICT projects and initiatives that take place within a broader framework of economic development. In the U.K., and specifically in the case of Sunderland in the Northeast of England, these projects often draw on traditional restructuring mechanisms, such as funding and programs initiated by the European and U.K. governments. ICTs therefore, become a strategic response to restructuring and, as witnessed above, the City of Sunderland Telematics Strategy is such a response.

The four themes of the Telematics Strategy reflect the orthodox and typical path toward a restructured local economy, with the added ingredient of ICTs. The focus on infrastructure seen in Sunderland was about providing a physical electronic architecture, complemented by the softer infrastructure of skilled and knowledgeable people who could develop the potential opportunities of the technology. This, it was suggested by local planners, would support new inward investors who are seeking to develop an economic advantage in a severely competitive world. The focus on lifelong learning in Sunderland is a recognition that skills will need constant updating in the informational mode of development as new business sectors emerge and new skills are required. The fourth area of the Telematics Strategy was about how the public sector could exploit the potential of the technology by creating better access to information services and improving the processes of local governance. The objective of connection becomes an inclusive process, and attempts are made to avoid further division amongst local groups. Not only are the four themes of the Telematics Strategy an extension of the economic development activity of the city, they are legitimized through the social and economic rationale that underpin them.

Legitimacy of ICT initiatives is important, and the scope of this legitimacy needs to be broad. It has to cover the day-to-day activities that take place in local communities, as well as fitting into the professional world of global trade. I provided two examples of this, which illustrated both the scope and the reach of legitimacy of ICT projects in Sunderland. The first, the computer recycling project, is run by a community enterprise and shows how groups that would otherwise be disenfranchized from the informational mode of development are responding and attempting to shape the way in which the space of flows will be used. I suggested that Castells's (1996) work on this provides us with a useful starting point to understand the defense of space by community groups through ICT initiatives. The second example I used was that of Doxford International Business Park. The teleport concept at Doxford is a representation of the future for many urban economies in the U.K., whether situated on science parks or business sites. This concept is about future development to connect the local economy to the global economy, resting on winning new inward investment and, in particular, on attracting information-processing industries. It also means stimulating new ICT-based small businesses and ensuring a capable labor market to support such industries. So the legitimacy of ICTs is provided through the broad church economic rationale in which projects are positioned.

Scope and legitimacy are important features of the local governance of ICTs. In Sunderland this is determined by the STWG, which acts under the auspices of the City of Sunderland Partnership, the main regeneration body in the city. The political importance of this can be seen as key local actors in the STWG try to deal with the contradiction of ICT development. That is, the more the global electronic architecture spreads, the more it has a placeless logic. Meanwhile, as we have seen above, urban economic restructuring includes connection to the electronic architecture, and as a consequence local players seek to shape what they see as potential benefits for their place. Sometimes this result in speculative and entrepreneurial activity involving public and private sectors, but always ICT activity that maintains the support of the ICTs governance groups, such as the STWG, and of their political paymasters, such as the U.K. and European governments. Shaping the space of flows is an important aim of local actors as they try to achieve an efficient and coordinated connection to the informational mode of development. Above all, the local governance of ICTs is an attempt to impose a local logic to the space of flows, and this is its political salience.

NOTES

1. By ICTs I refer to the convergence of computer processing power and digital telecommunications by land or by satellite. There are a number of terms used to represent this, such as information superhighway, informatics, telematics, and so on. Here the term "ICTs" is preferred.

2. This can be investigated in more depth by taking into account the work of long-wave theorists who map out waves of economic development based on technological advances (see, for instance, Hall and Preston, 1988). In turn, the ideas of Castells on symbol communication can also be examined further by considering the ways in which economic geographers are drawing on cultural studies to build understanding of current restructuring processes (see Lee and Willis, 1997). Neither of these are developed in any detail in this chapter.

3. The allocation of cable franchises in the U.K. is complicated because it has always been linked to the privatization of British Telecom. In 1984 the principle of allowing private operators into the U.K. telecomms market was established through the Telecommunications Act and the Cable and Broadcasting Act of the same year. After the Duopoly Review in 1991, the cable industry in the Northeast region began to establish itself through United Artists in nearby Newcastle.

4. Quango is a term used in the U.K. to refer to organizations from central governement on local areas. They are not directly accountable through local elections in this sense, constrast sharply with elected local government. Often they will have Executive Board that draws on the local business community and on other groups outside of the state, hence the term quasi-nongovernment organization.

REFERENCES

Aglietta, M. (1979). A Theory of Capitalist Regulation: The US Experience. London: New Left Books.

Allen, J. (1992). "Fordism and Modern Industry." In J. Allen, P. Braham, and P. Lewis, eds. Political and Economic Forms of Modernity. Cambridge, MA: Polity Press.

Andersen, K. V., ed. (1998). *EDI and Data Networking in the Public Sector*. Amsterdam: Kluwer Publishing.

Bailey, N. (1995). *Partnership Agencies in British Urban Policy*. London: UCL Press.

Batty M. (1990). "Intelligent Cities: Using Information Networks to Gain Competitive Advantage." *Environment and Planning B: Planning and Design* 17 (2): 247–256.

Bellamy, C. and J. A. Taylor. (1998). *Governing in the Information Age*. Buckingham: Open University Press.

Castells, M. (1989). *The Informational City*. Oxford: Basil Blackwell.

———. (1996). *The Rise of the Network Society*. Oxford: Basil Blackwell.

City of Sunderland Partnership. (1996). "The City of Sunderland Partnership Telematics Strategy."

Cooke, P., ed. (1989). *Localities: The Changing Face of Urban Britain*. London: Unwin Hyman.

Dabinett, G. and S. Graham. (1994). "Telematics and Industrial Change in Sheffield, UK." *Regional Studies* 28 (6): 605–617.

Ducatel, K. (1990). "Rethinking Retail Capital." *International Journal of Urban and Regional Research* 14 (2): 207–221.

Gibbs, D. and K. Tanner. (1997). "Information and Communication Technologies and Local Economic Development Policies: The British Case." *Regional Studies* (8): 765–774.

Giddens, A. (1990). *The Consequences of Modernity*. Cambridge, MA: Polity Press.

Gillespie, A. and H. Williams. (1988). "Telecommunications and the Reconstruction of Regional Comparative Advantage." *Environment and Planning* A 20: 1311–1321.

Graham, S. (1997). "Cities in the Real-Time Age: The Paradigm Challenge of Telecommunications to the Conception and Planning of Urban Space." *Environment and Planning* A 29 (1), (January): 105–128.

Graham, S. and S. Marvin. (1996). *Telecommunications and the City*. Routledge: London.

Hall, P. (1993). "Forces Shaping Urban Europe." *Urban Studies* 30 (6): 883–898.

Hall, P. and P. Preston. (1988). *The Carrier Wave: New Information Technology and the Geography of Innovation 1846–2003*. London: Unwin Hyman.

Harvey, D. (1989a). *The Condition of Post-Modernity*. Oxford: Basil Blackwell.

———. (1989b). "From Managerialism to Entrepreneurialism: The Transformation in Urban Governance in Late Capitalism." *Geografiska Annaler* 71B (1): 3–17.

Lee, R. and J. Willis (1997). *Geographies of Economies*. London: Arnold.

Luthe, R. (1993). "On the Political Economy of 'Post-Fordist' Telecommunications: The US Experience." *Capital and Class* 51: 81–120.

Mitchell, W. (1995). *City of Bits: Space, Place and the Infobahn*. Cambridge, MA: MIT Press.

Qvortrup, L. (1989). "The Nordic Telecottages: Community Teleservice Centres for Rural Regions." *Telecommunications Policy* March: 59–68.

Sassen, S. (1991). *The Global City*. Princeton, NJ: Princeton University Press.

Sayer, A. (1989). "Post-Fordism in Question." *The International Journal of Urban and Regional Research* 13 (4): 666–695.

Southern, A. (1997). "Re-Booting the Local Economy: Information and Communication Technologies in Local Economic Strategy." *Local Economy* 12 (1): 8–25.

Walker, G. (1997). "NewNet and Community Networking in Newcastle upon Tyne." *Local Economy* 12 (1): 81–84.

TRAVEL, GENDER, AND WORK
EMERGING COMMUTING CHOICES
IN INNER-CITY PHOENIX

Elizabeth K. Burns

At the forefront of public interest in changes in the workplace is the issue of flexibility in travel to work. The broad term "telework" describes "new forms of working associated with new technologies" of communications (Gillespie and Richardson, 1998, page 1). Present commuting patterns in U.S. metropolitan areas provide ample evidence that the need to travel persists and that physical travel to work increasingly occurs in a restricted range of modal choices, primarily driving in private vehicles. Telework offers the possibility of profound reshaping and even elimination of the journey to work. The experience of employees who now enjoy spatial and temporal flexibility demonstrates that the relationship between travel and work is already changing.

The character of metropolitan workplace changes—by industry classification, labor force composition, and location—and the nature of participating employees—by gender, occupation, and residential location—are empirical questions. In American inner cities, urban policy in the 1990s stresses the creation of new businesses and job opportunities (Porter, 1995). Many inner cities retain pockets of employment strength and comparative advantage in their metropolitan areas. They remain a focus of regional commuting flows. As work conditions change, inner-city commuting patterns reflect evolving functional, economic, and social connections with the rest of the metropolitan area. Increased use of telework in inner cities offers the promise of addressing continuing traffic congestion in the urban core and of providing increased employment opportunities for inner-city residents (U.S. Congress, 1995).

This study investigates commuting behavior at inner-city work sites in the specific setting of Phoenix, Arizona, using the Maricopa County Regional Trip Reduction Program (MCRTRP) survey. First I compare resident and nonresident commuting to determine the extent of physical travel and the use of travel alternatives, including compressed work schedules and telecommuting. Then I expand this aggregate study with two detailed cases: the first examines telecommuting, while the second examines commuting at a major employment center, Sky Harbor International Airport. While the findings apply most directly to Phoenix, they have wider relevance to the roles of commuting and telework in job creation and retention in inner cities.

TRAVEL, GENDER, AND WORK

Daily commuting travel derives from the need to connect spatially separated workplaces and residences. This shared understanding is based on the view that employment occurs within a single metropolitan labor market. The perspectives of feminist geographers over the past fifteen years have reshaped this understanding to include an appreciation of the local contexts that underlie gender differences in travel patterns. Women's commuting travel is constrained by their traditional roles as homemakers and housewives quite apart from their occupational roles. Their travel by private vehicles makes it possible to juggle daily demands of employment, household responsibilities, and child care, including trips that link multiple destinations and family members before and after work (Rosenbloom and Burns, 1994).

Starting from inquiries into the process of occupational segregation, studies in time-space geography and on the journey to work have documented the spatial constraints that women experience. This literature has synthesized the generalization that women in female-dominated occupations have shorter work trips than other women. More recently, there has been a focus on the varying conditions faced by specific groups of women and on the role of specific places in their work experience (Hanson and Pratt, 1995). This study extends the focus on intraurban labor markets as the specific locational context for the employment opportunities of different occupational groups and, by extension, for the men and women in these occupations.

Four themes provide connections between this feminist perspective and the widespread interest in changing urban work and travel conditions:

- intraurban labor market participation and commuting by specialized groups;
- substitutability of communications for personal travel through workplace flexibility;
- time-space discontinuities and distortions; and
- connections of inner-city disadvantaged populations to technological resources.

Spatial variations in the participation of specific social and demographic groups in intraurban labor markets are linked to their mobility and occupational status. Whether the variable of interest is gender, age, or race, disaggregate studies reflect a common concern that aggregate findings are not sufficient to explain current commuting behavior. In addition, findings for one group, such as women, may vary in urban settings with different spatial structures. In contrast to the generalization that women, especially in female-dominated occupations, travel shorter distances to work than men, many women in metropolitan Phoenix travel longer distances to work than men (Burns, 1996; Rosenbloom and Burns, 1993).

Similarly, participation in any form of telework is a decision made by individuals in a context of specific workplaces and personal circumstances. Home-based work, whether electronically mediated or not, is not expected to have a major impact on travel, but may well be linked to an employee's professional status (Gillespie and Richardson, 1998). Interestingly, Aiken and Carroll find that most telecommuters are men, a finding that merits additional empirical study in more urban settings and scales ranging from the individual to the household, workplace, and region (Aiken and Carroll, 1996).

These decisions also reflect the availability of work, home, and other sites for use at different days and times of day. This "timing of space" needs to be separated from the availability of technologies that access these spaces (Janelle, 1996). Janelle explores the potentials and limitations of geographic information systems and related technologies for visualizing the impacts of space-adjusting technologies. Travel times and other measures of connectivity can show how different parts of the urban system change their accessibility under the impact of these technologies.

Finally, inner-city locations have accessibility advantages through their accumulated transportation networks, while the urban edge appears to benefit most directly from improved accessibility related to highway traffic flow improvements. Inner cities, however, are also areas of spatial mismatch whose disadvantaged residents, both men and women, must commute to suburban jobs to participate in the metropolitan labor force. Telecommuting and other forms of telework have the potential both to improve work opportunities, allow easier sharing of job information, and to increase civic participation (Sawicki, 1996). Sui, among others, expresses the need to overcome the intraurban polarization of information-rich and information-poor places and groups (Sui, 1996).

These issues raise specific questions in the context of individual cities. Metropolitan Phoenix is a low-density, sprawling region where personal mobility is considered a core value of the individualistic Arizona lifestyle. At this time, private vehicles remain a necessity, not an option, for local mobility. The following trends suggest that dependence on personal vehicles is not entirely a matter of personal choice but reflects a lack of travel options, including the option to substitute communications for physical travel (Burns, 1998a). This dependence has uneven social and spatial impacts that shape local travel behavior, now and in the future.

METROPOLITAN PHOENIX MOBILITY

Across the United States, continuing local population and employment growth supports ever larger increases in the use of personal vehicles. Phoenix led the nation in the 1970s in growth in population, expansion in the labor force, and increased use of personal vehicles to travel to work (Pisarski, 1992). In the 1980s, the continuing high population growth rate placed it second only to Orlando, Florida, among high-growth metropolitan areas of more than one million (Pisarski, 1996). Personal mobility, as measured by the number of daily vehicle miles traveled, has grown at a rate of 4 percent every year since 1985 (Kihl, 1997). Compared with other Western urban regions, Phoenix travel has a low average of daily miles traveled per person (22.72 miles), lags in the use of public transit (1 percent of all trips), and occurs primarily on the local street network (Kihl, 1997; Morrison Institute, 1997).

Locally, as well as nationally, the use of private vehicles dominates metropolitan commuting. Their long-standing use, particularly in single-occupant trips, remains a difficult trend to slow or reverse. In 1990, driving alone and carpooling together accounted for 9 out of 10 work trips, a level that has remained steady since 1970 (Table 17.1). From 1980 to 1990, the percentage of drive-alone commutes increased, while carpooling declined from its 1980 peak after the energy-conscious 1970s. Regional one-way average travel times to work increased to 23 minutes between 1980 and 1990 (U.S. Census, 1984, 1993), reflecting the increasing separation of residences from employment. By 1990, there had been a long-term decline in nonvehicle commutes by bicycle and walking, modes well suited for nearby work locations. Bus use clearly remained necessary and served 2 percent of the increasing number of workers in 1980 and 1990. More people worked at home or walked to work, however, than used public transit in 1990.

These trends may be changing. Phoenix is one of the few United States metropolitan areas with a public policy effort to encourage alternatives to single-occupant trips. In 1997, close to 500,000 employees participated in the Maricopa County trip reduction program. These participants used alternative modes of transportation for nearly 30 percent of their commuting trips (Maricopa County Regional Trip Reduction Program, no date). The most commonly used options were car pools, compressed work schedules, and, to a lesser extent, working at home.

MARICOPA COUNTY REGIONAL TRIP REDUCTION PROGRAM SURVEY

In the 1990s, public agencies are creating and maintaining databases for regulatory and management purposes in the policy area of travel demand management. Measuring change in driving alone to work is a key program component. Researchers seeking current data sources for work environments therefore have a new resource. These agency databases have the advantages of recent data collection and an expanded set of variables. Their use raises several issues, however. The critical issue is that the data set is collected and maintained for nonresearch purposes. In the same way that individual researchers may be reluctant to share individual data sets, data-sharing benefits are not always clear to the agencies managing local databases (Porter and Callahan, 1994).

Even when access to agency data is possible, problems with definition standardization and data formats can be expected (Evans, 1994). Key procedures are outside the researcher's control, including question design, data maintenance, surveyed population, and timing of surveys. Research obstacles include the time needed to obtain permission for data sets at an individual, work site, or company level; delays in staff preparation of special data sets by geographic

Table 17.1 Means of Transportation to Work in Metropolitan Phoenix

	1990 (n=996,495)	1980 (n=658,834)	1970 (n=361,426)	1960 (n=217,670)
Drove alone	75.0%	70.2%	79.3%	82.2%
Carpooled	14.4%	19.0%	10.0%	(a)
Worked at home	2.9%	1.6%	2.2%	4.0%
Walked	2.6%	3.3%	3.9%	6.0%
Bus	2.0%	2.0%	1.2%	4.0%
Bicycle	1.4%	1.7%	(b)	(b)
All other means (b)	1.7%	2.4%	3.5%	3.7%

(a) Drove alone includes carpooled
(b) Other means includes motorcycle, taxi, and railroad.
Sources: U.S. Census of Population, 1993; 1984; 1973; 1963.

area and gender; and the effort involved in occasional preparation of collected but unprocessed raw data.

The Maricopa County Regional Trip Reduction Program monitors commuting travel in metropolitan Phoenix, Arizona, and hence progress toward meeting federal air-quality standards. In the 1980s, concerns over regional air quality and increasingly severe assessments by the Environmental Protection Agency of carbon monoxide, ozone, and particulate levels led to the 1989 passage of a key state environmental law. The trip reduction program was one of a list of ten measures designed to reduce vehicle emissions and bring the area into compliance with federal pollution standards. All large employers (fifty or more employees at a single work site) are required to survey their employees annually. In 1995, 495,000 employees and 2,300 employers participated. Employees report their current commute behavior, including mode of travel, use of telecommuting, weekly schedule, and daily hours, as well as gender, age, occupation, and preferred future travel options.

This ten-year metropolitan data set provides a rich research resource to explore spatial dimensions of commuting behavior and to assess the travel behavior of men and women of different occupational groups. Spatial information includes employer work sites by street address and employee residence by street address, major cross streets, and zip code. Each year, employers assign every employee a unique number to ensure survey confidentiality. It is not possible to track an individual's mobility over time through changes in workplace and residence locations. The agency provides data sets for specific locations and demographic groups as well as annual work-site reports on request.

THE JOB-RESIDENCE IMBALANCE OF INNER-CITY PHOENIX

Although Phoenix, like other major North American cities, has experienced a decentralization of new employment activity, the downtown and its environs remain the metropolitan area's largest concentration of employment. This concentration creates a regional jobs-residence imbalance that illustrates the need for and emergence of local commuting options.

Phoenix is a huge, sprawling city in a metropolitan area of 2.6 million people with a booming economy. In an effort to divide the city into more manageable planning districts that provide some sense of local identity, the City of Phoenix is divided into thirteen urban villages. Ideally, these units also provide a self-contained focus for daily activities of work, shopping, and socializing, and thus reduce the need to travel. Inner-city Phoenix is contained in the two urban villages, the Central City Village, which contains the downtown business district, and South Mountain Village, which extends immediately to the south (Figure 17.1).

In 1990, approximately 28 percent of the City of Phoenix's and 15 percent of the metropolitan area's jobs were located in the Central City and South Mountain Villages (U.S. Bureau of the Census, 1993). In 1990 there were 152,000 jobs in the inner city: 118,000 in the Central City Village and 34,000 in the South Mountain Village (U.S. Bureau of the Census, 1990).

The City of Phoenix's main office complex, Maricopa County's offices and medical center, state government offices and the state hospital, and several federal offices are located in and around the rejuvenating downtown area. The downtown area is also the focus for corporate headquarters, large legal firms, and local financial institutions. It has a convention center with two large downtown hotels and an emerging sports complex. Gentrifying, historic neighborhoods are primarily north of downtown. Two miles east of the downtown area is the metropolitan area's regional airport, an adjacent industrial park, and ancillary activities of airline ticket offices, maintenance services, car rental firms and passenger travel services, airport hotels, and air express services. South Mountain Village includes an industrial district containing activities attracted to the inner city by its centrality and good transportation access. The inner city covers an area approximately eight miles by eight miles.

The economic base of inner-city Phoenix has comparative and absolute advantages in the metropolitan economy. In 1995, there were 457,814 large-company employees in Maricopa County, of whom 81,499 were inner-city Phoenix employees. Basic inner-city economic sectors, when compared to total county employment, are public administration (location quotient of 2.50) and transportation (location quotient of 1.15). The inner city notably lacks strength, however, in three sectors that dominate the overall metropolitan economy: durable-goods manufacturing, including high-technology; wholesale and retail trade; and health and professional services. The largest numbers of inner-city jobs are in state and local public administration (24,512), health and professional services (10,428), banking services (5,256), and air transportation (5,031).

Many of the 135,000 inner-city residents are unable to take full opportunity of nearby employment, however (Gober and Burns, 1998). These two urban villages are areas of severe economic and social distress, designated Phoenix's Enterprise Community. In 1990, approximately 43 percent of Central City Village households and 24 percent of South Mountain Village households had incomes below the poverty line, compared to 12 percent of all Phoenix households. Minorities dominate the demography of both villages—Hispanics and African Americans constituted 67 percent of the population of

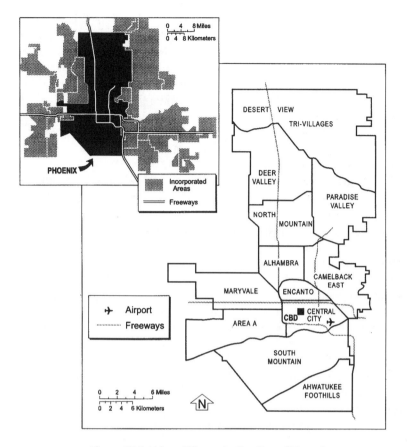

Figure 17.1 Urban Villages in the City of Phoenix

Source: Burns and Gober (1998). Reprinted by permission of *Urban Geography*, 19, 1: 12–23.

South Mountain Village and 73 percent of Central City Village. As compared to the city as a whole, the study area had many more persons who spoke a combination of Spanish and English, were without a high-school diploma, had high levels of unemployment, and had low household incomes. Also compared to the city as a whole, the study area had a higher proportion of households on public assistance and households with incomes below the poverty level.

INNER-CITY COMMUTING PATTERNS

Examining commuting patterns confirms the broad spatial mismatch of inner-city residents and nearby employment. Most residents find themselves in the unenviable position of proximity to a range of employment, but without the education or skills to be employed locally. There were 181 large employers within the boundaries of the Central City and South Mountain Villages in 1995. Residential addresses for 49,219 employees were sorted by zip code to identify inner-city residents and nonresidents. The boundaries of the nine zip codes used to identify the inner city are slightly larger than the two urban village boundaries and slightly overstate the number of inner-city residents.

More than 85 percent of inner-city jobs are held by nonresidents, confirming that relatively few jobs in the city's core were held by nearby residents (Burns and Gober, 1998). The link of residential and work location is quite weak for the city's urban villages in general and for the inner city in particular. As a result, work sites are dominated by nonresidents (Burns, 1998b). Sixty-four percent (39,439) of all inner-city employees work at a site where no inner-city residents are employed. Seventy-four percent (110) of the work sites have no employees who are inner-city residents.

Faced with this spatial separation of home and work, driving alone to work remains the dominant commute mode of all inner-city employees. They limit their commute travel by shifting work schedules far more than by shifting work locations. Although the five-day week/eight-hour day is the norm, one in five of the inner-city employees who do not telecommute (7,223 employees) has a flexible weekly or daily work schedule (Table 17.2). Only about 2 percent (684 employees) telecommute one or more days per week. The flexibility telecommuters enjoy through the spatial shift of their work location is paralleled by their schedules. More than a quarter of telecommuters have a work schedule that differs from a five-day week/eight-hour routine.

When employees are grouped by occupation, commute mode choice patterns emerge for inner-city residents and nonresidents (Table 17.3 and Table 17.4). For both residents and nonresidents, the professional/managerial and technical/research occupational groups have high drive alone rates, reflecting higher skills and education and presumably higher incomes. Nonresidents in sales/service jobs, which often require irregular daily and weekly schedules, have the highest drive alone rate. The lowest drive alone rates are for manufacturing/production employees and may reflect their low incomes. Nonresidents carpool at high rates except for resident manufacturing/production and sales/service employees, who also use the bus less than nonresidents. Although living relatively near their work sites, their commute choices appear to be limited by low incomes and work shift schedules as well as limited bus frequency and routes to specific work sites. Interestingly, about one in nine nonresident clerical/secretarial employees travels by bus, a pattern that reflects good express bus services from inner suburbs to downtown office complexes. Residents in all occupations walk and bicycle to work more than nonresidents.

Significant gender variations exist by occupation and work site, although almost equal numbers of men and women work in Phoenix's inner city (Burns, 1998b). Women are concentrated in three occupations: professional/managerial, clerical/secretarial, and sales/service. One result of this occupational concentration is that women employees are found in fewer inner-city work sites than men, notably in the large State of Arizona, Maricopa County, and City of Phoenix complexes. Compared to women, men work at numerous sites and are a higher proportion of professional/managerial, technical/research, manufacturing/production, and skilled crafts/trades occupations, and a lower proportion of clerical/sales employment.

These work-site variations are clearly linked to the use of travel options. The following sections discuss inner-city telecommuting and a case study of employee commuting patterns at Sky Harbor International Airport. In both examples, an employee's ability to have flexibility in the timing or spatial location of work depends on the travel context in place at his or her individual work site.

Telecommuting

Telecommuting, one of the most promising travel-demand reduction strategies, focuses on eliminating commuting trips by work at home or by reducing commuting travel distance by work at a site closer than the main workplace. In present-day Phoenix, residents can still live at a distance from work and not pay a comparable price in travel time. Future travelers are expected to find that increasing congestion in the metropolitan core provides a considerable incentive to change their travel behavior, especially to inner-city work sites. While it is possible to identify the gender and occupation of current telecommuters, the

Table 17.2 Inner-City Work Schedule and Location Flexibility

	Nontelecommuting Employees (n=37,237)	Telecommuters at least 1 day per week (n=684)
9 days/80 hours, 10th day off	3.4%	6.0%
3- or 4-day week/ 12 hour day	2.7%	3.8%
4-day week/ 10 hour day	8.7%	7.5%
5-day week/ 8 hour day	80.6%	75.6%
Work schedule varies	4.6%	7.2%

Source: 1995 Maricopa County Regional Trip Reduction Program.

Table 17.3 Nonresident Inner-City Employees' Commute Mode[a]

	Drive	Alone	Carpool	Bus	Other[b]
Professional/Manager	5447	82%	13%	4%	1%
Technical/Research	1,074	77%	16%	5%	1%
Sales/Service	1,616	88%	10%	2%	0%
Manufacturing/Production	440	67%	27%	3%	3%
Skilled Crafts/Trades	205	79%	17%	4%	0%
Clerical/Secretarial	5,261	68%	20%	11%	1%
Other	1,128	78%	16%	5%	1%
Total Number	15,171	11,664	2,443	95	109

[a] Calculated as a percentage of trips taken four or more days a week.
[b] Vanpool, walk, bicycle, motorcycle, and other, including telecommute.

Source: 1995 Maricopa County Regional Trip Reduction Program.

275

Table 17.4 Resident Inner-City Employees' Commute Mode[a]

	Drive	Alone	Carpool	Bus	Other[b]
Professional/Managerial	484	82%	12%	2%	3%
Technical/Research	117	77%	15%	3%	5%
Sales/Service	253	73%	13%	4%	10%
Manufacturing/Production	356	54%	32%	4%	10%
Skilled Crafts/Trades	62	70%	16%	5%	9%
Clerical/Secretarial	868	71%	18%	8%	3%
Other	402	64%	16%	8%	12%
Total Number	2,542	1,782	456	138	166

[a] Calculated as a percentage of trips taken four or more days a week.
[b] Vanpool, walk, bicycle, motorcycle, and other, including telecommute.
Source: 1995 Maricopa County Regional Trip Reduction Program.

ELIZABETH K. BURNS

survey did not ask employees to differentiate between home-based work and other forms of telework, including remote offices or mobile assignments. It is clear, however, that the gender and occupational composition at individual work sites provides a specific context for personal travel opportunities.

A single group, professional/managerial employees who work at home one day a week, dominates telecommuting in inner-city Phoenix. Their travel equals about 1 percent of all daily commute trips. Another 1 percent of all daily commute trips includes employees in this and other occupations who telecommute two or more days a week. Eight economic sectors had twenty-five or more telecommuters in 1995, with the majority working in public administration (Table 17.5). One of the largest inner-city employers, for example, is the State of Arizona, which has a strong commitment to encouraging 15 percent of its total labor force to telecommute at least one day per week (U.S. Department of Transportation, 1997). More women than men are telecommuters, both overall and in the public administration sector, but the gender balance shifts in other activities. The percentage of telecommuting men is highest in manufacturing, including the newspaper and bottled and canned soft drinks industries, while the highest percentage of telecommuting women occurs in educational services at colleges and universities.

Moreover, telecommuters vary by occupation and residence (Table 17.6). Only one in ten telecommuters is a resident of the inner city. The numerous nonresidents telecommute to jobs in high-status, high-paying professional/managerial, technical/research, and sales/service occupations. Telecommuting also occurs in routine and lower-paying activities. Nonresident women are more than three quarters of the clerical/secretarial telecommuters and have the highest percentage of both manufacturing/production and professional/managerial telecommuting jobs. Inner-city residents who telecommute hold a third of the manufacturing/production and other occupations positions without dominating any one occupational category.

Clearly, distant commuters find that telecommuting is an advantage. The distance savings, for both men and women, average sixteen miles for nonresidents and seven miles for inner-city residents. Finally, telecommuters are spatially concentrated in their residential locations (Figure 17.2). Many live south and east of the inner city, where Interstate-10 provides direct, but congested, access to new suburban neighborhoods in Phoenix, Tempe, and Chandler. Others live broadly north of the inner city, in the city of Phoenix, where freeways and multiple arterial streets provide access.

Sky Harbor International Airport Commuting

Commuting patterns at individual work sites illustrate the travel context provided by specific industry and occupational settings. Sky Harbor International Airport is the regional destination for the air transportation industry. Large air passenger companies share an interest in retaining longtime employees living at a distance and work together as a transportation management association to develop effective trip reduction programs. While carpooling at least once a week is the most common alternative to driving alone, compressed work schedules are the next choice. Employees at thirteen of the fifteen work sites use compressed schedules to eliminate trips. A positive culture of commuting options appears to be emerging at work sites, where multiple travel mode and schedule choices occur.

Table 17.5 Telecommuters' Gender by Standard Industrial Classification:
Employers with 25 or More Telecommuters

SIC	Category	Women	Men	Total
2086	Bottled and canned soft drinks	12%	88%	49
2711	Newspapers	33%	67%	39
4512	Air transportation, scheduled	48%	52%	27
6021	National commercial banks	58%	42%	31
6022	State commercial banks	60%	40%	48
8221	Colleges and universities	86%	14%	43
8222	Junior colleges	41%	59%	29
9111	Public administration, executive offices	55%	45%	374

Source: 1995 Maricopa County Regional Trip Reduction Program.

Table 17.6 Telecommuters' Occupations

	Nonresident Men (n=319)	Nonresident Women (n=355)	Residents (n=78)
Professional/Managerial	44.3%	50.0%	5.7%
Sales/Service	66.7%	27.2%	6.1%
Manufacturing/Production	24.0%	44.0%	32.0%
Skilled Crafts/Trade	60.9%	21.7%	17.4%
Clerical/Secretarial	5.9%	77.9%	16.2%
Technical/Research	48.6%	41.4%	10.0%
Other	31.7%	38.1%	30.2%

Source: 1995 Maricopa County Regional Trip Reduction Program.

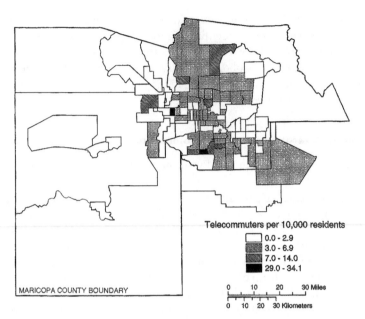

Figure 17.2 Home Zipcode of Inner-City Telecommuters
Source: 1995 Maricopa County Regional Trip Reduction Program.

Airport telecommuting occurs most at two local branches of national companies, a food service firm and a car rental, that employ low-paid workers from nearby zip codes. Nine Host Marriott workers telecommuted distances that averaged 11 miles. Similarly, ten workers at National Car Rental telecommuted distances that averaged 10 miles. Employees at these companies had the lowest drive-alone rates among airport employers (Host Marriott, 61 percent; National Car Rental, 67 percent), high carpool rates (Host Marriott, 14 percent; National Car Rental, 19 percent), and average (National Car Rental, 2 percent) or high (Host Marriott, 14 percent) bus use. Not coincidentally, Host Marriott met its travel reduction program goal of reducing the percentage of drive alone commutes in four of the past six years.

Reliance on carpooling and compressed work schedules varies not only by work site, but also by gender (Table 17.7). At America West Airlines, 87 female employees (7 percent) use a compressed schedule, while only men use a compressed schedule at United Airlines. Three large work sites for Southwest Airlines show that specific job responsibilities allow temporal flexibility. There are more employees with compressed work schedules at the mainte-

278

nance (149 employees, 15 percent) and personnel/reservations work sites (146 employees, 5 percent) than at the ground operations work site (37 employees, 2 percent). At these companies, men use compressed schedules more than women, while women are more likely to drive alone five days a week and to carpool than men. Employees with compressed work schedules live at average distances of 15 to 17 miles, approximately the commute length for non-resident telecommuters.

Table 17.7 Commuting Patterns for Selected Sky Harbor International Airport Employers

	Total Employees	Telecommute (a)	Compressed Schedule (b)	Carpool (a)	Drive Alone (c)
America West	880				
Men		1.6%	69.6%	16.2%	30.4%
Women		4.0%	43.9%	11.6%	61.0%
Southwest Airlines Ground Operations	620				
Men		—	5.1%	22.3%	75.3%
Women		—	2.9%	19.6%	77.1%
United Airlines	57				
Men		2.6%	12.5%	22.5%	59.0%
Women		—	—	33.3%	66.7%

(a) 1 or more days per week
(b) other than 5 day/8 hour schedule
(c) 5 or more days per week

Source: 1995 Maricopa County Regional Trip Reduction Program.

At this time, flexibility in work schedule rather than flexibility in work location eliminates commute trips. Telecommuting could clearly serve employees, given the large numbers of compressed work schedule users living at distances similar to other inner-city telecommuters. Some 106 of the 885 employees at the Southwest Airlines personnel/reservations work site state that they are interested in telecommuting from their Tempe, Phoenix, and Chandler neighborhoods south and east of the airport. The numbers of employees interested in telecommuting are low at all airport work sites, however, compared to the numbers of employees already using compressed schedules.

CONCLUSION

This study documents the travel flexibility in space and time for a large set of commuters, both men and women. Its limitations include examining only the behavior of large-company employees, who are estimated to be half the metropolitan labor force. The focus on the inner city does show the value of examining travel at the scale of submetropolitan districts. In Phoenix and elsewhere, the inner city is large enough that employees are drawn not only from distant locations but from a range of inner city neighborhoods, including gentrified enclaves as well as extensive but poorer communities. Travel distances are short, but inner-city residents still must travel to dispersed work sites.

279

High rates of commuting by driving alone confirm the importance of access to a personal vehicle for both residents and nonresidents. Commuters in sales, professional/managerial, and technical/research occupations are more likely to drive alone than to use another mode. Some employees clearly may be burdened by the cost of a vehicle. In inner-city Phoenix, manufacturing/production employees, both inner-city residents and nonresidents, drive

ELIZABETH K. BURNS

alone less and carpool more than other occupational groups. This pattern may reflect their limited economic circumstances rather than an independent choice to work near home. Residents do commute by alternative modes—walking, bicycling, bus, and carpooling—more than nonresidents do.

This study shows that flexible work scheduling is more prevalent than telecommuting, which provides variation in work location. Although 80 percent of these commuters have a five-day, eight-hour workweek, 20 percent have compressed schedules. Their separation of work and residence is accommodated by shifting toward longer blocks of work time, which has the effect of reducing the number of commute trips. Only 2 percent of all employees telecommute at least one day a week, and only half of those 2 percent telecommute more than one day a week. They are primarily nonresidents who live an average distance of 16 miles from their work sites. The one in ten telecommuters who are inner-city residents live an average of 7 miles from their work site. Although more women than men telecommute, the mix of genders and occupations at specific work sites contributes to distinct patterns of telecommuting. Women telecommute to public administration and education jobs, while men telecommute to manufacturing locations.

A positive culture of commuting options, including telecommuting, is emerging at individual work sites. Workers use a variety of travel options at locations where there is already a pattern of alternate mode use for carpooling, bus, walking, and bicycling, and a pattern of compressed schedules. Work sites at Sky Harbor International Airport include both inner-city resident and non-resident labor forces. Their employees' travel behavior confirms the importance of site-specific work and travel conditions for personal commuting behavior.

It is clear that present-day commuting in U.S. cities reflects a dependence on personal vehicles that individuals have only limited power to change. Decentralized development patterns in Phoenix are not particularly conducive to traditional commuting options such as public transit. Flexibility in the timing rather than the location of work is the dominant local response to the separation of home and work. Telecommuting at this time is an option limited to a small percentage of commuters in selected economic sectors and at limited work sites. For Phoenix and other metropolitan areas, this shift toward flexible work scheduling may be a short-term response to residential decentralization while employment is still concentrated centrally. These trends mitigate, but do not remove, the need for continuing physical travel between suburban residences and inner-city employment.

REFERENCES

Aitken, S. C. and M. Carroll. (1996). "Man's Place in the Home: Telecommuting, Identity and Urban Space." In Helen Couclelis, compiler, *Spatial Technologies, Geographic Information, and the City*, 36–41. Santa Barbara, CA: National Center for Geographic Information and Analysis, Technical Report 96-10.

Burns, E. K. (1996). "Automobile Dependence, Gender, and Inner-City Residence, and Travel Demand Management." In Helen Couclelis, compiler, *Spatial Technolo-*

gies, *Geographic Information, and the City*, 46–50. Santa Barbara, CA: National Center for Geographic Information and Analysis, Technical Report 96-10.

———. (1998a). "Participation of Employed Women in Telecommute Options: Evidence from Inner-City Phoenix." Paper presented at the Telecommunications and the City Conference, University of Georgia, Athens, GA, March 21–23.

———. (1998b). "Travel in Metropolitan Phoenix." In J. S. Hall, S. J. Cayer, and N. Welch, eds. *Arizona Policy Choices. Growth in Arizona: The Machine in the Garden.* Tempe, AZ: Morrison Institute for Public Policy, Arizona State University, 46–48.

———. (1998c). "Women's Travel to Inner-City Employment." *Women's Travel Issues.* Proceedings from the Second National Conference, October 1996. Publication No. FHWA-PL–97–024. Washington: U.S. Department of Transportation, 167–184.

Burns, E. K. and P. Gober. (1998). "Job Linkages in Inner-City Phoenix." *Urban Geography* Vol. 19: 12–23.

Evans, J. (1994). "Sharing Spatial Environmental Information Across Agencies, Regions and Scales: Issues and Solutions." In W. K. Michener, J. W. Blunt, and S. G. Stafford, eds. *Environmental Information Management and Analysis: Ecosystem to Global Scales.* London: Taylor & Francis Ltd., 203–219.

Gillespie, A. and R. Richardson. (1998). "Tele-Activities and the City: Emerging Technologies, Emerging Mythologies." Paper presented at the "Telecommunications and the City" Conference, Athens, GA, March 21–23.

Gober, P. and E. K. Burns. (1998). "Why Inner-City Job Linkages Won't Work in Phoenix." *Applied Geographic Studies* 2: 1–16.

Hanson, S. and G. Pratt (1995). *Gender, Work, and Space.* London: Routledge.

Janelle, D. E. (1996). "Space-Time Properties of Urban Life and Urban Structure: Discontinuities, Distortions, and Distance. In Helen Couclelis, compiler, *Spatial Technologies, Geographic Information and the City*, 156–161. Santa Barbara, CA: National Center for Geographic Information and Analysis, Technical Report 96–10.

Kihl, M. (1997). *Forging an Appropriate Transportation System for Arizona.* Seventieth Arizona Town Hall, May 4–7. Phoenix: Arizona Town Hall.

Maricopa County Regional Trip Reduction Program. (N.D.). 1997 *Annual Report.* Phoenix, AZ.

Morrison Institute for Public Policy. (1997). *What Matters in Greater Phoenix: 1997 Indicators of Our Quality of Life.* Tempe, AZ: Arizona State University.

Pisarski. (1992). *Commuting in America.* Westport, CT: Eno Transportation Foundation.

———. (1996). *Commuting in America II: The Second National Report on Commuting Patterns and Trends.* Lansdowne, VA: Eno Transportation Foundation.

Porter, J. J. and J. T. Callahan. (1994). "Circumventing a Dilemma: Historical Approaches to Data Sharing in Ecological Research." In W. K. Michener, J. W. Blunt, and S. G. Stafford, eds. *Environmental Information Management and Analysis: Ecosystem to Global Scales.* London: Taylor & Francis Ltd, 193–202.

Porter, M. E. (1995). "The Competitive Advantage of the Inner City." *Harvard Business Review* May–June: 55–71.

Rosenbloom, S. and E. K. Burns. (1993). *Do Environmental Measures and Travel Reduction Programs Hurt Working Women?* Final Report, Contract J–9–M–1–0075. Washington, DC: U.S. Department of Labor.

———. (1994). "Why Working Women Drive Alone: Implications for Travel Reduction Programs." *Transportation Research Record* No. 1459, 39–45.

Sawicki, D. S. (1996). "Information and Spatial Technologies and the Inner City." In Helen Couclelis, compiler, *Spatial Technologies, Geographic Information and the City*, 198–203. Santa Barbara, CA: National Center for Geographic Information and Analysis, Technical Report 96–10.

Sui, D. Z. (1996). "Information and Spatial Technologies and the Inner City." In Helen Couclelis, compiler, *Spatial Technologies, Geographic Information and the City*, 198–203. Santa Barbara, CA: National Center for Geographic Information and Analysis, Technical Report 96–10.

U.S. Bureau of the Census. (1963). *1960 Census of Population and Housing*. "Subject Reports, Journey to Work." Washington, DC: U.S. Department of Commerce, Bureau of the Census.

———. (1973). *1970 Census of Population and Housing*. "Subject Reports, Journey to Work." Washington, DC: U.S. Department of Commerce, Bureau of the Census.

———. (1984). *1980 Census of Population and Housing*. "Subject Reports. Journey to Work." Washington, DC: U.S. Department of Commerce, Bureau of the Census.

———. (1990). *1990 Census of Transportation Planning Package: Phoenix*. Washington, DC: U.S. Department of Commerce, Bureau of the Census, Journey-to-Work and Migration Statistics Branch.

———. (1993). *1990 Census of Population and Housing*. Social and Economic Characteristics. Metropolitan Areas. Washington, DC: U.S. Department of Commerce, Bureau of the Census.

U.S. Congress, Office of Technology Assessment. (1995). *The Technological Reshaping of Urban America*. Washington, DC: U.S. Government Printing Office.

U.S. Department of Transportation. (1997). *Successful Telecommuting Programs in the Public and Private Sectors: A Report to Congress*. Washington, DC: U.S. Department of Transportation.

ELIZABETH K. BURNS

282

RESTRUCTURING WRIT INVISIBLY

CELLULAR TELEPHONE SYSTEMS AS A MEANS FOR TRACKING URBAN CIRCULATION

Christopher Bertaut

One interpretive dichotomy from the geographic literature explores the primacy of spaces of flows and spaces of places. From Castells's (1996) perspective, IT is creating a new space of flows of information within and between the built infrastructure of cities. This encompasses the idea that new spaces are being created inside the telecommunications infrastructure that are at best loosely tied to actual physical places. Graham (1997) disagreed with Castells's (1996) argument that a space of flows is replacing the space of places. In Graham's conception, place still matters. This follows from the thesis that telecommunications facilities follow the existing built infrastructure. That is, places that are heavily built tend to have an underground or invisible infrastructure for telecommunications. He used this to argue that electronic spaces have come to rival physical space because people compete for them and interact through them. This argument is then used as a foundation for his hypothesis that place-based and electronic spaces form parallel networks.

This chapter examines the literatures on economic geography, communications, and information technology with a view toward forming a theoretical base for a case study of Gwinnett County, Georgia. One fundamental question is: How can we account for the observed spatial pattern of the cellular telephone infrastructure in American cities? Does it represent a worked out realization of the restructuring of business due to the impact of information technologies? Could it embody a new space where a highly mobile workforce will make its contribution to the urban economy of the near future? There is a divergence of opinion on the influence of telecommunications technology on urban form and the economy. Furthermore, there is little published work in geography that directly addresses the impact of wireless telecommunications on urban form and the present structure of the economic activity that cities support using data showing the actual locations of telecommunications infrastructure. This chapter will explore these issues and relate them to a case study of the spatial distribution of cellular telephone base station facilities and individual roaming users in Gwinnett County, Georgia.

The idea that telecommunications can influence urban form and its inter-action with business enterprise is not new. In discussing the United States in 1876, the year the telephone was invented, Casson (1910) wrote:

> It is one of the few social laws of which we are fairly sure, that a nation orga-nizes in proportion to its velocity. We know that a four-mile-an-hour nation must remain a huge inert mass of peasants and villagers; or if, after centuries of slow toil, it should pile up a great city, the city will sooner or later fall to pieces of its own weight. . . . Mere bulk, unorganized, becomes its own destroyer. It dies of clogging and congestion. But when . . . Morse's telegraph clicked its signals from Washington to Baltimore, and Bell's telephone flashed the vibrations of speech between Boston and Salem, a new era began. . . . In came cities of unprecedented bulk, but held together so closely by a web-work of steel rails and copper wires that they have become more alert and cooper-ative than any tiny hamlet of mud huts on the banks of the Congo.
>
> That the telephone is now doing most of all, is this binding together of all manner of men. . . . It is the telephone which does most to link together cot-tage and skyscraper and mansion and factory and farm.

Notwithstanding such hyperbole, there is evidence to show that Informa-tion Technology (IT) is better understood as an infrastructure that follows the development of the built urban environment than as one that leads it. IT is an *enabling* technology rather than a technology that defines urban form and its economic structure.

Burton (1992) defined IT as the convergence of computers and commu-nications technologies. A closely related term is "telematics," which for Gra-ham (1997) meant computers communicating over advanced *digital* telecommunications links. More precisely, for Burton, IT cannot exist in iso-lation but can have achieved what it has only through the creation of vast net-works of computers linked by telecommunications. Thus telecommunications has facilitated the flow of information from branch to head offices and back again while allowing access to vast corporate resources from readily available terminals and telecommunications links. He also noted that early computers were accessed only through terminals located in the same building. The pre-sent spread of networks over broader geographic scales was accompanied by the geographic dispersal of organizations themselves.

WHY IS INFORMATION TECHNOLOGY USE INCREASING?

There are now more than 55 million (Riezenman, 1998) users of cellular tele-phones in the United States, counting older analog and newer digital system users. This huge market penetration is important because *cellular telephony serves to compress in time many of the same communications functions that wire-line telephones with automated answering devices support while enabling their dispersal across space.*

Eliasson (1989) commented that ". . . what drives economic growth is the creation, diffusion and application of industrial knowledge. Internal education and knowledge transfer are critical components of industrial knowledge because much of the internal knowledge base of a firm is tacit, embodied in people and the way they work." For Eliasson, the production, distribution, and use of knowledge provide the best explanation for economic growth.

Cornish (1992) discussed several trends in business that have increased use of information in the production of goods and services facilities. These included formal and informal liaisons between business organizations, the increasing rate of product innovation, and contracting out of goods and services production. The latter trend of outsourcing of goods and services production has specific relevance for cellular telephone use since it has the potential to increase usage in ways that will be discussed below.

In summary, then, IT use is increasing for two specific reasons. First, it permits different, more flexible sorts of business organizations by allowing the internal knowledge base of an organization to be routinized and dispersed to peripheral locations or outsourcing firms. Second, it allows rapid and ready access to knowledge, whether by facilitating *anyone-anywhere* communication between individuals, or by giving workers the means rapidly to search for information in databases.

STRUCTURAL CHANGES AND THE DISTRIBUTION OF EMPLOYMENT AMONG ECONOMIC SECTORS

It is useful to begin this part of the discussion with mention of the Clark-Fisher (Clark, 1957) model of sectoral shifts in developing economies. In discussing the distribution of workers across the agricultural, manufacturing, and service sectors, Clark (1957) noted that as the Western economies that he studied advanced economically over time, the number of workers engaged in agriculture declined steadily while those employed in manufacturing first rose, then fell. The service sector showed steady gains in the relative number of people employed throughout the time frames of his analyses. As Pandit and Casetti (1989) noted, increases in income at a national level have been associated with small increases in agricultural output, moderate increases in manufacturing output, and large increases in services output. While these trends have been associated with differing levels of productivity gains across the sectors (Clark, 1957; Pandit and Casetti, 1989), structural and sectoral changes in economies over time are not invariant across cultures and time frames (Pandit and Casetti, 1989).

Because it is a dominant perspective in this area, the post-Fordist model of capitalist production deserves some consideration. Cooke (1992) began with a discussion of the change from a Fordist economy to a post-Fordist economy. Cooke listed several salient attributes of post-Fordist capital processes:

- Investment in flexible plants and human resources
- Competition through collaborative product innovation
- Organization using flexible integration
- Markets that are both based on volume and differentiated
- Labor that relies on both technical and social skills

How can the flexibility in the use of human resources mandated by post-Fordism be accomplished? There appear to be at least two methods for doing so. First, employees must change their contractual relationship with a company and, second, employees must communicate better across the horizontal corporate hierarchy. Available-anywhere mobile communications can play a role in both methods. Forge (1996) predicted that some business processes will be redesigned for people, who as roaming "free agents," rely on wireless telephony. Collaborative product innovation requires greater communications capabilities between firms and individual agents. Flexible integration is especially aided by the ability of wireless services to reduce uncertainty in interpersonal interactions. Differentiating products for specific niche markets can be achieved through better use of IT. Finally, while technical and social skills refinement does not specifically require more use of IT, that is one way to accomplish a skills upgrade among workers.

Hepworth (1990) contrasted the growth in the information occupations with other noteworthy trends in labor markets, particularly the growth of lower order service jobs and "flexible work." Malone and Rockart (1991) argued that the new organizational structures featuring decentralization of routine administrative functions mean more and faster decision-making which, combined with IT, improves the flexibility of firms with respect to labor and commerce markets.

THE "NEW" INFORMATION ECONOMY

According to Hepworth (1990), the information sector of the economy is hardly new, only its prominence is. Citing Beniger (1986), he noted that this sector grew from 0.2 percent to 46.6 percent of the U.S. labor force when services were considered separately. This long history of change culminating in the present economic structure is also recounted by Burton (1992). Hepworth went on to state that the share of information workers has grown in all of Europe and North America since World War II. For her part, Cornish (1992) reinforced the idea that an information-based economy is old by pointing to evidence that we have always had an economy that depended on information flows. The misnomer "information economy" is harmful since it may mislead geographers into examining qualitative changes to the exclusion of quantitative changes in the urban economy.

Castells and Aoyama (1994) did an analysis of employment trends in the G-7 countries covering a fifty-year span of recent history. With some reservations concerning the lingering influence of craft trades in Japan and Germany, they found an across-the-board increase over time in the proportion of the workforce employed in white-collar, information-intensive occupations. They also found that this increase has not caused a polarized society where the middle range of occupations (and pay levels) shrink as white-collar and menial jobs increase. They also recognized the formation of a new "white-collar proletariat" consisting of semiskilled clerical and sales workers.

Hepworth (1990) noted declines in employment in routine information-handling by clerical, support, and administrative staff. The decline in "pink-collar" employment has perhaps been caused by automation of such routinized tasks. This trend has been countered by a rise in flexible employment (Hakim, 1987) consisting of temporary, part-time, and self-employed workers. These and other trends noted by Hepworth argue for a vertical disintegration of the firm and increased use of information and communications technologies by both the fixed-employment and flexible-employment sectors of the labor force.

For their part, Graham and Marvin (1996) noted that modern tele-communications networks have sprung up alongside older types of urban infra-structure, including water and sewerage services. While wireless services are clearly not limited to the existing infrastructure by considerations of economy of installation, they are constrained to it by their customer base who are them-selves so bounded in the transaction of their daily affairs.

One prevalent notion concerning the impact of information technology and especially advanced telecommunications networks is that instantaneous communications will lead to a world in which no place is more important than another. The general idea here is that, like a roadway that reduces the effec-tive economic distance between two places (Taafee, Gauthier, O'Kelley, 1996), the nearly instantaneous nature of telecommunications links erases the eco-nomic distance for some types of interfirm transactions. As Graham (1997) pointed out, there is distance decay even with an "instantaneous" communi-cation link, since 60 percent of telephone calls occur within single buildings. Hepworth (1990) emphatically denied that we are anywhere near having a "fric-tionless surface" with respect to location decisions by firms.

The notion of telecommunications networks as analogous to "highways" in terms of their ability to produce added value is problematic. With respect to advanced producer services it seems like a workable analogy, because of the concentration of such service providers in major cities and the limited num-ber of pathways between these centers. When considering advanced manu-facturing that benefits from telecommunications-aided technologies such as just-in-time (JIT) and computer-aided design (CAD), the analogy is more stretched, because such manufacturing centers are spread worldwide with lit-tle clear concentration.

Castells (1989) has influenced the way that geographers consider the rela-tionship between information technologies, including telecommunications, and urban form. Castells noted the decentralization of information activities linked to producer and consumer services to the new industrial perimeter. This took place largely due to the availability of cheap office space and the way that IT allowed the removal of routine tasks to service centers on the urban edge. Castells also said that information technologies play a role in facilitating this movement because the new nodal areas would be unable to compete with the established metropolitan centers if not for their access to communication and information networks that keep them in close and constant contact with their command and control centers. In doing this, businesses are taking advantage of a cheaper and more flexible business environment. Castells attributes this environment to several structural factors. First, large corporations that decen-tralize internal parts of themselves to the suburbs are dominated by internal linkages over external ones. Private communications systems that aid internal and external business communication can readily allow relocation of specific corporate functions to peripheral urban areas. Castells also cited the availability of well-educated women who work below their skill levels. Nonetheless, Castells emphasized corporate functions that locate in the suburbs do so primarily because of the presence of a labor market that "fulfills the needs of the automated office."

Castells noted that decentralization is countered by three factors: first, electric power still comes from centralized facilities, and facilities at great distances from power generation facilities are at the greatest risk of losing the electrical power their IT investment needs to function. Second, peripheral areas are often inaccessible by air, which prevents face-to-face interaction between command and control management and lower-level management at peripheral facilities. Finally, rural areas lack the telecommunications infrastructure needed to support an automated branch office of a firm. Specifically, rural areas tend to be distant from their nearest central office switch, which makes provision of advanced telecommunications services such as T1 lines expensive or impossible.

Forge (1996) predicted the demise of the traditional command-and-control-centered organization to one where horizontal communication is most important. Forge also foresaw less emphasis in the future on the physical location of the office and more on the "logical" location of the office as paper files are made available through database management systems and workers are located via universal telephone numbers.

Taken together, all of these perspectives suggest that IT is a permissive factor in allowing urban subcenters to spring up around large cities. This allows decentralization of routinized tasks to office parks on the urban periphery while maintaining much of the urban hierarchy in its present form. Thus IT follows urban development and is dependent on it. IT is permitting the development of "edge cities" but doing little to promote growth outside traditional urban areas.

SOCIAL CONSTRAINTS ON THE DISPERSAL OF LABOR

Dörrenbächer (1993) noted that the actual use of a mobile telecommunications system depends on the *social compact* between employees and employers, exemplified by the case of a messenger service that in theory could have used cellular telephones to give the employees greater flexibility in the performance of their jobs but in practice used them to place relentless time pressure on the employees. Dörrenbächer argued that new technological infrastructure is not sufficient to change the social relations and geographic dispersal of labor.

Using the assumption that work tasks that require strong coordination must remain in close physical proximity, Rallet (1997) wrote that some categories of tasks may be geographically separated if they can be carried out according to preestablished procedures. Wherever a work unit has the freedom to organize its own work, the need for direct proximity to centers of control is lessened.

Rallet also remarked that employees may be ambivalent about whether telework is the best means to advance themselves in an organization. Thus, in organizations with a strong possibility for internal advancement, telework may be constrained. Rallet stressed the importance of socialization and social roles in the physically concentrated workplace. "The reconstitution of new forms of sociability supported by Information and Communications Technologies (ICTs) cannot completely replace socialization based on physical work relations." Rallet further argued that ICTs can more readily relax proximity constraints for organization and control of work than for incentives to work and the representation of the firm.

Proximity constraints are stronger when work organizational units are integrated. Less horizontal coordination is needed. Administrative work is far more amenable to the relaxation of proximity constraints than industrial work. IT supports the relocation of administrative work to alternative locations due to its strong information-processing component.

SPATIAL IMPLICATIONS OF INFORMATION TECHNOLOGIES

With respect to predictions of a decentralized workforce or greater centralization, Burton (1992) noted that both exist. Burton laid out a three-part scheme for the use of IT by modern firms. First, IT automates basic clerical and accounting routines. Here change is limited to these organizational functions. In the second phase, organizations use IT to provide services that are unfeasible using manual means. Finally, organizations use IT to provide completely new services that are impossible without IT.

Li (1995) looked at corporate reorganizations occurring in the 1980s and later. Although IT has been used to enhance existing organizational structures and processes, Li found that it is often used in *reaction* to organizational change toward a more horizontally organized firm than to generate the changes themselves. Li used this perspective to develop a framework for understanding the impact of IT and networks on the spatial and functional organization of companies. Li also noted that another important trend is the flattening of organizations to reduce hierarchical relationships, and the concomitant decentralization of decision-making.

Furthermore, Li found the trend toward horizontal reorganization most evident at the lowest levels of the corporate hierarchy. Thus back-office activities are more commonly segregated from front-office activities than had been the case in earlier years. Corporate IT networks can reintegrate back-office and front-office activities into a functional—if not spatial—whole.

Although Li noted that cities are more than the agglomeration of large firms, changes in their spatial organization can influence city and regional spatial organization. There are costs involved with physically moving workers, so at this time IT may change lines of control and information flow instead of simplifying the relocation of corporate employees. Thus IT may substitute for either physical relocation of employees or for some of their mobility. With that said, however, IT gives corporations a new tool for flexibly locating human resources to their best competitive advantage. Another form of employee flexibility in organizations and between cooperating organizations is flexible teamwork, where teams form, disband, and reform to work on specific projects (Malone and Rockart, 1991).

Castells (1989) also wrote that new communications technologies make it possible to relocate back-office activities even further from the traditional core of major cities than the suburbs—to remote areas and even offshore locations. This will, in Castells's view, lead to even more relocation of activities to minor metropolitan and nonmetropolitan areas of the country. It will also demand greater use of IT by firms.

Burton (1992) pointed to two reinforcing trends for IT use by firms. First, the amount of information required at all levels of organizations is increasing, and second, the use of IT has spread as it has been applied to problems previously thought intractable using "manual" methods.

Berkeley, Clark, and Ilbery (1996) did a case study that compared business practices and telecommunications and IT use between south Warwickshire and north Lancashire in England. The former is situated between several urban agglomerations and is considered closer to the core while the latter is at the periphery of the urban development of England. While the authors stated that telematics have the potential to open up rural areas for business purposes, the firms interviewed in this study show a marked contrast in uptake rates for both information technology and even simple telecommunications services such as facsimile machines. Even when allowing for a more favorable sectoral split in favor of information-intensive firms in south Warwickshire, the authors found firms in north Lancashire were less likely to serve other firms in distant places.

HIERARCHY OF INFORMATION FLOWS

Graham (1997) argued that in spite of much theoretical work on the impact of IT on urban form, there is little good empirical evidence to date concerning the actual directions, origins, and destinations of information flow within and between cities. One exception this researcher cites is the work of Mitchelson and Wheeler (1994), which used Federal Express package data to show dominance relationships between a hierarchy of American command-and-control centers. However, if voice traffic can be considered evidence of information flows, then Graham and Marvin pointed to another metropolitan dominance effect of interest; in 1994 the New York metropolitan area had about 6 percent of the U.S. population, yet it accounted for 35 percent of all outgoing calls on the U.S. Public Switched Telephone Network (Graham and Marvin , 1996).

In a similar vein, Rey (1983) looked at traffic between telephone exchanges in the United States. Using as his criteria whether telephone traffic originated and terminated within the same central office or between central offices, the large differences shown in Table 18.1 resulted. The proportion of calls that originated and terminated on the same switch varied between communities depending on their character. In rural areas, all customers in an exchange are typically served by one switch. For larger cities, the local exchange company normally

Table 18.1 Proportion of Originating Calls That Terminate in Same Central Office Switch

Community Type	Percent Terminating in Same CO Switch
Rural	66
Suburban	54
Urban	31

Source: Rey, 1983, page 125.

deploys many switches. Finally, as Graham (1997) remarked, 60 percent of telephone calls take place within individual buildings, showing a strong level of intrafirm communication.

These four studies provide empirical evidence that place still matters, that urban areas are different in the way that their inhabitants communicate, and that some urban areas function as command-and-control centers for others. All four lend support to Noyelle and Stanback's (1984) assertions concerning the existence of a hierarchy of corporate information flows. Within individual urban areas, this would enforce a tendency toward more telecommunications traffic with distant nodes while simultaneously boosting the amount of interexchange traffic through interfirm and intrafirm communications traffic.

THE ROLE OF WIRELESS TECHNOLOGY

Much of the current literature deals specifically with IT and only inferentially with the role of wireless technology. This is unfortunate, since Forge (1996) predicted that by the year 2000, one third of voice communication and all major IT applications will use the radio spectrum. Dörrenbächer (1993) reported that the Organization for Economic Cooperation and Development (OECD) has estimated that by the year 2000, 60 percent of all telephone calls in Europe will have at least one mobile party. In 1991, 10 percent of professionals in Germany were using mobile telecommunications; by the year 2000, 40 percent are predicted to have the same capability. Furthermore, mobile telecommunications represented a larger source of revenue than international calling—12 percent versus 9 percent as reported by the OECD (Wireless, 1997).

The role of voice communication itself requires some explanation. Burton (1992) mentioned that satellite communications have lent global reach to a basic means of transferring information—the voice telephone call. Hepworth (1990) made a careful distinction between voice and data communications. For Hepworth, the former represented flows of labor services and the latter flows of capital services within and between firms and governments. As a distant echo of Casson (1910), Hepworth noted that: "in different historical periods, telex and the telephone have played a critical enabling role in providing for production and locational flexibility in firms and government." Dörrenbächer (1993) said that mobile telephones are used to make it easier to control some jobs at a distance. He also noted that the effectiveness of a par-

291

ticular wireless communications system depends on the number of mobile subordinates that a supervisor must control. For large numbers, private mobile radio systems are more effective since they allow instructions to be given to multiple employees simultaneously. Thus for firms that typically use one-to-many supervisor-employee relationships, cellular telephones are less useful since they allow only two parties to attend to a single conversation at once.

Some insight into the type of user of the North American cellular system can be found in a report by Newman (1997). Residential cellular telephone customers used their mobile phones 82 percent of the time for outgoing calls. Of outgoing calls, 98 percent terminated on the wired telephone network. Newman reported that calling records indicated that during the peak usage hour of 4 P.M. to 5 P.M., 86 percent of all cellular minutes were used for outgoing calls.

Forge (1996) saw two forces acting within organizations that are of interest to this discussion of wireless facilities use. First, companies are beginning to build their competitive edge by improving their time to market and customizing products for local markets. This also requires more internal communications. Also, firms are beginning to specialize in the parts of the market chain where they compete most strongly. This leads to an increased need for external communications. As Forge put it: "Ubiquitous direct interpersonal communications are needed to reduce the risks in this deverticalization. These new post-Fordist global corporations possess a duality in that they need to remain responsive to local conditions while using their global resources for R&D and other leveraging resources."

DISCUSSION OF THEORETICAL PERSPECTIVES

While it is difficult to choose from among the theoretical perspectives presented here, the available empirical data suggest several worthwhile approaches to discussing the impact and influence of wireless telephone service on American cities. First, there seems little reason to believe that the presence of cellular telephone technology can be unequivocally linked to specific observed changes in the economic structure of cities and their morphology. In line with observations by Burton (1992), Graham (1997) and Cornish (1992), wireless telephony is at most an enabling factor. Even Castells (1989) said that telematics are an enabling technology, not a determining one for the economic structure and form of cities. Second, structural changes in the economy have wrought changes that are likely to increase the amount of cellular telephone use by both businesses and individuals. Third, wireless services are tied into the built infrastructure in ways that we seldom fully appreciate (Graham and Marvin, 1996). Mobile telephone use in the United States can be tied to the roadway network since cellular service is tolled and ready access to wireline network alternatives [i.e., Plain Old Telephone System (POTS)] should have a strong negative influence on cellular use by account holders. Furthermore, the movement-dominated lifestyles of urban dwellers (Burton, 1992) ties in nicely with the physical requirements of the North American cellular systems.

In the same way that voice telephone service vastly expanded the use of electronic communication over usage observed when only the telegraph existed, mobile telephony may eventually surpass fixed telephony for transacting many forms of personal and paid-sector business. Voice communication represents an extraordinarily easily learned user interface that changes little with the changing task requirements of modern employment. With the rapid improvement of voice processing automation at the individual firm level (Child, 1997), mobile workers can flexibly interact with corporate databases from nearly any urbanized location. Thus, telephony is coming to have the same ease-of-use advantages presently held by personal computers over earlier mainframe systems, and represents an attractive alternative to some forms of business communication that presently rely on face-to-face communication.

The idea that telecommunications has aided the presently observed pattern of suburban sprawl has merit. With the spread of routine office functions to suburban office parks, information technology provided a valuable means of maintaining a command-and-control structure in firms. Nonetheless, as Li (1996), Rallet (1997), and Forge (1996) showed, more horizontal spreading of corporate functions may prevail in the future. While this may do little to alter present U.S. urban morphology, it is quite likely to increase demand for IT and wireless communications services in particular. Furthermore, the upcoming PCS digital cellular telephone services possess one important attribute that will doubtless speed their acceptance by firms; conversations on them are encoded in a way that makes casual eavesdropping far more difficult than with the present analog cellular telephone system. In much the same ways that encryption techniques are helping to make private WANs unnecessary in many instances, wireless privacy is likely to increase the range and extent of cellular telephone use by firms. Taken together, these show that wireless telephone service can perform the useful function of reducing uncertainty among cooperative and often ad hoc work groups. This may in turn lead to a decrease in the perceived need for face-to-face contact in business matters.

As shown by the empirical information presented by Rey (1983), Mitchelson and Wheeler (1994), and Graham and Marvin (1996), place still matters in this context. IT users are not free to communicate with other firms and individuals across a featureless plain. There are hubs and nodes amongst the built urban infrastructure, and the wireless network in the United States closely conforms to the roadway network.

The preceding discussion serves as a springboard for consideration of my research into the spatial dependence of cellular telephony on traffic flows. If American urban areas have become diffused centers for economic interaction among horizontally organized firms, then cellular telephone traffic is likely to increase in lockstep with the layout of the road network and its available carrying capacity. This finding is in line with Graham's (1997) advancement of the notion of "telemediated urban change," since cellular infrastructure must follow cellular traffic patterns for both regulatory and competitive reasons.

The predictions of Forge (1996) and Dörrenbächer (1993) concerning increases in mobile telecommunications tie in with projections of Li (1995), Rallet (1997), and Forge (1996) for further horizontal reorganization of businesses, and together predict near-saturation of the market in some urban areas in the near future. This prediction is further bolstered by Haddad's (1997) data for Atlanta. In the Atlanta metropolitan area, the combination of rapid economic growth among smaller companies and lengthy average commuting times has boosted the market penetration for cellular service to 50 percent, with predictions for 100 percent household penetration by the year 2000.

Furthermore, Dörrenbächer's (1993) argument that cellular systems are less effective for organizations based on a one-to-many relationship between supervisors and their subordinates cuts both ways. Cellular systems are more effective for organizations composed of one-to-one or many-to-many authority relationships. The shift in business structures toward horizontally defined firms is more likely to favor cellular systems than the Specialized Mobile Radio (SMR) platforms currently favored by many businesses in the United States.

A CASE STUDY OF GWINNETT COUNTY, GEORGIA

Study Area

Gwinnett County, Georgia, is one of twenty counties in the Atlanta metropolitan area (see Figure 18.1). It encompasses an area of 1,130 square kilometers and, according to the U.S. Census Bureau, had a residential population of 478,001 in 1996. As shown in various Census reports from 1980, 1990, and 1995, Gwinnett County had the highest growth rate of all counties in the Atlanta metropolitan area between 1980 and 1990. Even as growth slowed in the 1990s, Gwinnett still grew 35.4 percent between 1990 and 1995 (U.S. Census Bureau, 1996). I selected Gwinnett County because I believe that such booming growth rates present a challenge for anyone who must plan services for an urban population. Atlanta has a combination of intense growth coupled with urban sprawl throughout the study area. Thus as a rapidly growing and spreading urban area, Atlanta makes a good test city for the central hypothesis of this study: roadway usage determines the areal extent and spatial patterning of cellular telephone base-station facilities.

The economic segmentation of Gwinnett County differs from that of the United States generally and the Atlanta metropolitan area in particular. While Gwinnett is notably weak in the Services and FIRE sectors, it has an unusual sectoral bias toward the Wholesale Trade sector of the economy defined by the U.S. Census Bureau. And while the United States had a sectoral concentration of about 7 percent for Wholesale Trade, Atlanta is closer to 10 percent and Gwinnett was even more strongly concentrated in Wholesale Trade at 17 percent in 1995. Furthermore, census figures also show that total employment growth was stronger in Gwinnett in the 1985–90 and 1990–95 periods than in Atlanta as an area and the United States as a whole.

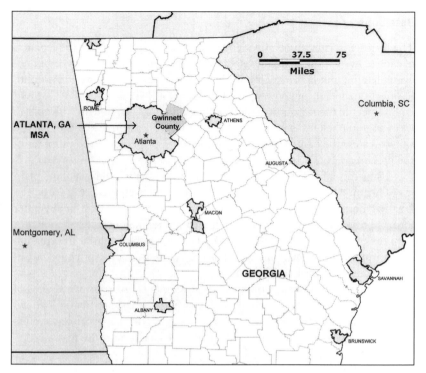

Figure 18.1 Atlanta, Georgia Metropolitan Statistical Area

Method

There is no readily available source of data that shows cellular telephone infra-structure in the United States. The data available for this study include:

- An engineering database of cellular tower facilities in Gwinnett County, Georgia, provided by AirTouch Cellular.
- TIGER/Line data showing the roadway network for Gwinnett County from the 1990 U.S. Census.
- Traffic counts provided by the Georgia Department of Transportation.

The cellular engineering database contains locational information as well as specific characteristics of each antenna site that has a bearing on the pre-sent study. This allows analysis of the aggregation of towers in the study area.

The roadway use data are comprised of several hundred observations taken by the Georgia Department of Transportation (DOT) along roadways in Gwinnett County. The raw traffic counts are adjusted for the average number of axles on a vehicle, Seasonal Factors and Daily Factors to produce an esti-mated Annual Average Daily Traffic (AADT) count for each tested roadway seg-ment. I used AADT counts as my basic measure of traffic along roadways. Furthermore, I used a map supplied by the Gwinnett County DOT to find and digitize the location of each traffic count point for analysis.

295

Data Sources

The engineering database provided by AirTouch Cellular shows the location of each of twenty-four cellular base-station towers in the county, and other relevant data including the height of each radiating antenna above the ground, its direction, and output power. The towers vary little in height at the base and with respect to the radiation centers of their antennas. The relative invariability of antenna heights is important because it gives reason to assume that the study area can be treated as a topographically even plane for the purposes of the present analysis. (See Table 18.2.)

Using this information it is possible to construct a tessellation of the plain over Gwinnett County, Georgia that shows which towers can cover particular areal segments of the county. This tower database does not exist in any other form at present for Gwinnett County since their regulatory structure does not require the registration of antenna heights along with structural information relevant to other planning purposes. The engineering database provided by Airtouch is current as of July 30, 1997.

The TIGER/Line data contains linear segments representing lengths of roadway that are rated in a general way according to their capacity. This allows the construction for the present study of a roadway network that can have vehicular traffic allocated along it according to the areal patterns of the roadway network.

For traffic volume data, I obtained roadway traffic counts gathered by the Georgia DOT for 1997. These are taken along major arterials, connectors, and feeder roadways in the county. As such, they do not represent traffic along smaller residential streets. Since the distribution of the counted roadways is relatively even throughout the county, this did not seem to be a factor that should prevent the use of the DOT data. I digitized the locations of each count point to allow them to be assigned to coverage areas. This was necessary because traffic counts for specific types of roadways (for example, interstate highways) showed a high rate of variance that suggested that traffic data must be considered separately for each coverage area analyzed.

"Natural Neighbor" Tessellation of a Plain

It is necessary to determine the coverage of individual towers in order to test the applicability of using the road network of Gwinnett County, Georgia, to model cellular telephone population. The dependent variable in this study is the actual location of cellular telephone facilities found in that county in July 1997.

I constructed a Voronoi tessellation (Watson, 1992; Bailey and Gartrell, 1995) of the network of tower locations. The tessellated plain is shown in Figure 18.2. This shows areal coverages enclosing sets of locations that are closer to the tower they are assigned to than to any other tower. Thus I have created a graph theoretical model of *areas of influence* of cellular telephone fixed facilities. These areas of influence only approximate the coverage of each tower since cellular base stations use a "strongest signal" criteria to decide

Table 18.2 Cellular System Antenna Heights for Gwinnett County, Georgia

Site AMSL[a]—Meters	Trans. Height—Meters	RCAMSL[b]—Meters
310.0	51.70	364.7
22.95	16.68	35.9

[a] AMSL = above mean sea level.
[b] RCAMSL = radiation center above mean sea level.
Data Courtesy of AirTouch Cellular, Inc.

which tower should serve any given system user. Nonetheless, given relatively even terrain and the absence of extremely high buildings, the coverage areas shown in this Voronoi tesselation should serve for the purposes of the present analysis.

Voronoi diagrams were first described in a general mathematical form by Dirichlet in 1850 and Voronoi in 1908 (Okabe, et al., 1992). The usefulness of Voronoi polygons was recognized early in this century in the earth sciences by researchers studying the distribution of rainfall and ore deposits (Watson, 1992, Okabe, et. al., 1992). One early application of Voronoi diagrams in urban geography was Bogue (1949) who used them to define surrogates for U.S. metropolitan market areas. The most commonly used term for Voronoi diagrams among geographers is *Thiessen polygons*. However, the use of the term "Thiessen polygons" is problematic since so many other fields of endeavor in the natural and social sciences refer to the same mathematical entities as

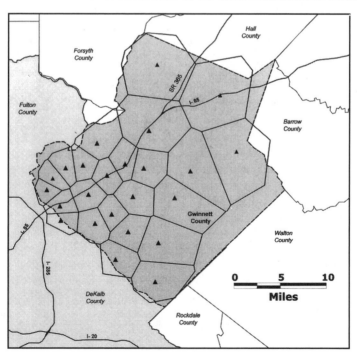

Figure 18.2 Voronoi Tessellation of Gwinnett County Cellular Tower Array

Voronoi diagrams (Okabe, et al., 1992). Thus geographers can avail themselves of a larger and more diverse literature on the subject by searching for published research using the more common term.

In order to develop the tessellation shown in Figure 18.2, it is necessary to calculate the nearest neighbors for each datum; all natural neighbors of each datum; and the convex hull encompassing the nearest neighbors of each datum. I used a commercial software package developed by Robert Edwards and marketed as TriTools (Edwards, 1998) to generate Voronoi polygons around each of the 24 Airtouch towers in Gwinnett County. Polygons at the edge of an area tend to be misshapen because they have no exterior neighbors. In order to counter this tendency, I placed a series of dummy points distributed according to the relative population density in areas surrounding the Gwinnett study area.

With Voronoi polygons for each of the towers in hand, I then created overlays of the census roadway data for Gwinnett and enough of each of the surrounding counties to assure complete roadway data for each polygon overlay. Once the overlay roadways were calculated, I then divided the roadway data into four classes corresponding to basic divisions of the Census Feature Classification Codes (CFCC):

- Class 10—Interstate highways and limited access roads
- Class 20—Primary roads including state highways
- Class 30—Secondary roads and connectors
- Class 40—Neighborhood and local roads

Once I had created separate roadway networks for each of the twenty-four overlay zones, I then used the GIS to calculate the area of each converage polygon. Finally, I took the digitized locations of each vehicular traffic count point and assigned them to individual "Natural Neighbor" coverage areas using GIS overlay.

Case Study Results

There is considerable variability in the traffic count data. The sharpest contrast is seen in interstate highway traffic counts for rural tower cells such as Buford and Hog Mountain when compared with the Jimmy Carter cell. Along Interstate-85, there is Average Annual Daily Traffic (AADT) of 43,265 vehicles in the Hog Mountain cell and 247,736 at the other end of Gwinnett County in the Jimmy Carter cell.

Using these disparities as a cue, I allocated all DOT roadway counts to each of the twenty-four specific cells and obtained median values of AADT within each cell for each of the four Census roadway classes. Here too there were no clear linear trends observed between roadway length by class, capacity measured in AADT and the area of cell coverages. There were strong and statistically significant associations between AADT by roadway class and coverage areas. These are shown in Table 18.3. The strongest was that between Class 10 (interstate highway) and coverage areas and showed a statistical association approaching unity. In the case of Class 10 roadways, there were only seven cellular coverages in Gwinnett County that contained Interstate Highways. The other roadway classes had larger numbers of included coverages.

Multiple regression analysis showed moderate-to-strong values for the coefficients of determination, or R^2, when traffic counts for roadway classes 20–40, 20–30, and 30–40 were compared to "natural neighbor" areas. These results are shown in Table 18.4.

THEORETICAL FINDINGS

This research project supports the notion that cellular services are at most an enabling factor in the restructuring of American cities by showing a strong correspondence between the traffic carried by the roadway network in the vicinity of a tower and the local pattern of tower spacing and location. This correspondence suggests a system of circular and cumulative influences beginning with the roadway network and ending with the location of facilities designed to serve cellular telephone traffic. Such a pattern of circular and cumulative causation strongly supports Graham's (1997) perspective of a space of places in telecommunications that is strongly tied to existing urban infrastructure.

Therefore, "natural neigbor" cellular analysis shows promise for charting the influence of aspects of the built environment on cellular service infrastructure. In doing so, it helps to show the new space of flows of information between, within, and among the built urban infrastructure (Castells, 1989). Structural changes in the economy are bringing changes that are likely to increase the amount of cellular telephone use by both businesses and individuals. This is because organizations are becoming more horizontally organized (Forge, 1996) and at the same time are dividing into smaller functional units. These structural factors are likely to increase cellular telephone

Table 18.3 Correlation of Traffic Counts by Roadway Class with Areas of Voronoi Tesselation Coverages

Road Class	Pearson's r	df	t	p <
10	-0.98	6	10.85	.001
20	-0.53	14	2.23	0.05
30	-0.61	13	2.67	0.05
40	-0.61	23	3.56	0.05

Table 18.4 Multiple Regression of Traffic by Roadway Classes against Natural Neighbor Areas

299

Road Classes vs. NN Area	IVs	R^2	F	df	p<
20–40	3	0.7228	5.2148	6	.05
20–30	2	0.6252	6.6715	8	.05
30–40	2	0.7054	13.1718	11	.01

traffic as an ever-increasing proportion of business activity takes place between business instead of within large, vertically organized operations. Since there is no evidence that the desire for face-to-face contact between individuals has decreased, traffic congestion and travel demands in urban environments will help to propel further growth in cellular traffic, as individuals struggle to maintain personal and business contacts while circulating on the roadway networks in our urban areas.

REFERENCES

Beniger, J. (1986). *The Control Revolution: Technological and Economic Origins of the Information Society*. Cambridge, MA: Harvard University Press.

Berkeley, N., D. Clark, and B. Ilbery. (1996). "Regional Variations in Business Use of Information and Communications Technologies and Their Implications for Policy: Case Study Evidence from Rural England." *Geoforum* 27: 75–86.

Bogue, D. J. (1949). *The Structure of the Metropolitan Community: A Study of Dominance and Subdominance*. Ann Arbor: Horace M. Rackham School of Graduate Studies, University of Michigan.

Burton, P. F. (1992). *Information Technology and Society: Implications for the Information Professions*. London: Library Association Publishing.

Carter, R. (1997). "A Telecommuting in the Real World." *The Atlanta Journal/Constitution*, August 11.

Casson, Herbert N. (1910). *The History of the Telephone*. Project Gutenberg e-text.

Castells, M. (1989). *The Informational City*. Oxford: Blackwell.

———. (1996). *The Rise of the Network Society. The Information Age: Economy, Society and Culture, Vol. I*. Cambridge, MA: Blackwell Publishers.

Castells, M. and Y. Aoyama. (1994). "Paths Toward the Informational Society: Employment Structure in G-7 Countries, 1920–90." *International Labor Review* 133: 5–33.

Child, J. (1997). "Computer Telephony Expanding Into a New Phase." *Computer Design*, June: 104–107.

Clark, C. (1957). *The Condition of Economic Progress*. 3d ed. London: Macmillan.

Cooke, P. (1992). "Some Spatial Aspects of Regulatory and Technological Change in Telecommunications Industries." *Environment and Planning* A 24: 683–703.

Cornish, S. (1992). "The 'Information Economy': Implications for Organizations, Cities and Regions." Unpublished paper.

Dörrenbächer, C. (1993). "Mobile Communications in Germany." *Telecommunications Policy* 17: 107–117.

Edwards, Robert. (1998). TriTools. A software add-on for Mapinfo, available from the Maptools Company, Oak Ridge, Tennessee.

Eliasson, G. (1989). "The Dynamics of Supply and Economic Growth." In B. Carlsson, ed. *Industrial Dynamics: Technological, Organizational, and Structural Changes in Industries and Firms*. Boston: Kluwer Academic Publishers, 21–54.

Forge, S. (1996). "The Radio Spectrum and the Organization of the Future." *Telecommunications Policy* 20: 53–75.

Graham, S. (1997). "Cities in the Real-Time Age: The Paradigm Challenge of Telecommunications to the Conception and Planning of Urban Space." *Environment and Planning* A 29: 105–127.

Graham, S. and S. Marvin (1996). *Telecommunications and the City: Electronic Spaces, Urban Places.* New York: Routledge.

Haddad, C. (1997). "Is Everybody Wired?" *Atlanta Journal/Atlanta Constitution* June 2.

Hakim, C. (1987). "Trends in the Flexible Workhouse." *Employment Gazette* 95: 549–560.

Hepworth, M. E. (1990). *Geography of the Information Economy.* New York: Guilford Press.

Li, F. (1995). "Corporate Networks and the Spatial and Functional Reorganization of Large Firms." *Environment and Planning* A 27: 1627–1645.

Malone, T. W. and J. F. Rockart. (1991). "Computers, Networks, and Corporations." *Scientific American* 256: 92–99.

Mitchelson, R. and J. O. Wheeler. (1994). "The Flow of Information in a Global Economy: The Role of the American Urban System in 1990." *Annals of the Association of American Geographers* 84: 87–107.

Newman, W. (1997). "Reality Check on Bill & Keep." *Cellular Business* 14: 78–86.

Noyelle, T. J. and T. M. Stanback, Jr. (1984). *The Economic Transformation of American Cities.* Totowa: Rowan and Allanheld.

Okabe, A., B. Boots, and K. Sugihara. (1992). *Spatial Tessellations: Concepts and Applications of Voronoi Diagrams.* New York: John Wiley & Sons.

Pandit, K. and E. Casetti. (1989). "The Shifting Patterns of Sectoral Labor Allocation During Development: Developed Versus Developing Countries." *Annals of the Association of American Geographers* 79: 329–344.

Rallet, A. (1997). "Labor Relationship and Geographical Proximity: The Case of Telework." Paper presented at 93rd Annual AAG Meeting, Fort Worth, Texas.

Rey, R. F., ed. (1983). *Engineering Operations in the Bell System.* Murray Hill: Bell Laboratories.

Riezenman, M. J. (1998). "Technology 1998 Analysis and Forecast." *IEEE Spectrum* 35: 29–41.

Taafee, E. J., H. L. Gauthier, and M. E. O'Kelley. (1996). *Geography of Transportation.* Upper Saddle River: Prentice-Hall.

Watson, D. F. (1992). *Contouring: A Guide to the Analysis and Display of Spatial Data.* New York: Pergamon Press.

"Wireless Sector Leads Growth in Telecom Market." (1997). *Telepathy*, a periodic supplement to *Communications Week.* 661.

PEOPLE VERSUS PLACE

TELECOMMUNICATIONS AND FLEXIBILITY REQUIREMENTS OF THE CBD

Nancey Green Leigh

INTRODUCTION

In this chapter, I explore the influence of new flexibility and technology requirements in the delivery of advanced services on central-city land use devoted to office property. Historically, the key determinant for land use devoted to the office-using industry sector has been employment, particularly in Finance, Insurance, Real Estate, and the subsector "Services." However, the degree to which the correlation between employment growth in these sectors and the demand for office buildings and related infrastructure can be used to forecast land use patterns in the future is less predictable due to technological changes occurring in the office workplace.

Why is this an issue of concern? From an economic development as well as urban and regional planning perspective, there are a number of reasons. To begin with, office-sector land use is an essential component of a healthy central-city economy. It provides high employment densities that in turn facilitate the efficient provision of urban services such as mass transit. Office-sector employment typically encompasses a range or hierarchy of occupational levels, from low-level clerical to upper-level managers and executives. It therefore helps to meet the needs of a cross section of the labor force. In particular, it is an important source of employment for inner city residents who have lower education levels, income, and mobility. Beyond this "captive" labor market, for cities that seek to promote a stronger middle class, professional workers occupying office buildings are an important group to "capture" for central-city middle-income housing development. A final point is that office-sector land use creates demand for ancillary business-support services as well as retail services, in turn generating additional employment and revenue for the central city.

To understand trends in the office market, it is necessary to recognize its heterogeneous nature: distinctions in age, building services, building materials, and location are used to assign office buildings to Class A, B, or C status. Vacancy rates among the different classes of office buildings typically vary, but are linked. For example, overbuilding in the Class A sector, such as that which occurred in the speculative frenzy of the late 1980s, can lead to a softening in rents for Class A space and thereby induce movement out of the Class B sector.

An issue central to this study's focus is whether the recent and future technological requirements of the key central-city office using sectors—advanced services—may promote growing vacancy rates. These rates could stem from: declining numbers of employees in firms resulting in less square footage required for the average firm; and/or movement out of office buildings that do not meet the technological requirements of advanced services.

It has been suggested that telecommuting and electronic data storage are resulting in decreased work and file-storage space requirements overall. Further, technology changes are facilitating the movement toward "hoteling," "virtual offices," and "virtual corporations," all of which decrease firm's space requirements. These trends parallel, in the organization of services production, the search for increased flexibility observed for industrial production manifested in vertical disintegration and specialized subcontracting.

Trends toward increased flexibility in the office market, on the one hand, also suggest further impetus for suburbanization of work and home, thereby reducing the demand for in-place infrastructure of the central city and dimming prospects for revitalization efforts. On the other hand, the desirability and/or necessity of a CBD location and face-to-face contact within and among firms may never disappear for certain advanced services.

The influence of requirements by advanced services for telecommunications and other advanced information technologies on central-city land use and economic development is a neglected area of study. In particular, there is a striking lack of empirical analysis of this area. Graham and Marvin, in *Telecommunications and the City*, do raise questions about the future role of the central-city but they do not undertake any empirical investigation to answer their questions. Castells, in *The Rise of the Network Society*, attempts to make the case for the continued primacy of CBDs, but also offers no empirical proof.

RECENT DISCOURSE ON THE FUTURE OF THE CBD

Graham and Marvin's *Telecommunications and the City* is an attempt to lay out and examine the implications for cities of an era increasingly dominated by telematic-based electronic flows and networks. The authors define telematics as "services and infrastructures, which link computer and digital media equipment over telecommunications links."[1] Their introductory chapter poses a number of key questions about the urban impacts of telecommunications, of which two are particularly relevant for this chapter's focus on the CBD:

> How are cities to sustain themselves economically given that more and more of their traditional economic advantages seem to be accessible, "online," from virtually any location? Are cities being affected physically by advances in telecommunications as many claim they were in previous eras by the railway and the automobile? (page 4)

In considering these questions, Graham and Marvin write:

> Arguments that this will mean the dissolution of the cities and the emergence of decentralized networks of small-scale communities or "electronic cottages" are widespread. In fact they are so common that visions of the end of cities seem almost to have reached the status of accepted orthodoxy within some elements of the popular media. (page 5)

At the same time, while they note "actual telecommunications-based developments in real contemporary cities are rarely analysed in detail," the authors have compiled a list (Table 19.1) of "metaphors and grand scenarios ... [recently coined] to describe the increasingly telecommunications-based city" (page 9).

Clearly, the list conveys a negation of the centrality of cities. But Graham and Marvin refute the idea that the "spatial 'glue'" that concentrates large cities is automatically undermined by the ability to have instantaneous communication across distance. Instead, a new type of "telegeography" (a term they borrow from Staple) is being formed by the differences in the extent to which telecommunications investments vary across nations, regions, cities, rural areas, neighborhoods, and households. For example, they note that fiber-optic networks—because of costs and technical barriers—are concentrated as trunks in national and global grids, as local lines to the largest users, or in the largest cities. This can be seen as a force for increasing concentration of economic activity in large cities.

Table 19.1 Metaphors of the Telecommunications City

The "invisible city" (Batty, 1990)
The "informational city" (Castells, 1989)
The "weak metropolis" (Dematteis, 1988)
The "wired city" (Dutton, et. al., 1987)
The "telecity" (Fathy, 1991)
The "city in the electronic age" (Harris, 1987)
The "information city" (Hepworth, 1987)
The "knowledge-based city" (Knight, 1989)
The "intelligent city" (Martin, 1978)
"Electronic communities" (Poster, 1990)
"Communities without boundaries" (Pool, 1980)
"Electronic cottage" (Toffler, 1981)
The city as "electronic spaces" (Robins and Hepworth, 1988)
The "overexposed city" (Virilio, 1987)
The "Flexicity" (Hillman, 1993)
The "Virtual Community" (Rheingold, 1994)
The "non-place urban realm" (Webber, 1964)
"Teletopia" (Piorunski, 1991)
"Cyberville" (Von Schuber, 1994, quoted in Channel, 4 ,1994, 1)

Source: "Metaphorical Characterisations of the Contemporary City," Figure 1.1 in Graham and Marvin, 1996.

Furthermore, while they do not contest that the urban landscape and physical urban forms of advanced industrial cities are now being radically reshaped, notably into polycentric urban areas, the "end of cities as we know them" does not automatically follow. There are emerging combinations of decentralization and centralization in which, they assert, world cities are a particular focus for increased centralization due to their acquisition of layers of telematics (that is, the not mutually exclusive categories of fiber optic networks, wireless and mobile communications networks, broadband cable networks, and satellite and microwave systems).

Graham and Marvin are critical of the widespread and technologically deterministic generalizations of telematics' impacts on urban form. However, when focusing specifically on the urban area's core, the CBD, they appear guilty of their own accusations, albeit from a "socially deterministic" viewpoint. They assert that there will be continued dominance of cities as global command centers in spite of the fact that much of the formal information cities traditionally dominated can be widely accessed online. Tacit information exchange will continue to require face-to-face contact for "the people involved at the apex of corporate power, and also those at the apex of financial markets and professional services need to be 'in the thick of it' in ways that cannot be substituted by telematics" (page 142). Hence, the social and cultural production of urban places in the form of financial services, offices, and corporate and service professionals will continue to underpin global command centers.

Are we to take such assertions, however, to mean that those at the apex of corporate power, of financial markets, and of professional services will still be tied to the *central business districts* of global cities? The continuing development of major metropolitan areas in the last quarter of this century has been characterized by a polycentric urbanization resulting in "edge cities" and multiple high-rise skylines. Further, there is significant literature on business location that suggests that the residential location preference of the corporate executive accounts for the growing suburbanization of corporate headquarters and other firms. Past studies have shown that the relocation choices of manufacturing plants and offices are influenced by the residential location of the chief executive officers. Schmenner reported that 40 to 50 percent of the officers overseeing manufacturing plant relocations admitted that the location of the chief executive's house had an influence on the decision process (Schmenner, 1982, page 162). In a study of relocations from New York City at the height of the office exodus, Whyte showed the same trend is true for front offices. Out of thirty-eight relocating companies, thirty-one moved to within an average of 8 miles from the CEO's home (Whyte, 1988, pages 287–289)

Two additional forces for decentralization or polycentric concentration are worth considering. First, the building stock in suburban edge city centers is newer and more likely to have the floorplates and technology capabilities required by today's firms. Second, traditional models of urban land prices suggest office lease rates of comparable-quality buildings would be less expensive in the edge city than in the CBD, as would be the costs of commuting and parking for the suburban office worker compared to those in the downtown.

In Castells's *Rise of Network Society* we can find another notable discourse over the future of the CBD within his description of a new spatial logic characterizing recent urban form evolution. This new logic is that of "the space of flows" as opposed to "the historically rooted spatial organization of our common experience: *the space of places*" (pages 377–378). The global (what he calls informational) economy is organized around global and command centers (that is, cities) that "coordinate, innovate, and manage the intertwined activities of networks of firms."

At the core of this economic process are advanced services, those sectors and/or activities in the economy that produce knowledge "generation and information flows." Advanced services include: finance, insurance, real estate, consulting, legal services, advertising, design, marketing, public relations, security, information gathering, management of information systems. They also include research and development activity and scientific innovation.

While advanced telecommunications systems could enable advanced services to be dispersed around the world, Castells observes that there has been, instead, a spatial concentration of the highest-order advanced services in major world cities. Further, the advanced services are distributed according to urban hierarchy logic. However, following Michelson and Wheeler (1994), Castells suggests that as international markets become more regulated, thereby reducing market uncertainty, "the concentration of the information industry will slow and certain aspects of production and distribution will filter into lower levels of an internationalized urban hierarchy" (page 381).

Advanced service systems will continue to be dependent on agglomeration because cities' business districts are "information-based, value production complexes, where corporate headquarters and advanced financial firms can find both the suppliers and the highly skilled, specialized labor they require." CBDs are networks of production and management ". . . whose flexibility needs *not* to internalize workers and suppliers, but to be able to access them when it fits, and in the time and quantities that are required in each particular instance" (page 381). There is, as a result, an agglomeration of core global networks that interact with each other and also have secondary networks that are dispersed and reached via telecommunications and air transport.

Castells also suggests that heavy investment in valuable real estate by corporations makes firms reluctant to leave CBDs because it would devalue their fixed assets. This notion, at least in the United States, deserves critical appraisal. There are many well-known examples of major headquarters choosing to leave their CBD locations for suburban office parks, with, perhaps, the relocation of Sears out of Chicago to the northern suburb of Oak Park being the best known. In an age of "lean and mean," highly expensive downtown "trophy" spaces are luxuries that many firms will not maintain. They are better off selling the real estate, even if there is some loss involved, because, on net, their costs are significantly reduced in the suburban location. In the move to achieve increased flexibility, corporations may tend toward leasing space that is customized for their needs as opposed to making outright purchases.

Further, the advent of REITs, or Real Estate Investment Trusts, offers even more flexibility to corporate location decisions. The multicity REIT ownership of office property releases firms from space leases that are much longer than product cycles by allowing them to transfer between office buildings owned by the same REIT. Although REITs managed only 8.3 percent of commercial real estate in midyear 1997, most analysts expect the REIT management system to dominate real estate investments in the near future. Further, the majority of REITs are located in the suburbs, which creates another disincentive for remaining in the CBD.

While Castells acknowledges that services, advanced and other, do decentralize within metropolitan areas and to smaller metropolitan areas, he cites his and others' work to support the notion that this is almost exclusively limited to back-office work: that is, semiskilled office workers (largely suburban female) who do the "mass processing of transactions that execute strategies decided and designed in the corporate centers of high finance and advanced services." If this is indeed the case, then we should not expect to find corporate headquarters of advanced services in suburban locations. Further, we should expect the price of suburban office space to be cheaper than that of downtown space, the average number of employees to be greater, and the square feet of space per employee to be smaller. This may be, for example, because the employees are lower level, may not have their own dedicated office space, or may be assigned cubicles rather than individual offices in which to work.

DEMANDS FOR SMART BUILDINGS

Increasingly, it appears that Class A buildings are expected to be "smart" or "intelligent" buildings. And it is this expectation that raised original concerns that Class B buildings might become increasingly obsolete, leading to rising vacancy levels in the central city. Intelligent buildings have been defined as those which have "adaptive environments of high quality, energy efficiency, security and safety, permitting optimised internal and external communications" (Gann, 1992). The three areas of technology identified with intelligent buildings are described in Table 19.2.

Although there were predictions ten years ago that new technology requirements and the costs of upgrading were making Class B buildings obsolete, the subsequent evolution of information technology has seemed to make it easier to make the upgrades. As there are typically ten to fifteen years of economic life for various tenant improvements (carpet, lighting, air conditioning, and so on), many Class Bs are at the end of their economic cycle and are ready for improvements that can make them competitive for new demands (Schlesinger, 1997).

Further, the issue of installing cabling for enhanced telecommunications is less of a problem than it was previously. Today, only two pairs of wires are required for digital communications: one pair for the phone line and one pair for the data line. Previously, analog phone wiring required 24 pairs of wires. Thus the wiring is simplified, it takes up less space, and the wiring itself is also smaller making it easier to run between floors (Schlesinger, 1997).

Table 19.2 Intelligent Building Technologies

Building Automation	Energy management, temperature control, humidity control, fire protection, lighting management, maintenance management, security management, access control, space planning and management.
Office Automation	Local Area Networks (LANS), electronic mail, data processing, word processing, management reporting and executive information systems, document image processing, and other internal communications such as audiovisual.
Enhanced Telecommunications—connections between buildings	Digital PABX, routing cost analysis where the landlord acts as public utility for the building, teleconferencing, value-added data services (VADS), ring networks, satellite uplinks.

Source: Gann (1992) and supplemental information provided by BellSouth, Atlanta, 1998.

Some industry experts consider wiring and information infrastructure to be less important issues in retrofitting a building than upgrading air conditioning and vertical transportation systems. This is because the A/C systems of most Class Bs were designed to accommodate a ratio of one person per 175 square feet. Today, with team approaches, ratios are closer to one person per 150 square feet. This means A/C systems need upgrading (more BTUs), because there are more bodies per square foot, and accompanying these bodies are more pieces of equipment that give off heat. However, due to changing chlorofluorocarbon (CFC) requirements and the fact that chillers wear out and need replacing, it is normal to replace A/C systems in B buildings, and this will typically not be seen as a cost-prohibitive capital expenditure.

As more employees are put into B buildings, demands on the vertical transportation system (that is, elevators) also increase. Further, elevator systems are expected to work more quickly or efficiently. It is now possible to update elevator systems through overlaying rather than replacement. Overlaying involves taking out the old relay and controller technologies and replacing them with state-of-the-art solid-state microelectronics technology. This technology can increase the vertical transportation capacity of a building by 25 percent without requiring the installation of new elevators because it has artificial intelligence: that is, it learns the traffic pattern of a building and adjusts for it, automatically going to floors where peak traffic occurs at specific points of the day. Hence, microelectronics technology is not only affecting the organization of office work—resulting in fewer clerical personal per professional staff—it affects the utility of buildings as well.

KEY DATA SOURCES FOR EXAMINING TELEFLEX GEOGRAPHY

While not openly accessible to the public, there are two databases that have real potential to provide insight into economic trends that drive the evolution of metropolitan land use and property markets.

The first database is one that is generated in the public sector, specifically by state-level departments of employment security. Commonly referred to as the ES202 database, this is an administrative database collected for the federally mandated unemployment compensation reports filed quarterly by all employers with one or more employees. From the database, it is possible to get information by firm on exact location, number of employees, annual payroll, and industry type. This data is generally not published or made publicly available below the county level. Nor does the U.S. Department of Labor collect the data and publish it as part of its national economic series. Each state makes its own decisions on what data to publish, as well as setting its own standards and eligibility requirements for research access to its ES202 database.

With special aggregation of the ES202 data, however, we can obtain a picture of the distribution of industries between the CBD and suburbs of a metropolitan area. Thus, this data can provide valuable insight into which firms and industries choose central-city over suburban locations. For the purposes of this study, ES202 data was aggregated to compare the central cities of the Atlanta and Chicago metropolitan regions with their suburbs.

The second database with potential to provide insight into the case study cities' teleflex geography is that of proprietary information collected by real estate research firms and sold primarily to real-estate marketing and development firms. The information collected typically includes building space inventories and available space for the office and industrial markets, tenant firm characteristics (number of employees and industry sector), lease rates, and building ownership information.

This database permits us to compute employee to square feet of office space ratios, which are seen as a key indicator of reengineering the organization of office work. Increased use of telecommunications and information technology is permitting the adoption of practices such as hotelling and virtual offices. Adoption of these practices can result in employee space ratios one fifth to one tenth of previous standards. For Andersen Consulting, this ratio has been reduced to 15 to 20 square feet per employee (Strohm, 1995).

PROFILE OF THE CASE STUDY CITIES, ATLANTA AND CHICAGO

Atlanta's recent redevelopment has, of course, benefited from the 1996 Olympic Games. It is a high growth region that has seen significant portions of its central city transformed by new development and redevelopment activity over the last decade. At the same time, it has experienced even faster rates of growth outside the central city. Atlanta is gaining stature as a corporate headquarters city and was acclaimed to have reached world city status in 1994 in publications such as *Fortune* magazine and the London *Financial Times*.

While the skyline of downtown Atlanta has changed dramatically over the last decade with the addition of a number of new skyscrapers, even more dramatic has been the development from scratch of skylines of several edge cities in the metropolitan region.

Chicago, in contrast to Atlanta, has long been recognized as a world city. It is also one of the nation's oldest and largest cities, and its urban history exemplifies this century's industrial and spatial restructuring patterns. Chicago's losses to the suburbs in recent years of corporate headquarters and CBD activity—most notably Sears—have been highly profiled. Yet today, the central city appears to be experiencing a renaissance. This is most visible in redevelopment activity that is residential and commercially oriented.

Chicago and Atlanta are ranked, respectively, third and thirteenth among U.S. cities in population, though Atlanta's land area is only 10 percent less than Chicago's. (See Table 19.3.) Chicago's central city holds nearly one third of its eleven-county CMSA's population while Atlanta's central-city population is slightly more than one tenth of the eighteen-county MSA. Yet Chicago's central city land area (4 percent of the CMSA) is not much bigger than Atlanta's (2.7 percent of the MSA), indicating a much denser pattern of development.

The percentage of blacks living in Atlanta's suburbs is more than twice that of Chicago's suburbs but, still less than 20 percent of the suburban population. In contrast, two thirds of Atlanta's and less than two fifths of Chicago's central-city population, is black.

There is less than $150 difference in median annual income between the Atlanta and Chicago metropolitan areas overall, but Atlanta's central-city median annual income is only 85 percent of Chicago's ($4000 less). This runs counter to what we would expect based on levels of educational attainment: the distribution of suburban populations by levels of educational attainment is quite similar, but Atlanta's central-city population is more educated than Chicago's. Nearly 24 percent of Atlanta's central-city residents have a bachelor's or higher degree and the population of those who are not high school graduates is just under 29 percent; in contrast, nearly 34 percent of Chicago's central-city residents are high school dropouts and a little more than 18 percent have a bachelor's or higher degree. Given that Atlanta's central-city has a majority black population, the income discrepancy may be more accurately explained by the Southern legacy of racism.

That Chicago has been, and continues to be, a more industrial city than Atlanta can be seen in its distribution of employment by industry. In both the central city and suburbs of Chicago, around one fifth of workers are employed in manufacturing (durable or nondurable production), while less than a tenth of Atlanta's central-city workers are employed in manufacturing, and less than 15 percent of suburban workers are in manufacturing. While the distribution of workers by occupation is quite similar between the suburbs of the two cities, Atlanta's central-city workers are more likely to be in managerial and professional positions and less likely to be working as operators, fabricators, and laborers than Chicago's.

Both cities' origins lie in their serving as transshipment points, and both

Table 19.3 Statistical Comparison of Chicago and Atlanta

	Chicago CMSA	Atlanta MSA
Size Rank among U.S. Cities (1996)	3	13
Number of Counties	11	18
Transportation System (1996)		
Total Highway Miles	23,642	12,117
Freeway Miles Per Urbanized Population	59,7	121.7
Daily Vehicle Miles Per Capital	19.1	36.5

(*Source:* FHWA Highway Performance Monitoring System, 1996)

	Chicago		Atlanta	
	Central City	Suburbs	Central City	Suburbs
Population				
1990	2,783,726	5,456,094	393,929	2,565,571
1996	2,721,547	5,878,227	401,907	3,139,323
% Change (1990–96)	–2.2%	7.7%	2.0%	22.4%
% of CMSA (1996)	31.6%	68.4%	11.3%	88.7%
Land Area (sq miles, 1990)	227.2	5,391.7	131.8	4,989.7
% of CMSA	4.0%	96.0%	2.6%	97.4%
Racial Distribution (1990)				
White	45.5%	85.4%	31.1 %	77.9%
Black	39.0%	8.7%	67.1%	19.3%
Other	15.5%	5.9%	1.9%	2.8%
Annual Income (1990)				
Median Annual Income	$26,301	$35,918 (CMSA)	$22,275	$36,051 (MSA)
Annual Income Group Distribution				
Less than $10,000	20.8%	8.0%	26.4%	8.4%
$10,000-$19,999	18.0%	11.3%	19.3%	12.4%
$20,000-$29,999	16.7%	13.7%	15.7%	15.9%
$30,000-$39,999	14.0%	14.9%	11.1%	15.8%
$40,000-$59,999	10.0%	13.8%	7.2%	13.6%
$60,000-$99,999	16.8%	30.7%	14.0%	28.0%
$100,000 or more	3.5%	7.6%	6.3%	5.8%
Unemployment Rate (annual ave, 1997)	6.02%	4.48% (CMSA)	5.92%	3.53% (MSA)

(*Source:* Bureau of Labor Statistics, 1997)

Percent of Population Working in Indicated Occupation (1990)				
Manag and prof specialty occupations	24.9%	29.6%	28.8%	29.3%
Technical, sales, and admin support	33.0%	35.1%	31.3%	37.1%
Service occupations	24.5%	22.2%	25.9%	21.6%
Farming, forestry, and fishing	0.5%	0.8%	1.2%	1.0%
Precision production, craft, and repair,	8.9%	11.2%	6.8%	10.6%
Operators, fabricators, and laborers.	17.6%	13.1%	13.9%	12.0%

Percent of Population Working in Indicated Industry* (1990)				
Agriculture, forestry, and fisheries	0.4%	1.0%	1.2%	1.2%
Mining	0.1%	0.1%	0.1%	0.1%
Construction	3.8%	5.9%	5.1%	7.0%
Manufacturing, nondurable goods	8.1%	7.6%	5.5%	6.4%
Manufacturing, durable goods	10.6%	12.8%	3.9%	7.5%
Transportation	6.2%	5.3%	6.2%	6.7%
Communications & other public utilities	2.3%	2.7%	3.4%	4.3%
Wholesale trade	4.5%	5.9%	4.4%	6.9%
Retail trade	15.0%	16.6%	16.0%	16.8%
Finance, insurance, and real estate	9.2%	8.6%	8.8%	8.7%
Business and repair services	6.1%	5.1%	7.3%	6.4%
Personal services	3.4%	2.4%	6.0%	2.8%
Entertainment and recreation services	1.4%	1.3%	1.4%	1.2%
Health services	8.4%	7.8%	7.7%	6.3%
Educational services	7.3%	7.2%	8.6%	6.3%
Other professional and related services	8.2%	7.0%	8.8%	6.6%
Public administration	5.0%	2.8%	5.7%	4.8%

*SIC Code groupings: 000–039, 040–059, 060–099, 100–229, 230–399, 400–439, 440–499, 500–579, 580–699, 700–720, 721–760, 761–799, 800–811, 812–840, 842–860, 841 & 861–899, 900–939.

Educational Attainment (1990)				
Less than 9th grade	13.8%	6.3%	9.5%	6.0%
9th to 12th grade, no diploma	19.8%	11.8%	19.1%	13.5%
High school graduate (incl. equivalency)	24.9%	29.3%	24.1%	27.8%
Some college, no degree	18.9%	22 7%	19.7%	22.3%
Associate degree	4.5%	6.0%	3.8%	5.9%
Bachelor's degree	11.7%	16.0%	15.4%	17.5%
Graduate or professional degree	6.5%	7.8%	8.5%	7.0%

Source unless otherwise noted: US Census Bureau, 1990 Census, 1996 Estimates [STF3A (Central City), STF3C Part 1 (MSA)].

were destroyed by fire before the end of the nineteenth century. And both even adopted the symbol of the Phoenix rising from the ashes to symbolize and inspire their postfire reconstructions.

Atlanta's original name, "Terminus," came from its beginning as a railroad juncture in 1837. The city's name change to Atlanta in 1847, resulted from a feminization of the "Atlantic" in the Western and Atlantic railroad juncture that it was. Atlanta's centrality on the "South's underdeveloped rail network [made it] a key industrial, medical, and logistical center for the Confederacy" (Rutheiser, 1996). It also made the city a target of destruction for General Sherman, with Atlanta's burning to the ground depicted in one of the most popular films of all time, *Gone with the Wind*.

Chicago's transshipment role derived from its natural advantages of being located on Lake Michigan and the Chicago River, along with the subsequent development of the railroad. In essence, Chicago became the country's gateway to the West as it was located:

> at the breaking point between eastern and western rail networks. Already by 1852, the pattern had clearly emerged that eastern railroads operating south of the Great Lakes would find their eastern terminal in Chicago, while the various western railroads fanning out from the city would locate their Western terminal. No single railroad company operated trains both east and west of Chicago. Out of this seemingly trivial fact flowed many consequences that maintained Chicago's railroad hegemony for the rest of the century. (Cronon, 1991, page 83)

The "Great Fire" of 1871, which started in a barn behind the cottage of Patrick O'Leary (hence the well-known song lyrics attributing the start of the fire to the lantern knocked over by Mrs. O'Leary's cow) destroyed the entire downtown. Unlike Atlanta's postfire position, however, Chicago still held its regional advantage as the gateway to the West. As a consequence, capital to rebuild flowed into the city quickly from Eastern and European mercantile and business interests. Further:

> By clearing away the old wooden building stock, the catastrophe enabled businesses to erect new structures using the latest techniques for fire prevention; these safety measures were enforced by the passage of new ordinances imposing strict new building codes and fire limits. More important, the burn produced a construction boom that drove up the price of downtown real estate. (Cronon, 1991, page 346)

Land values had risen well above their prefire levels by the first anniversary of the fire, encouraging architects to design taller structures. This, in turn, led to the invention of the skyscraper (Cronon, 1991). Many if not all of the earliest skyscrapers designed by the "Chicago School of Architecture" are still standing; in fact, two are among the older buildings discussed in the Chicago case study. The architects identified with the Chicago School include John Root, Dankmar Adler, Louis Sullivan, and Daniel Burnham (Cronon, 1991).

While the cities of Atlanta and Chicago are similar in age, their current pattern of development and the way in which this pattern influences redevelopment prospects of these city region's cores are very much dependent upon the difference in when their primary growth phase took place. Chicago is a "preauto" city—its defining growth phase occurred when goods and workers were transported primarily by passenger and freight rail, intracity trucking, and street cars. Atlanta is still in its defining growth phase. This phase began in the 1970s with the national movement of industry and jobs to the sunbelt, and it continues today.

The contrast in when the two cities experienced their defining growth phases—pre- or postauto—has resulted in very different transportation system patterns. While Atlanta's total land area is 90 percent of Chicago's, Atlanta has more than two freeway miles per capita than does Chicago. Atlanta's drivers travel nearly twice as many miles a day—36.5 versus 19.1 (see Table 19.3). In contrast, the annual transit vehicles miles ridden by Atlantans are only 27 percent of those of Chicagoans. Atlanta's mass transit system (buses and rapid transit) is underdeveloped and underutilized. The MARTA system (Metro Atlanta Rapid Transit Authority) is not well distributed throughout the area, and while the Olympic Games provided fuel for some expansion, key high-growth counties of the area have refused to allow MARTA to expand to them. In contrast, the Chicago Metro area has a very well-developed transit system, and easy access to the central city is available via trains, rapid transit, or multiple bus systems. Further, unlike Atlanta, the areas around mass transit stations have good commercial development to meet the needs of commuters.

The transportation *similarity* between the two cities is found in their air service. Chicago and Atlanta are, respectively, the first and second busiest airports in the United States, and their international status truly links them to the global economy. The decision made in the 1950s by Atlanta boosters and city leaders to invest in an airport far beyond that which they needed is seen as one of the key strategic moves that allowed Atlanta to ascend rapidly to its Southern, and then national, leadership position. The city was able to reinvent itself as a transshipment node based on air transport, having had its original rail transshipment role destroyed in the Civil War and having gone so far as even to demolish its classic Union Depot rail station in the 1950s. In contrast, Chicago has maintained its train stations and recently completed an elegant renovation of its Union Station. Further, its airport serves to continue Chicago's historic *raison d'être* as a gateway between the East and West of the nation.

OFFICE LAND USE IN ATLANTA AND CHICAGO

There is a lack of empirical evidence on how the shifts toward increased flexibility and information technology usage are affecting key cities' CBDs in the United States. What evidence there is focuses largely on New York City, the United States' first-order world city. The cities focused on in this research, Chicago and Atlanta, are also global cities, albeit secondary. Atlanta's population size of only around four million for the metropolitan area might suggest it be pushed down to a tertiary level. However, Atlanta has recently taken a leadership role in the global marketplace. In this decade alone, 249 foreign-based firms have opened new offices, taking their cue from the Association of Foreign Investors and *World Trade* magazine, which ranked Atlanta on top for, respectively, viable foreign investment and sites for global companies. The 249 foreign-based firms joined the thirteen Fortune 500 firms headquartered in the Atlanta region (see Table 19.4), helping to generate the 63.3 million passenger flights at Hartsfield International Airport in 1996.

In looking at the two cities' CBDs, this chapter explores the previously described assertion that the need for face-to-face contact, to be "in the thick of it" in ways unsubstitutable by telematics, gives the CBD a "comparative advantage" or a place of fixed importance in a flexible global telegeography. Perhaps the reason there is so little empirical evidence on this question—and the larger question of what exactly is this evolving pattern of telegeography—is connected with the difficulty of obtaining data that can shed light on the topic. This is particularly the case when we seek to explore the evolving teleflex geography *within* global cities. This is due to the lack of published secondary data by detailed industry and employment below the county level.[2] It is also because the government does not collect *property* data specifically on office and industrial use. This accounts for why the empirical evidence on the evolving pattern of telegeography and flexible space, or "teleflex geography," is largely case study, survey research, and/or anecdotal.

Data on property markets (office and industrial) is privately collected by a number of real estate research firms and associations. There is no government mandate that a census of all properties be made, which means that the data the researcher has to rely upon does not produce nearly the confidence for analysis that, for example, federally collected employment or housing statistics warrant. The coverage and the methodology for producing property data varies widely amongst the numerous firms covering the major urban markets.

Table 19.4 Atlanta's Fortune 500 Headquarters

Firm Name	Industry	Metro Location
Alumax	Nonferrous Metals	Suburban
BellSouth	Telecom carrier	CBD
Coca-Cola	Beverages	CBD
Coca-Cola Enterprises	Beverages	Suburban
Cox Communications	Broadcasting	Suburban
Delta Air Lines	Airline	Suburban
Equifax	Business Services	CBD
Genuine Parts	Automobile Parts	Suburban
Georgia-Pacific Group	Paper and Lumber	CBD
HBO & Company	Health Care Services	Suburban
Home Depot	Home Improvement	Suburban
Southern Company	Electric Utility	CBD
Sun Trust Banks	Regional Banking	CBD

Source: Forbes 500 1998 (*www.forbes.com*) and Atlanta telephone records.

Consequently, one has to be cautious in performing time series analyses and/or making comparisons between cities, and it is best to look for major trends. That said, this study attempts to establish what the trends in the office-property market have been for Atlanta and Chicago during this decade.

Data from Table 19.5 suggest that Chicago's CBD office market is nearly five times the size of Atlanta's, while its suburban market is closer to twice the size of Atlanta's. Further, 1997 figures indicate that Atlanta's Class A suburban market is twice the size of the CBD's, while its Class B inventory is four times that of the CBD's. In contrast, Chicago's CBD has nearly twice as much Class A space as its suburbs, while its CBD Class B space is only around two fifths of that found in the suburbs. Further, Class B space in the suburbs of Chicago appears to have quadrupled between 1990 and 1997. CBD vacancy rates for both cities are substantially higher than suburban rates. Notably, the CBD vacancy rates in Class B buildings of 18 percent for both cities is at least 9 percent greater than those for CBD Class A space, or both kinds of suburban space. Chicago has actually been experiencing a negative net absorption of Class B space, that is, the amount of Class B space occupied actually fell over the last year.

Defining whether a building is Class A or Class B is not an exact science. While Class A buildings are more likely to be of newer construction, a new building can be built to Class B standards. This appears to be a major trend in the Chicago suburbs, as noted above. Typically, a Class A building is characterized by a prime location, high-quality finish, and high level of maintenance. It commands a relatively high rental rate within its market area. Class B buildings are characterized by quality finish and maintenance, lower levels of amenities (for instance, parking that is not covered, interior finish, retail services), and lower lease rates. Over time, Class A buildings that are not updated can shift down into the Class B category, and the opposite can occur: Class B buildings can be upgraded to Class A status, which we discuss below.

Table 19.5 Atlanta and Chicago Comparison of Office Market, 1990–1997

Atlanta	1990 CBD		1990 Outside CBD		1997 CBD		1997 Outside CBD	
Building Type	Class A	Class B	Class A	Class B	Class A	Class B	Class A	Class B
Total	18,161,436	na	56,390,398	na	16,456,738	8,068,362	33,294,548	32,928,637
Vacant	2,834,517	na	9,840,163	na	1,820,344	1,454,493	1,690,061	3,041,606
Vacancy Rate	15.6	na	17.5	na	11.1	18	5.1	9.2
Under Construction	2,801,500	na	2,164,200	na	na	na	950,000	na
Net Absorption	457,148	na	2,722,697	na	38,022	22,076	1,832,798	101,726

Chicago	1990 CBD		1990 Outside CBD		1997 CBD		1997 Outside CBD	
Building Type	Class A	Class B	Class A	Class B	Class A	Class B	Class A	Class B
Total	45,583,000	44,104,000	29,623,000	22,277,000	44,118,432	40,092,965	23,239,976	96,417,574
Vacant	5,077,000	6,427,000	6,225,000	4,616,000	4,129,594	7,535,366	1,600,726	6,174,571
Vacancy Rate	11.1	14.6	21	20.7	9.4	18.8	6.9	6.4
Under Construction	5,567,000	0	3,617,000	0	0	0	300,000	0
Net Absorption	1,648,000	na	1,724,000	na	1,205,222	(257,294)	312,178	37,150

Source: Society of Industrial and Office Realtors: 1990 Guide to Industrial and Office Real Estate Markets; Comparative Statistics of Industrial and Office Real Estate Markets (1997).

CITY-SUBURBAN DISTRIBUTION OF ADVANCED SERVICES

Tenants drive the demand for office space, and thus to understand the trends in the use of land for office buildings between the CBD and suburbs of the metropolitan area, it is helpful to have a profile of the office-using sectors in the two subregions. In keeping with this chapter's focus on advanced services use and technology requirements for office use in the CBD, Table 19.6 shows the city and suburban distribution of establishments and the average number of employees per establishment for selected industry sectors in the Chicago metro area. The data indicate that the city does dominate the metro area in advanced services activity: out of thirteen 3-digit SIC advanced services categories, the city has more establishments in all but four. Three of these four are residential-market-oriented, suggesting they have followed the population to the suburbs: mortgage banking, insurance, and real-estate services. The city particularly dominates in legal services (3 times more firms than the suburbs), management and public relations (2.4 times more firms), and personnel supply services (2 times more firms). Furthermore, in all thirteen subsectors, the average number of employees per establishment in the city is greater than that in the suburbs. City firm employment sizes are double or more those of the suburbs in communications, securities and commodity services, insurance, advertising, miscellaneous business services, legal services, and accounting services.

The City of Atlanta does not play as dominant a role in the provision of advanced services as does Chicago. From Table 19.7, we see that only three of the thirteen services subsectors have more establishments in the city: security and commodity brokers, advertising, and management and public relations.

Table 19.6 Chicago Advanced Services
(Number of Establishments, Average Number of Employees per Establishment)

| SIC* | Description | Number of Establishments | | | Avg. Employee/Est. | |
		City	Suburbs	City%	City	Suburbs
480-489	Communications	730	411	64.0%	42.4	22.6
616**	Mortgage Bankers and Brokers	133	505	20.8%	17.3	12.5
628**	Security and Commodity Services	366	451	44.8%	14.8	3.0
641**	Insurance Agents, Brokers, and Service	875	2,848	23.5%	12.3	5.5
653**	Real Estate Agents and Managers	1,625	2,825	36.5%	8.5	4.3
731	Advertising	826	286	74.3%	16.9	8.3
736	Personnel Supply Services	1,056	536	66.3%	66.7	62.2
737	Computer and Data Processing Services	1,961	1,497	56.7%	15.4	11.0
738	Misc Business Services	1,736	1,109	61.0%	26.3	11.8
81	Legal Services	4,034	1,317	75.4%	8.8	3.6
871	Engineering and Architectural Services	1,347	916	59.5%	13.3	9.8
872	Accounting, Auditing, and Bookkeeping	1,737	950	64.6%	13.9	6.4
874	Management and Public Relations	3,385	1,414	70.5%	8.9	8.0

* SIC = Standard Industrial Classification
   Source: U.S. Census, County Business Patterns, 1995, unless otherwise noted. *City* = Cook County.
   Suburbs = Chicago PMSA Total—Cook County
** *Source:* ES202 Data, Economic Information and Analysis, Illinois Department of Employment Security. *City* = City of Chicago ZIP codes. *Suburbs* = Balance of Region, 1996.

The city's advanced services firms do all have higher average numbers of employees, and, in most sectors, average employment in city firms is two to three times that of firms in the suburbs.

Atlanta Office Market Insights from Property Market Data

Extracting data from the Jamison proprietary real-estate information database provides additional insight for Atlanta on the question of whether advanced services and their highest order functions are continuing to make the CBD their location as suggested by Castells and others.

For the purposes of this analysis, two office submarkets have been aggregated to reflect the CBD of Atlanta. These markets are referred to as the down-

Table19.7 Atlanta Advanced Services
(Number of Establishments, Average Number of Employees per Establishment)

SIC*	Description	# of Establishments		Av Emp/Establish	
		City*	Sub*	City*	Sub*
480–489	Communications				
	1990	116	110	309.85	24.96
	1996	294	316	113.86	43.26
616	Mortgage Bankers and Brokers				
	1990	137	118	14.22	8.07
	1996	212	238	17.83	8.16
628	Security and Commodity Services				
	1990	79	34	8.57	3.91
	1996	134	50	8.00	4.80
641	Insurance Agents, Brokers, and Service				
	1990	508	781	12.93	8.61
	1996	644	960	12.45	7.21
653	Real Estate Agents and Managers				
	1990	529	603	11.12	5.76
	1996	745	937	9.80	4.88
731	Advertising				
	1990	244	155	11.44	10.86
	1996	280	172	12.50	9.84
736	Personnel Supply Services				
	1990	262	247	97.30	37.42
	1996	420	434	77.49	72.53
737	Computer and Data Processing Services				
	1990	376	595	32.00	9.60
	1996	690	1,264	35.81	9.82
738	Misc Business Services				
	1990	595	859	25.85	11.68
	1996	679	1,018	24.10	11.53
81	Legal Services				
	1990	825	668	11.68	4.63
	1996	1,058	814	10.45	3.76
871	Engineering and Architectural Services				
	1990	384	470	19.35	14.41
	1996	446	627	21.66	11.66
872	Accounting, Auditing, and Bookkeeping				
	1990	351	466	16.91	5.79
	1996	449	672	16.07	5.31
874	Management and Public Relations				
	1990	661	640	10.68	5.87
	1996	870	1,001	12.19	5.69

*SIC = Standard Industrial Classification, City=ZIP Codes of the City of Atlanta, Sub = Balance of Region
Source: ES202, 1990 and 1996, Georgia Department of Labor.

317

town and midtown markets, respectively. The downtown submarket is the city's original CBD, and some of its buildings date back to the 1890s. Expansion of this district, particularly in the 1980s and 1990s, has encompassed the adjacent midtown submarket. These two submarkets are at the center of the metropolitan region's transportation system. Interstates 75, 85, and 20 pass through them, as does MARTA, the region's rapid transit system. These two submarkets contain the greatest concentration of MARTA stations in the metro area: 13 of the total 36 stations. Together the two submarkets contain 432 office buildings, for a total of 21.1 million square feet of the metro area's office space.

Beginning with an examination of the distribution of tenants across the metro area by whether their intrafirm function is that of a branch unit, headquarters, or regional headquarters, as headquarters are the highest-order function, we would expect to find them predominantly located in the CBD. However, for the distribution of office tenants across all industries, the suburbs have nearly as high a proportion (more than 80 percent) of headquarters as they do regional and branch units. Moreover, the suburbs are the location of 82 percent of the headquarters firms in the advanced services sectors.

Second, examining the distribution of office tenants by five categories of administrative function—government, international, local, national, and regional—we would expect tenants that are international and national to be located in the CBD if the CBD continues to hold its primacy for high order functions. However, for the distribution of office tenants across all industry sectors, the only function found predominantly in the CBD is government. Almost 60 percent of government office tenants are located in the CBD, while more than 80 percent of office tenants in the four remaining administrative functions are located in suburban office space (Table 19.8). The predominance of government office tenants in the CBD is due to Atlanta being a state capital, as well

Table 19.8 Distribution of Office Tenants within Metro Atlanta by Interfirm and Administrative Function
Classes A & B Combined

	Metro Total		Metro Adv Services		CBD Total		CBD Adv Services		Suburban Total		Suburban Adv Total	
	#	%	#	%	#	%	#	%	#	%	#	%
Intra-Firm Function												
Branch	1,473	29%	668	28%	207	25%	86	22%	1,238	29%	578	29%
Headquarters	3,300	65%	1644	68%	597	71%	305	76%	2,751	65%	1349	67%
Regional Headquarters	325	6%	117	5%	33	4%	8	2%	275	6%	100	5%
Total	5,098	100%	2429	100%	837	100%	399	100%	4,264	100%	2027	100%
Administrative Function												
International	652	13%	253	10%	81	10%	36	9%	606	14%	211	10%
Regional	271	5%	125	5%	42	5%	18	4%	281	6%	114	6%
National	924	18%	442	18%	100	12%	47	12%	841	19%	388	19%
Local	3,147	62%	1604	66%	554	66%	297	74%	2,655	59%	1310	65%
Government	97	2%	4	0%	62	7%	3	1%	86	2%	0	0%
Total	5,091	100%	2,428	100%	839	100%	401	100%	4,469	100%	2023	100%

Note: Class C buildings excluded from analysis as there are only 35 in the entire Metro Atlanta area.
Class A buildings are "prime quality office product, characterized by quality finish and high level of maintenance."
Class B buildings are "good quality office product, characterized by quality finish and maintenance but lacking somewhat in the level of amenities (including covered parking, interior finish, retail services, etc.")."
Source: Leasetrac 6.1, Jamison Research, Inc. Data current as of March 6, 1998.

as the location of regional headquarters of a number of federal government agencies, including the U.S. Department of Housing and Urban Development, U.S. Environmental Protection Agency, and the Southeast Federal Reserve Bank. That these agencies remain in the CBD is undoubtedly influenced by Executive Order No. 12072 which, seeking to "strengthen our Nation's cities," requires them to first consider CBD locations when choosing their offices.

Examining the average number of employees per tenant can provide insight on whether firm reorganization trends such as the growth of the back-office movement are occurring. If the suburbs are indeed the recipient of lower-level functions in advanced services, as a result of firms seeking lower real-estate and overhead costs to house employees for whom face-to-face contact is not primary, then we would expect the average number of employees per tenant to be greater in the suburbs than in the CBD. Figure 19.1 indicates just the opposite for the Atlanta metropolitan area: the average number of employees per tenant for firms in the CBD is larger than the suburbs (50 versus 36 in Class A space, and 36 versus 19 in Class B space).

Examining specific sectors within advanced services, computer and data processing (SIC 737) does have higher average numbers of employees per tenant in the suburbs, and nearly all of the tenants are located in the suburbs (Table 19.9). Thus it would appear to fit the notion of back office activity. However, the average number of employees per tenant is higher in the CBD than it is in the suburbs in Legal Services (SIC 81), Insurance (SIC 641) and Accounting (SIC 872) sectors. These are key advanced services sectors associated with firm reorganization trends such as hoteling.

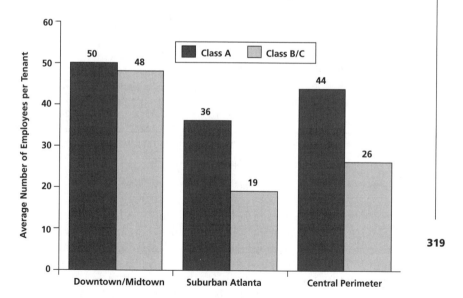

Figure 19.1 Average Number of Employees per Tenant for Advanced Services by Class/Location

Source: Leasetrac 6.1, Jamison Research, Inc. Data current as of March 8, 1998.

Table 19.9 Atlanta Advanced Services
(Number of Tenants, Average Number of Employees per Tenant)

SIC*	Description	Number of Tenants			Av Employee/Tenant		
		CBD*	Sub*	CP*	CBD*	Sub*	CP*
480–489	Communications						
	Class A	9	55	21	75	113	185
	Class B/C	11	54	12	603	120	386
616	Mortgage Bankers and Brokers						
	Class A	3	33	16	103	19	13
	Class B/C	5	76	27	13	12	12
628	Security and Commodity Services						
	Class A	14	38	11	13	19	48
	Class B/C	6	82	16	7	14	18
641	Insurance Agents, Brokers, and Service						
	Class A	6	78	32	63	45	45
	Class B/C	5	159	33	202	19	12
653	Real Estate Agents and Managers						
	Class A	18	66	30	11	12	13
	Class B/C	31	207	51	6	10	12
731	Advertising						
	Class A	7	22	4	51	18	22
	Class B/C	10	45	14	7	30	8
736	Personnel Supply Services						
	Class A	18	48	18	10	12	15
	Class B/C	4	82	13	3	8	10
737	Computer and Data Processing Services						
	Class A	5	96	51	6	73	62
	Class B/C	9	131	28	42	54	20
738	Misc Business Services						
	Class A	8	41	13	32	18	16
	Class B/C	26	121	22	55	15	12
81	Legal Services						
	Class A	79	89	22	31	11	7
	Class B/C	63	200	43	7	5	7
871	Engineering and Architectural Services						
	Class A	14	23	3	72	42	31
	Class B/C	25	117	15	22	17	21
872	Accounting, Auditing, and Bookkeeping						
	Class A	7	24	12	528	14	15
	Class B/C	9	119	27	6	5	5
874	Management and Public Relations						
	Class A	16	67	25	24	24	27
	Class B/C	32	124	24	12	11	10

*SIC= Standard Industrial Classification, CBD=Downtown/Midtown, Sub=Suburban Atlanta,
CP= Central Perimeter.
The CBD and Sub categories are geographically mutually exclusive.
The CP category is a subset of the Sub category.
Source: Leasetrac 6.1, Jamison Research, Inc. Data current as of March 18, 1998.

In addition, the average square footage per employee for advanced services is higher in the CBD than in the suburbs, another contraindication of increasing intensity of office space use associated with firm reorganization trends (Figure 19.2). Thus, at least in the case of Atlanta, indirect evidence does not suggest a shift toward hoteling. This appears to be the case, despite the fact that the city's average commute is the longest in the nation, and the city is also one of the most wired in the nation.

One of the most significant urban spatial trends of the last quarter-century has been the shift to multicentric metropolitan areas. Once bedroom

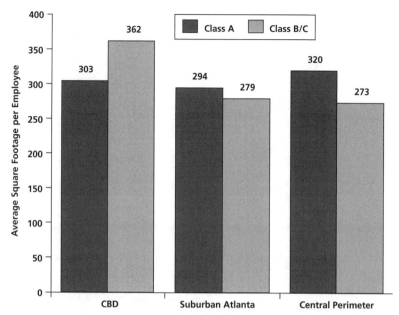

**Figure 19.2 Average Square Footage per Employee
for Advanced Services by Class/Location, Atlanta**
Source: Leasetrac 6.1, Jamison Research, Inc. Data current as of March 18, 1998.

communities, many suburbs have developed downtowns of high-rise skylines that are centers of employment. The Atlanta metropolitan region is no exception. In particular, the Dunwoody suburb has become an edge city on the 285 freeway that circles Atlanta. Its office market, known as Central Perimeter, is larger (19.6 million square feet) than the original downtown market of the CBD (15.5 million square feet). The quality of the office space, as indicated by lease rates, appears to rival, if not exceed, that of Atlanta's CBD. Figure 19.3 shows that average lease rates paid by Central Perimeter advanced services tenants in both Class A and B space were higher than those for the CBD or downtown/midtown markets.

Out of the categories of advanced services displayed in Table 19.9, only four have more tenants located in the CBD than in the Central Perimeter area: Legal Services, Security and Commodity Services, Engineering/Architectural Services, and Advertising. We would expect back-office-type employment to be located in less expensive space, that is, Class B and C office buildngs. However, the Central Perimeter area average employment per tenant in advanced services does not suggest the area is a center of back-office employment. Average employment per tenant is twenty or less for nearly all of the SICs, the exception being Communications. But even then, average employment per tenant in the Central Perimeter is 386, compared to 603 for the downtown area.

If we take average lease rates paid as an indicator of the quality of office space and highest order of advanced services users, the finding that the aver-

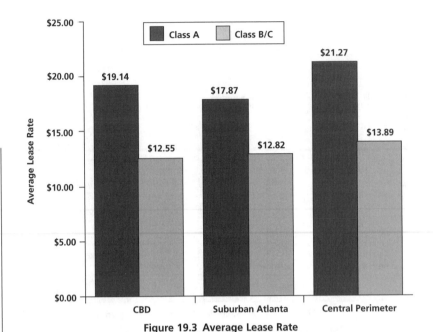

**Figure 19.3 Average Lease Rate
for Advanced Services by Class/Location, Atlanta**
Source: Leasetrac 6.1, Jamison Research, Inc. Data current as of March 18, 1998.

age lease rate paid by advanced services in both Class A and B buildings is lower in the CBD than the Central Perimeter offers further evidence that highest-order services are not compelled to stay in the downtown location.

Atlanta's pattern of advanced services location suggests that in the post-war, auto-dependent metropolitan form, the business district of the historic center does not hold its primacy for those at the apex of corporate power, financial markets, and professional services who need to be "in the thick of it." Instead, a new business district can be created closer to executive housing and other suburban amenities while the advanced services elite can still enjoy the advantages of being located in an international city intricately tied to the global economy.

What kinds of firms may always stay downtown? An obvious answer is those that need proximity to the courts, city hall (thus, law firms especially), and centrally located federal facilities. Those that seek to draw on the technical resources and labor of central-city located universities are another group. An area near the Georgia Institute of Technology that has been experiencing revitalization by information technology firms, many started by Tech graduates, has recently been labeled Atlanta's Fiber-Optic Alley.

Further, as the overall costs of occupancy in the downtown area are now more in line with those of the suburbs, in large part due to the suburban space becoming tight enough that rents have been rising, those seeking less expensive space may stay in or return to the downtown area. In Chicago, one real estate analyst noted that even with the add-on charges such as higher property taxes in the city, a downtown lag in rent escalation has helped it stay attractive (Ludgin, 1997).

Hoteling Hype?

Much attention has been given in the real estate literature to the adoption of hoteling and virtual offices. Talking with real estate analysts and looking for evidence of the trends leads this researcher to conclude that it is not a widespread trend. For example the director of investment research at Heitman Capital Investment, Mary Ludgin, has not seen average lease sizes decreasing. She theorizes this is due to increases in the ratio of professional to support staff. The greater weight of professional staff in a firm's makeup is associated with higher average space per employee. Further, the professional staff are now doing more things for themselves with the aid of equipment (that is, computers, printers, faxes, and so on) that in turn require more space. Her company continues to work with a planning ratio of 200 square feet per employee.

The most highly profiled examples of hoteling have been amongst the largest accounting firms, such as Arthur Andersen and Ernst & Young. It may be that their adoption of hoteling is more the exception—suited to one particular industry subsector—than the rule amongst all advanced services. These megafirms must keep an army of accountants to service their clients. They hire continuously, their staff are on the road much of the time, and they are not known for emphasizing quality of work life. Still, there appears to be only anecdotal evidence on this trend and recent examples have not been forthcoming. While the survey discussed below does not provide broad trend data on hoteling, it did seek space utilization information, among other issues, on downtown firms in a broader range of advanced services.

SURVEY ANALYSIS

In an effort to gain greater insight into why firms choose a central-city location, a survey was conducted on two buildings, one Class A and one Class B, in each of the case study cities. The purpose of surveying tenants in selected Class A and Class B office buildings was to create a profile of their location decision process, space utilization, and technology requirements. The criterion for building selection was to find a good mix of tenants representing the various industries of the service sector—for example legal services, accounting and financial, insurance, marketing, real estate, and publishing.

The survey sought to shed light on the three areas below:

I. What kind of tenant chooses a central-city location over a suburban one?
Why a central-city location instead of suburban?
What is the tenant or firms's SIC?
Are its clients/customers from a local, regional, or national market?
Does the firm conduct business activity away from its central-city location? In another office it owns or leases? And/or at client locations?
What are the characteristics of the firm's labor force? Occupational breakdowns? Residential location of employees? (that is, central-city versus suburb).

II. Recent trends in space requirements of tenants:

Is the firm using more or less space per employee now than in 1990? At this location? All locations combined?

What is the average square footage per employee? By administrative/clerical versus manager/professional category?

What is the square footage per employee dedicated specifically to office use? To common/shared space?

III. What are the technology requirements of the firms?

Computers per employees

Vertical transportation

Automated systems for lighting/air

Energy consumption

Wiring

The buildings selected for surveying were chosen through discussion with local real-estate professionals and by examining building profiles in office market guides. Permission and cooperation in administering the surveys were obtained from the property managers of the buildings. In the Chicago survey administration, surveys were mailed directly to the tenants from lists provided by the property managers with a cover letter explaining the survey's intent. This yielded satisfactory results in percentage response from the tenants in the Class B building (with one reminder postcard mailed as follow-up to the original mailing), but did not yield enough responses to make the Class A survey analysis possible. In the Atlanta survey administration, the property managers distributed the survey instrument directly to the tenants with the cover letter, along with their own cover letter sanctioning the survey. This strategy was more successful and yielded enough responses to make analysis of both buildings possible.

The Chicago Class B building surveyed was built in 1972 and renovated in 1997. Average rental rates for the building were $18 to $20 per square foot. The building has thirty-two floors and 536,000 square feet of space. It had a 70 percent occupancy rate in 1997. Of the fifteen tenant firms who responded to the survey, average tenure in the building was just under five years. The primary reason tenants gave for choosing the Class B building was its location or proximity to those they did business with. Lower costs and the building's image or appearance were the second and third most cited reasons.

The principal business identified most by tenants were: law (three tenants), real estate (three), management consulting (two) or insurance (two). Forty-two percent of the firms stated the majority of their clients were located nationwide, while another 21 percent identified the central loop area as their clients' main location. Eighty-one percent of the firms stated their principal business was conducted at their central loop office. Furthermore, 62 percent stated the space per employee in their offices had *increased* since 1990. These firms do not seem to be "hotelers." The average space employees in these firms had for their own use was 242 square feet—285 square feet for professionals/managers, and 213 square feet for administrative/clerical workers. More employees in the Class B building firms took transit to work than drove in all occupational categories except technical workers.

From questions about technology usage, the survey responses indicated nearly 70 percent of the firms used computers that were part of a networked system as opposed to stand-alone PCs, and employees in 80 percent of the firms made use of the Internet/World Wide Web connections. A little more than half the firms responding indicated there was individual control of the heat and air conditioning in the office, and nearly 90 percent were satisfied with the response of the vertical transportation (elevator system) of the building.

The Class A Atlanta office building surveyed is a trophy Portman building completed in 1992. It has 60 stories and 1.2 million square feet of space. It leases for $26 a square foot, is near a MARTA station, and has high-end amenities. Tenants responding to the survey (50-percent response rate) had been in the building over five years on average, and had been in a downtown location for nearly twenty-six years overall. "Location, convenience, access to MARTA" were the primary reasons firms stated for leasing space in the building. Four of the tenants gave their principal business as law, while three were in banking and the remaining were advanced services activities, including a diplomatic office. Thirty-six percent of the firms stated the majority of their clients were located nationwide, while 17 percent identified the twenty country metro area and another 14 percent identified the downtown area as their clients' main location. Eighty-three percent of the firms stated their principal business was conducted at their central loop office.

The total space occupied by firms in the building averaged 100,682 square feet, and 42 percent of the firms said the space per employee occupied in their downtown location had increased since 1990. One of the major accounting firms leases space in this building and it stated it was using less space than it did in 1990. The average space employees in these firms had for their own use was 213 square feet—226 square feet for professionals/managers and 143 square feet for administrative/clerical workers. Far fewer employees in the Class A building firms took transit to work than drove in all occupational categories.

More than 90 percent of firms' employees used the World Wide Web, 71 percent of firms used computers that were part of a networked system, and 67 percent used in-house teleconferencing. All but one of the firms stated they intended to stay in downtown Atlanta upon the expiration of their lease, and 86 percent of those responding said they were *not* considering locating administrative function to less expensive space.

The Class B Atlanta office building surveyed could be classified as a B+ or A– building. It has 28 stories and 380,000 square feet of space. It leases for $18.50 a square foot, is near a MARTA station, as well as exits to the main interstates traveling through the city, and has good amenities. The building was constructed in 1968 and renovated in 1986. It is located in the midtown portion of the CBD, just a couple of blocks from Georgia Tech. Tenants responding to the survey (nearly a 33 percent response rate) had been in the building more than six years on average, and had been in a downtown location for ten years overall. Proximity to business, access to highways, and parking were the primary reasons firms stated for leasing space in the building. Two of the tenants gave their principal business as law, while the remaining firms were an eclectic group of advanced services activities (banking, advertising, engineering, commercial real estate, viatical settlement[3]), and retail. Twenty-four percent of the firms stated the majority of their clients were located nationwide, while another 24 percent identified the 20-country metro area and another 18 percent identified the downtown area as their clients' main location. Ninety-two percent of the firms stated their principal business was conducted at their central loop office.

The total space occupied by firms in the building averaged 6,859 square feet—less than a tenth of that in the Atlanta Class A building, and 55 percent of the firms said the space per employee occupied in their downtown location had stayed the same since 1990. The average space employees of these firms had for their own use was much higher than in the Class A building: it was 327 square feet, 236 square feet for professionals/managers, and 239 square feet for administrative/clerical workers. Driving to work was the dominant commute mode for employees.

More than 70 percent of firms' employees used the World Wide Web, 63 percent of firms used computers that were part of a networked system, and 54 percent used in-house teleconferencing. Again, all but one of the firms stated they intended to stay in downtown Atlanta upon the expiration of their lease, and 92 percent of those responding said they were *not* considering locating administrative function to less expensive space.

Response rates were low to a number of the more detailed questions in the surveys, but satisfactory response rates on many questions do provide insight into the three questions posed above. First, the firms in the surveyed business choose to locate in the central city for reasons of proximity to business and/or location. Second, the amount of space firms use today is either the same or more per employee than it was in 1990. And, third, employees of the firms are high-technology users and appear to be satisfied with the technology provided within their buildings.

Rationales and Strategies for Retrofitting Older Office Buildings

Good design and historical significance, examples from the case studies show, provide strong incentives for retrofitting older office buildings. Many of Chicago's Class B buildings have unique architectural designs and historical landmark designations that have helped them to maintain their lasting attraction. Atlanta has not been nearly as protective of its historical buildings as has Chicago over the years, but a significant exception is now taking place as the historic Biltmore Hotel is being retrofitted as an office and retail complex.

The Rookery Building on LaSalle Street is a good example of Chicago's historic buildings remaking themselves to stay attractive for office use. It was rehabilitated in 1992 and had a 94 percent occupancy rate in 1997, with advertised rental rates of $12 to $15 a square foot. Originally designed by Daniel H. Burnham and John Wellborn Root, it was built by the Central Safety Deposit Company, which had obtained a long-term lease for the site from the city (expiration date of 1982). When completed in 1888, it had 12 floors and was the world's tallest building. Less than twenty years after it was built, Frank Lloyd Wright was commissioned to redo the interior and the atrium (which suggests a heated office property market at the time). In 1931, William Drummond brought mechanical improvements to the building, updating the elevator banks. Upon lease expiration, the city put the property on the market and it was eventually acquired and renovated by Baldwin Development Company. The Rookery Building was placed on the National Register of Historic Places in 1970 and it was designated an official Chicago Landmark in 1972.

Another example of an early office building that warranted renovations to meet today's demands is the Marquette Building. This building was designed by Holabird and Roche, and completed in 1894. Named for Pere Marquette, the building's lobby is a memorial in honor of the Frenchman's expedition to Illinois and to important Indian chiefs of the Mississippi Valley. This 17-floor building was restored in 1980 by a company owned by John D. MacArthur. The John D. and Catherine T. MacArthur Foundation now owns the building, which had an 80 percent occupancy rate in 1997 and leased at from $17 to $20 a square foot.

The Biltmore Hotel in Atlanta is a 1921 brick structure with 250,000 square feet of space. The brick façade of the building and its two ballrooms will be kept intact, all the rest of the space is being demolished and rebuilt with new walls, elevators, HVAC systems, and plumbing. In addition, fiber optic capacity is being added to the building.

While older Class B office buildings may be very beautiful or have great architectural features, their floorplates can be simply too small to work for today's needs. One example in Chicago is an Art Deco building located a little outside of the prime office sector that was converted to residential use (Ludgin 1997). In addition, downtown Chicago has a wealth of Class C buildings (they constitute nearly 60 percent of the stock), and many do not warrant retrofitting for continued office use. This is because the net effective market rents average $1 to $2 per square foot per year for the Class C stock, and it simply is not cost effective to modernize the buildings (Chanen, 1997).

The vacancy rate among the downtown Class C buildings was 23 percent in 1997 (*Metro-Chicago Office Guide*, 1997). Increasingly, these Class C buildings are being converted into residential lofts and condominiums. One of the current conversions underway is that of the former corporate headquarters of the Florsheim Shoe Company. It is located at 130 S. Canal St. in a commercial area. Profiles of the first seventy individuals to reserve one of the planned 212 units in the building indicate that it is attracting an older house-buying group of empty-nesters who no longer desire the large, single family home lifestyle of the suburbs (Kerch, 1997).

Another amenity-offering strategy that appears to help older downtown office buildings maintain their appeal is to upgrade the level of information technology they offer. Profiled in detail below is the 55 Marietta Building in Atlanta. Another example is the rehabilitation taking place on a 400,000-square-foot, 27-floor building at 230 Peachtree St. in downtown Atlanta. The building is being renovated cosmetically to update its 1960s look. Its redevelopers have also put in several options for access to the information superhighway. Electrical service is being upgraded throughout the building to support the added high-tech amenities as well as smart utilities. The renovating expense of $600,000 comes on top of an asbestos abatement project for the building that is costing $120,000 per floor (Silver, 1997).

A CLASS B BUILDING MADE SMART

The office building at 55 Marietta Street in Atlanta was of typical Class B 1970s construction. It was bought out of bankruptcy by its present owners. Due to the strategic decisions of the new owner, the building has become a telecommunications hub—a vertical telecommunications cluster that is home to firms such as Quest, LCI, MCI, Media One, Vartec, and Avdata. The building provides technical space, not image making space. Its new owners decided to invest heavily in telecommunications network hookups—it is on a fiber-optic ring served by Metro Fiber, MCI, and Media One. It also has a satellite earth station on its roof. The building's leasing agent says the investments have paid off well—the lease rates of this "B" building exceed that of some "A" buildings in Atlanta, and, the building now has an $11 to $12 million value in excess of its original purchase price.

Fifty-five Marietta has attracted data-intensive firms but not those associated with back-office activity. Tenants are secondary-market telecommunications companies which take telecommunications data, bundle it, and transmit it over long-haul fiber to other cities. To them, connectivity to the outside fiber-optic network is important, but so is the interconnection within the building to one another. They are part of the bill and rebill trend in telecommunications services. They have a symbiotic relationship with one another.

That 55 Marietta has been successful in colocating data-intensive firms stems from the tenant firms' need to engage in "peering," whereby telecom companies have to interconnect with one another in order to get data from one company's customers to another company's customers. Public peering points—buildings with fiber from lots of companies coming into a building where they are all connected—are usually very congested with traffic, yielding slow performance in data transmission. In many cases, a company will have private peering arrangements with other companies, and those companies will colocate in a building where the physical connection is made.

CONCLUSION AND PROGNOSIS

The strength of the national economy has done much to fuel revitalization efforts for office property markets. The case study cities of Atlanta and Chicago are good examples of how heated the markets have become. The two metropolitan areas' respective central cities have both benefited from strong invest-

328

ment activity, but not to the same degree. Further, when the national economy slows down, the ability to sustain the momentum each has experienced in central-city redevelopment may be quite different.

Chicago has taken a far more proactive approach to redeveloping its central-city office markets in terms of strategic and land-use planning, zoning development, financial incentives, and environmental remediation. Further, the demand for greater residential stock in the central city, that is, to make it a "live and work" central city, may do much to sustain long-term viability.

Chicago's well-developed mass transit system contributes to the demand for the central city as a live-and-work space. In contrast, Atlanta's under-developed mass transit system is a major barrier to efforts to create greater density and strengthen the central-city economy. This will become more apparent when the national economy slows down.

The technological requirements for today's business (particularly information technology) do not seem to pose a barrier to the reuse of most central-city stock. Advances in technology and ongoing research will continue to make it easier to retrofit existing structures.

In terms of the original questions of this study's focus on whether vacancies and underutilization of office properties due to *technological* obsolescence will be a significant factor contributing to central-city decline, my prognosis is that it this will not be the case. It has become easier to retrofit older office buildings, and those that do not warrant retrofitting can be converted to residential use. Furthermore, softening demand or rising downtown vacancies stemming from widespread adoption of "hoteling" does not appear to be a real threat.

The answer to the "people versus place" question, however, is not as straightforward. In fact, the question itself has become more complicated over the process of this research. Technology is reducing the number of employees per office-sector firm, particularly at the lower occupational levels. However, the technology itself and the larger space given to higher-level employees appear to be countering any overall tendency for firms to use less space.

While CBDs' continued primacy has been asserted because face-to-face contact is still needed for those at the apex of corporate power, financial markets, and professional services, insights from Atlanta suggest that edge-city office-sector development is not so much back-office development as, instead, the recreation of the CBD on the metro fringe. The primacy of the original CBD holds only for select sectors: those that need proximity to courts, city hall, other federal facilities, and/or to technical labor and resources of central-city-located universities. The recreation of the CBD in edge cities for certain advanced services stems largely from executive and worker preferences for suburban living. However, if central cities can provide unique design environments for business activity, as well as housing coupled with good transit systems and supporting commercial activity, Chicago, in particular, shows that many suburbanites can be lured back to the city.

NOTES

1. Graham, Stephen and Simon Marvin (1995) *Telecommunications and the City* London: Routledge, p. 5.
2. The Census Bureau has just started releasing industry data by zip-code level; it is available for 1994 and 1995. Employment figures are given by firm size category instead of actual numbers for each industry in a zip code. Proprietary databases such as TRW-Redi and Dunn & Bradstreet are available, but are expensive and can have issues of quality and reliability.
3. This term refers to the purchase of a terminally ill person's life insurance policy for a certain percentage of the policy's face value (*www.investorwords.com*).

ACKNOWLEDGMENTS

The research discussed in this chapter was funded by the Lincoln Institute for Land Policy, Cambridge, MA. Jamsion Research, Inc. kindly provided access to its real-estate database for the Atlanta portion of this study. The author is grateful for the cooperation of Wim Wiewel and the University of Illinois at Chicago's Great Cities Institute, which generously provided space and adminstrative assistance to facilitate the Chicago portion of this research. Jean Templeton, UIC doctoral student, assisted in portions of the Chicago research. Finally, the author wants to acknowledge the research assistance provided Jonathan Hoffman, Georgia Tech graduate student, whose dedication, initiative, and intellectual contributions greatly enhanced this research effort.

REFERENCES

Adams, L. and D. W. Parham. (1995). "Repositioning the Office Building." In *Reinventing Real Estate*. Washington, DC: Urban Land Institute.

Alexander, H. (1998). Architect with McClier Corporation, Chicago, IL. Interview with Jean Templeton, May.

Bartsch, C., et al. (1991). "New Life for Old Buildings: Confronting Environmental and Economic Issues to Industrial Reuse." Washington, DC: Northeast-Midwest Institute.

Batty, M. (1990). "Invisible Cities." *Environment and Planning* 13: *Planning and Design*. Vol. 17: 127–130.

Bell, M. (1993). "The Virtual Office: Hit or Myth?" *Site Selection* December: 1296–1302.

Black, T. J. (1995). "The Economics of Renovation in the Commercial Property Sector." In *Reinventing Real Estate*. Washington, DC: Urban Land Institute.

The Business Journal (1992). "Grand Avenue TIF to Cash Out Early." Vol. 9, No. 8.

Carver, Bill. (1998). Economic Development Manager, Bell South Telecommunications, Inc., Interview with Nancey Green Leigh and Jonathan Hoffman, June 2.

Castells, M. (1989). *The Informational City: Information Technology, Economic Restructuring and the Urban-Regional Process*. Oxford: Blackwell.

———. (1996). *The Rise of the Network Society*, Malden, MA: Blackwell.

Dematteis, G. (1988). "The Weak Metropolis." In L. Mazza, ed. *World Cities and the Future of the Metropolis*. Milan: Electra.

Dutton, W., J. Blumler, and K. Kraemer, eds. (1987). *World Cities: Shaping the Future of Communications*. Washington, DC: Communications Library.

Chanen, H. S. (1997). "In Chicago's Loop, Conversions to Condos." *New York Times*, Sunday, July 27.

Cronon, W. (1991). *Nature's Metropolis*. New York: W.W. Norton.

The Economist (1995). "The Kindergarten That Will Change the World," March 4: 63–64.

Ewing, Reid. (1997). "Counterpoint: Is Los Angeles-Style Sprawl Desirable?" *Journal of the American Planning Association* Vol. 63, No. 1, Winter: 107–126.

Fathy, T. (1991). *Telecity*: Information Technology and Its Impact on City Form. London: Praeger.

Gann, D. (1992). *Intelligent Buildings: Producers and Users*. University of Sussex: Science Policy Research Unit.

Goodman, L. (1997). Goodman Williams Real Estate Research, Chicago, IL. Interview with Nancey Green Leigh, July 17.

Graham, S. and S. Marvin. (1996). *Telecommunications and the City*. London: Routledge.

Harris, B. (1987). "Cities and Regions in the Electronic Age." In J. Brotchle, et al., eds. *The Spatial Implications of Technological Change*. London: CroomHelm.

Hepworth, M. (1987). "The Information City." *Cities*. August: 253–262.

Hillman, J. (1991). *Telelifestyles and the Flexicity: A European Study*. Dublin: European Foundation for the Improvment of Living and Working Conditions.

Jamison Research, Inc. (1997). *The Office Jamison File*: the Metroplitan Atlanta Market, Year End 1997.

Kerch, S. (1997). "Loft Conversion Binds Generations to Urban Housing." *Chicago Tribune*, July 6.

Knight, R. (1989). "City Development and Urbanization: Building a Knowledge-Based City." In R. Knight and G. Gappert. eds. *Cities in a Global Society*. London: Sage, 223–242.

Leigh, N. G. (1993). "The Making and Unmaking of Industrial Wasteland: Economic Development Insights from Two Milwaukee Chronicles." *Economic Development Commentary* Spring.

———. (1994). "Introduction to Environmental Constraints to Brownfield Redevelopment." *Economic Development Quarterly* November.

———. (1996). "Fixed Structures in Transition: The Changing Demand for Office and Industrial Infrastructure." In *The Transition to Flexicity*, Chapter 9. Daniel C. Knudsen, ed. Boston, Mass.: Kluwer Boston Academic Press.

Leigh, N. G. and R. Hise. (1997). *Community Brownfield Guidebook: Assessing and Resolving Barriers to Redevelopment*. Atlanta: Georgia Tech Research Corporation.

Lorette, G. (1998). Leasing Agent with Ultima R.E. Services, Atlanta, GA. Interview with Nancey Green Leigh, March.

Ludgin, M. (1997). Director of Research with Heitman J & B, Chicago, IL. Interview with Nancey Green Leigh, July 22.

Lydon, A. (1997). National Director of Industrial Services for Grubb & Ellis. Interview with Nancey Green Leigh, July 17.

McIntosh, W. and W. Whitaker (1998). "What REITs Mean to You." *Corporate Real Estate Executive* January/February: 24–27.

Metro-Chicago Office Guide, Second Quarter. (1997),Vol. VII, No. 2. Chicago, IL: Law Bulletin Publishing Company.

Mitchelson, R. L. and J. O. Wheeler. (1994). "The Flow of Information in a Global Economy: The Role of the American Urban System in 1990." *Annals of the Association of American Geographers* Vol. 84, No. 1 (March): 87–107.

Nelson, K. (1986). "Labor Demand, Labor Supply, and the Suburbanization of Low-Wage Office Work." In A. J. Scott and M. Storper, eds. *Production, Work, Territory*. Boston: Allen & Unwin.

Noonan, F. and C. Vidich. (1992). "Decision Analysis for Utilizing Hazardous Waste Site Assessments in Real Estate Acquisition." *Risk Analysis* Vol. 12, No. 2 (June): 245–251.

Nunnink, K. K., ed. (1994). *Viewpoint 1994.* Minneapolis: Valuation International, Ltd. February.

Ogilvie, H. (1995). "This Old Office." *Journal of Business Strategy* Vol. 15, No. 5: 27–34.

Piorinski, R. (1991). "Teletopia: Nouvelles Technologies et Aménagement de Territoire." *Futuribles* November, 47–65.

Pool, I. de Sola, ed. (1980). *Communities without Boundaries.* Cambridge, MA: MIT Press.

Poster, M. (1990). *The Mode of Information: Poststructuralism and Social Context.* London: Polity Press.

Read, W. H. and J. L. Youtie (1996). *Telecommunications Strategy for Economic Development.* Westport, CT: Praeger.

Rheingold, H. (1994). *The Virtual Community.* London: Sicker and Warburg.

Robins, K. and M. Hepworth. (1988). "Electronic Spaces: New Technologies and the Future of Cities." *Futures* (April): 155–156.

Rutheiser, C. (1996). *Imagineering Atlanta.* New York: Verso.

Schlesinger, B. (1997). Facilities planner with Heitman, J&B, Los Angeles Office. Interview with Nancey Green Leigh, September 27.

Schmenner, R. W. (1982). *Making Business Location Decisions.* Englewood Cliffs, NJ: Prentice-Hall.

Silver, J. (1997). "Rehabilitation Propels Building into Cyber Era." *Atlanta Business Chronicle,* December 5–11.

Strohm, P. (1995). "The Quest for Efficient Space." In *Office Trends 95,* pp. 10–12, supplement to the *Estates Gazette.*

Toffler, A. (1981). *The Third Wave* New York: Morrow.

Virilio, O. "The Overexposed City." *Zone* 1(2): 14–31.

Webber, M. (1964). "The Urban Place and the Non Place Urban realm." In M. Webber, J. Dyckman, D. Foley, A. Guttenberg, W. Wheaton, and C. Whurster, eds. *Explorations into Urban Structure.* Philadelphia: University of Pennsylvania, 79–153.

Whyte, W. H. (1988). *City: Rediscovering the Center.* New York: Doubleday.

ABOUT THE CONTRIBUTORS

Yuko Aoyama is Assistant Professor of Geography and affiliate faculty member at the Center for Asian Studies, University of Georgia. She obtained her Ph.D. in City and Regional Planning at University of California, Berkeley in 1996. Her area of research includes Informational Economy and Technological Change, Globalization, Entrepreneurship, and Asia's Industrialization. She has written on the locational dynamics of Japan's high-tech industry, comparative development of information intensive industries, and the historical legacy of small business policy in Japan and the United States.

David B. Audretsch is the Ameritech Chair of Economic Development and Director of the Institute for Development Strategies at Indiana University. He was at the Wissenschaftszentrum Berlin fuer Sozialforschung in Berlin, Germany, which is a government-funded research think tank between 1984 and 1997. Between 1989 and 1991 he served as Acting Director of the Institute. In 1991 he became the Research Professor. Audretsch's research has focused on the links between entrepreneurship, government policy, innovation, economic development, and global competitiveness. He has consulted with the World Bank, National Academy of Sciences, National Science Foundation, United States Federal Trade Commission, General Accounting Office, and International Trade Commission as well as the United Nations, Commission of the European Union, the European Parliament, the OECD, as well as numerous private corporations and a number of European governments. His research has been published in more than one hundred scholarly articles in the leading academic journals. He has published nineteen books including, *Innovation and Industry Evolution*, with MIT Press in 1995. He is founder and editor of the premier journal on small business and economic development, *Small Business Economics: An International Journal*.

Lon Berquist (M.A. Stanford University) is a Ph.D. candidate studying Communication Technology and Policy in the Department of Radio-Television-Film at the University of Texas at Austin where he is a Research Associate for the Telecommunications and Information Policy Institute (http://www.utexas.edu/research/tipi). He has worked for the City of Austin's Telecommunications and Regulatory Affairs Office, Stanford University's Networking Systems, and Viacom Cable. He has taught at the University of Texas, De Anza College, and Foothill College. His e-mail address is berquist@uts.cc.utexas.edu.

Christopher Bertaut received his B.A. from the University of South Florida and an M.A. from The University of Georgia (1998). His Master's thesis examined the spatial relationship between cellular facilities siting and vehicular traffic in a suburban Atlanta county along with their implications for the relative roles of space vs. place in urban economic development. His interests include Urban Geography, Economic Geography, and the part played by Telecommunications in shaping the urban milieu. He is presently employed as an infrastructure planner in the cellular telephone industry.

William B. Beyers is a Professor of Geography at the University of Washington in Seattle, WA. He received his B.A. and Ph.D. from the University of Washington, and has Specialized in economic geography and regional science, with research interests in regional economic development processes, models of regional and interregional economic systems, and the geography of advanced service industries. He has been involved with research on the rural rebound in the United States, especially in relation to the growth of information-intensive economic activities. His recent research has also focused on forces related to the rapid growth of producer services in urban areas.

Stanley D. Brunn (M.A. University of Wisconsin, Madison; Ph.D. Ohio State University) is Professor of Geography at the University of Kentucky. He has published numerous articles, chapters, and books during the past three decades on social, political, and economic geography and on human/environment futures. He is past editor of The Professional Geographer and the Annals of the Association of American Geographers. He has taught at the University of Florida, Michigan State University, and a half-dozen universities in Europe. His current interests are in information and communications technologies as used by scholars, scientific organizations, and the state.

Elizabeth K. Burns received the Ph.D. degree in geography in 1974 from the University of California, Berkeley. She is currently professor of geography at Arizona State University, Tempe. Her areas of specialization are urban and transportation geography with more specific interests in travel behavior and the impacts of urban growth, spatial mismatch, the geography of women's employment, and spatial technologies. Recent publications on inner-city employment and commuting appeared in the *Transportation Research Record*, *Urban Geography*, and *Applied Geographic Studies*. Burns served as associate editor of the *Professional Geographer*, treasurer of the Association of American Geographers, and president of the Association of Pacific Coast Geographers. Integrating urban geography, planning, and transportation in her professional practice as a member of the American Institute of Certified Planners, she led studies in Arizona, California, and Utah, including the City of Phoenix Urban

Village plan adopted in 1987. She is currently the Arizona State University Executive on Loan to the City of Phoenix.

Manuel Castells, born in Spain in 1942, is Professor of Sociology and of Planning at the University of California, Berkeley, where he was appointed in 1979, after teaching sociology for twelve years at the University of Paris. He has also taught and researched at the Universities of Madrid, Chile, Montreal, Campinas, Caracas, Mexico, Geneva, Copenhagen, Wisconsin-Madison, Boston, Southern California, Hong Kong, Singapore, Taiwan, Amsterdam, Moscow, Novosibirsk, Hitotsubashi (Tokyo), and Barcelona. He has published over 20 books, including *The Economic Crisis and American Society* (Princeton, 1980); *The City and the Grassroots,* winner of the 1983 C. Wring Mills Award. *The Informational City* (Blackwell, 1989); and the trilogy, *The Information Age: Economy, Society and Culture* (Blackwell, 1996–98). He has been a Guggenheim Fellow, as well as a member of the European Commission's High Level Expert Group on the Information Society. He was appointed to the European Academy in 1994.

Martin Dodge is a researcher and part-time Ph.D. student in the Centre for Advanced Spatial Analysis (CASA), University College London, United Kingdom. He is interested in the geography of the Internet. He maintains the Cyber-Geography Research Web site at http://www.cybergeography.org/. He can be contacted at the Centre for Advanced Spatial Analysis, University College London, Gower Street, London, WC 1E 6BT, United Kingdom. E-mail: m.dodge@ucl.ac.uk. http://www.casa.ucl.ac.uk/.

Maryann P. Feldman is Research Scientist at the Institute for Policy Studies and Assistant Professor of Economics at Johns Hopkins University. She received her B.A. from Ohio State University, and her Ph.D. from Carnegie Mellon University. She is the author of more than twenty academic articles that have been published in such journals as the *American Economic Review, The Review of Economics and Statistics,* and *The Annals of the Association of American Geographers.* Her Ph.D. dissertation, *The Geography of Innovation,* was published in 1994 by Kluwer Academic Publishers. She is currently editing the forthcoming *Handbook of Economic Geography* for Oxford University Press. She has also served as a consultant to private business, various federal, state, and local agencies and non-profit organizations. She has received grants from the National Science Foundation, the German Marshall Fund, the U.S. Small Business Administration and the Edison Electric Institute, among others.

Andrew Gillespie is Professor of Communications Geography at the University of Newcastle, and Director of the Centre for Urban and Regional Development Studies (CURDS), United Kingdom. His research interests focus on the implications of information and communications technologies for the development of cities, regions, and rural areas. He is a policy adviser to the Commission of the European Union.

Stephen Graham is a Reader in the Centre for Urban Technology (CUT) in Newcastle University's Department of Town and Country Planning, in the United Kingdom. His research addresses the relations between new information technologies, urban development, urban theory, and urban policy. He is the joint author, with Simon Marvin, of *Telecommunications and the City: Electronic Spaces, Urban Places.*

August E. Grant, Ph.D., is Director of Entertainment Services for 2Wire, Inc. in Milpitas, California. Grant is a former broadcaster and academic who specializes in research on new media technologies and consumer behavior. After completing his doctorate at the Annenberg School for Communications at the University of Southern California, he spent nine years with the Department of Radio-Television-Film at the University of Texas at Austin. He then became the rounding Director of the Center for Mass Communication Research in the College of Journalism and Mass Communications at the University of South Carolina. Although his primary interest is mass communication technology, his research and teaching reflects the convergence of communication forms through the application of new technologies. He has written numerous articles and conference papers dealing with high-definition television, television audience behavior, television shopping services, theories of new media, and emerging communication technologies. He is the editor of the *Communication Technology Update* (now in its sixth edition), a semi-annual review of the latest developments in more than three dozen technologies in electronic mass media, telephony, consumer electronics, computers, and satellites. He has also served as a consultant to various media organizations regarding new communication technologies and consumer behavior. His e-mail address is agrant@wire.com.

Darrene Hackler is a Senior Research Associate at the Claremont Graduate University Research Institute. Her main research areas are on the spatial, economic, and transportation of information technology. She has a Master's in Public Policy and is a doctoral candidate in Political Science as and Economics at the Claremont Graduate University. Her dissertation research analyzes the effect of regional and local economic development policies on industrial location patterns of high technology manufacturing in the metropolitan areas of Los Angeles, California; New York City, New York; Phoenix, Arizona; Minneapolis-St. Paul, Minnesota; and El Paso, Texas. She is co-author of "Spatial Impact of Information Technology on Economic Development in Minnesota," *Journal of Urban Technology*, special edition on Urban Livability, with Lee Munnich and Thomas Horan, forthcoming December, 1999; and coauthored *Stalking the Invisible Revolution: The Impact of Information Technology on Human Settlement Patterns* with Benjamin Chinitz and Thomas Horan for Lincoln Institute of Land Policy.

336

Nancey Green Leigh is an Associate Professor in the Graduate City Planning Program at the Georgia Institute of Technology where she teaches and conducts research on urban and regional development, industrial restructuring, local economic development planning, and brownfield redevelopment. She obtained her Ph.D. in City and Regional Planning (1989) and Master's in Economics (1984) from the University of California at Berkeley where she was a Regents Fellow, National Science Dissertation Fellow, and Woodrow Wilson Rural Development Policy Fellow. She is the author of Stemming *Middle Class Decline: The Challenges to Economic Development Planning* (Rutgers: CUPR Press, 1994). She recently completed a research project for the Lincoln Institute for Land Policy on "The Influence of New Flexibility and Technology Requirements on Central City Office and Industrial Markets."

Thomas R Leinbach is Professor, Department of Geography, University of Kentucky and coeditor of the journal, *Growth and Change: A Journal of Urban and Regional Policy.* His interests focus on issues of regional and urban development but especially those related to transportation, communications, technology impact, and industrialization in both Asia and Europe. His is coeditor of *Collapsing Space and Time: Geographic Aspects of Communications and Information* (Routledge, 1991). He was formerly Director, Geography and Regional Science Program, National Science Foundation and is currently Director, Office of International Affairs, University of Kentucky. His e-mail address is leinbach@pop.uky.edu.

Simon Marvin is Director of the Centre for Urban Technology at the Department of Town and Country Planning, University of Newcastle, United Kingdom. Simon has research interests in the relationships between infrastructure networks and urban and regional governance in developed and developing cities. In particular he is interested in the implications of new logics of infrastructure provision on the social, economic, and environmental development of ; contemporary cities. His research program has received funding from the UK Research Councils, the European Commission, private companies, and governmental organizations. Simon has published widely on the changing relations between cities and technical networks and was coauthor with Stephen Graham of *Telecommunications and the City* (Routledge, 1997).

Stephen D. McDowell teaches in the Department of Communication at Florida State University in Tallahassee in the areas of communication policy, new technology and society, and mass media. His research has dealt with new communication technology, and with communication policies in India, Canada, and the United States. He held a Congressional Fellowship in Washington D.C. in 1994–95, sponsored by the American Political Science Association, a Shastri Indo-Canadian Institute fellowship in 1989–90, and was a post-doctoral fellow at the Canadian federal Department of Communications in Ottawa from 1987 to 1989.

Mitchell L. Moss is the Henry Hart Rice Professor of Urban Policy and Planning and Director of the Taub Urban Research Center at New York University. He is the principal investigator of an interdisciplinary research project, "Telecommunications and the Future of Urban Environments" sponsored by the National Science Foundation. Professor Moss has written extensively on technological change and urban development, and he has served as a consultant to leading communications companies.

Robert Mugerauer is Sid Richardson Professor of Architecture and Planning at The University of Texas at Austin, where he is also a faculty member in the Departments of Geography, Philosophy, and American Civilization. His most recent books are *Environmental Interpretations* and *High-Tech Downtown*. A specialist in the impact of high-technology on the physical environment and technology's qualitative dimensions, he can be reached at drbob@mail.utexas.edu

Ranald Richardson is a senior research associate at the Centre for Urban and Regional Development Studies, Newcastle University, United Kingdom. Trained as a town and country planner, his recent research focuses on the implications of information and communications technologies for changing patterns of work and employment, particularly in the service sector.

Bishwapriya Sanyal (Ph.D. in Urban and Regional Planning) is Department Chair, Department of Urban Studies & Planning, Massachusetts Institute of Technology. He is also a former Vice-President, American Planning Association, International Division, and has been appointed to the National Task Force on Doctoral Planning Education. He served as a consultant to Ford Foundation, World Bank, International Labour Organization, United Nations Center for Human Settlements, and the United States Agency for International Development. Research experience in India, Bangladesh, Zambia, Kenya, Jordan, Brazil, and Curacao. He is currently supervising a twelve-country study of administrative decentralization, which is sponsored by United Nations Development Program. Most recent publications include: *The Profession of City Planning: Changes, Successes, Failures and Challenges (1900–2000)* (edited by L. Rodwin and B. Sanyal), Rutgers University Press; *High Technology and Low-Income Communitie Prospects for the Positive Use of Advanced Information Technology* (edited with W. Mitchell and D. Schön), MIT Press, 1998.

Narushige Shiode is a graduate student in Centre for Advanced Spatial Analysis (CASA), University College London, United Kingdom. His Ph.D. topic is "modelling cyberspace." He can be contacted at the Centre for Advanced. Spatial Analysis, University College London Gower Street, London, WC I E 6BT, United Kingdom. His email address is n.shiode@ucl.ac.uk.http://www.easa.ucl.ac.uk/.

Alan Southern is Lecturer in the Management of Economic Development at the University of Durham Business School in the United Kingdom. He teaches courses on social research methods, and on issues relating to economic development and technology. His B.A. degree was in Urban Policy and he received an M.Sc. in Computation from the University of Manchester, Institute of Science and Technology. His Ph.D. work is focused on information and communications technology (ICTs) in local economic restructuring, undertaken at the Geography Department in Durham. Recent research projects include regional development and technology strategy and on ICTs in small business.

Barney Warf (Ph.D. 1985, University of Washington) is Professor and Chair of Geography at Florida State University. His research and teaching interests lie within the broad domain of regional development, straddling contemporary political economy and social theory on the one hand and traditional quantitative, empirical approaches on the other. In the first topic area he has written on structuration theory, postmodernism, and the localities issues; in the second, his work centers on producer services, telecommunications, military spending, and international trade. He has coauthored one book, seventeen book chapters, and fifty-two refereed articles. His teaching interests include urban and economic geography, social theory, and East Asia.

James O. Wheeler is the Merle Prunty Professor of Geography at the University of Georgia, where he served as Department Head from 1975–1983. He is co-editor of Urban *Geography*, an international academic journal, and the *Southeastern Geographer*, published by the Southeastern Division of the Association of American Geographers. He is author of more than one hundred refereed articles and book chapters, and has authored, coauthored, or edited seven books.

INDEX

information superhighway, 148
information systems; hub and spoke schematic, 259; urban activity patterns and, 34
information technology (IT); citywide new media and, 85–87; decentralization trend, 201; as enabling technology, 284; firm location and, 200; increased use of, 284–285; industrial spatial pattern, 202; location theory and, 202–203; new economy and, 169–170; spatial implications of, 289–290; urban growth and, 31–32; urban poverty and, 14
information technology (IT) intensity, defined, 201
information technology (IT) intensive industries, 203–204; central and outer counties, 211–213; decentralization, 212; geographical concentration, 204; industrial location, 205; US individual states, 207–211
The Informational City (Castells), 3
informational mode of development, 250–259; connection to, 253–254
infrastructure (*see* telecommunications infrastructure)
innovation, 10–11, 130; defined, 183; geographic activity of, 183–185; geographic region and, 193; industry life cycle and, 189–190; significance of, 183; specialization vs. diversity, 192
innovation cluster, 185–196; agglomerating influence of, 190; congestion effect, 190; culture of, 191
Integrated Services Digital Network (ISDN), 7
integrated transport, telecommunications strategies and, 82–85
Intel, 138
intelligent buildings, 328; technologies for, 307–308
interactive services, 109
Internet, 139, 172–173, 229 (*see also* Internet real estate); global cities and, 6; grassroots activities and, 85; growth of, 3, 7; home-schooling and, 38; horizontal communication, 22; linkages of, 24–25; local communities and, 86; metropolitan dominance of, 79; personal interaction, 22; social bias of, 25–26; social movements, 23; as social product, 9; solidarity and cooperation, 22; telecommunications competition and, 99; as transformation agent, 5

Internet Assigned Number Authority (IANA), 45
Internet banks, 35
Internet real estate; data sources and limitations, 45–47; defined, 42; ownership of, 44–45; relevant research for, 43–44; UK IP address space analysis, 46–51; what is it?, 44–45
Internet service provider (ISP), 43
introductory stage, industry life cycle, 190
IP address (Internet Protocol address), 44
IriScan, 61
"Is There a Body in the Net?" (Argyle and Shields), 65

Jacobs, Jane, 192
Jacobsen, K. N., 231
Jacobs's diversity theory, 195–197
Jaffe, Adam B., 182, 185, 187
Jameson, F., 56
Janelle, Donald, 57, 161, 269
just-in-time production, 124

Kairamo, Kari, 132–133, 137
Kallal, Hedi D., 191–192, 195–196
Kalsdottir, A., 231
Kaplan, Rachel, 219
Kaplan, Stephen, 219
Kapor, Mitchell, 149
Kellerman, Aharon, 4
Kennard, William, 121
Kick Start Initiative, 148–149
Kim, Duckjoon, 204
Klevorick, A. K., 193
knowledge-based service industries, 161
knowledge-based workers, 15
knowledge production function, 181 (*see also* innovations); economic knowledge, 182; knowledge spillovers, 181–182, 197; spatial and product dimensions, 185
knowledge spillovers, 181–182, 197; geographic region and, 191–192; innovation clusters and, 186; tacit knowledge, 189
Kolko, Jed, 34
Korte, W. B., 229
Krugman, Paul, 10, 182, 186

La Neta, 23
Lakeland, Florida, 104
land use (*see* location theory); urban planning
Lansing, John B., 219

in, 164–165; traditional sectors and, 177–178

new industrial spaces, 165

new information economy, 286–288

New Jersey, IT-intensive industries, 211

New Urbanism movement, 88

New York, IT-intensive industries, 211

New York Information Technology Center, 35

Newman, W., 292

Nguyen, D., 59, 65

niches, 162, 165, 192

Nilles, Jack, 74

Nissan, 253

nodes and hubs, 19

Nokia; cellular communications, 133–134, 137–138; competitive advantages, 134, 136–139; corporate history of, 131–133; corporate profile, 134–136; fast second strategy, 138; future of, 139–140; global markets and, 131; government relations and, 137; government support of, 132; R&D, 137; refocusing strategy, 133; telecommunications competitiveness, 133–134

nomadic/mobile workers, 236, 238–240

Noyelle, T. J., 291

office automation, 308

office property (*see also* central business districts (CBDs)); future technological requirements of, 303; as investment, 306; land use and, 302; trends in, 302; vacancy rates, 303

Olds, Kris, 76

Ollila, Jorma, 133

online communities, 229

open platform, 103

open video systems (OVS), 98

Organization for Economic Cooperation and Development (OECD), 291

Pacific Telesis, 152

Palo Alto, California, 104

Pandit, K., 285

personal communications services (PCSs), 118, 123

personal mobility, 269

Pestle, John W., 123

phenomenological investigations, 220

Phoenix mobility case study, 269–270; gender variations, 274–275; inner-city commuting patterns, 273–275; job-residence imbalance, 271–273; Sky Harbor International Airport commuting, 277–279; telecommuting, 275–277

pink-collar employment, 287

polycentric concentration, 305

Pope, Kyle, 130

Porrit, Jonathan, 74

Porter, Michael E., 14, 130–131, 140, 176, 192

post-Fordist model, 124, 285–286

Power, Thomas, 224

Press, Larry, 43

producer services, employment growth, 166

The Production of Space (Lefebvre), 55

public space, 38–40

quality of life factors, 175; location decisions and, 224

Quarterman, John S., 44

Quigley, Phil, 152

R&D; economic knowledge and, 182, 187; knowledge spillovers and, 197

radio pagers, 123

radiofrequency (RF) radiation, 116

radiomagnetic spectrum, 114–115

Rallet, A., 288–289, 293–294

regional fountainhead, 131

regional Internet registries (RIRs), 45

REITs (Real Estate Investment Trusts), 307

remote offices, 236, 241

Request for Information (RFI), 105

Request for Strategic Partners (RFSP), 105

Requests for Proposals (RFPs), 104

residential location, electronic homework (EHW) and, 238

restructuring, Sutherland case study, 253–256

Rey, R. F., 290, 293

Richardson, Harry W., 32, 202

Richardson, Ronald, 14, 228

Rifkin, J., 171

rights-of-way (ROW), 101, 103, 113; as public trust, 116–118

RIPE (Réseaux IP Européens), 45–46, 52

The Rise of the Network Society (Castells), 303, 306

Road Transport Informatics (RTI), 84

Robinson, S., 229

Rockart, J. F., 286

Root, John Wellborn, 312, 326

Rose, S., 164–165

Rural Electrification Administration, 120

123–124; shifts in governance, 121–123; tower siting/placement, 118; universal access and, 148–149; universal availability and, 103; universal service provision, 120; zoning authority, 118

telecommunications city, metaphors of, 304

"Telecommunications and the City" (Conference), 3

Telecommunications and the City (Graham and Marvin), 13, 303

Telecommunications for Clean Air, 82

telecommunications infrastructure, 103; local municipalities and, 97–98; municipal initiatives, 104–107

telecommunications regulation; construction permits and street cuts, 101–102; economic development, 102–103; environmental impacts, 102; franchising, 101; role of local governments, 100–102; universal availability, 103; zoning location, 102

telecommunications research, new approach to, 33–34

telecommuting, 7–8, 15, 75, 82–83, 107–108; gender and, 269; Phoenix mobility case study, 275–277

telecottages, 236

teleflex geography, data sources for, 309

telegeography, 304

TeleGeography Inc., 43

telemantics, defined, 303

telematics strategy, 254–255, 260, 284; Sutherland case study, 261–263; themes of, 264

telemediated urban change, 293

telemedicine, 60

teleport, 257

teleport communications hub, 258

teleservices, 231

televillage, 88–89

telework, 8, 15, 230; classification of, 235–236; defined, 229; definition of, 267; electronic homework, 235–238; gender and, 269; group/team telework, 236; management and, 230–232; mobile teleworking, 238–240; nomadic/mobile workers, 236; remote offices, 236; telecottages, 236; travel need and, 235–236, 242

Telework Facilities Exchange, 82

territorial innovation complex, 10

Thiessen polygons, 297

Thrift, Nigel, 33, 65, 76, 234

Thurow, L., 171

time-space convergence model, 161

Tomas, D., 56

tower siting/placement, 118

Townsend, Anthony M., 12, 31, 79

Trajtenberg, Manuel, 182, 185, 187

Transactional City, 171

transport-telecommunications, 74–76

transportation, Road Transport Informatics (RTI), 84–85

travel (*see also* commuting patterns); electronic homework (EHW) and, 237–238; telecommunications and, 38, 74–76; telework and, 235–236, 242

trip chaining, 237

uniform business rates (UBR), 257

United States v. Robert Alan Thomas, 63

universal access, 109; ensuring access, 151; government policies, 148–150; key policy objective, 150; lack of social infrastructure, 147–148; market provision of, 146–147; public education and, 151–152

Universal Service Fund, 120

universal service provisions, 120

urban centers; agglomeration of, 306; cyberspace and, 7–10; decentralization, 305; digital age and, 71–72; historical overview of, 4–5 information economy and, 76–78; polycentric concentration, 305; technological determinism, 72; telecommunications and, 4–6, 305; virtual communities and, 80–81; workplace transcendence myth and, 228–229

urban cultures, cybercultures and, 78–80

urban planning; communication corridors, 83–84; emerging telecommunications strategies, 81–82; future of cities and, 73; information district, 88; new technologies and, 73; Road Transport Informatics (RTI), 84–85; smart city strategies, 87; telecommunications policy and, 89–94; televillage, 88–89; teleworking initiatives, 82–83

urban poverty; advanced information technology (AIT) and, 143–144; digital redlining, 147; social activism and, 144–146; universal access and, 146–147

urban televillages, 82

urbanization, megacity and, 234

Urry, J., 77

Usenet groups, 80